Jean Arthur

Jean Arthur

The Actress Nobody Knew

John Oller

Limelight Editions
New York

First Limelight Edition February 1997
First Limelight paperback editon April 1999

Copyright © 1997 by John R. Oller

Manufactured in Canada

Library of Congress Cataloging-in-Publication Data

Oller, John.
    Jean Arthur : the actress nobody knew / John Oller. — 1st pbk.
ed.
       p.   cm.
    Filmography: p.
    Includes bibliographical references and index.
    ISBN 0-87910-278-0
    1. Arthur, Jean, 1905-   . 2. Actors—United States—Biography.
I. Title.
    [PN2287.A75043   1999]
    791.43'028'092—dc21
    [B]   99-11144
                                                  CIP

To my parents

CONTENTS

THE AMERICAN GARBO

"Next to Garbo, Jean Arthur is Hollywood's reigning mystery woman," observed *Life* magazine in 1940, and there were many who thought it the other way around. Garson Kanin, who scripted her for stage and screen, called Arthur "the most fascinating mystery in the entire entertainment world." Columnist Sheilah Graham found her "the hardest-to-understand star in Hollywood." Louella Parsons, who knew everything about everyone, confessed that after thirty years of trying, "I really hadn't learned anything about her." No one else had, either, concluded Parsons, who declared Arthur's private life "a baffling mystery."

The titles of the articles written about her told it all: "Leave the Lady Be," "Disappearing Jean Arthur," "The Actress Nobody Knows." She was the American Garbo—the actress nobody knew.

On screen, Arthur was known to millions as the quintessential working girl heroine of Hollywood's "screwball" comedies of the thirties and early forties—the smart-talking, good-looking gal Friday who could be tough and cynical one moment, soft and loving the next. Cast opposite nearly all of Hollywood's leading men at one time or another, in most of her films she labored in a masculine environment, as, for example, in two of her best-remembered roles: a newspaperwoman trailing Gary Cooper in *Mr. Deeds Goes to Town* (1936), and a congressional secretary to James Stewart in *Mr. Smith Goes to Washington* (1939). Frank Capra, the director of both of these classics, called her "my favorite actress," while George Stevens, who directed her best later work, noted that "this mysteriousness about her private life doesn't keep her from being one of the greatest comediennes the screen has ever seen."

That was the Jean Arthur of the movies: winsome, charming and consistently appealing to audiences as were few actresses of her time. "Every movie star is disliked by some people," said John Cromwell, another director with whom she worked, "but everyone liked Jean Arthur." Nevertheless, the questions persisted. As Garson Kanin put it, "When she's not acting, who is she, what is she?"

Arthur did her best to ensure that no one could find out. From her first silent picture in 1923 to her final screen appearance, nearly ninety films later, in *Shane* (1953), Arthur worked assiduously at placing herself beyond Hollywood's usual grasp. She recoiled from interviews, shunned photographers and declined to participate in the standard publicity gimmicks. She avoided parties and nightclubs and the glamour set that inhabited the likes of Club Mocambo and the Troc. Instead, she chose to live as a virtual recluse. As her one-time husband, movie producer Frank Ross, once affirmed, "She really wants to be left alone."

2

In part, Arthur eschewed the usual star treatment because she was simply bored by it. She sought stimulation instead in the world of ideas, and was continually seeking out intellectual heroes, like Erich Fromm and George Bernard Shaw, upon whom she could fasten her admiration. Indeed, at the peak of her career, after her first and only nomination for an Academy Award, Arthur abruptly quit films to become a college student.

In part, too, Arthur rejected the trappings of stardom because her only interest was in being a good actress. "If people don't like your work, all the still pictures in the world can't help you and nothing written about you, even oceans of it, will make you popular," she once explained. For this attitude she was ostracized by the press and voted by the Hollywood Women's Press Club as filmdom's least cooperative actress.

But for more than any other reason, Jean Arthur shrank from public attention because of a pathological shyness born of fear and self-doubt. Often this was mistaken for aloofness or temperamentalism; Arthur had a reputation in the business for being "difficult." But whatever difficulties she caused others were rarely deliberate, and instead arose from conflicts that lay hidden below her surface.

Arthur's inner conflicts manifested themselves both on and off the set. For one, she was plagued by stage and camera fright throughout her career. Capra claimed that she vomited before and after every scene, and hid crying in her dressing room between takes. When called for the next scene, she would drum up every sort of excuse for not being ready. "And it wasn't an act," he said. "Those weren't butterflies in her stomach. They were wasps. But push that neurotic girl forcibly, but gently, in front of the camera and turn out the lights—and the whining mop would magically blossom into a warm, lovely, poised and confident actress."

Perhaps out of that same camera fright, or simply out of good judgment, Arthur repeatedly refused to play roles that she disliked, explaining that it made her physically sick even to think about acting in a bad picture. Every time she turned down a script, she was suspended by her home studio, Columbia Pictures, with the result that her five-year contract was extended to nine long years. For nearly a decade, she continued to reign, reluctantly, as queen of the Columbia lot, appearing in a nearly unbroken string of box-office hits.

After completing her Columbia contract in 1944 (she reportedly ran through the studio's streets shouting "I'm free! I'm free!"), Arthur returned five times over the next thirty years to the legitimate stage, where she had briefly appeared in the early 1930s. On each of these five occasions, however, she withdrew from the production, often just before opening night, citing various illnesses. The symptoms in each case were real, not feigned, and Arthur always found a reason to declare the situation professionally intolerable. But this pattern of behavior, psychosomatic in origin, must inevitably be linked to her core feelings of uncertainty.

These feelings manifested themselves, as well, in Arthur's most memorable attribute, her famous voice. Impossible to appreciate without being heard, it was at once squeaky and husky, and has been described as like "corduroy," like "butter being churned," "grated like fresh peppermint," or (in Capra's words) "low, husky—at times it broke pleasingly into the higher octaves like a thousand tinkling bells." Arthur's voice shifted unpredictably according to her mood—hesitant and trembling at one moment, firm and comforting the next. Considered a liability when sound first arrived, Arthur's distinctive voice proved to be her greatest asset.

If her voice reflected a certain paradoxical quality, then so did Arthur's screen personality. In both comedy and drama, she projected an unusual mix of toughness and vulnerability, of skepticism and idealism, of confidence and fear. The Arthur heroine's pluckiness is almost always accompanied by a nagging sense of anxiety and bewilderment. Comparing her to another famous Jean, author James Harvey has aptly observed that "if Harlow is the tough girl who doesn't know what it is to be nervous, Arthur is the tough girl who does."

What was it, then, that Jean Arthur feared? Certainly she was afraid of people, or at least those she did not already know. With her closest friends, most of whom were from outside the entertainment world, she could be spontaneous, opinionated, full of impish humor; almost everyone who knew her well found Jean Arthur endlessly fascinating and delightful.

4

But there were precious few such people over the years, due to her near-total aversion to meeting strangers.

"Inferiority complex" was a phrase frequently applied to Arthur by friends and observers alike, and she was inclined to accept that assessment:

> I am not an adult, that's my explanation of myself. Except when I am working on a set, I have all the inhibitions and shyness of the bashful, backward child.... Unless I have something very much in common with a person, I am lost. I am swallowed up in my own silence.

Wary of strangers, Arthur also feared failure, or more precisely, anything short of utter success. A fundamentally modest woman, Arthur nevertheless sought perfection in her work, and feared what might come from not performing as superbly as her exacting standards demanded.

Sadly, Arthur regarded her career as something of a failure, in that she never became the type of dramatic actress she aspired to be. Although justly proud of some of her work, particularly in the Capra social comedies, she wanted something more: to play a role by which people would remember her forever. She nearly had that opportunity when, in 1938, she came within an eyelash of gaining the part of Scarlett O'Hara in *Gone With the Wind*; of the four finalists, she was the most established star. She was so distraught at losing out that she reportedly burned her screen test.

"She always thought she should have been a more serious actress," said her longtime friend, educator Nell Eurich. "She felt she should have done Shakespeare, she should have been in a repertory company. There was a general dissatisfaction with the kind of roles she played. She certainly didn't hide it at all."

There were, however, two roles from her stage career that Arthur cherished above all others. And in her love of these two roles—Peter Pan and Joan of Arc—Jean Arthur revealed the greatest of all her fears: conformity. More than anything, she feared losing her own uniqueness amidst the pressure to become what Erich Fromm, her one-time psychoanalyst, would call a "conforming automaton." Correspondingly, to maintain her individuality, to preserve intact her inner integrity, she felt an almost obsessive need to assert her freedom and independence. The same could be said of her two favorite characters who, not coincidentally, were both children who refused to accept the strictures of the adult world.

All her life, Arthur had wanted to play Peter Pan, and when she finally got the chance—at the age of almost fifty—she enjoyed a Broadway run that broke all previous records for any production of the play, and indeed ran longer than the later and better-known version starring her friend Mary Martin. Not only did Arthur achieve her greatest triumph in *Peter Pan*, but she also found, in the whimsical and androgynous title character, her true kindred spirit.

"Nobody is going to catch me, lady, and make me a man," was Arthur's favorite line from the play, and it might easily have been uttered by her with the genders reversed. But the meaning of J.M. Barrie's play, for Arthur, went beyond the literal story of the boy who refused to grow up. "It means nonconformity and freedom of the imagination and the individual," she once said. "If you can hang on to your individuality, hold tight to your freedom, and not get squigged-out as you grow older, then and only then are you mature," she said during the play's run, later adding that "people who aren't free like Peter, or at least hunger to be free, aren't aware of the adventure of living. They're walking around dead."

If Peter Pan provided Arthur with a fictional affirmation of her values, then the historical embodiment of her thinking was surely Joan of Arc. "She was a nonconformist too," said Jean of Joan, "a believer in her own intuition. Intuition, that's what Joan's voices were. She never killed anybody. She just wanted everybody to go home and mind their own business," which is all that Arthur wanted, as well.

As with Peter Pan, Arthur had wanted all her life to play Joan of Arc, and specifically, the Saint Joan of Shaw's play of the same name. In the case of Joan, however, the attachment was more personal. In 1923, a budding young actress named Gladys Greene had to select a name for use in her first Hollywood film. For her surname she chose "Arthur," after the legendary English king. For her first name she thought immediately of her personal heroine, the French Jeanne d'Arc, and settled upon the derivative "Jean."

It is probable that Arthur saw something of herself in the young Maid of Orleans. Like Joan, Jean was born to a family of modest means and rustic background. Though not illiterate, as Joan was, Arthur suffered a comparative lack of formal education in her youth, which she overcame, as Joan did, with great natural intelligence and insight. Each was born into a family of three older brothers, and from their respective male-dominated atmospheres each acquired a taste for doing masculine things, for leading a man's life. "It's hardly fair for women to do the same things at the same hours every day of their lives, while men have new experiences, meet new people every day," Arthur once lamented early in her career. Years later, she would state with a hint of envy that "men have always been more important than women."

Through the roles of Peter Pan and Saint Joan, and in her choices of other then-typically male roles throughout her career—reporter, lawyer, congressperson and Supreme Court justice—Arthur did manage to achieve a sort of vicarious masculine success. She was, as feminist writer Marjorie Rosen has written, the only one among her peers who remotely embodied the truly accomplished women of the thirties, such as Frances Perkins and Jane Addams, who were otherwise completely without representation on the screen. Playing directly on men's professional turf, Arthur came across as a direct and no-nonsense—but still feminine—companion. The resulting screen character was a kind of pre-feminist ideal.

If Arthur was breaking new ground—if she was a transitional female image—she herself was not especially conscious of it. Asked in 1975 to comment upon the women's liberation movement, she responded that "I don't know much about it because I've always sort of fought my own way. Yet, when I see these things and realize how most women live, I realize I've been liberated all my life just because I did it. Because I couldn't do anything else."

Arthur's philosophy of life was perhaps best summed up in a line from Keats that appeared below a portrait of the poet in her apartment at the Carlyle Hotel in New York, where she lived during *Peter Pan*. It read, "He ne'er was crowned with immortality who fears to follow where airy voices

7

lead." In following her own "airy voices," Jean Arthur certainly achieved, as did her beloved Peter Pan and Joan of Arc, a form of immortality. But sometimes those voices led her directly into trouble....

Part One

A·I·R·Y
V·O·I·C·E·S

CHAPTER ONE

ANIMAL INSTINCTS

*I*t was 6 a.m. on Sunday, April 1, 1973, when the phone rang in Pete Ballard's apartment in Winston-Salem, North Carolina, waking him from a sleep that had begun only three hours earlier. Ballard, a teacher at the North Carolina School of the Arts, had been out late celebrating his forty-second birthday and he was in no mood for any April Fool's jokes. He soon learned that this was no joking matter.

Ballard immediately recognized the cracked, child-woman voice at the other end of the line. But he could not fathom why his friend Jean Arthur would be calling at such an hour.

"Well, how was your party?" she asked, softly. "Fine," he responded, half-asleep.

"What did you have to eat," she inquired further, sounding distracted.

"Jean, not at six o'clock in the morning," he snapped, and paused before adding, "and where the hell were *you*?"

Despite the irritation in his voice, Ballard was neither surprised nor offended by Arthur's failure to show at his birthday party after promising to attend; he was aware of her track record in such matters. What did take him aback was her response.

"I was in jail," she said, so matter-of-factly that it did not register at first. Then she said, in a suddenly plaintive voice, "I really *was* in jail and I need to talk to you right *now*!" Whereupon Ballard shot out of bed, threw a coat over his pajamas and raced over to Arthur's apartment to hear her story.

It had started a few weeks earlier and it had to do with a certain German shepherd dog named Major, whose owners were a young working couple living in Winston-Salem. They generally kept the year-old puppy chained up in the backyard, from where it could frequently be heard barking and crying, much to the chagrin of a certain elderly woman who lived next door. The couple did not know that she was a once-famous movie star now teaching drama as an artist-in-residence at the School of the Arts.

They also did not know that Jean Arthur had a legendary reputation for refusing to tolerate inhumane treatment of any creature, however lowly, that fell within her reach. At one point in the filming of *Shane*, for example, she refused to do another scene until dummy chickens were substituted for the real ones whose eyes had begun to bleed during rehearsals from being carried upside down the way farmers do. While on location for the picture *Arizona*, she hired a veterinarian, at her expense, to cure the pigs of a skin disease which she noticed was afflicting them. Another time, she spent nearly four hours on a Long Island beach picking up horseshoe crabs that lay helplessly overturned on their backs, and throwing them back into the water; she proudly counted more than six hundred whose lives she had saved.

Thus, when Jean Arthur saw a young pup whimpering sadly next door to her, she naturally took action. Her overtures began innocently enough, with her taking the dog food each day, as she did with other animals in the neighborhood. The dog's owners, however, were not amused by these acts of charity. She next offered to build a fenced run for the dog so that it could roam the backyard without having to be tied up all day while the couple was at work. But they did not appreciate their lives being intruded upon, and they told her to stop coming over. She accused them of mistreating the dog, and threatened to call the Humane Society. They in turn threatened to call the police if she set foot on their property again.

On the afternoon of March 31, 1973, she was in the couple's yard again, making the rounds, when they pulled in the driveway and saw her, barefoot, consoling the dog. Twenty-five-year-old Ronald Ray Douglas got out of the car and twice told the nameless old woman to get off his land. After she finally left, he called the police and said he wanted to prosecute.

Arthur always left the front and back doors to her apartment open so her cats could come and go as they pleased. Thus, when two officers showed up at her doorstep to serve a trespass warrant upon her, they went right in and found her in the kitchen, fixing dinner for her three cats and two canaries.

Arthur tried to explain her side of the story, but Officer H.N. Thomas cut her off, saying he was not there to judge the merits of the case. She called him "goddamned stupid," whereupon he told her she was under arrest for cursing and abusing an officer. When she asked if she could put on some shoes and check on the meal she had cooking on the stove, her requests were denied.

The ensuing scene might have been right out of one of Arthur's screwball comedies were it not so serious. The two burly police officers, having no clue as to the identity of their prisoner, placed her hands behind her back, handcuffed her and tossed her in the back seat of the patrol car parked outside. Once at the county jail, they threw her in a cell with a group of prostitutes, just as the police had done with Arthur and her eccentric family, some thirty-five years earlier, in the film *You Can't Take It With You.*

In that movie, Arthur's character was released from jail when the lawyer of fiancé Jimmy Stewart's wealthy father arrived on the scene with bail in hand. In real life, it was not so easy. Arthur knew virtually no one in town except Pete Ballard, and she had no way of getting in touch with him, as he had gone to his birthday party. No one knew who she was, nor had she told them (she gave the police an assumed name). So she sat in jail, barefoot and in baggy clothes, bumming cigarettes from the prostitutes.

The jailkeepers called a bail bondsman for her but he declined to put up the $100 necessary for her release. After a second bondsman came through with bail approximately forty minutes later, she was allowed to leave. For a while she sat nervously in the station waiting for her taxicab to arrive, but when she rose and started pacing back and forth, one of the officers pushed her back down, saying, "You sit there." When the taxi arrived, she ran to the door, turned around and said, "You wouldn't do this to me if I were Katharine Hepburn!" Once back in her apartment, she sat by herself all night until she woke her friend Ballard.

By the time she finished telling Ballard this story, it was almost 8 a.m. They agreed that the entire incident had to be kept away from the press. Ballard called Weston Hatfield, the legal advisor to the School of the Arts, who came over and agreed to represent her. A trial was booked for ten days later in a North Carolina district court, the lowest level state court for the trial of misdemeanors.

The low-profile stratagem worked for a while, but a few days before the trial word of Arthur's arrest leaked to the press and the story was all over the country. Hatfield began receiving calls of support from well-known animal rights activists like Cleveland Amory and Amanda Blake. Richard Burton and Elizabeth Taylor cabled to offer their assistance. Several Fondas sent the same message from Europe. Then mail began arriving by the bagful, all of which Arthur proceeded to throw out, as was her habit.

Ballard retrieved it, however, and found a thousand-dollar check from a judge in California, along with several marriage proposals.

On the morning of the trial, April 11, 1973, a surprisingly relaxed Arthur met for breakfast with Helen Hayes, who happened to be in Winston-Salem visiting friends. Ballard, a costume designer by background, had exhorted Arthur to wear a dress that day, something she had not done in years. But she declined his advice, put on a pantsuit instead and headed over to the courthouse with him at the appointed hour.

After ramming through a throng that was waiting at the courthouse entrance, Arthur and Ballard were met inside by Hatfield, a tall, dapper man in his early fifties. Ballard took a seat in the audience, which he had managed to pack with friends. "I had called everyone I knew in town who had a respectable look to them to come and fill up this little courtroom," he recalled.

The presiding judge was one Abraham Lincoln Sherk. According to Hatfield, Sherk had a reputation for being a tough judge—a man who was not going to be interested in any technical defenses. Not that Arthur's defenses were that strong, technically speaking: In response to her neighbor's charge, the defense plea was justifiable trespass; to the charge of abusing an officer, Hatfield invoked the First Amendment.

Douglas, the prosecution's first witness, recounted how he had warned the elderly defendant to stay off his property and finally called the police when she appeared again on March 31. Douglas claimed the woman had been drinking both that day and on the prior occasions when she showed up in his yard. Each time he mentioned her drinking, Arthur let out an "Ahhh," her way of disputing the allegation. After the second "Ahhh," Sherk turned in his chair toward Hatfield, eyes half-closed, and drawled, "One more time, counselor. That's all it's going to take." She did do it softly, one more time, but the judge let it pass. Otherwise Arthur sat quietly through the testimony with a pleasant look on her face.

Following Douglas, Officer H.N. Thomas took the stand and told the story of the arrest. He claimed he had never entered Arthur's apartment, but, lacking an arrest warrant, had stayed outside on the porch instead.

He further testified that he handcuffed the woman because the patrol car did not have a glass partition between the driver's seat and the prisoner's seat in the rear.

Now it was Arthur's turn to testify. Before parting from Ballard earlier in the courtroom, she had asked if he had any advice and he had told her to play it like a scene out of a Frank Capra movie. With that in mind, she walked politely up the aisle, said good morning to the policemen and to the judge and took the stand. She then testified that she had become concerned about the dog because "he barked all day and most of the night and he cried—like a child. It kind of broke my heart." She said she went out to pet the dog in the yard about six times and had taken him calves' liver and chicken on a couple of occasions, but that she returned only once after Douglas told her to stay away. Asked by the prosecuting attorney why she hadn't left immediately on March 31 when told to, she responded, "But I love the dog and the dog loves me." It was, at least, faintly Capra-esque.

Although his client admitted to having called Thomas "damn stupid" (which was slightly milder than the phrase the officer recalled) Hatfield argued that such a remark was constitutionally protected by freedom of speech unless it could be shown to have actually obstructed justice. To demonstrate how ridiculous the abuse charge was under these circumstances, he had the diminutive Arthur stand up beside the two large arresting officers. He also said the use of handcuffs on the elderly woman was "shocking," and asked the judge to imagine his own mother being similarly treated.

Whether good Capra or bad theater, Abraham Lincoln Sherk was having none of it. He found Arthur guilty on two misdemeanor counts, fined her fifty dollars and court costs for cursing and abusing an officer, and tacked on an additional twenty-five dollars and a three-year suspended sentence with probation on the charge of trespassing.

"None of the people involved fully realized who she was," recalled Hatfield two decades later. He said everyone in Winston-Salem was surprised at the negative press the city received when news of the arrest of Jean Arthur broke, and that, he speculated, may have affected the prosecution of the case.

Arthur, on the other hand, was relieved not to have received a stiffer sentence. "But for the fact that it was discovered it was 'me,' instead of just a little old lady, I would have been put in jail," she reflected later.

Not only was she not jailed, but Arthur ultimately was vindicated. Six months into her appeal, after she had moved back to California, the state elected to dismiss the case. By that time, Ronald Ray Douglas and wife Joan had also left town, victims of a series of threatening anonymous phone calls and letters.

Avenged or not, the dog incident reaffirmed for Jean Arthur her belief that animals, not people, are the world's most trustworthy inhabitants. "Animals have no chips on their shoulders—they're never mad at you, and they never misunderstand you," she once explained. "When I'm walking down the street I don't pay much attention to the people," she said another time. "I only see the animals and I go up to them like old friends."

Indeed, even more than the compassion she felt for animals, Jean Arthur felt a certain kinship with them. Speaking of her adopted mongrel dog Pat in 1938, in terms that might have been reserved for herself, she said, "I wouldn't have a trained show dog or trick dog for the world. I believe that dogs should be allowed to be natural—then if they do have any personality it will show itself in its own individual way."

Arthur herself felt most natural in front of the camera; it was acting, rather than "real life," that brought out her individuality. "I've never been self-conscious acting," she once explained. "The only times I'm self-conscious are—when I'm Jean Arthur. In front of a camera I lose my identity completely, and with it I lose my timidity. As a character in a play I feel as if I can be what people expect. As Jean Arthur, I never feel as if I know what people expect." In 1972, in one of her last published interviews, she explained it even more succinctly: "I guess I became an actress because I didn't want to be myself."

The person Jean Arthur did not want to be, and from whom she sought to escape through acting, was a person nobody knew. The scarcity of knowledge about Jean Arthur begins with the most basic information about her life: when she was born, and where. Both are facts she managed to keep from people, even those closest to her, for almost her entire life.

CHAPTER TWO

HIDDEN HERITAGE

*T*t was the week before Thanksgiving in 1950, and Jean Arthur was furious. The object of her wrath was *Collier's* magazine, which had recently run one of the few in-depth articles ever published about the actress. It was not the article itself that had upset Arthur, but rather the following letter to the editor in its November 18 issue, under the caption, "Miss Arthur's Chronology":

Editor: Just how old is Jean Arthur? In [the October 7 *Collier's*], it is stated that Jean Arthur was born on October 17, 1908; but later on, we find the statement, "In 1923, at the age of 18, she became an actress in silent films." However, whether she be 42 or 45, I still think Miss Arthur an excellent actress and the story very interesting.

Ed. Note: Well, let's see—*Who's Who in the Theatre* gives Miss Arthur's birth date as October 17, 1905; *Who's Who in America* says she was born October 17, 1908. Maybe we're all a little confused.

Eleanor (Harris) Howard, the author of the original article, recalled that Arthur telephoned the magazine's editor to complain about this seemingly innocuous item. Arthur had consented to an interview, had even allowed its writer a rare glimpse into her private life, and now the magazine had gone and betrayed her by exposing a hole in her story. Never again would she agree to be interviewed, she vowed.

Mrs. Howard, who managed to escape Arthur's personal ire, recalled her subject as "charming, but very neurotic." The actress refused to talk about some things at all, like her age and the details of her childhood, about which she seemed to harbor a sense of shame. While dutifully reporting the actress's birthplace as New York City, as Arthur always claimed, Mrs. Howard suspected humbler origins.

Nearly forty years later, author Elizabeth Kendall sensed the same thing in analyzing the famous park bench scene between Arthur and Gary Cooper in *Mr. Deeds Goes to Town*. As big-city reporter Babe Bennett, Arthur confesses to Cooper's Longfellow Deeds of mythical Mandrake Falls, Vermont, that she, too, is from a small town. After telling him that he reminds her of her father, she breaks into a rendition of "Way Down Upon the Swanee River" with man-made drumsticks on a garbage can, the way her father taught her. "The scene is so well acted that we have the impression we are seeing the 'real' Jean Arthur, too, before she got into this artificial business of making movies," Kendall wrote, but added, "That's not true, of course: Jean Arthur came from New York City, not a small town."

Upon Arthur's death in 1991, much of the media continued to record her birthplace as New York City, and her birthdate as either 1905 or 1908. Although a few publications discovered the correct facts, no one managed to learn of Jean Arthur's hidden heritage, which reflected a combination of pioneer strains that contributed to her fiercely independent nature.

By coincidence, Jean Arthur's father did come from a small town in Vermont, but he would not have reminded anyone of Gary Cooper. Hubert Sidney Greene was short (about five-foot-five) and slight of build. A flamboyant handlebar mustache helped supply character to the gentle face he had inherited from his Anglo-Saxon ancestors.

Greene's roots were traceable to the year 1202 in Northampton, England, where King John bestowed upon Alexander, a knight in his court, the estate of Boketon. It had a spacious green, which a century later was used by Alexander's descendants for the family name of "de Grene" ("of the green"), and eventually simply "Greene."

In the early 1600s, the descendants of these knightly Greenes left England, victims of religious persecution, and settled in Rhode Island, where they followed the preacher Roger Williams into the wilderness. They migrated throughout New England, fought in the French and Indian Wars and became rock-ribbed Yankee pioneers. By the time of the Revolutionary War they were living in Bennington, Vermont, where the Americans won a crucial battle in 1777. During the encounter a fourth-generation colonist named Job Greene was taken prisoner and narrowly saved from an Indian scalping by the intervention of a British officer. Greene's luck continued the following night when he escaped during a chase of runaway cattle and made his return to the American lines.

Just after the war, Job Greene was dispossessed of his farmland near Bennington as part of a continuing boundary dispute between New York and New Hampshire over the New Hampshire Grants, as Vermont was then known. Unable to provide for his teenaged sons, the elder Job sent them off to fend for themselves.

The two boys, Nathan and Job, set out north and arrived at the settlement of St. Albans, Vermont, which they helped pioneer in the late 1780s. Then a complete wilderness, St. Albans lay on a hill sloping high above Lake Champlain, only a few miles from the Canadian border. The Greenes who settled here were probably proficient in both French and English, as was Jean Arthur a century and a half later.

Nathan and Job Greene became influential and respected citizens of St. Albans and fathered twenty-three children between them. One of Nathan's sons, Henry Collamer Greene, was a judge with an independent (some thought stubborn) mind. One night a disgruntled litigant interrupted Judge Greene's supper by shooting him in the chest at his doorstep, a wound from which he luckily recovered.

Among Henry Collamer Greene's thirteen children was a son named Sidney Thomas Greene, Jean Arthur's paternal grandfather. Born in St. Albans in 1841, Sidney Greene served in the First Vermont Cavalry in the Civil War and laid guns at Fort Monroe, outside Norfolk, Virginia. In 1862, during a break in the fighting, he returned to St. Albans to wed Mary Clark, another native of the town.

When the war ended, Sidney Greene returned to his wife and one-year-old son, Hubert, who had been born just after the battle of Gettysburg in 1863. Another son and twin daughters later came along. The family eventually settled in Schenectady, New York, where Sidney Greene pursued his livelihood as a cabinetmaker and building contractor.

Sidney's son Hubert had no interest in following in his father's footsteps. Around the time of his eighteenth birthday, Hubert headed west, intending to become a cowboy. He arrived in Kansas City, walked into a saloon and asked for Ike Morgan, a prosperous rancher of the day. Morgan stepped forward and asked, "What do you want?" When Greene replied, "A job," Morgan inquired, "What can you do?" "Nothing," the young man responded, whereupon Morgan exclaimed, "You're hired. You're the first damn man who didn't say he knows everything!"

After working the range for Morgan for a few years in the 1880s,

Hubert Greene made his way to Billings, Montana, where he continued to work as a cowboy. On the side he pursued an interest in painting and photography; his favorite subjects were Indians and landscapes.

It was at a rodeo in Billings that Greene met his future wife, a young woman named Johannah Augusta Nelson. The courtship was not an easy one. In an effort to impress the girl, Greene paraded his horse in front of her father's hotel and performed riding tricks, which she studiously ignored. He persisted in wooing her, however, and they were married in Billings on July 7, 1890, when he was twenty-six and she was nineteen.

"Hannah" Nelson, as she was known, was the youngest child of Hans P. Neilson, a Norwegian immigrant who arrived in 1866 with his wife and a daughter born during the Atlantic voyage. Rechristened with the surname Nelson, they drifted west, across Wisconsin, adding a second daughter along the way. Eventually they made their way to the Dakota Territory, which was heavily populated by Indian tribes. There, in 1871, Hannah was brought into the world by an Indian midwife.

When she was a young girl, Hannah's family moved to Lawrence County in the Black Hills of South Dakota, where gold had been discovered in 1874. Though not a gold miner himself, Hans figured he would find a market there for his skills as a builder and commercial painter. He settled the family near Deadwood, a colorful mining town full of saloons, brothels and dance halls. As a young girl, Hannah walked the same streets as Wild Bill Hickok and Calamity Jane.

By 1878, Hannah's mother had died and her father had married a girl barely half his age, a fellow Norwegian named Georgianna Svennes. Descended from the early Vikings, Georgianna was strong-boned and taller than her husband. At eighteen, she was also only four years older than Hans's eldest daughter, and only eleven years older than Hannah, which created certain inevitable rivalries. In time, Georgianna bore Hans another eight children: four sons and four daughters.

When the South Dakota gold rush had spent itself, Hans Nelson placed his family in a covered wagon and headed north for the new Montana Territory. The area had just recently been opened to settlers following the final defeat of the Sioux Indians, victors over Custer in the great battle of 1876. The coming of the Northern Pacific Railroad to the Eastern Montana valley in 1882 brought a surge of population, and in 1883, in the town of Billings, the Nelsons made their new home. Hans built them a large, rambling residence and became a partner in a business offering "house and sign painting, graining, glazing and paper-hanging."

Hans Nelson was a man of varied talents who dabbled in several different business ventures during his lifetime. Easygoing to a fault, he was also an alcoholic who was unable to sustain any endeavor for long. He ran a hotel and saloon in Billings that was frequented by Jeremiah Johnson and Buffalo Bill Cody; made and lost several small fortunes in sheepherding; and ran off for a time with Cody's Wild West Show. In 1899, Hans deserted his wife and children—guilty, according to the divorce papers later filed by Georgianna—of "profligacy and dissipation," the latter term a euphemism for his excessive drinking. Hans lived another twenty years after their parting, eventually helping to found the nearby town of Roundup, Montana, but Georgianna thereafter always listed herself as "widowed."

As a result of Hans's waywardness, it was left to Georgianna to raise a family of eight young children. She was not unequal to the task. As her relatives recalled, Georgianna was a strong-willed, obstinate woman who survived out of sheer determination—"a real Norwegian trouper," in the words of a granddaughter. Georgianna ran a boarding house in Billings for income, turning it into the first European-style bed and breakfast in the area. While ensuring that all of her children were properly educated, she managed to travel frequently throughout the West. As another granddaughter recalled, Georgianna "liked to control everyone" and dominated family get-togethers, which usually ended in arguments. "There was a lot of verbal abuse in the family, but that's Norwegian," added John Nelson, Georgianna's self-described favorite grandson.

The Nelsons were indeed a tough bunch. Georgianna used to down a shot of 180-proof grain alcohol with a teaspoon full of water each morning just to get herself going. Daughter Palma smoked, drank and performed all types of "men's work," like roofing and wallpapering. She became the first female steam engineer in the state of Montana and the first woman in the entire country to hold a steam engineering license.

Hannah Nelson was a more temperate, serious woman than the others in her family—somewhat distant, even. Tall, fair, with handsome Nordic features, Hannah was also better-looking than most of them. But like the others, she too was independent and strong-willed. "Like a Viking princess when she got mad," her famous daughter later described her.

It is not surprising, then, that Hannah Nelson initially professed disinterest in the short, comical figure of Hubert Greene as he pranced about on horseback before her. But Miss Nelson found something attractive in young Mr. Greene, namely, the similarity that he bore to her father. Like Hans Nelson, Hubert Greene was charismatic, happy-go-lucky and a bit of a showman; his usual garb was a suit of gleaming white buckskin. "Hube," as he was known to friends, was described as a "humorist" and "optimist" by his second cousin, Ferdinand Greene.

In addition to painting and photography, Hubert Greene loved animals, especially dogs, which he took with him in groups of half a dozen or more wherever he went. As a cowboy, he also liked his liquor, and eventually became an alcoholic. Certainly, the similarities between Hubert and her father were too strong to escape Hannah's detection.

Drawn to Hubert, she eventually had to face another consideration: six months before the wedding, a son, Don Hubert Greene, was born to Hannah. To obscure this fact, she later generally misstated the date of her son's birth and of her marriage.

Following the birth of their first son, the Greenes moved across the Montana border to North Dakota, where a second son, Robert, was born to them in March 1892. By 1894 they had returned to Montana, where Hannah gave birth to Albert, their third son, in December of that year.

Sometime thereafter the Greenes left Montana with their three boys and a pack of dogs, barged down the Missouri River and then the Mississippi to New Orleans, and made their way to Florida, where property was cheap. But by 1898 they had returned to the area near Hubert's native St. Albans, settling just across Lake Champlain in the small town of Plattsburgh, New York. It was there, two years later, that the Greene family welcomed another member. On October 17, 1900, Hannah gave birth to a daughter, Gladys Georgianna Greene. One day, that daughter would cast that name aside, along with everything associated with it, and become known to the world as Jean Arthur.

CHAPTER THREE

UNCERTAIN BEGINNINGS

With its picturesque setting among gentle, tree-covered hills overlooking Lake Champlain, Plattsburgh was a good location for a young photographer like Hubert Greene; less dramatic than the West he had left, but accommodating nonetheless. Greene joined the George T. Woodward studio in downtown Plattsburgh, which advertised itself as among the "leaders in northern New York" for "photographs…frames, etchings, engravings and art goods generally."

With his new job Greene was able to provide a modest living for his family, but little more. During their five years in Plattsburgh, the Greenes lived in rental dwellings in middle-class districts, beginning at South Platt Street on the edge of town, then moving to 94 Oak Street, on a tree-lined thoroughfare near the center of town, where Gladys was born.

Her early childhood was a lonely one. The youngest child by several years and the only girl, she was forced to create her own world of play. At first she was interested in dolls, spending countless solitary hours patiently stitching together tiny wardrobes for her large doll family. However, her interests soon turned to boys' games, like cowboys and Indians, partly from jealousy of her older brothers. "It seemed to me that they led adventurous lives compared to mine," she once explained. "I felt cheated, frustrated. I became a tom-boy, in self-defense. I decided I was going to do things that were exciting, or at least interesting."

Although it was not true, as she later claimed, that the youngest of her brothers was ten years older than she, Arthur nevertheless vividly remembered how inferior she had been made to feel growing up with three older male siblings. "It was like having four fathers," she said. "They all told me what to do. I was entirely dependent on their opinions. Even after I was fully grown up, I always deferred to a man, any older man."

Young Gladys's feelings of loneliness were exacerbated by the nomadic existence her family led. Because Hubert Greene's work took him on location seasonally to Florida and New England, the Greenes moved about frequently, leaving Gladys to attend school wherever they happened to land. Constantly forced into the role of the newcomer, Gladys was ill at ease with her peers, who seemed more confident, more clever, more accomplished than she was. Gladys never went to children's parties or belonged to girls' clubs. Instead, she withdrew into herself and made no lasting friends. "I've never had a single close, intimate girl friend in all my life," she lamented when she was nearly forty. "I never had a chum to whom I could confide my secrets. I suppose that accounts for the fact that now it is so painfully difficult for me to open my heart and confide in people who are, so often, almost strangers. You have to learn so very young to open your heart."

For all her insecurities, Gladys was an intelligent girl and an excellent student. And despite her awkward demeanor, she sensed deep down that she was somehow special, even unique. Gladys, according to her grandmother, Mary Greene, "thought she was better than everybody else." Her paternal aunts concurred, thinking her spoiled. To her mother, she was merely eccentric: "When are you going to start acting like a lady?" Hannah frequently asked her only daughter, in exasperation.

But other relatives noticed a spark of imagination beneath her timid exterior. "A very venturesome girl" was how Marcus Greene, a cousin three years her junior, remembered her. William Wernecke, a second cousin whose family Gladys lived with for a time in Schenectady, recalled his sisters telling him that Gladys "was born an actress." Shedding her natural shyness, she put on plays on her grandparents' front porch and walked the "tightrope" across their fence. As a Greene family genealogy later recorded it, in a single cryptic reference to their most famous member:

> GLADYS9. Mrs. Vivian Greene Isham said she loved to dance and perform, talents of which her grandfather, Sidney Greene, did not approve. She lived for a time with her cousin, Grace Greene Wernecke, and went to school. Later she performed on the stage in New York, changing her name to JEAN ARTHUR, and becoming a popular Hollywood actress. However, her family never approved of her profession.

This disapproval came not from her immediate family, but instead from certain older relatives. The Greenes were strait-laced "proper people," said Mary (Greene) Fraenckel of her elders. To them, Hollywood was a place where only "naughty girls" went. Gladys would not forget their attitude. Often in later years, distant relatives from the Schenectady area sought her out to introduce themselves, only to be turned away without so much as a hello. Mary Fraenckel recalled that when she was a young woman living in California in the 1960s, she drove up to Arthur's Carmel residence twice, identified herself at the doorstep as someone whose father had been a cousin and childhood playmate of Arthur's, and was refused an audience both times. "It was a terrible experience for me," she said.

In fairness to the Greenes, Arthur distrusted all strangers, and with few exceptions, she kept an equal distance from relations on her mother's side in later years. Still, Arthur seems to have harbored especially chilly feelings toward the Greenes. "I've come away with the impression that they were a hopelessly lower-middle-class bunch," theorized Abbott Lowell Cummings, a Greene on his mother's side who became an architectural historian and professor at Yale University. Cummings' mother, Louise Lowell Greene, a sensitive, intelligent woman who was disenchanted with her environment and eventually escaped, later described her contemporary Gladys as "different" and as estranged from the family. The atmosphere for both young women, Cummings said, "must have been absolutely stifling."

Surrounded by relatives who bored her, nagged by a mother who misunderstood her and ignored by brothers who had little use for her, Gladys could still turn to one person for genuine affection—her father. She adored Hubert Greene, and he seems to have felt the same way toward her. In several photographs taken of Gladys as a child, it is evident that her father has very carefully and lovingly posed his daughter, and that she quite enjoys being the object of his attention.

Hubert Greene's relationship with his wife was more problematic. While opposites in temperament, they shared fierce independent streaks. As one relative put it, "He was a great one to do what he wanted and she was a great one to do what she wanted....She was more interested in society, and that was the last thing he was interested in."

Hannah Greene was a pragmatic woman, gracious in manner, who saw her moral betterment as her most worthwhile goal. She became a Christian Scientist, and later a practitioner, or authorized healer, within that faith. Like her Nordic family, she was strong and resilient, but she was more refined than the West in which she had grown up.

Hubert Greene, by contrast, was an impractical artist. His true love was painting, not photography, and he preferred liquor to religion. He refused to clean his boots before entering the house, despite his wife's frequent admonishments. Nor was he good with money; his purchase of unnecessary items like flower bouquets was scorned by his more practical spouse.

By 1908 the Greenes had moved to Congress Street in Portland, Maine, another harbor town. Now forty-five, Hubert Greene had taken over as manager of the Lamson Studio, an established and successful portrait gallery in downtown Portland. For the first time, the Greenes began to experience a measure of financial security.

But it was not to last long. In the spring of 1909, the family was down in Jacksonville, Florida for the season when Hubert Greene suddenly walked out on them. For Hannah Greene it was a repeat of the fate suffered by her stepmother before her. But it was an even more traumatic event for young Gladys, who was only eight at the time. The person she revered most in the world, the one person who always returned her love without condition, had inexplicably abandoned her. She was, in her mind at least, very much alone.

As it turned out, Hubert Greene would be back, for by 1910 the Greenes were together again in Portland. But he could never stay with his family for long. He repeatedly wandered off from time to time, destination undisclosed. "I don't know where he went on his apparent 'forays,'" said Arthur's close friend Ellen Mastroianni, one of the few people the actress ever told about her parents' marital difficulties. His behavioral pattern was consistent with that of an alcoholic, which his oldest son later became. Jean Arthur would also struggle with the same addiction for much of her life.

Given the precarious nature of her husband's support, it behooved Hannah Greene to develop an independent earning capacity. In Portland, she opened a boarding house where eleven-year-old Gladys helped by laying out the dining tables, polishing the silver and making the beds. Mrs. Greene was also a skilled seamstress who could make almost anything with her hands. "On a hunting trip with my father, she made soap, candles, and even a deerskin suit," Arthur later said. "She made all my clothes until I was grown up, and once sewed me a dress in an hour before I went to school in the morning."

In September 1912, Gladys returned to classes at Portland's North School, resuming her place in the sixth grade, where she had left off the prior year. Her marks for health, conduct and scholarship were all good. But in October, just after her twelfth birthday, the Greenes uprooted again and moved to Jacksonville. Perhaps because Hubert Greene was unable to manage a business of his own, he elected to rejoin his former Plattsburgh employer, George T. Woodward, who had relocated his studio to Jacksonville earlier that year.

Within a year or two, Gladys was the only child still living at home. Her youngest brother, Albert, had learned photography and moved back to Portland, where Bob Greene, the middle brother, was working as a clerk and traveling salesman. Oldest brother Don had become a drifter like his father, and his whereabouts were often unknown. Meanwhile, Gladys was left alone with her estranged parents, who literally lived in separate parts of the same house.

To overcome her loneliness, Gladys cast about for a role model—someone removed from her immediate life, someone even larger than life, whom she could admire without fear of rejection. She found one such person in a girl whose real name was also Gladys, and who appeared to have faced all the same familial and financial difficulties. Recalling her object of affection years later, when asked to name her favorite girlhood movie crushes, Arthur responded unequivocally: "Mary Pickford and Mary Pickford."

The second role model Gladys chose was a real woman, her Aunt Pearl Nelson. The youngest of Georgianna's girls, Pearl was also the closest among them to their half-sister, Hannah. In 1913, when she was in her late twenties, Pearl moved from Billings to Jacksonville in order to live with Hannah, while continuing her career as a teacher.

Gladys Greene had never known a woman like Pearl Nelson. Educated and well-read, Pearl was interested in things with which Gladys had little familiarity, like theater and culture. Unlike Gladys's mother, who was often cool and aloof, Pearl was outgoing and charismatic; as evidence of her enormous popularity with her students, she continued to receive cards and letters from them throughout a forty-year teaching career.

Pearl filled a void in Gladys's life by providing an example of what an intelligent woman was capable of accomplishing on her own. She did not marry until she was thirty-five, unusually late for that time. Her independence was all the more impressive given her physical handicap: ever since an accident during her infancy, she had been without the use of her right hand.

Pearl was also a great source of comfort to Hannah, whose marriage continued to deteriorate. Relations between Hubert and Hannah soon became so difficult that Gladys was sent to live with her grandparents in Schenectady, where she entered the eighth grade at Howe Elementary School in the fall of 1914. Somehow she managed to score excellent grades that year. But as always, she kept to herself. George Osan, a neighbor, remembered her as "a very timid girl" who "minded her own business."

She ventured out only once, to attend a graduation-birthday party for George's older brother, Charles, a member of Gladys's eighth-grade class. George, who was twelve at the time, still remembered seventy-five years later how surprised everyone was that Gladys had showed up. "The only time any of us saw her was at this party," he recalled. A photograph from the occasion shows Gladys to be of plain appearance and seemingly less at ease than her classmates. It was the last time she would ever see them.

❧

New York City in 1915 was teaming with vitality and optimism, a place that offered a cultural feast for artists, entertainers and writers. Bohemianism flourished in Greenwich Village, where free-thinking radicals debated politics and poetry. The cosmopolitan spirit that infused the city was like nothing Gladys Greene had ever experienced in places like Plattsburgh and Portland. New York, she concluded, was not only a more exciting city in which to live, but also a better place for people to think you were from.

She moved there in the summer of 1915, when her father accepted a job with photographer Ira L. Hill, who ran a prosperous studio on Fifth Avenue. This turn of events led to another reconciliation between Hubert and Hannah Greene, who settled into an apartment at 573 West 159th Street in the new Washington Heights section of northern Manhattan. Today the area is poor and run-down, a haven for drug dealers, but eighty years ago it was blessed with open, grassy spaces that gave it a vaguely rural feel and made it an attractive residential neighborhood for newcomers to the city. The five-story walk-up building into which the Greenes moved was on a steeply-sloping street with a view of the Hudson River. A short walk to the east lay the Polo Grounds, home of baseball's New York Giants and, at that time, the Yankees. Just down the street was the Audubon Theater, an impressive vaudeville and movie house opened by pioneering film producer William Fox. For ten cents a seat, Gladys could get her fill of the Fox Film Corporation's latest stars, such as Theda Bara, the original movie vamp, and western heroes William Farnum and Tom Mix.

That fall, Gladys entered high school, where she learned shorthand and developed an interest in foreign languages. She thought of becoming a teacher of romance languages, or perhaps a clerk in a publishing house. Although nothing so exotic as the notion of acting for a living had yet entered her head, Gladys could not content herself with the dreams of her peers, most of whom simply wanted "to get husbands and furnish apartments on the installment plan," she later recalled. "I knew that I would never have become just a wife," she said. "My imagination would have seen to that. I would have felt stifled with only housework to do."

She did not finish high school, having been forced by a "change in family circumstances" to drop out in her junior year and seek work. A movie studio press book later alluded, just as cryptically, to "family financial reverses" as the reason she left school. Although no one knows precisely what happened, evidently Hubert Greene's employment did not pan out as hoped, leading to further strains in the Greene household. As a result, Gladys took a job as a stenographer on Bond Street in downtown Manhattan during the First World War. At war's end, a cousin returning from the service found Gladys and Hannah dwelling together on 159th Street, with no sign of Hubert. Her brother Bob also soon returned from the service, but Albert Greene was not so fortunate: he died in his midtwenties, apparently as a result of injuries sustained in battle.

By the end of the war, Gladys, now eighteen, had blossomed from an unexceptional-looking schoolgirl into an attractive young woman. A five-foot-three, blue-eyed brunette, she wore her dark hair in a short bob, a symbol of independence in the era of suffragettes. Soon she and millions of other girls started turning their bobs into the "Jeanne D'Arc," named for the French maid canonized by the Church in 1920, the year American women acquired the vote.

Around the same time, the comely young stenographer began a new career as a commercial model. Most likely her new calling came to her as a result of her father's professional contacts. She nevertheless later maintained that she stumbled onto her first modeling job when a friend who was posing for a commercial photographer took her along to the man's studio, where someone supposedly noticed the shy Miss Greene sitting in the background. "They asked me whether I would care to pose for girl's hats, and with some diffidence I consented," Arthur said.

As part of her effort to obscure her age, Arthur also claimed that her modeling career began when she quit high school in her junior year, and that she was offered a movie contract at age sixteen by a talent scout who noticed some of her posing. But while she may have done some posing on the side during high school, modeling did not become a serious occupation for her until after 1920. Certainly it did not bring her a Hollywood movie contract as early as age sixteen. But it did bring her money (five dollars a sitting, with as many as five or six sittings a day), and a brush with New York's glamour society. She modeled at the Hotel des Artistes for the celebrated magazine illustrator Howard Chandler Christy, whose "Christy Girl" idealized the young American woman of the period. She also sat for photographer Alfred Cheney Johnston, who transformed cheesecake into an art form. Hired by Florenz Ziegfeld in 1918 to photograph his Follies girls, Johnston went on to glorify the beauty and eroticism of women of the Jazz Age. He draped his often nude or bare-breasted subjects in lavish silks, laces and velvets, and posed them as gypsies, harem girls or goddesses. Arthur probably received the standard treatment.

Occasionally Arthur ran into another of Johnston's subjects, a struggling but determined young woman from Montreal named Norma Shearer. Norma had come to New York with her mother and sister in early 1920, when she was nineteen, to look for work. She found a job playing piano in a small Eighth Avenue movie theater near her $7.50 a week ramshackle room on 57th Street, then began modeling for illustrators such as James Montgomery Flagg and Charles Dana Gibson, and for Johnston and other photographers. She became the "Miss Lotta Miles" of the Springfield Tire ads, and had her picture plastered on a billboard above Columbus Circle. "Norma Shearer gained my whole-hearted admiration for her business ability," Arthur later said. "She made people realize her time was valuable. She was always prompt herself, and therefore got promptness and attention in return."

Alfred Cheney Johnston later only vaguely recalled Gladys Greene as a shy, attractive girl, but he vividly remembered Norma Shearer. "Now...there was an outstanding personality," he said of her. Others thought so, too. By 1922 Norma had landed several roles in low-budget independent films shot in upstate New York, and in early 1923, after signing a contract with Louis B. Mayer arranged by Mayer's young assistant (and her future husband) Irving Thalberg, Norma was off to Hollywood.

Her acquaintance Gladys Greene, for all her reserve, was not far behind. In mid-1923, she was given a screen test by Fox Film's New York studio after being "selected by a prominent group of New York artists in an unpublicized campaign by William Fox for new leading lady material." Though the bashful young model was unable to project much of an image on film, she was photogenic enough to be offered a one-year contract.

Arthur would later tell friends that her father took her and Norma Shearer to Hollywood by train when both girls were still teenagers, but this was simply another story Arthur invented to hide her real age. In reality, it was twenty-two-year-old Gladys and her mother who boarded the train for California. From now on the pictures for which Gladys posed would be moving ones.

CHAPTER FOUR

SUFFERING IN SILENTS

‘

Gladys and Hannah Greene arrived in Hollywood during the summer of 1923, only a few weeks after Norma Shearer and her mother had stepped off the same train. It is unlikely that the Greenes were greeted any more royally upon their arrival than were the Shearers, who had fully expected a veritable welcoming party to meet them at the station, only to find that no one was there. But such treatment was the rule, not the exception, in those days. The once-sleepy village of Hollywood had grown into the undisputed capital of the motion picture industry, and it could hardly be expected to busy itself with each of the thousands of girls who flooded the place in search of stardom. They usually showed up fresh from some hometown triumph in a school play or beauty pageant, chaperoned by expectant stage mothers, many of whom, like Hannah Greene, had been divorced, widowed or abandoned by their husbands. All too often, the aspiring stars came with too-lofty expectations, only to be ignored and sent back home brokenhearted.

But it was not for nothing that Hollywood remained a mecca for every girl who thought she ought to be in pictures, and for every mother who encouraged such a belief. For those who succeeded, the rewards were ample indeed; a young woman who had been earning twenty dollars a week as a shopgirl or secretary could make twenty times that as a beginning actress, and many thousands more if real stardom were to come her way. The biggest stars, like Gloria Swanson, commanded astronomical salaries, and came as close to attaining the status of royalty as any group of Americans, before or since. Thanks largely to the star system, by 1923 the Hollywood silent film had become the greatest cultural influence on the face of the earth, and the most popular form of entertainment the world had ever known.

But Hollywood was not without its problems, or its detractors. It had a seamy side of prostitution, gambling, bootlegging and blackmail that brought forth a drumbeat of criticism from church and other civic groups. While the forces of cultural opposition were kept at bay by the sheer popularity of the movies, a series of headline-grabbing scandals beginning in 1921 started to expose Hollywood's rear flank. "Fatty" Arbuckle, an immensely popular (and immense) comedian, was arrested and put on trial for sexual manslaughter in the death of a young woman he allegedly raped during a party thrown to celebrate his new multi-million dollar contract. Despite an eventual acquittal, the incident effectively ended Arbuckle's career. In 1922, Wallace Reid, a dashing young matinee idol, was revealed to be a drug addict; he died, disgraced and debilitated, a year later. And most shocking of all, the prominent director William

Desmond Taylor was murdered in a suspected love triangle that implicated the comedienne Mabel Normand and a rising young star, Mary Miles Minter—a mystery unsolved to this day. The sweetly virginal Minter's reputation was ruined as a result of the discovery of her silky nightgown, monogrammed "M.M.M.," in Taylor's bedroom. Normand, too, was driven from the screen when it was soon discovered that she had been supporting a $2,000-a-month cocaine habit.

Armed with fresh proof of Hollywood's depravity, its opponents began organizing local censorship movements and threatening boycotts of the movies, while Congress took up calls for a crackdown at the federal level. To head off these developments, which were beginning to adversely affect the box office, industry leaders moved quickly. Within a month of the Taylor murder they had organized the Motion Picture Producers and Distributors of America, to establish a written code of self-censorship. Will Hays, the Harding Administration's conservative Postmaster General, was hired to head up the unit.

In appointing a motion picture czar to clean up the industry, the producers were taking a cue from the professional baseball owners, who had recently created the position of Commissioner to help restore the integrity of the game and revive sagging attendance following the 1919 Black Sox scandal. And as it had in baseball, the strategy worked. Though many of the "reforms" imposed by Hays would not be enforced in earnest for another decade, when the infamous Production Code went into effect, no new earth-shattering scandals emerged in Hollywood. The storms of protest thus quieted, movie attendance began to climb once again.

To help sustain its appeal, though, Hollywood needed fresh-faced young innocents to carry on the tradition begun by Mary Pickford and advanced so promisingly, until her abrupt collapse, by the unfortunate Miss Minter. The market for sophisticated sultriness had been cornered by Gloria Swanson and her exotic new rival, Polish import Pola Negri. For those in search of sheer beauty there was Billie Dove, a former Ziegfeld Follies girl who, like Gladys Greene and Norma Shearer, had gotten her start as a commercial model in New York. And for weepy romances, no one could touch Norma Talmadge. What the studios needed most were new American sweethearts, but with sufficient sex appeal to interest Jazz Age audiences. In a word, flappers.

The first of them burst to stardom in early 1923, just as Gladys Greene was heading off to California. Colleen Moore had been in movies for six years, playing leading lady to cowboy Tom Mix, among others, when she appeared in *Flaming Youth*, the film that gave birth to the movie flapper. In it, she smoked, drank, danced daring dances and showed off her startling new Dutch "bob," all the while preserving her virtue intact. Within three years, she was the number-one box office attraction in America, having paved the way for new flapper heroines such as Louise Brooks and the "It" Girl, Clara Bow. As F. Scott Fitzgerald later remarked, "I was the spark that lit up flaming youth. Colleen Moore was the torch." Now the search was on for other torch-bearers.

And so it was this niche that Fox had in mind for its most recent find, Gladys Georgianna Greene. That name, of course, would never do, and soon after her arrival the young starlet rechristened herself Jean Arthur.

Fox wasted no time in putting the name Jean Arthur out for public consumption. On the cover of the September 8, 1923 *Movie Weekly*, the smiling and dark-haired beauty was shown looking very much the jazz baby in a low-cut minidress, her bare leg draped across the front of the chair on which she is perched. A month later another fan magazine displayed her in a filmy, Egyptian-style outfit and announced her as a potential new star. And a Fox press kit described her as "one of the most beautiful leading women in motion pictures, whose charm and histrionic ability will win her thousands of new admirers."

For her movie debut, the studio paired Arthur with future western superstar Ken Maynard in a two-reel comedy short called *Somebody Lied*, about which little else is known. That same summer, Arthur completed a small part in a major feature, *Cameo Kirby*, starring a young John Gilbert. Usually credited as Arthur's first picture, *Cameo Kirby* was also the first film in which the director listed his screen name as John Ford, rather than "Jack."

Based on a Booth Tarkington play that had been filmed in 1914 by Cecil B. DeMille, *Cameo Kirby* told the story of a Mississippi riverboat gambler (Gilbert) who was a southern gentleman at heart. The film itself was popular and well-regarded, especially for its paddlewheel race scenes. But Arthur's role, as a friend of the heroine, Gertrude Olmstead, was too small to receive any mention.

After completing her assignment in *Cameo Kirby*, Arthur was given her first chance at stardom as the female lead in Fox's *The Temple of Venus*. Featuring a cast of "1,000 West Coast Beauties," the film was a plotless tale about a group of dancing nymphs, with a few jazz-modern interior scenes patched in for effect. Nothing more than a screen beauty contest, it was nevertheless a good vehicle for showcasing the kind of innocent sexuality that Arthur was being groomed to project.

The initial scenes were to be shot on Santa Cruz Island off the coast of Santa Barbara, and it was with a mixture of anxiety and pride that Arthur kissed her mother goodbye as she left for her assignment. The experience that awaited her proved to be an unmitigated disaster. Her lines prepared, Arthur eagerly awaited director Henry Otto's instructions, but when they came, her efforts to slavishly follow them fell flat. Repeated rehearsals failed to yield any improvement. As Arthur later explained, "There wasn't a spark from within. I was acting like a mechanical doll personality."

Three days into shooting, an exasperated Otto called a recess and went to phone the studio. When he returned, the director called Arthur aside and said she simply wasn't working out and that the studio would be sending over a more experienced actress to replace her. The new female lead was going to be Mary Philbin, who had come to Hollywood with her mother in 1920 as the sixteen-year-old runner-up in a beauty contest won by Gertrude Olmstead, the co-star of *Cameo Kirby*.

"I thought I was disgraced for life," Arthur later recalled. "I wanted to throw myself over the cliff." Informed by Otto that there were no more ferries back to the mainland that day, Arthur panicked, unable to bear the thought of staying on the island a minute longer or facing her replacement. So she hopped aboard the only returning vessel, a fishing boat piled high with the day's catch and commanded by a crusty old angler.

"I almost forgot my misery on that trip," she recalled. "It was rough and I was deadly sick and I was soaked to the skin. I got home on the trolley at five o'clock that morning and frightened my mother almost to death by staggering into her room and begging her to start back to New York." As Arthur later said, the episode left her with an "inferiority complex." It was small solace that both the picture and Mary Philbin's performance in it were panned by critics. (Philbin would go on to co-star with Lon Chaney in the 1925 version of *Phantom of the Opera* before disappearing from film, like Gertrude Olmstead, with the advent of sound.)

Although Arthur was ready to pack her bags and return to New York, she had signed a year's contract with Fox. "So I stayed and made comedies," she said. They were strictly custard pie, two-reeler shorts. As often as not, Arthur's leading man was an orangutan, a lion or a dog. "One of the 'stars' I played opposite bit my finger nearly off," she later recounted, displaying the scar from an ill-tempered chimpanzee. But she dutifully played out her contract with Fox and made a couple of comedy shorts on loanout to Universal, one of which gained her notice as "a pretty girl with a personality that registers on the screen."

Although she was not yet very good at it, Arthur truly enjoyed acting. "I like to act because I've never been or done anything myself, so it gives me an outlet," she explained about that time. She listed herself as a "photoplayer" in the Los Angeles city directory, but it was not easy to find work. Once she toiled for free for eighteen straight hours in a promotional film for a new Encino nightclub, in hopes that someone would notice. But nobody did.

Then one day, while still getting by on income from freelance acting jobs and her mother's dressmaking, Arthur wandered onto the lot at Action Pictures, a producer and distributor of "B" western films. Lester F. Scott Jr., the company's aggressive and entrepreneurial head, was about to launch a series of "quickie" westerns and was looking for new talent. For his leading men he lined up a trio of daredevil riders whom he colorfully rechristened Buffalo Bill Jr., Buddy Roosevelt and Wally Wales. To direct these horse operas, as they were affectionately called, he hired Richard Thorpe, who later achieved success as an MGM contract director of swashbucklers, comedies and Tarzan films.

Finally, to serve as leading lady to his cowboy heroes, Scott took a chance on a complete unknown. At age ninety-three, director Thorpe could still remember the day a "beautiful, charming" Jean Arthur showed up unemployed and looking for work. Had he not been married, he recalled, she would have been exactly the kind of girl he would have been interested in romancing. Despite her shy manner, she had a certain pluckiness and a willingness to become one of the boys if that was what it took to make a western.

That it took, and more. For about twenty-five dollars a picture, Arthur churned out nearly twenty low-budget westerns over a two-year period, all of them filmed under crude conditions not much better than those found on the range. The films were generally shot on location, often in the desert near Los Angeles, under a scorching sun that caused throats to parch and makeup to run. Running water was nowhere to be found, and even outhouses were a luxury not always present. The extras on these films were often real cowboys, tough men who were used to roughing it and who had little use for those who were not.

Even more cheaply made than most B westerns, the Action Pictures films were eminently forgettable. The titles pretty much tell the story: *Roaring Rider*, *Fast and Fearless*, *Thundering Through*. The main ingredients were hard and fast riding, plenty of fistfighting and occasional gunslinging (but little onscreen killing) to ensure that good prevailed over evil. Add a touch of deadpan humor, a little romance and the final kiss, and the formula was set. They weren't art, but they were nonetheless a popular diversion, particularly in the small farm and coal-mining towns of the Midwest where they played in second-rate theaters.

Arthur's job in all these pictures was to be saved from the villain by the dashing hero. As Thorpe put it, "She just had to be there and both guys just had to want her." Still, the films provided Arthur with steady work and an opportunity to hone her skills in playing mildly romantic situations. Surviving prints show her evidently enjoying herself as a spunky heroine who sports stylish clothes and hats. She is also seen doing her own riding, a talent that would prove useful much later in her career.

While Arthur seldom attracted any official attention at this time, what little there was was positive. *The Fighting Cheat* (1926), starring Wally

Wales (named after the popular Prince of Wales), prompted *Motion Picture News* to observe that the girl "is daintily played by Jean Arthur, who registers as a very sweet and winning heroine." The same publication, remarking on *The Hurricane Horseman*, another Wales vehicle from that period, proclaimed Arthur "not only a pretty heroine but a worthy match for 'her man' when it comes to a question of daring equine stunts."

That last comment was clearly hyperbole, for Wales was an authentic horseman who acquired his riding skills on the Montana ranch where he was born and raised as Floyd T. Alderson. Buffalo Bill Jr. (Jay Wilsey), another of Arthur's frequent co-stars, was also a former rodeo cowpuncher and rider, while the third of the Action Pictures heroes, Buddy Roosevelt (Kent Sanderson), had been a stuntman doubling for the likes of Rudolph Valentino in *The Sheik*. None of these three approached the status of the greatest western stars of the day; each was a poor man's version of Tom Mix. And of the trio, only Wales, the "Cowboy Prince," displayed any real flair for acting. But they left a legacy of entertainment that is fondly recalled today by western film historians, and in which Arthur played a small but essential part.

During the two-year period from 1924-26, Arthur made twelve features for Action Pictures, plus several independent westerns starring the popular Tom Tyler, one of which (*The Drug Store Cowboy*, 1925) counted a young Gary Cooper among its extras. She also appeared in a few non-western films for "Poverty Row" studios, none of which did much to advance her career. She had an uncredited bit part in Buster Keaton's *Seven Chances* (1925), in which she rejected Keaton's marriage proposal; a few good comic scenes in *The College Boob* (1926), an attempted cash-in on Harold Lloyd's *The Freshman*; and the female lead the same year in *The Block Signal*, a railroad romance in which, according to *Variety*, she looked merely "ok."

Then in early 1927 she began to attract a little more attention, playing a gold-digging chorus girl in the independently-made *Husband Hunters*, which *Exhibitors' Daily* said "serves to bring Jean Arthur into the spotlight." She was also tapped by comedian Monte Banks as his female lead in *Horseshoes*, a farce that generally pleased the public, if not the critics.

Banks, a diminutive Italian who tried, not terribly successfully, to mimic the Chaplin style, had seen Arthur in one of her westerns and was impressed enough to give her a full-length comedy role, for which she was paid the cast-high salary of $700.

But after four years in Hollywood, Arthur was discouraged with her progress. She likened her roles to "a diet of spinach" and was frustrated that no one trusted her to play anything but an ingenue or western heroine. "My mother says I'm ungrateful because I'm not satisfied," she said at the time. "She says thousands of girls would be glad to get the parts I've had...leading lady to slapstick comedians, leading lady to cowboys in westerns, leading lady in independents." After all, her mother reminded her, how many other girls had been sent home without so much as a film credit to their name? But Arthur craved something else: she wanted to be an actress, not just a worker in films.

Hannah Greene's professed satisfaction with her daughter's mediocre career was a little condescending. Indeed, even after Arthur achieved success in later years her mother felt a need to put her down, according to several of the actress's closest friends. The reasons for Hannah's feelings toward her daughter are unclear, though they may have stemmed from self-doubts she harbored as a result of her failed marriage. She may also have been influenced by religious differences: Hannah was an ardent Christian Scientist, while her daughter never embraced the faith (though she was not uninfluenced by it). For whatever reason, the relationship between Hannah and Gladys Greene, while generally loving, was a tentative and difficult one.

Shortly after she completed *Horseshoes*, Arthur landed her first important role. Over the objections of executives at First National Pictures, who were looking for someone more experienced, director Richard Wallace picked her for the female lead in *The Poor Nut*, opposite popular actor Jack Mulhall. A college comedy adapted from a play by J.C. and Elliott Nugent, this box-office draw gave Arthur her widest exposure to date and led to her first mention in the New York *Times*, which listed "the appeal of Jean Arthur" as among the film's high points. But *Variety* offered a scathing dissent. "With everybody in Hollywood bragging about the tremendous overflow of charming young women all battering upon the directorial doors leading to an appearance in pictures," its review began, "it seems strange that from all these should have been selected two flat specimens such as Jean Arthur and Jane Winton. Neither of the girls has screen presence. Even under the kindliest treatment from the camera they are far from attractive and in one or two side shots almost impossible."

Though she was at least being noticed, Arthur had severe doubts that she would ever make it in Hollywood. Many times she was encouraged after testing for desirable roles at major studios, only to be told she was not right for the part.

Following each rejection Arthur returned home to cry behind closed doors. "It would have been better business if I cried in front of the producers," she said in an interview in 1928, her first for publication. "It isn't a bad idea to get angry and chew up the scenery." Bitterly, she continued: "I've had to learn to be a different person since I've been out here. Anybody that sticks it out in Hollywood for four years is bound to change in self-defense…. Oh, I'm hard-boiled now. I don't expect anything. But it took me a long time to get over hoping, and believing, people's promises. That's the worst of this business, everyone is such a good promisor."

Arthur's interviewer was plainly intrigued by this young woman, so unlike her peers and seemingly wise beyond her years. "She sits there slim, controlled—oddly controlled for a girl of twenty," the writer noted, unaware that Arthur was closer to thirty. "There are none of the flutterings, the aimless gestures, the italicized exclamations of youth about Jean Arthur. Her face is childish, with young curves and coloring. Her eyes are older than the rest of her."

"I want my break," Arthur said in conclusion. "I've got to get it before I quit. If I do get it, perhaps I won't be able to quit."

She got her break, at last, with a baseball picture. Entitled *Warming Up*, the film was produced by a major studio, Famous Players-Lasky (soon to be known as Paramount), and starred the handsome and popular Richard Dix. Arthur was skeptical about the project due to her relatively small role, another ingenue part, and the story, which was formulaic and uninspired. But when the picture was released in the summer of 1928, it was a box office success and was held over at many theaters.

The reason can be summarized in a single word: sound. *Warming Up* had originally been shot as a silent film, but was hastily retrofitted with a synchronized sound track and musical score in order to capitalize on the latest rage. Billed as Paramount's first sound picture (a slight misnomer, since no dialogue was included), the film was promoted with ads promising "Hear What You See!" As one exclaimed, "Above the roar of the crowd you hear a high sweet voice! What was she trying to say?" As an added promotional touch, the film was preceded by the release of a sound trailer, the first of its kind, which was greeted with tremendous applause whenever it was shown.

Critics dismissed the movie's hackneyed plot, but they were mesmerized by the novel effect of sound. "Without sound effects," *Variety* asserted, "the picture is one of the worst duds to ever come out of the Hollywood factory." But with them, the picture was "lift[ed]...unbelievably." The Boston *Traveler* called it "a brilliant forerunner of what to expect in the future," and reported that by the time of the film's climactic World Series finish, the audience was on its feet, joining in the audible cheering of the stadium crowd. No one seemed to care that the synchronization was so poor that the sound of the bat hitting the ball was heard seconds before the pitch was even thrown.

Fortunately for Arthur, the critics' enthusiasm for the picture spilled over into their appraisal of her performance as the clubowner's daughter. *Variety* opined that "Dix and June [sic] Arthur are splendid in spite of the wretched material," while *Screenland* gushed that Arthur "is one of the most charming young kissees who ever officiated in a Dix film. Jean is winsome; she neither looks nor acts like the regular movie heroine. She's a Nice Girl—but she has her moments."

As a result of *Warming Up*, Arthur was given a three-year contract with Paramount. Starting off, she was to be paid about $150 a week, modest by Hollywood standards, but more money than anyone in her family had ever seen. Her good fortune was probably one reason Hubert Greene went west to rejoin his wife and daughter, moving in with them at their bungalow at 1727 Courtney Avenue just outside Hollywood. Brothers Don and Bob were soon to follow.

With a contract in hand, and a box office hit under her belt, Jean Arthur was finally in a position to grasp that which had so far eluded her. The title of the film had it right: she was just now warming up for her bid for genuine success.

CHAPTER FIVE

FALLEN STARLET

Paramount Pictures was the largest and most profitable Hollywood studio in the late 1920s. Formed through a series of mergers spearheaded by Adolph Zukor, Paramount was the very model of efficiency, churning out a number and variety of features each year that no other studio could match.

The original studio of Mary Pickford and Cecil B. DeMille,

Paramount was home to a proud and glorious past. Its reputation was enhanced in the early twenties by such megastars as Valentino and Swanson and by the release in 1923 of the blockbuster epics *The Covered Wagon* and DeMille's *The Ten Commandments*. The studio had also weathered the Arbuckle/Taylor/Reid scandals, the principals of which were all affiliated with Paramount.

By 1928, with Valentino dead and with Pickford, Swanson and DeMille having moved on, the studio was in the process of revamping its roster of creative personnel. B.P. Schulberg, Paramount's head of productions, had managed to assemble a group of younger players who captured the studio's exuberant spirit, including his personal discovery, Clara Bow. With the release of *It* in 1927, this Brooklyn-born redhead became the new queen of the flappers and the industry's biggest box-office draw. Bow's sometime lover, Gary Cooper, was an up-and-coming star at this time, as were Richard Arlen and Charles "Buddy" Rogers. Among the promising young actresses recruited by Paramount were slapstick comedienne Thelma Todd, vivacious Nancy Carroll, lovely Fay Wray and playgirl Louise Brooks, whose jet-black bobbed "Look" was the most striking of all the movie flappers.

To complement this youth movement, Paramount kept under contract a number of veteran actors, such as Adolph Menjou, Richard Dix and Clive Brook, as well as comedians W.C. Fields and Harold Lloyd. It had also recently scored a coup by signing up the acclaimed German actor Emil Jannings, who went on to win the first Academy Award for Best Actor. And to direct its stars, the studio acquired a remarkable and diverse group of talent, including stylish foreigners Joseph von Sternberg, Ernst Lubitsch and Rouben Mamoulian, action/adventure specialists William Wellman and Rowland V. Lee and contract directors Frank Tuttle, Eddie Sutherland and Dorothy Arzner.

But for all its well-oiled success, the Paramount that Jean Arthur joined in 1928 was a studio very much in limbo. For unless its legion of actors and directors could work in sound pictures, none of the assembled talent would be worth the price of a single admission. Less than a year after Jolson sang in *The Jazz Singer*, talkies were no longer a novelty; they were a necessity for a demanding public. While thousands of theaters remained to be wired for sound (requiring the studio to promise "a continuous supply of silent pictures of full Paramount quality"), the many that had already been retooled made it imperative to start producing talking pictures.

To aid this process, Paramount outdid all other studios in raiding Broadway for talented actors and actresses whose vocal skills were already established. Fredric March, Claudette Colbert and Ruth Chatterton were among the "legits" who were persuaded to leave the footlights of the Great White Way for the klieg lights of Marathon Avenue. Sound also put a new premium on singing ability, prompting Paramount to recruit such musical stars as Maurice Chevalier and Jeanette MacDonald.

But by far the most eagerly-awaited, or in many cases dreaded, development in the conversion to sound was the voice testing of existing silent film players. Having initially convinced themselves that sound was a short-term gimmick, the stars were now panicking at the thought that their untrained voices would be judged unworthy and their talkie careers pronounced dead on arrival. An entire cottage industry of voice coaches and seminars sprung up overnight in Hollywood as actors and actresses learned "how to talk."

As Buddy Rogers later recalled, he and Gary Cooper watched from their dressing rooms one morning as Harold Lloyd was brought in for testing. They waited, past lunch; two, three and four o'clock came and went; finally the doors flung open and a young boy came out and exclaimed, "He has a voice!" Rogers and Cooper, together with Jack Oakie and Richard Arlen, promised each other that if any of them failed their voice test, the others would contribute ten percent of their salaries to him. (None failed.) Equally apprehensive, a group of Paramount's young female stars, including Clara Bow, Fay Wray, Louise Brooks and newcomer Jean Arthur, gathered in front of the dressing room complex one evening after shooting and declared that they were "not going to talk in films."

As it turned out, few silent actors failed to make the transition to talkies for purely voice-related reasons. But Arthur was convinced she would be among the unchosen few; after testing with Paramount's much-feared sound wizard Roy Pomeroy, she listened to her playback and cried in despair, "a foghorn!" But while Arthur may not have realized it at the time, Adolph Zukor recalled in his autobiography, "It was that foghorn quality which made her a greater star than she might have become on the silent screen."

In Arthur's earliest talkies her distinctive, throaty "catch" seems missing, either because it had not yet emerged or because she consciously kept it submerged. In reality, said Arthur Jacobson, then an assistant director at Paramount, no one knew whether an actor's voice would prove good, bad or indifferent to his or her career, save in the extremes. Thus it is probable that Arthur "passed" her voice test without much fanfare.

The Canary Murder Case, Arthur's first all-talking picture, is best remembered today as the film which both launched William Powell's career as a screen detective and destroyed Louise Brooks' Hollywood career as anything. The film was based on the novel by S.S. Van Dine, author of the popular Philo Vance detective series and the best-selling mystery writer of his time. Van Dine's on-set pronouncement that the movie was even better than the book set off a rush of publicity that had audiences eagerly awaiting its release.

Arthur was fourth-billed behind Powell, Brooks and James Hall, a Paramount junior star whose jealous girlfriend she played. The object of her envy is the "Canary," a showgirl played by Brooks, who is killed off early in the film. The suave Powell assembles the suspects and methodically eliminates each from consideration the way he would time and again as both Philo Vance and later Nick Charles in *The Thin Man* series. With Powell onto him, the murderer reveals himself in a surprise ending that audiences were asked to keep a secret.

Completed as a silent by director Malcolm St. Clair in the fall of 1928, *The Canary Murder Case* was extensively reshot by Frank Tuttle in December to make it a "100% talkie" rather than another mere synchronization. But the iconoclastic Brooks, back in New York after completing *Pandora's Box* for G.W. Pabst in Berlin, refused to return to California to shoot the retakes. Substitute actress Margaret Livingston doubled for Brooks in some reshot scenes and dubbed her voice in others, but neither the audiences nor the critics were fooled. For her obstinacy, Brooks was pilloried by Paramount and blackballed by the rest of the industry. She was forgotten until the 1970s, when her fabled "Look," her writings on Hollywood and the rediscovery of her Pabst films combined to turn her into a cult figure.

Arthur, meanwhile, attracted little attention for her role in *Canary*. In truth, she was not good. Stilted both in manner and voice, she was like an aimless, chirping bird. As she later admitted:

> I was a very poor actress in those days. You know—blah! I was awfully anxious to improve, but I was inexperienced so far as genuine training was concerned; I was horribly meek and not of sufficient consequence to be bothered with...only if you're a great hit do they give you the attention you need. If you've learned some acting techniques on the stage, you have a background of references. I presumed there was only one way to enact every emotion, and so I plugged along pretty blindly.

Luckily, Arthur had at least one powerful ally in Hollywood at this time. David O. Selznick, a rising young Paramount executive, had come to the studio as an assistant production supervisor under B.P. Schulberg in early 1928 and quickly began to make his mark. Literate and intellectual, Selznick despised the assembly-line manner of production that prevailed at Paramount, and he worked constantly to upgrade the quality of the studio's featured releases.

The burly and bespectacled Selznick was hardly handsome by conventional standards, but his enthusiasm and intelligence made him attractive to women. Considered one of Hollywood's most eligible bachelors, he escorted a number of young starlets about town. But he was particularly smitten with Jean Arthur, whose quirky personality fascinated him and led him to pursue her in earnest.

"He was crazy about her," Selznick's son Danny recalled. "My father loved women with a sense of fantasy and romance, which Jean Arthur certainly had," Danny said. "She had an otherworldly quality."

Selznick's infatuation with Arthur drove him to engage in fisticuffs with his brother Myron after the latter made a pass at the young actress at the Selznick home. On another occasion Selznick chased her around his house until she became enraged and complained to his mother. But it was not long before she fell for him, for David Selznick was exactly the kind of man to appeal to her: articulate, opinionated, profound—a man of ideas. His rebellious spirit also dovetailed with attitudes that Arthur shared, but was too inhibited to express.

That Selznick succeeded in winning her over is evident from an anxious letter she wrote him while she was traveling back East (in which she enclosed a photograph of herself):

> Please write—I think you might have written any way (I shall tell you personally why you are such a difficult person to write to).

The influence Selznick exerted on Arthur's behalf at Paramount appears to have been substantial. In May 1928, when he had just started at Paramount and Arthur was preparing to film *Warming Up*, Selznick wrote B.P. Schulberg that "the terms you spoke of for Jean Arthur are agreeable to her," suggesting that he had already taken her under his wing. Schulberg's son Budd later wrote that when he was a teenager, Selznick often dropped by the Schulberg house "with a young actress who was very pretty and very shy.... I remember a Sunday afternoon when she sat on the floor and listened with a lovely and I thought loyal intensity while David was busy talking enthusiastically, as was his style, about some new picture idea."

Their relationship was encumbered, however, by Selznick's romance with Irene Mayer, daughter of movie mogul Louis B. Mayer, for whom Selznick had briefly worked at MGM. A studio employee whose office was next to Selznick's told author David Thomson that Arthur would be there on some nights, and Mayer on others. And as Fay Wray recounted in her memoirs, she and husband John Monk Saunders were at the Beverly Wilshire one summer night in 1928, to attend a party being given for David and Irene in the hotel ballroom, when they "heard David Selznick's voice talking to Jean Arthur through a wide open door in the hallway." Wray recalled that Mayer danced the Charleston by herself that evening, and that "considering the recently heard voices in the hallway, the solo dance that night seemed very, very solo." Mayer wrote in her memoirs that she "desperately didn't want to know" about her competition at the time, but that Selznick did little to hide it.

Selznick was in fact genuinely torn between them. Arthur was appealingly whimsical, and the more attractive of the two. But Mayer was the more practical choice; like Selznick, she was Jewish, and she represented the proverbial boss's daughter. For an ambitious young executive like Selznick, these were important considerations.

But if Selznick was hedging his bets at that time, so was Arthur. Whether due to genuine ambivalence or as part of a strategy to keep him off balance, Arthur blew hot and cold in her attachment to Selznick. Briefly she became involved with Oscar Levant, a witty, neurotic young pianist and songwriter who had just come to Hollywood from Tin Pan Alley. The playful Levant escorted her to prizefights and speakeasies, one of which was raided while they were there. In later years, Arthur spent entire parties talking alone in a corner with Levant, whom she once called "the only brain in Hollywood." The leading interpreter of George Gershwin's music, Levant eventually fell victim to drug addiction and never reached his full potential.

Arthur's fickleness only served to make her even more attractive to Selznick. "He liked the fact that she was slightly unattainable, that she kept him guessing," Selznick's son Danny said. "Whatever other women he was seeing were falling all over him, whereas she wasn't totally committed." Danny believes that Arthur may have been looking for a marriage proposal, and his father once told him that they had been "practically engaged." But Selznick was reluctant to make the ultimate commitment at that point; he was young, without a great deal of money and still primarily focused upon advancing his career.

Unmarried and still living with her parents as she approached the age of twenty-eight, Arthur was clearly feeling restless. Although she had no desire to become a housewife, she acknowledged that "someone who could understand, someone to whom I could turn, would have been invaluable to me." Increasingly it began to look as if David Selznick would not be that man; he seemed to be moving inevitably toward Irene Mayer. And so, when another love came along for Arthur, she quickly, even impetuously, married him.

Julian Ancker, like Hubert Greene, was a photographer by trade. And like Arthur's father, he was a happy-go-lucky sort, full of romantic charm. They shared the trait of optimism, as well; Arthur recalled that "Julian dreamed of becoming a millionaire," and "had a lot of good ideas." But he differed sharply from Hubert Greene both in appearance and lineage: Julian was tall, curly-haired, and reminded Arthur of Abraham Lincoln. Ancker was also Jewish, as were both David Selznick and Oscar Levant. Perhaps this pattern was coincidental, but it may have reflected some subconscious act of rebellion by Arthur against her mother's Christian Science fervor.

Following a spur of the moment proposal and quick acceptance, Arthur and Ancker eloped to Santa Barbara in the latter part of 1928. "You should have heard our families' reactions—all sorts of screaming and shouting and carrying on about suicide," Arthur recalled. And so, she claimed many years later, because neither of them had enough money to enable them to live together on their own, the marriage lasted all of one day and was annulled. Shortly thereafter, Ancker suffered sunstroke while fishing and died.

That story, told by Arthur more than forty years after the fact, is not the one that circulated at the time. The fan magazines reported that Arthur separated from Ancker when she discovered a clause in her contract that forbade marriage without the studio's consent, which it withheld, thereby forcing her to choose between a husband and a career. According to one publication, Ancker then sued and obtained an annulment a month later on the grounds that she had failed to fulfill her marital vows. Arthur called these stories ridiculous and said the contract had nothing to do with the annulment. "I'd marry a man I loved this second and count my career well lost," she was reported to have said. "But I made a mistake and realized it. I thought it best to correct it before it muddied my mind with bitterness." Asked about it again in 1950, Arthur was positively cryptic about the cause of the breakup. "There was nothing tragic about it—it was a case of willfulness," is all she would say. Perhaps she had married Ancker only to catch David Selznick's attention.

Her marriage undone, Arthur got a break of sorts in early 1929, when the Western Association of Motion Picture Advertisers, better known as W.A.M.P.U.S., named her one of its "Baby Stars" for that year. Begun in 1922 as a promotional gimmick, the W.A.M.P.U.S. awards were given annually to thirteen promising starlets who were presented to the press at a formal evening celebration. Past recipients read like a "Who's Who" of accomplished young actresses: Colleen Moore, Clara Bow, Mary Astor, Joan Crawford, Janet Gaynor, Dolores Del Rio—and the lineup of 1929 Baby Stars put Jean Arthur in the company of such future stars as Anita Page, Helen Twelvetrees and Loretta Young. Though a W.A.M.P.U.S. award was no guarantee of success, it was as good a predictor as any in random Hollywood.

With such a hot commodity on its hands, Paramount should have followed up by hurrying Arthur into some good roles. But her next movie, a Zane Grey western called *Stairs of Sand*, was decidedly mediocre. The only interest it held for her derived from her co-star, Phillips Holmes, a handsome, twenty-year-old Princeton man who became her latest infatuation. But Holmes did nothing to encourage Arthur's adoration, and he quickly faded from her thoughts. He later died, at age thirty-two, in a World War II military air collision.

After *Stairs of Sand*, Arthur was tossed into an outrageously racist film called *The Mysterious Dr. Fu Manchu*. This all-talking picture concerned the evil doctor's scheme to obtain revenge upon the British army officers he holds responsible for the deaths of his wife and son during the Boxer Rebellion. Arthur played Fu's adopted white daughter, whom he hypnotizes to help carry out his diabolical plot, until she is rescued by her fiancé.

The Mysterious Dr. Fu Manchu was well produced for its day, with lavish costumes, authentic interiors and eerily lit sets. Ironically, the title role was played by a Scandinavian, Warner Oland, whose thick Swedish accent was indecipherable enough to let him pass for Hollywood's idea of an Asian. (Oland was so convincing as Fu Manchu that he was given the role of Charlie Chan in the movie series of the thirties.) And for the first time in her young talkie career, Arthur received some actual positive notices. *Variety* commented that in *Fu Manchu*, "Jean Arthur makes an appealing heroine, a girl who can act and handle lines without over-playing." The New York *Herald Tribune* added that "Miss Arthur has a winsome and appealing way about her." Director Rowland V. Lee thought he had hit upon the reason:

> Jean Arthur was a lovely looking girl but had a low, rather husky
> voice. So, with the advent of sound no one on the lot would cast
> her. I thought the quality of her voice would be an added attrac-
> tion and give color to her performance—which it did.

Whatever Lee managed to stimulate in Arthur seems largely untapped, however, in *The Greene Murder Case* (1929), another Philo Vance detective movie starring William Powell. This time Arthur is the murderess, a deceptively sweet young thing who tries to kill off the entire family. Though she is given substantial screen time, Arthur's role is insipid, her performance unnatural, her diction overly deliberate and theatrical. She comes alive only in the film's climactic moment, when she convincingly displays the desperation expected of a crazed, trapped murderess before she falls to an icy death.

The Greene Murder Case was Arthur's eighth picture in a little over a year under her contract with Paramount. "In those days we worked constantly—eight days a week, thirty hours a day, Saturday and Sunday," said Arthur Jacobson with only slight exaggeration. On days they were not shooting, actors were in the photographer's stills gallery or being interviewed by the publicity department. "They didn't let you sit around. They paid you and they expected to take that pound of flesh every day," Jacobson said.

In the beginning, Arthur dutifully went along with "the starlet bit," as Paramount publicity man Teet Carle called it. This meant posing on the sand with beach balls, in the gym lifting dumbbells or in a bunny suit when Easter came around. But she intensely disliked it. As time went on she sought to dodge such commitments, or at least to turn them into something off the beaten path, like posing as David Copperfield.

Arthur's aversion to the camera extended to the shooting set, recalled Arthur Jacobson, her assistant director on several Paramount pictures. "She was very shy about exposing her body," he remembered. Though blessed with an excellent figure, she declined to bare her legs and resisted appearing in revealing outfits. Occasionally the directors reworked the scenes to accommodate her, and eventually they learned not to ask her to do anything too risqué. "Nobody ever understood why" she felt this way, Jacobson said.

Indeed, Arthur's reticence before the camera is difficult to explain. She was the daughter of a still photographer, for whom she had posed many times, and she earned her very livelihood for several years modeling lingerie and other items. If anyone should have been accustomed to having her picture taken, it was Jean Arthur.

Arthur's friend Roddy McDowall has attributed her aversion to cheesecake to her earnestness over her acting craft. "To a very original personality it was deeply offensive because it had nothing to do with the work for which one is employed," he said. "It all seemed a terrible lie. I can certainly appreciate how she felt about it, except that because Jean was never casual in her emotional fervors she couldn't just let it roll off—there was no such thing as water off a duck's back with her."

But to assistant director Jacobson the feeling seemed more deeply rooted. He perceived it as a genuine phobia that related to something that had happened in her past, perhaps during her years as a photographer's model.

Whatever the reasons, Arthur certainly wasn't talking about them. For that matter, she was doing her best not to talk about anything, least of all herself, to anyone who didn't know her. That included not only outside interviewers but the studio's own publicity agents. "I probably knew less about her than any other person I ever worked with, she was so reserved," said Teet Carle, whose job included writing short star biographies for distribution to newspapers and film exhibitors. One such write-up on Jean Arthur from around this time makes clear the difficulty the publicity department faced:

Jean Arthur probably leads a more secluded life than any other girl in pictures. With her father and mother she lives in a roomy California bungalow. She seldom goes to public places, but keeps with a small group of friends. Horseback riding is her favorite outdoor sport, but she is [an] omnivorous reader, and her collection of books is notable for such a young person.... Her ambition is to own a large ranch somewhere in Southern California, and run it on a systematic and paying basis. Noise, confusion, glitter and crowds are her aversions. Peace, quiet, good books, music and congenial friends are her delight.

"She was nothing like any of the others," confirmed Arthur Jacobson. "She was her own individual, not cut out of a mold."

Arthur's penchant for privacy acted as a brake on her career in Hollywood where, then as now, networking was an important part of getting ahead. Unlike her colleagues, Arthur stubbornly continued to go it alone. "I have a negative personality. I'm too repressed," she explained in a moment of introspection at the time. *Photoplay* magazine, which fed on the stars' relentless desire for self-promotion, found such talk confounding, to say the least. "She has been called somewhat of a dumbbell in Hollywood because she isn't a whoopee girl," the magazine said of her. "A self-admitted negative personality is not understood in the cinema city. Calmness and the ability to reflect are unknown qualities."

But these were qualities that continued to appeal to David Selznick. Even after he became secretly engaged to Irene Mayer in the summer of 1929, he kept a steady stream of flowers flowing to Arthur and continued to promote her career. With Selznick's help, Arthur soon received her best role to date, that of Clara Bow's younger sister in *The Saturday Night Kid*. Any Bow picture at that time was a guaranteed box-office hit, and Arthur finally made the most of the opportunity she was given. *The Saturday Night Kid* was a remake of the 1926 Paramount silent *Love 'em and Leave 'em*, in which Louise Brooks played the part in which Arthur was now cast. The story was about a shopgirl (Bow) who sacrifices everything to her younger, conniving sister, who thanks her by stealing her money and her man. Some thought Arthur even stole the picture. Mordaunt Hall of the New York *Times* declared that the film would have been merely commonplace "were it not for Jean Arthur, who plays the catty sister with a great deal of skill." He called it "a thoroughly believable and natural portrayal, in contrast with her screen sister's, whose every other scene is shot through with heavy dramatics and thick sentiment."

While Bow might have resented being upstaged by her lesser-known co-star, she was actually quite supportive. "She was so generous, no snootiness or anything. She was wonderful to me," Arthur recalled for author David Stenn nearly sixty years later. Bow also lent a helping hand to another Jean in that picture, a sexy blonde newcomer named Harlow. "We were all friends on that picture and had a lot of fun," assistant director Arthur Jacobson recalled.

For Arthur, though, the fun was short-lived. She continued to mark time in her next few films, including *Half Way to Heaven*, released in December 1929, in which she and Buddy Rogers were romantically paired as tightrope walkers. *Variety* granted that Arthur was "a good looking girl who, given a chance to slip in a little more s.a. [sex appeal] may be going somewhere." The trade weekly also took note of her "soft husky voice which isn't hard to take."

David Selznick then got Arthur a part in *Street of Chance* (1930), a loosely biographical story of famed New York gambler Arnold Rothstein (played by William Powell). Selznick later called this "my first personal film, one I really worked on and cared about." But Arthur's role as the naive newlywed of the gambler's brother (Regis Toomey) was inconsequential. Director John Cromwell bluntly told her she should go back to New York because she would never make it in Hollywood.

Paramount on Parade (1930), the only musical of Arthur's career, was an all-star revue featuring more than twenty of Paramount's contract stars under the guidance of eleven directors in a variety of song and dance numbers and comedy sketches. Among them were Maurice Chevalier doing an Apache dance with Evelyn Brent, and Clara Bow talk-singing a nautical number, "I'm True to the Navy Now." Arthur appeared twice in the film, first in a brief comedy skit as an annoying nurse, then in a technicolor interlude in which she, Fay Wray and Mary Brian waltzed to a song called "Let Us Drink to the Girl of My Dreams" sung by Gary Cooper, Richard Arlen and Phillips Holmes.

That the musically talentless Arthur was included twice in *Paramount on Parade* may have been a parting favor from David O. Selznick, who married Irene Mayer on April 29, 1930, eleven days after the film's release. In her autobiography, Irene Mayer Selznick recalled her one-time rival as "a girl in whose talents no one then believed but David. She was not one of the cuties who came and went, but a girl with whom he'd been in love and broken off. He couldn't bait me with her, and when I refused to listen to her reactions about me, he stopped talking about it. I never even knew when she left the scene and his thoughts."

Selznick's son Danny disputed his mother's version that it was David who ended the romance with Arthur, rather than the other way around. "He clearly would have hung around," the younger Selznick averred, but Arthur could not tolerate the uncertainty. Danny also recalled that despite his mother's efforts to dismiss Selznick's feelings for Arthur as "just an infatuation," Irene was extremely concerned about her competition at the time. "It hurt her to believe that my father was seriously interested in Jean Arthur," Danny said. Irene Mayer was "very aware of the hold Jean Arthur had on David and she set out in their first year of marriage to obliterate her from his consciousness."

Years later, the thought of Jean Arthur could still bring a smile to David Selznick's face. Dancing with Fay Wray one night at the Mocambo, he saw his one-time heartthrob pass across the dance floor, prompting him to comment wistfully to Wray, "Oh, lost ecstasy." Characteristically, Arthur never mentioned their romance once it was over; when Danny Selznick tried sixty years later to gain her cooperation for David Thomson's biography of his father, she declined, telling an intermediary that their relationship was "a brief little thing" that "wasn't important."

With her mentor effectively lost to her, Arthur's career at Paramount began to ebb. She appeared in several more mediocre films over the course of the next year, including *The Return of Dr. Fu Manchu* ("Heavens, they were dreadful," she later said of the Fu Manchu pictures) and she continued to be stuck in lifeless ingenue roles. *Motion Picture Magazine* summed up her dilemma:

> The success story of Jean Arthur is always being written. But it always turns out to be a little premature. Every so often she seems to have beaten the game, and things that she does are hailed with enthusiasm and excitement. But afterwards nothing ever seems to happen.

In the same article, Arthur expressed a sense of both appreciation and resignation concerning her plight:

> They've been awfully sweet to me here. Mr. Schulberg told me not to feel discouraged, because my time was coming. But it'll have to come pretty soon. I'm not going to spend my whole life waiting around for a chance that never comes.... I've seen so many girls even after they get married, keep hanging on, taking little parts, hoping for a break. There are so many things I would like to do that I can't do when I'm working. I'd never just do nothing. I'd study—or maybe go on the stage. I've had several good offers.

One such offer she jumped at was a theatrical role in a production by the Pasadena Playhouse, where such future talents as William Holden, David Niven and Frances Farmer got their starts. On December 11, 1930, she made her stage debut in a three-act drama called *Spring Song*. Cast in the role of Florrie, the youngest daughter of lead Vera Gordon, Arthur came down with her first case of opening night jitters. Her hands were literally trembling, her appearance faint, when she told the director she didn't think she could go on. But she did and gave a praiseworthy performance, throwing her hands around her leading man and kissing him when she exited the stage to enthusiastic applause.

Back in Hollywood after the play finished its limited ten-day run, Arthur began to see the writing on the wall. It seemed that promising young female stars like Carole Lombard and Tallulah Bankhead were arriving at Paramount every day to take the place of the hangers-on, like

Jean Arthur, who had never quite made it. Broadway imports were increasingly dominating Paramount's casts, enabling the studio to loan out its contract players to lesser studios. As Arthur lamented at the time, "There just aren't enough parts to go around."

In an effort to spruce up her image and escape her fate, Arthur began dying her hair slightly blonde. "Mary Brian was the ace ingenue on the lot and somehow it was said we looked like each other," Arthur explained. "That was hard on me, for Mary was so much better than I was, and so much bigger box-office, that she was inevitably first choice. I got the ultra insipid assignments. It dawned on me that if I lightened my hair a little, it would lessen any resemblance."

But it was not enough. "So far as the studio was concerned, I dyed in vain!" Arthur recounted. In mid-1931, Arthur's three-year contract with Paramount expired, and she was given her release, along with Fay Wray and, ironically, Mary Brian. David Selznick told Wray that it was due to economic circumstances (the Depression was beginning to take its toll on Paramount's finances) and that she shouldn't take it personally. No record of what he said to Arthur exists, but undoubtedly it was an awkward moment for both of them. Within days, Selznick also left Paramount, when he quit rather than participate in an across-the-board executive salary cut.

With her contract up, Arthur faced the prospect of continuing as a free-lance journeywoman actress, scraping by from part to part. But her future changed when she met a young actor whose option Paramount likewise failed to pick up. Frank J. Ross Jr., a Boston-born, Princeton-educated man, had come to Hollywood a few years earlier from Long Island, where he had been running his family's profitable construction business. On the side, Ross was an amateur singer who became a regular in New York's high society by entertaining at parties thrown by the Vanderbilts and Whitneys. With Irving Berlin and other top songwriters of the day at the piano, Ross would give the composers' new works their first public rendition. Eventually, Ross's talent came to the attention of Paramount's Adolph Zukor, who thought the new sound pictures could use a voice like

Ross's. In 1929, Paramount signed the twenty-five-year-old singer to a short-term contract.

Hedging their bets, Ross and his brother, Richard, moved their construction operations to Los Angeles, where Frank Jr. awaited his first film assignment. The "singing realtor," as Paramount soon dubbed him, was first cast in a small, non-singing part in *The Saturday Night Kid*. According to several movie magazines, and as Ross told Bow biographer David Stenn in 1987, that was how he met the starlet Jean Arthur.

In a slightly different story he told in 1943, Ross said that he and Arthur said hello to each other on the Paramount lot for about three months, until the studio decided to let him go without having put him in a single picture. "I was to go East the next day," he recalled. "So I rambled around to the set of *The Saturday Night Kid* and there was Jean, and I asked her for a date, and she said okay."

But according to still another version, recounted by Ross in 1936, he and Arthur met by "accident" as neighbors, after failing to notice each other for about six months. This version appears closer to the truth, as it comports with what Ross later related to his niece. As told by Wendy Ross, daughter of Richard, it was her father who first met the young actress. According to Ms. Ross, the two young men were renting an apartment together in the same neighborhood where Arthur was living, a fact corroborated by Los Angeles directories indicating that the Ross brothers lived on Courtney Avenue in Hollywood, right down the street from Hubert and Hannah Greene. Richard Ross "kept telling Frank about this cute girl" he had seen walking around, Wendy Ross recalled, but "it was my uncle who put the moves on her first."

It therefore appears that Frank Ross and Jean Arthur began dating even before *The Saturday Night Kid*, and it was probably Arthur, the co-star of the picture and Selznick's protégée, who got her beau a bit part in the film. A few months later Ross was given another small role in Paramount's *Young Eagles*, an aviation picture in which Arthur also co-starred. It was to be the second and last film in an acting career that ended without Ross singing a single note.

But none of that mattered to Jean Arthur, who found in Ross a man unlike any who had previously attracted her. Short but handsome, Ross combined a pleasant sociability with an earnest and quiet manner. Like David Selznick, Ross was intelligent and well-read, and he possessed a serious, idealistic streak. But Ross lacked both Selznick's showy brilliance and his arrogance. Wendy Ross described him as "a total gentleman" who "didn't like coarse behavior." Though he enjoyed parties, which posed a potential barrier to any relationship with Jean Arthur, he was a private person who did not like to talk about himself, even among intimate friends.

In other fundamental respects, too, the two of them had much in common. The son of Irish Protestants, Frank Ross was the first non-Jewish man Arthur seriously dated. More than that, he was a Christian Scientist whose mother and sister were both practitioners. And like Hubert Greene, Ross's father was an alcoholic who separated from the family when his children were still being brought up. Though the Rosses were more well-to-do than the Greenes, Frank Ross was a man with whom Jean Arthur could empathize. And he seemed to understand her in a way no one else had.

By the time Arthur was given her release by Paramount, Ross had already abandoned his fledgling acting career and returned to the building business on Long Island, from where he carried on a long-distance courtship with Arthur by mail and telephone. So when she got the word from David Selznick that her Paramount days were over, Arthur simply packed her bags and headed back east, with few regrets about quitting the profession that she had pursued so hopefully, but painfully, for the past eight years. "Playing those colorless, vapid ingenues had bored me so that I just couldn't go on," she said. "The salary I could have earned by hanging on and taking whatever I could get in the same sickly sweet rut wasn't enough lure."

Before long, Arthur had settled again in New York and *Motion Picture Almanac*, the industry annual, was listing her as being "no longer in motion pictures." For all that she or Hollywood knew or cared, she would never be back again.

CHAPTER SIX
BROADWAY REVIVAL

*T*he New York City to which Jean Arthur returned in late 1931 was a far less happy place than the one she had left nearly nine years earlier. Physically, it was much more impressive and imposing: the soaring Empire State Building, the Chrysler Building and many other splendid Art Deco skyscrapers had sprung up since her departure. The Rockefeller Center complex was under construction, including Radio City Music

Hall, which would open in 1932 to rival the spectacular Roxy Theatre as Manhattan's greatest movie palace.

But while its buildings stood tall, New York's spirit was sunken. The city was now in the throes of the Great Depression, which was about to enter its grimmest year. Men sold apples on the street corner for a nickel apiece or shoveled snow for a quarter. Manhattan's department stores required college degrees for their elevator operators, so far did demand for jobs exceed supply. Many of the financial institutions in downtown New York, where Gladys Greene had worked as a stenographer at the dawn of the boom years, were now broke.

Amidst the panic Jean Arthur counted herself lucky. She had no job yet but she had money to live on. She was also virtually engaged to a man who appeared capable of riding out the crisis. Although the real estate business was stalled for the time being, Frank Ross's family wealth put him in a position to buy up land cheaply on Long Island for eventual development at a hefty profit.

In later years, Arthur maintained that she returned to New York to learn how to act. But in fact she was so disillusioned by her Hollywood experience that she thought it might be time to try something completely different. She thought of pursuing her original goal of becoming a foreign languages teacher, or perhaps taking up interior designing. But neither of these options was feasible. Because of the Depression, the New York City schools were not hiring, nor were New York's apartment dwellers, even the well-to-do, in any hurry to refurbish their living quarters. And so, Arthur found herself gravitating to the theater.

Hollywood experience carried with it a certain cachet, and it was on that basis that a Broadway agent helped Arthur obtain a supporting role in an adaptation of Aristophanes' *Lysistrata*. The play opened "uptown" at the Riviera Theater at Broadway and 96th Street on January 24, 1932, and toured the area until early March, when it closed in Mount Vernon. For her part as Kalonika, Arthur received fifty dollars a week—meager in comparison with what she had been earning when she left Hollywood, but more than three times the national average weekly wage of those who had jobs. Indeed, with nearly two-thirds of Manhattan's theaters shut down, Arthur was lucky to be getting any paycheck at all.

Shortly after *Lysistrata* ended its tour, Arthur landed a role in her first Broadway play. *Foreign Affairs* was a romantic comedy set in a provincial Italian mountain inn. The play starred veterans Dorothy Gish (sister of Lillian), Osgood Perkins (father of Anthony) and Henry Hull as criss-crossed lovers, with Arthur as a kitchen maid who falls for the sophisticated Hull. When the opening-night curtain rose at the Avon Theatre on April 13, 1932, Arthur was, in her words, "numb....When I walked on I wasn't sure any noise would emerge from my lips." But critics liked the newcomer. "Miss Arthur, making her stage debut, fresh from the talkies, is a vivid Anna," reported the New York *World Telegram*. "She and Mr. Perkins easily outshine the others." The New York *Sun* called her "dryly witty." Taking note of her unusual voice, the New York *Post* termed Arthur "not only charming to look at but amusing to listen to."

The play fared less well, closing after only twenty-three performances. A month after it closed Jean Arthur married Frank J. Ross Jr. The ceremony took place on June 11, 1932, at the Church-In-The-Gardens in Forest Hills, Queens, chosen because it lay halfway between Ross's residence on Long Island and Arthur's in Manhattan. They told no one of their plans, as evidenced by the following item that appeared four months later in the Los Angeles *Herald-Examiner*:

> If "grapevine" reports which were received here yesterday from New York may be believed, Jean Arthur, former Paramount featured player, has for some months been the secret bride of Frank Ross, millionaire Long Island real estate man. Miss Arthur is in New York. However, H.L. Greene, Miss Arthur's father, declared in Hollywood yesterday that he knew nothing of his daughter's reported secret marriage.

The new Mr. and Mrs. Frank Ross postponed any honeymoon while Arthur tried out for, and won, the female lead in *The Man Who Reclaimed His Head*. The play was a historical fiction set in pre-World War I Paris, and was scheduled to open on Broadway that fall. She then threw herself immediately into summer stock in Red Bank, New Jersey, and appeared in three plays with the Monmouth County Players.

On September 8, 1932, *The Man Who Reclaimed His Head* opened at the Broadhurst Theatre, with Claude Rains in the title role. He played a hideously deformed ghostwriter for a shallow French politician who steals his beautiful wife (Arthur), setting off a tale of revenge and murder. A precursor of such modern Broadway extravaganzas as *Phantom of the Opera* and *Les Misérables*, *The Man Who Reclaimed His Head* was an ostentatious production featuring a revolving stage, an enormous cast, stirring music and spectacular scenes of mobs, carnivals, air raids and Parisian boulevards. Unfortunately the plot was hopelessly muddled and the play closed to negative reviews after only twenty-eight performances.

Arthur's work received mixed notices, largely due to conflicting reactions to her peculiar voice. The New York *Herald Tribune* found her "endowed with charm of voice and beauty of figure...a pleasant breeze," but the *Post*, while allowing that she was a "personable young actress," thought she showed "a noticeable lack of vocal flexibility." Brooks Atkinson of the *Times* concurred, proclaiming that "her voice needs considerable cultivation."

While visiting her parents in California over the Thanksgiving and Christmas holidays, Arthur shot her first film in two years, an RKO production called *The Past of Mary Holmes.* The New York *Times* thought her "better than usual." This may have been due to improved spirits; during her visit, Hannah Greene wrote in a letter that her daughter "looks wonderful and is very happy." Her professional stock also seemed to be on the rise, for Mrs. Greene boasted to her sister Pearl that the studio paid her daughter's expenses and train fare both ways, "with compartment," which may explain how she was persuaded to make this inconsequential film.

Back in New York, Arthur continued to receive critical plaudits for her stage work, even if the plays she appeared in were nothing special. Commenting on her performance in *$25 An Hour,* which opened May 10, 1933, and closed three weeks later, the *Herald Tribune's* reviewer wrote:

"Twice this season I have seen her in stage dramas of no importance and each time she has shown herself as an interesting and attractive actress." The New York *Times* declared *$25 An Hour* a "tedious" comedy, but added that Thomas Mitchell's direction was "one of the play's two good parts, and Miss Jean Arthur is the other."

After shooting an ill-conceived independent film, *Get That Venus*, in Fort Lee, New Jersey, Arthur joined her husband for a long-delayed honeymoon that July. They spent it in the Adirondack mountains at Sagamore Lodge, an estate owned by Alfred Gwynne Vanderbilt, a millionaire friend from Ross's New York singing days. Then the Rosses headed to Long Island, he to resume his building business and she to do summer stock in Southampton with the Hampton Players, a group of Broadway regulars that included Esther Dale and Granville Bates. Arthur's performance that August as Dale's daughter in the new comedy *Perhaps We Are* drew raves from the Southampton *Press*, which observed that she "was very attractive and brought to her scenes some of the finest, [most] restrained acting that has ever been seen" on the local stage.

For the first time, Arthur was beginning to develop confidence about her craft. In the theater she had time to study her part and build a character, whereas in Hollywood she had been expected to know everything the moment she stepped in front of the camera. "I don't think Hollywood is the place to be yourself," she later said. "The individual ought to find herself before coming to Hollywood.... On the stage I found myself to be in a different world. The individual counted. The director encouraged me and I learned how to be myself."

Arthur's theater reviews from this period confirm that she had cast off the mousey demeanor that had plagued her screen performances, and that she had developed a knack for light comedy. Above all she had learned to relax her acting style and become involved in the world of the play. As Arthur herself later put it, "I learned to face audiences and to forget them. To see the footlights and not to see them; to gauge the reactions of hundreds of people, and yet to throw myself so completely into a role that I was oblivious to their reaction."

What her career still lacked, in theater or film, was a chance at a starring role. She had played any number of female leads, but had never yet been the undisputed center of attention. It was thus appropriate that her first such opportunity came in *The Curtain Rises*, a Pygmalion story about a spinster transformed by play's end into a beautiful and talented actress.

The Curtain Rises was a three-act comedy written by Wall Street lawyer Benjamin M. Kaye under the pen name Oskar Rempel. The heroine Elsa Karling (Arthur) initially hires a famous Viennese actor to tutor her so she can play love scenes with him and obtain some vicarious pleasure. After taking one look at her, however, the matinee idol turns her over to his more patient, less colorful understudy (Donald Foster). Naturally she falls in love with the understudy and, when both are summoned to the stage as last-minute replacements one night, a new star is born.

The same could have been said of Arthur herself. The New York *Herald Tribune* called her "a fair girl with a throaty voice and sincere manner [who] managed these transformations adroitly." To the New York *American* she was a "natural"; to John Mason Brown of the *Post* she was "the chief pleasure of the evening"; and Brooks Atkinson, who previously found her voice lacking in "cultivation," was now prepared to endorse her wholeheartedly:

> When Jean Arthur and Donald Foster are together on the stage it is remarkable to observe how interested the audience becomes in what they are doing, for they are the only forthright actors in the cast. Miss Arthur is a fair-haired, contralto young exile from the motion pictures who has appeared here in "Foreign Affairs," and "The Man Who Reclaimed His Head," and who is gradually outgrowing the monotony of her first appearances and becoming an actress.

The Curtain Rises was Arthur's favorite Broadway play from that period, and her most successful. It ran a respectable sixty-one performances, from October to December 1933, and might have lasted longer had it not been for what *Variety* reported as Arthur's "temperament." She refused to pose with the cast for publicity pictures, arguing that if any producers saw her in her frumpy first-act costume it would jeopardize her chances for future parts. She also complained of fatigue and had a theater hand spread a mat on the floor after each scene so she might lie down and rest. Then, on a freezing December day, she insisted on keeping the back stage door open during the matinee performance despite objections from the audience and cast. She even refused to appear for the second act until the management promised the door would remain open. After that evening's performance, the play unexpectedly folded, probably because the management would not risk lawsuits from patrons who might claim to have caught pneumonia as a result of the theater's negligence. It would not be the last show Jean Arthur closed.

With the run ended, Arthur headed to California, again to spend Christmas with her parents. Impressed with her latest notices, a number of movie executives approached her with contract offers, all of which she turned down. As she was preparing to leave, however, Arthur was asked to stay and shoot an upcoming film for a small but growing studio known as Columbia Pictures. Housed with other shoestring producers on the block near Hollywood known as "Poverty Row," Columbia could not match the prestige of a Paramount or MGM, but it did offer her a good dramatic role in a picture called *Whirlpool*, alongside the studio's bread-and-butter male star, Jack Holt. Finding the temptation too great, she agreed to stay and began shooting the film after the new year began.

Partway through production, Columbia liked what it saw and offered Arthur a long-term contract. The arrangement promised her steady work when much of her profession was unemployed, more money than she had ever made and proximity to her parents. But returning to Hollywood would mean long absences from her husband, to whom she was blissfully married, an uprooting from New York, which she preferred over Los Angeles, and interruption of a budding stage career.

It was this last consideration, more than any other, that made Arthur hesitant to jump at Columbia's offer. Her two years on Broadway had been "the happiest years of my life," as she later called them. They had allowed her to bury the "negative personality" that had doomed her in Hollywood. "I'm staying here on Broadway," she had insisted earlier. "You see, they let me act."

And yet she again found herself pulled inevitably in the direction of the screen. For all that could be said of the theater, it could not compete with Hollywood in its potential for bestowing mass acclaim on an actress's work. So Arthur agreed to sign on Columbia's dotted line. On February 14, 1934, she penned a five-year contract that gave the studio an option to employ her for up to four pictures a year. She hedged her bets by inserting a clause that allowed her to return to Broadway once a year for stage appearances, but for all practical purposes she was a film actress again. Once a Hollywood has-been, Jean Arthur was back in the town she despised, hoping that this time she would be allowed to be herself.

CHAPTER SEVEN

GOING TO TOWN

T here was no use mincing words: Harry Cohn, the head of Columbia Pictures, was a son of a bitch. That's what John Wayne, who made one film for Columbia before being dropped, called him; and that's what everyone else in Hollywood thought, whether or not they were willing to say so in public. Gossip columnist Hedda Hopper refined her description of Cohn only slightly: to her, he was a "sadistic son of a bitch."

Without fear of retribution, Red Skelton was able to say after Cohn's funeral, which thousands attended, "Well, it only proves what they always say—give the public something they want to see, and they'll come out for it."

Harry Cohn was the prototypical Hollywood studio mogul: ruthless, tyrannical and vulgar. A product of New York's Lower East Side, Cohn spent a resourceful youth fencing furs, pocketing fares as a trolley conductor and plugging songs in vaudeville houses and cabarets. From New York he went west to become one of the "Jews who invented Hollywood," as author Neal Gabler has called them. His C.B.C. Film Sales Company, disparagingly nicknamed "Corned Beef and Cabbage," was renamed Columbia Pictures Corporation in 1924 and, within ten years, carved out a niche for itself as the best of the small "B" picture studios.

Writer Garson Kanin said of Cohn, "He believed instinctively that it was only out of hostility, conflict, and abrasiveness that superior work could be created." He ran Columbia like a virtual police state, monitoring his employees' comings and goings and personally touring the studio to make sure they were at work. At night, he went from office to office looking for lights that had been left on; those responsible were excoriated the following day. He developed an elaborate spy system to keep tabs on his employees' personal lives, and was reputed to have installed eavesdropping devices that enabled him to listen in on their conversations. "You were a commodity, and he was very concerned to know everything about you," recalled Ann Doran, one of Columbia's contract players. But the rumor that he bugged the set was false, she said. "He bugged it personally. He was always there."

A man of intense sexual drive, Cohn was notorious for using his position as studio head to indulge his passion for young, beautiful actresses. There is, however, nothing to suggest that Jean Arthur ever became one of Cohn's many conquests or that his roving eye even settled upon her. Since it would be difficult to imagine two less compatible people than the gruff, domineering Cohn and the introspective, retiring Arthur, clearly what drew them to one another was not sex but symbiosis. Anxious to turn his studio into a major player, Cohn needed talented actors he could call Columbia's own, while Arthur wanted the opportunity he offered to validate her newly-honed talents.

Validation came, soon enough, with the release of *Whirlpool* in May 1934. In this sentimental drama, Arthur played a reporter assigned to interview racketeer nightclub owner Duke Sheldon (Jack Holt), only to discover that he is her father, who is presumed to have drowned himself in prison twenty-five years earlier. Father and daughter proceed to re-acquaint themselves and are virtually inseparable over the next few days. Sheldon insists, though, that she keep his secret to avoid disgracing and disrupting the life of her mother, who is comfortably remarried to a re-spected judge. To preserve his secret, Sheldon ends up committing suicide rather than testify as an alibi witness in a highly-publicized gangster trial.

Although *Whirlpool* flirted with mawkishness, Arthur's playing kept it from drifting over the edge. The New York *Herald Tribune's* Howard Barnes proclaimed hers a "brilliant and thoroughly plausible portrayal of a difficult role, marking her as a first-rate actress." The veteran Holt's per-formance, Barnes wrote, was "quite overshadowed by that of Miss Arthur. In a role calling for subtle inflections and a sure sense of the values in human relationships, she is altogether admirable, giving the whole produc-tion most of the poignancy and inevitable tragedy to which it pretends."

Indeed, it was evident that this Jean Arthur was a completely different person from the one who had left Hollywood only three years before. Now nearly bleach blonde, there was a confidence and piquancy to her manner that was entirely missing in all previous film appearances. Her new image was best displayed in a scene in which she jauntily bounces into breakfast with her mother and stepfather after being out nearly all night with Holt. The judge asks her in a scolding tone, "Don't you think that coming home at four in the morning requires some kind of explana-tion?" to which she responds saucily, "4 a.m. should never be explained, my dear!" When the judge follows up by asking whether she would mind telling him and her mother who she was with, she quickly retorts with obvious enjoyment, "The witness refuses to answer, Your Honor!" This was the first scene in the movies that allowed Arthur to engage in genuine repartee.

Whirlpool was also the first film in which Arthur played a traditionally masculine role—here, a big-city newspaper reporter. She appears relaxed and confident, almost brash at times. While critics have tended to over-look *Whirlpool* in tracing Arthur's metamorphosis as a film actress, it remains the earliest film in which one can recognize the Jean Arthur of the classic movies of later years.

Unfortunately, Columbia failed to capitalize on its talented new actress. Harry Cohn had lured Arthur back to Hollywood by promising to put her only in big-time productions, but her first few films after *Whirlpool* failed to live up to his word. She was reteamed with Jack Holt in a mediocre melodrama, *The Defense Never Rests*, in which she played a young law school graduate who sets out to expose lawyer Holt's unethical tactics and ends up falling in love with him. *The Most Precious Thing in Life*, released in late 1934, was a complete misfire, a tearjerker featuring Arthur as a middle-aged college scrubwoman. The twist is that she cleans the room of a spoiled and wealthy student (Richard Cromwell) who is unaware that she is really his mother.

Arthur had been eager to take on the part, which required her to don a grayish wig and apply makeup to make her appear older. But despite her sincerity in the role, the critics found her lacking in authenticity. Arthur agreed with their assessment, and later explained her miscalculation:

> Some of our most famous screen actresses had done roles sim-
> ilar. Such as Irene Dunne, Norma Shearer and Helen Hayes. I
> fought for a chance to do such a characterization. Above every-
> thing else I wanted to do that part. Unfortunately, for me, it
> was wrong. And if my eagerness had not blinded me, I would
> have realized the mistake I was making.

After this debacle, Arthur exercised her contractual right to appear in another Broadway play and returned to New York to rehearse for the title role in a comedy called *The Bride of Torozko*. Like all her previous Broadway plays, this one was set in Europe. Arthur played Klari, a Hungarian peasant girl whose Catholic fiancé (a young Van Heflin) calls off the wedding when a birth certificate search reveals that she was born

Jewish. A sympathetic Jewish tavern keeper played by Sam Jaffe then takes her under his wing and instructs her in the ways of the Hebrew faith, until it turns out that she is really Protestant and that she is free to wed after all. The play was "ineffectual," thought John Mason Brown of the New York *Post*, but again Arthur was the highlight. "In spite of the fact that she is still wasted on a play that is unworthy of her, Miss Arthur is a young actress who matches her sincerity and her skill with her charm and beauty," he wrote. Brooks Atkinson opined in the *Times* that Arthur "may still be a trifle too heavy for ideal comedy acting, but this is the best acting of her career, and it is modestly enchanting."

The Bride of Torozko had a short run, closing in September 1934 after only twelve performances. Arthur said shortly afterward that she would have given up movies for a long run on the stage if the chance had presented itself, and she still yearned for such an opportunity. But back in Hollywood, something better was about to come along.

❧

Nineteen-thirty-four was a watershed year for comedy in Hollywood, and for Columbia Pictures in particular. In February of that year, just as Arthur was finishing *Whirlpool*, a seemingly run-of-the-mill bus picture entitled *It Happened One Night* opened at Radio City Music Hall under the Columbia logo. Though the film was directed by Harry Cohn's hot young director, Frank Capra, there was little to suggest that this unpretentious romantic comedy would cause much of a stir. But the following year it unexpectedly swept the major Academy Awards, becoming the first film to win each of Best Picture, Best Actor (Clark Gable) and Best Actress (Claudette Colbert), a feat equalled only twice since (by *One Flew Over the Cuckoo's Nest* in 1975 and *The Silence of the Lambs* in 1991).

It Happened One Night ushered in a new film genre in Hollywood: the screwball comedy. Its dominant features were irreverent dialogue, good-natured sparring and a breakdown of traditional barriers between sex and class. Its protagonists exhibited a cheerful and sophisticated humor in the face of adversity and anarchy. And its consistent moral, in an age of unrelieved economic depression, was that love and laughter were the twin solutions to life's problems.

The engine that drove the thirties romantic comedies was the screwball heroine. The leading men in these films were charming, playful types, but it was the women who reveled most in the surrounding chaos. Beneath their surface eccentricity, they were the ones who possessed the strength of character necessary to deal with, and make sense of, their crisis-ridden world. At a time when men had begun to doubt themselves, the screwball heroines helped forge a new understanding between the sexes, one that allowed men and women to view each other in a more truthful and respectful light. And in the process they created, as author Roger Dooley has written:

> a new, peculiarly American kind of comedienne, the attractive girl who could be funny without losing her feminine charm.... Whether debutantes or secretaries, the true '30s heroines were breezy without being brassy, quick-witted but never smart-aleck, capable of meeting the hero on his own terms without putting him down...a breed of heroine never seen before in American films and seldom enough since.

Oddly, nothing in their acting backgrounds could have forecast the success of some of the greatest female stars of the screwball genre. Claudette Colbert had often been miscast as a femme fatale before she (reluctantly) accepted the runaway heiress role in *It Happened One Night*. Myrna Loy played Asian vamps for nine years before rocketing to fame as Nora Charles in the *Thin Man* series. And prior to her classic madcap roles in *Twentieth Century* (1934) and *My Man Godfrey* (1936), Carole Lombard's career looked much like Jean Arthur's: she began as a decorative leading lady in silent westerns, caught pies in the face in slapstick comedies, then languished in ingenue roles at Paramount.

On February 28, 1935, the day after *It Happened One Night*'s surprise Oscar showing, Jean Arthur officially joined the ranks of the screwball comediennes. Opening that day at Radio City Music Hall was Columbia's *The Whole Town's Talking*, which paired Arthur with tough guy Edward G. Robinson, on loan from Warner Brothers and in search of an opportunity to display a little-known comic touch. John Ford, who had achieved success directing westerns since he guided Arthur's screen debut in *Cameo Kirby*, was an equally unlikely choice as director of this urban comedy. But the screenplay was by two of the best comedy writers in the business: Robert Riskin (who had won the Oscar for scripting *It Happened One Night*), and Jo Swerling.

The film proved to be a tour-de-force for Robinson, who excelled in the double role of a milquetoast bookkeeper and the look-alike gangster for whom he is mistaken. But it was an equally breakthrough performance for Arthur, which became evident in the film's very first scene.

Robinson's character Jonesie, a usually punctual office clerk, is threatened with the loss of his job after he slithers into work twenty-five minutes late, the victim of a failed alarm clock. Moments later a pretty blonde coworker breezes into the office, tosses aside the cigarette she has been puffing and noisily punches the time clock before she is accosted by her boss. "You're late!" he screeches, and she replies, quizzically, "What for—has something happened?" "I want to know why you see fit to step in at 9:30 this morning," he demands, to which she pertly responds, "Well if you *must* know, it's because I saw fit to step out at 9:30 last night." She is fired on the spot, but this only seems to make her day. At that moment, a new screen comedienne was born.

The Whole Town's Talking was the first of Arthur's films to feature her in the type of role with which she would always be associated: the hardboiled working girl with a heart of gold, who successfully urges a meek but good man on to glory. Even if the role seems stereotyped today, it is a stereotype that Arthur helped invent, and it was exhilarating at the time. As *Variety* observed, after first praising Robinson's performance:

> Second in unusualness in the cast is Jean Arthur, now with some legit experience behind her. She's gone blonde and fresh. Effect on her personality is to produce a new girl. But a better type. She's more individualistic, more typically the young American self-reliant, rather sassy stenog. She will get other

opportunities as a result of this auspicious baptism in flippancy. Whoever guided her in the metamorphosis was canny in reading production trends.

Recalling the reviews, Robinson wrote in his autobiography:

> They were handsome in their comments about me, but their raves were really for Jean Arthur—that curious, neurotic actress with so touching and appealing a nature that she really brought a new dimension to the screen. No curlylocks was Jean Arthur; hardly pretty by ancient Hollywood standards, with a voice that grated like fresh peppermint, she seemed to me to be living—off and on screen—in a dream world of her own devising. She was whimsical without being silly, unique without being nutty, a theatrical personality who was an untheatrical person. She was a delight to work with and know.

Arthur enjoyed the experience as well, except that she had trouble following what her director and co-star were saying most of the time. As she explained about John Ford, "He's got this handkerchief in his mouth and chews on it while he's talking to you. And Eddie Robinson always has a pipe in his mouth. Between the two of them I couldn't understand a word. I finally said would you please take that stuff out of your mouths so I can know what you're talking about."

Although Arthur's next few films failed to match the success of *The Whole Town's Talking*, they brought her good reviews and kept her career moving forward. She was a convincing victim of small-town gossip in *Party Wire* (her first top-billed role), a sympathetic sister of gangster Joseph Calleia in *Public Hero # 1*, and a whimsical job seeker in *If You Could Only Cook*, released Christmas Day 1935, in which she breathed life into the usually doleful Herbert Marshall. One critic wrote that Marshall's "tendency for melancholia is so well concealed by Miss Jean Arthur's playing…that he takes on new life as one of the debonair, heart-throb boys."

By this time, Arthur's growing importance to Columbia enabled her to extract several important contractual concessions from Harry Cohn, including script and director approval and the right to make films for other studios. But Cohn had yet to deliver on his promise to cast her in only top-rank films. Moreover, she was still hungry for a starring vehicle suitable to her developing talent. And then it happened one night—she was discovered by Frank Capra.

Like Harry Cohn, Frank Capra came up the hard way. The son of Sicilian immigrants who arrived in America when he was six, Capra had to scrape and fight his way to the top. He put himself through high school and college by factory work, then, after a brief Army stint, he found himself unable to secure a job in his chosen field of engineering. He bummed around the West for a time, hopping freight trains, peddling products door to door, hustling poker, before he stumbled into the film business in 1921. After directing a few shorts he became a gag writer for Hal Roach and Mack Sennett, and then went on to direct the popular silent comedian Harry Langdon in several successful releases before Langdon let him go (Langdon had decided to direct himself, a move that led to his swift decline). In 1928, the unemployed Capra was hired on the rebound by Harry Cohn; the salary was paltry, but the quid pro quo was a substantial measure of creative control.

Capra's career rose steadily at Columbia, culminating in the Academy Award—the first for both him and studio—for *It Happened One Night*. But by that Oscar night in the spring of 1935, Capra was a physical wreck, having nearly died from complications following an operation for appendicitis. After he recuperated, Capra determined that for the rest of his life he would make movies to promote the brotherhood of man; as he put it in his autobiography, his films "had to *say* something."

Capra's new focus on socially-conscious filmmaking began when he acquired the rights to a magazine serial entitled *Opera Hat*, by popular novelist Clarence Budington Kelland. The story concerned a greeting card poet from Mandrake Falls, Vermont, who inherits millions of dollars and a New York City opera house, but prefers the values of small-town America over the corruption of the big city. Capra and screenwriter Riskin rewrote the plot to give it a Depression twist: the hero gives away his millions to the unemployed poor, prompting his cynical detractors to accuse him of insanity. The film went into production in December 1935 with the working title *Opera Hat,* and later emerged as *Mr. Deeds Goes to Town.*

Mr. Deeds was a sort of *It Happened One Night* with the genders reversed. Instead of a runaway heiress and a crafty male reporter as the protagonists, here the heir was a man and the reporter a woman. For the part of the rural innocent Longfellow Deeds, Capra's first and only choice was Gary Cooper, the tall, quiet leading man of western fame. But casting the role of the cynical newspaperwoman Babe Bennett, who exposes Deeds's foibles and ends up falling in love with him, proved to be more difficult. Carole Lombard was signed for the part but turned it down three days before shooting began in order to make *My Man Godfrey.* Production began without a leading lady, leaving Capra frantic. Then, as he later recalled, he stuck his head into a Columbia projection room and there, on the screen, was a lovely young woman with a quirky voice playing a western scene opposite Jack Holt. "Who's the girl?" he asked the film cutters, to which one of them responded, "Jean Arthur. Good, isn't she?"

Although Arthur never appeared in a western with Holt, Capra's recollection that the scene was an "offbeat quiet love scene" involving "something about a ring" unmistakably identifies the film as *Whirlpool,* for in that movie Arthur recognizes Holt as her father from the inscription in his ring. It is doubtful, though, that Capra stumbled upon these rushes by chance, since *Whirlpool* had finished filming nearly two years earlier. Most likely Arthur's name was brought to Capra's attention at Columbia and he asked to see a screening of her work.

According to Capra, the word around Columbia was that Arthur was a bit "cuckoo." But he liked her style—and her voice—and signed her for *Mr. Deeds* over the objection of Harry Cohn. "Great voice?" Cohn bellowed. "D'ja see her *face?* Half of it's angel, and the other half horse." Cohn accurately observed that the left, "feminine" side of Arthur's visage was appreciably more attractive than her "masculine" right. But Capra fixed the problem, as he did for Claudette Colbert, by making sure his cameraman Joe Walker always shot the actress with her best face forward. It was a move to which Arthur later attributed much of her movie success.

However she happened to be cast, Arthur was perfect for *Mr. Deeds*, and for her, it was the part of a lifetime. The film, released in 1936, was voted Best Picture by both the New York Film Critics and the National Board of Review and won Capra his second Oscar as Best Director. *Mr. Deeds* was the first true classic of the many in which Arthur was to appear, and it propelled her to international stardom. Watching the picture today, it is not hard to see why.

In her opening scene, her exasperated city editor is tossing out story angles to the male reporters, who are bemoaning the fact that Deeds's savvy press agent has been successfully shielding him from them. Arthur, barely listening to the editor's harangue, is off in a corner of the office, engrossed in playing a little game with a rope. After the other reporters are dispatched to pursue the elusive Deeds, the editor wonders aloud what he can do to motivate his star female reporter to join in the hunt. When he offers her a month's vacation with pay, she suddenly perks up. "With pay!" she exclaims, then barks an order to her boss to "Leave four columns open on the front page tomorrow." As she starts to leave, the excited editor asks her what she is going to do next. "Have lunch," comes the nonchalant reply on her way out the door.

Although Arthur has far less screen time in *Mr. Deeds* than her co-star Cooper, the characterization she created is just as indelible. With an adroitness scarcely imaginable a few years earlier, she manages an utterly convincing transformation from cynic to romantic over the course of the film. She begins as the jaded female reporter who will do anything to get a story. After gaining Deeds's sympathy and confidence by pretending to be a starving lady in distress, she writes a series of exclusive pseudonymous articles ridiculing the "Cinderella Man," as she's dubbed him. But then she begins to fear that she is crucifying an innocent man; she starts to see in him an innate "goodness" that calls up a long-submerged nostalgia for her small-town past. By the end of the film, when she testifies on his behalf in the climactic insanity trial, Babe is in love with Longfellow and is championing him as a friend of the common man. "When I was crying and working so hard at the end in the courtroom in *Mr. Deeds*, well it's funny but I forgot about it being a picture. I mean completely," Arthur told an interviewer in 1972.

Capra came to regard Arthur as the finest actress of her day, and it was her performance in *Mr. Deeds* that provided the foundation for his belief. "Some actresses could have played the cynical part, while others could have done the romantic ending," he commented. "But no one could have done them both as well as Jean."

Her other colleagues' impressions of her cover a wide gamut. Veteran character actor Charles Lane called her "a delightful woman to work with," and Lionel Stander thought her "a real pro" who "always knew her lines and hit her marks." But sound mixer Edward Bernds remembered her as "kind of an unhappy girl" who "didn't fraternize with the crew or other actors." And actress Ann Doran, who appeared in four pictures with Arthur, said that the star "was never sure of herself." Doran vividly recalled that Arthur was deathly afraid of visitors on the set or strangers in the studio's beauty parlor. Whenever another woman appeared while Arthur was having her hair done, she insisted on going into a separate room with hairdresser Helen Hunt.

"Never have I seen a performer plagued with such a chronic case of stage jitters," Capra wrote of Arthur in his autobiography. His claim that she cried and vomited in her dressing room between every scene may be exaggerated, but not by much. Gary Cooper witnessed several of her bouts of nausea, as did later co-star Cary Grant. Said cameraman Joseph Walker, "She stalled and just couldn't bring herself to do it. There was nothing wrong with her except insecurity."

"I'm sure she had immense self-doubts," confirmed Arthur's close friend Roddy McDowall. He recalled hearing that "you could never say, 'Miss Arthur, you're wanted on the set.' You had to break it to her softly, gently. You'd talk about how 'it's a lovely day, oh Jean, by the way, if you're ready....' You couldn't say, 'all right come on let's get going.' You couldn't do that to her. And it wasn't an affectation."

In *Mr. Deeds*, the easygoing Cooper elected simply to ignore Arthur's idiosyncrasies so as not to be fazed by them. In fact, the two stars' scenes together have an extraordinary quality of sincerity and tenderness, particularly in the quieter moments. In one such scene, Deeds declares his love for Babe Bennett by reciting a poem to her on her apartment steps as she weeps in response. Capra almost cut the sequence for fear it would be too corny, but Arthur had been working on the scene for weeks and she convinced him at least to try it. To release any pent-up audience snickers at the oversentimentality, Capra had Cooper trip over a garbage can as he ran away, prompting Arthur to laugh through her tears.

Those were not the last tears Arthur would shed on account of *Mr. Deeds*. According to a much-repeated story, she burst out crying at the film's preview because she noticed so many things she thought she could have done better. Many years later, viewing the picture during a rare personal appearance at a film festival, she had a similar reaction, but for different reasons. Commenting on the final emotional courtroom scene in which Babe Bennett is crying almost in hysteria, Arthur said, "Now I look up at the screen and my face starts to do the same things. I feel the feeling all over again."

CHAPTER EIGHT

MAKING HISTORY

After her success in *Mr. Deeds*, Jean Arthur was not only famous; she was rich, as well. In 1936 she earned $119,000—far more than the President of the United States, and three times as much as the greatest player in baseball that year, Lou Gehrig. Though well short of the nearly $500,000 a year commanded by the highest-paid Hollywood actress, Mae West, Arthur's salary was still a staggering sum of money in those days, when America was still groping its way out of the Great Depression.

Arthur immediately channeled part of her new fortune into her family. She sent her mother on her first trip to Europe, bought her father a camping trailer for use on his painting expeditions throughout the West and helped finance a new and larger home for them at 7750 Hollywood Boulevard—"the rambling old house under the pepper tree," as Hannah Greene once called it. Arthur also secured a studio stagehand job for her brother Bob and helped her oldest brother, Don, open a restaurant in Los Angeles.

Arthur's now-cemented stardom also led Frank Ross to abandon his Long Island building business in order to join his wife full-time on the West Coast. For the previous two-and-a-half years the Rosses had been apart an average of six months a year, and the shuttling back and forth had become tiresome for both. "Finally I decided that a builder could build anywhere but a film actress had to be in Hollywood," Ross later explained. "So, in 1936, I came out here to build." Though Arthur actually preferred New York to Los Angeles as a place to live, she agreed that "our happiness lay out here—and together."

Arthur had been living with her parents ever since returning to Hollywood, so the Rosses' first order of business upon their reunion was to find a place of their own. They rented a mansion in Beverly Hills, redoing the old Spanish interior in Colonial style, and acquired a glass beach house in Malibu. Among their oceanfront neighbors were two people responsible for Arthur's career resurgence, Frank Capra and Jo Swerling (co-screenwriter of *The Whole Town's Talking*), and two others from her Paramount days, B.P. Schulberg and Clara Bow, both of whom were now considered has-beens.

With Arthur's fame and fortune came something else that had previously been absent from her career: media attention. In her twelve years as an actress, fewer than half a dozen feature-length fan magazine articles about Arthur had seen print; invariably, their theme was to question when her streak of hard luck might end. Now that she was a bona fide star, journalists were suddenly clamoring for interviews and churning out stories with exclamatory titles like "Jean Arthur Defeats Her Jinx!," "The Girl's a Natural!" and "Blonde Dynamite!" Trying hard to Harlow-ize her, one such piece described her as the most exciting new blonde in Hollywood; "verily, the Blonde of the Month."

Despite their burst of enthusiasm, the Hollywood press merchants were perplexed by Arthur's indifference to the perquisites and demands of stardom. "You don't see her cocktailing about or dining at the Troc, except on rare occasions," observed one puzzled scribe. Another writer expressed bewilderment at her aborted appearance at an exclusive Hollywood tennis club. Arriving with her husband, Arthur took one look at the photographers lined up for informal star shots, turned on her heels and walked out. She later explained that she felt underdressed in slacks and sneakers, and that her lack of makeup made her unsuitable to be photographed. Indeed, she was forever terrified of being caught off guard by any photographer, for fear of being seen at less than her best. "Believe me, it's a strenuous job to have to live up to the way you look on the screen every day of your life," she once said.

Arthur also attributed her inhibitions to a painful, childlike shyness. "I can't seem to be able to do the things grown-up people do," she said. "I can't go to parties. When I do go, it's because I force myself to go, because Frank, my husband, wants me to go, thinks I should go for my own good. Sometimes I have fun when I actually get to a place. More often, I don't. I suffer."

As for interviews, Arthur protested that she had so little to say that it was hardly worth any writer's time to see her. She also found that it was impossible to open up to someone she had never met, and equally difficult for a stranger to interpret correctly what she had to say. "How can anyone in an interview really understand your thoughts, your ideas, when even people who know each other often can't really tell?" she asked one reporter.

Once, while filming on location, she turned away a writer who had driven forty miles in the sweltering heat for an interview; she sent word, without apology, that she had spent a sleepless night worrying about the interview and needed to rest over lunch for the afternoon's shooting. She later agreed to reschedule the appointment at her Malibu beach house, but nothing much came of it. Greeting the writer at the door with tear-reddened eyes, she explained that a kitten had been hit by a car nearby. She went on nervously to answer his questions, except for those decreed off limits by Frank Ross, who carefully monitored the session. Several times he addressed the more personal questions himself, interposing with an explanation that "Jean doesn't want to answer that."

Arthur's aversion to publicity would eventually cause the mainstream Hollywood press to turn on her, but for the time being journalists were more intrigued than anything else. Many saw her as a sort of American Garbo, only even harder to reach. "With Garbo talking right out loud in interviews, receiving the press and even welcoming an occasional chance to say her say in the public prints, the palm for elusiveness among screen stars now goes to Jean Arthur," declared *Movie Classic* in January 1937. "It is Miss Arthur, even more than the divine Garbo, who wants to be alone."

Arthur felt a certain kinship with the famous Swedish recluse. "I like to think that I understand Garbo a little," she said. "Her seclusion. Her refusal to talk for publication. Her belief that only her work is important to her public. I feel that way, too."

The two of them met only once, when a friend of Garbo's approached Arthur in New York and asked her to take a package back to Los Angeles and deliver it to the reclusive actress, who was renting a house up the hill from where Arthur lived. After holding the small box for a few days, Arthur summoned the courage to go up the hill. She knocked on Garbo's door, was let into the residence by a servant and stood in the foyer until the great woman descended the stairway. Awestruck and tongue-tied, Arthur introduced herself, explained why she had come, then watched as Garbo opened the package. In it was a huge diamond pin that caused Arthur's eyes to bulge with astonishment at the realization of what she had been carrying around. Garbo then turned to Arthur, said "Vy don't you mind your own business," and walked back upstairs. Whereupon Arthur beat it out of the house as fast as she could.

When left alone, Arthur spent most of her time at home, working in her gardens, tending to her pets, playing classical symphonies to herself on the phonograph. Above all else, she read. She typically "discovered" an author then devoured everything the person had ever written.

For physical diversion Arthur enjoyed long walks along the beach and dips in the icy ocean, where she swam, alone, at 6 a.m. each day. She and Frank Ross also loved to jump in their car Saturday mornings and take off impetuously for destinations unknown, not returning until late Sunday night. They frequented the theater and the movies, but never her own, which she was too self-conscious to sit through.

Though Arthur had no desire to see herself on screen, millions of other moviegoers did. After *Mr. Deeds*, she scored another success with RKO's *The Ex-Mrs. Bradford*, a screwball murder mystery that paired her with William Powell in a barely-disguised imitation of Powell's own previous hit, *The Thin Man*. Of all the attempted copies of that classic, this was perhaps the best. The delightful interplay between Powell and Arthur, as a divorced couple still obviously in love, approximated that between Powell and Myrna Loy. Indeed, as Frank Nugent of the New York *Times* wrote, "Disdaining the cries of 'treason' from the loyal Loyites, we must proclaim our complete satisfaction with the change. Miss Arthur is an amusing little clown who manages to be Mr. Powell's best friend and severest handicap without ever quite convincing us that she is just a nitwit." It did not hurt, either, that Arthur was outfitted in this film with some of the most flattering gowns of her career, courtesy of RKO's Bernard Newman, who designed Ginger Rogers' costumes for her greatest dance numbers with Fred Astaire.

Having made three films in rapid succession, Arthur was hoping now to take an extended vacation. But Harry Cohn insisted on rushing her into two more pictures, *Adventure in Manhattan*, a comedy-mystery co-starring Joel McCrea, and *More Than a Secretary*, a modestly amusing farce with George Brent. Neither film attracted much attention. Then, again without interruption, she was loaned to Paramount for her favorite role of her career thus far—that of Calamity Jane in Cecil B. DeMille's *The Plainsman*.

With the release of this wildly popular big-budget western in January 1937, starring Gary Cooper as the legendary Wild Bill Hickok, Arthur's career was truly in orbit. Her perfectly coiffed and well-scrubbed

Calamity was an almost laughably inaccurate characterization of the real Martha Jane Canary, a coarse, ugly woman who cut a wide swath of drunkenness and prostitution across the Great Plains as an army scout and stagecoach driver. Nor is there any historical evidence for the love affair between Calamity and Wild Bill as portrayed by Arthur and Cooper on the screen. But as with most of the historical hokum perpetrated by DeMille over the years, audiences didn't care in the least; they adored the film.

DeMille, who tried unsuccessfully to obtain Mae West for the part, admitted in his autobiography to "taking some liberties with authenticity" in casting Arthur as Calamity Jane. But the famed director found himself pleased that Arthur "threw herself into the role with appropriate gusto." Actually, she wanted to play it more or less straight at first, without makeup and with close-cropped hair, but Paramount opted for a more glamorous, Hollywoodized version. DeMille did require that Arthur learn how to crack a bullwhip, which she did, by cutting him across the wrist in practice sessions and leaving lash marks that he bore for days. "He wouldn't let me strike an extra he had hired to be struck until I had first practiced on *him*," Arthur explained.

Arthur's enthusiasm for the role was partly the result of her re-teaming with Gary Cooper, whom she described in later years as her favorite leading man. Cooper, a native Montanan whose parents had known some of Arthur's relatives, was a consummate professional in the actress's eyes. "He never went up on his lines—he was always there," she told publicist John Springer in 1972. As she later recalled for biographer Joseph McBride, "I can't remember Cooper saying much of anything. But it's very comfortable working with him. You feel like you're resting on the Rock of Gibraltar." Arthur may also have harbored a small crush on the handsome actor ("If I had married him he wouldn't have gotten cancer and died," she once told a friend), but despite Cooper's tendency to court his leading ladies there was never anything between them.

On screen, though, they were a convincing romantic couple. In *The Plainsman's* most dramatic scene, she and Cooper are tied by their wrists to a pole inside a tepee, facing each other, as they await a certain death at the hands of their Indian captors (led by DeMille's soon-to-be son-in-law, Anthony Quinn, in his first featured role). Although Calamity knows that Wild Bill loves her, he has never openly declared his feelings, so she is importuning him to do so in their last moments together. DeMille called their "brief, laconic, almost inarticulate exchange" one of the most touching love scenes ever filmed.

Another reason Arthur may have fancied the role of Calamity Jane was the connection between the famous plainswoman and Arthur's own relatives. Growing up in Deadwood, Hannah Greene would have known Calamity by sight, and her family likely had some contact with the itinerant legend in South Dakota or in Billings, a town frequented by Calamity at the same time Hans and Georgianna Nelson were living there. This connection was not enough, however, to draw a favorable local review for *The Plainsman* when it reached Montana in the summer of 1937. While proudly noting that Arthur's maternal grandmother was a long-time resident of Billings, the Montana Newspaper Association declared that the actress's "peaches and cream" portrayal of Calamity was "none too good."

Of all the reasons Arthur coveted her role in *The Plainsman*, the most important was her conviction that the character she portrayed was a symbol of emancipated womanhood. So strong was Arthur's belief on this subject that she was moved to write a full-length article for publication in order to promote her new film. In a revealing essay entitled "Who Wants to Be a Lady?" which appeared in the September 20, 1936 issue of *Screen and Radio Weekly*, Arthur wrote as follows:

> What I like about this day and age is that it doesn't trouble itself very much about what is or what is not "[l]adylike." Several years ago a great critic said: "No great lady can be an actress." Meaning, no doubt, that it was very hard for very well brought up Victorian ladies to tear their hair in drama, roll over the stage, shriek and otherwise go into tantrums for the sake of art.
>
> Well, time has proved him wrong. Most great actresses today

are ladies. So they were in the past, for that matter. Mrs.
Siddons, Ellen Terry, Julia Marlowe, Signora Duse—anything
wrong with them? I'll say not.

Women would have been emancipated long ago if it hadn't
been for the tyranny of the "ladylike," a false ideal and standard
of deportment. Their emancipators weren't men, but pioneers
of their own sex [Arthur listed Florence Nightingale and the
suffragettes as examples].

Arthur went on to note her own deep interest, as an actress, in the role
movies had played in the emancipation of women. As she pointed out,
millions of women wore slacks simply because Greta Garbo and Marlene
Dietrich did, and the movies showed women a world of automobiles,
electric refrigerators and other modern inventions and customs. "Isn't it
true," she asked rhetorically, "that Mae West's heroines, Katharine
Hepburn's tomboy characters, Bette Davis's waitresses and other tough
characterizations have helped millions to be more indulgent toward
women who are not coy, kittenish or too gentle? The movies have made
the world more tolerant, proved that this is as much a woman's world as
man's."

She included her own Calamity Jane among the list of women who
blazed the trail toward emancipation. "For one thing, Calamity Jane
smoked," wrote Arthur, herself a chain smoker for many years. "And
whenever she felt in need of a stimulating nip, she went into a bar and got
good service by banging the wood with a revolver butt. And she wore
trousers," added the actress, who likewise had a taste for alcohol and preferred to tramp around in pants.

Arthur concluded her essay with a paean to those modern women who
followed in the footsteps of their emancipators, without necessarily mim-
icking them:

> Really emancipated women are always natural, because they do
> what they want to do. They're not dulled with "culture," either,
> because there's nothing false or "put on" with them. They may
> be smart and well informed, but they are not stuffy. Because of

this there are thousands of emancipated women who don't wear slacks, smoke or drink cocktails, but type, clerk, keep house, raise children.

Doing what they want to do, they are emancipated without knowing it.

Following *The Plainsman*, Arthur's success continued unabated with the opening in March 1937 of United Artists' *History is Made at Night*, in which she co-starred with the suave Charles Boyer. A hodge-podge of melodrama and farce, the film was nevertheless well-received for the smooth romancing by the leading players and for the spectacular finale in which they survive the sinking of a *Titanic*-like oceanliner following a collision with an iceberg. The vaguely intelligible plot, involving an attempt by Arthur's sadistic husband (Colin Clive) to frame Boyer for a murder he himself committed, takes a back seat to the love scenes between the two main characters, who dance and romance their way through the film in evening clothes designed by Bernard Newman. Arthur would later remember *History is Made at Night* as giving her her most elegant and sophisticated role.

Director Frank Borzage recalled that Arthur and Boyer were business-like and professional on the set, without a trace of chumminess. "But in their scenes you'd swear they're the absolute real thing," marveled Borzage's friend and fellow director John Cromwell, who had once advised Arthur to leave the acting profession. "You'd suspect he had something going on the side with her," continued Cromwell, "but then you'd have to say no, not Charles Boyer, and definitely not with Jean Arthur."

Film Daily had predicted that "Jean Arthur will zoom to the heights on this performance," and she did. But ever since *Mr. Deeds*, Arthur was finding her best roles and films on loanout from Columbia, and she was beginning to question the value of her affiliation with her home studio. She particularly resented Columbia's ability to make money by loaning her to other studios for substantially more than her weekly salary, while she saw none of the profit. She also detested being told when, where and how often she had to work. Not only did this impinge on her freedom, but she discovered that she lacked the physical stamina required to go non-stop from one picture to the next. Now that she was approaching forty, she found the experience of having to carry large segments of each film a physical and emotional drain.

Deciding enough was enough, Arthur suddenly and unilaterally declared her independence. In March 1937, she signed with Paramount for her next film, called *Easy Living*, and simultaneously let it be known that she had no intention of returning to her home lot. Instead, she would work on a freelance basis, picking and choosing her own roles.

When Harry Cohn learned of Arthur's decision, he immediately filed suit to prevent her from joining Paramount for *Easy Living* and to obtain a ruling on her contractual status. Because Arthur's contract permitted her to make two outside pictures a year, he could not enjoin her from doing the film. But Cohn continued to try to hold the star to her contract, which still had three years to run. Arthur promptly counterclaimed to seek a termination of the agreement on the grounds that the studio had breached its promise to provide her with satisfactory roles. As she stated in a deposition in June 1937, referring to a conference with Columbia representatives in 1933, "I told them that I would not go back into pictures just to make money. I wanted to make quality pictures and to amount to something, or else not be in the business." She further testified that "being forced to do the kind of things you are ashamed to do is about the worst ill treatment one can possibly go through," adding that if necessary she would abandon her film career in favor of stage and radio work.

On June 25, Columbia won a ruling preventing Arthur from acting in radio or stage plays for one year. Meanwhile, she went ahead with filming *Easy Living*, a slapstick farce written by Preston Sturges and directed by Paramount's stylish Mitchell Leisen. Most critics found the film nonsensical and overwrought, and it was only moderately popular with audiences. Today, however, *Easy Living* is regarded as one of the classic screwball comedies of the thirties, and Arthur's performance one of the best of the genre. "We took the curse off the English drawing room type of thing, which I was getting kind of bored with," Leisen later explained.

"We just took off from there and went completely berserk."

The film's most famous scenes are the opening one, in which a fur coat thrown from an apartment penthouse lands upon working girl Mary Smith (Arthur), and the Automat scene, featuring a chaotic food fight among the patrons. But Arthur shone as well in several less frenetic moments, as when she arrives at a Waldorf-style hotel for what she thinks is a job interview (in fact she has been summoned by the hotel's owner, who has mistaken her for a millionaire's mistress). After receiving a tour of the palatial, gleaming-white, luxury suite the owner has set aside for her, Arthur's Mary flops down in a chair with a look of bewilderment, sighs softly to herself, "golly"—then springs to her feet and races back through the apartment to re-tour her fantastic surroundings.

Director Leisen called this delayed reaction an example of Arthur's "fabulous sense of timing." The most obvious thing, he thought, would have been for her to react to every detail of the apartment as it was being shown. Instead, she did just the opposite, saving her scrutiny for when she could be alone.

Later in the film, Arthur and co-star Ray Milland (the millionaire's son) end up sleeping with each other, Production Code-style. As Leisen recalled, to get around the censors he had the two stars lie with their heads together, feet apart, instead of side-by-side, as they were falling asleep on the drawing room couch. They say good night, he kisses her, she rolls over, and then comes another delayed reaction from her. She is about to drift off to sleep when suddenly she realizes they are lying together on the couch. "Say!" she protests, bolting upright. After a moment's hesitation, she breaks into a growing smile, deciding that she likes it, after all.

Easy Living was the first of Arthur's major films to revolve around her character, to be seen by the audience principally through her eyes. Though Mary Smith is ostensibly less intelligent than many of the professional women Arthur played, her sweet-tempered, wide-eyed bemusement at her surroundings stamps her as an appealing screwball character. And in Mary's very plainness lay the essential Arthur paradox—what James Harvey called her "special talent for making ordinary niceness on the screen seem somehow remarkable—and interesting." As Harvey observed, "In a way, she completes the cycle of screwball heroines, confirming the tendency to move their glamour closer to ordinary life."

While Mary Smith's troubles appear over at the end of *Easy Living*, Jean Arthur's were not. As soon as filming was completed, Harry Cohn decided to escalate warfare with his star. He ordered her to appear at Warner Bros. on loanout on a certain date, without telling her the title, director or cast of the film. Arthur refused to report, enabling Cohn to formally place her on suspension. The effect of this was twofold. Officially, it extended her contract for as long as she remained absent—a draconion penalty that studios could impose until Olivia de Havilland won a landmark court case in the 1940s. Unofficially, Arthur's suspension ensured that no one else in Hollywood would hire her.

By now, Arthur had been pushed to the breaking point. She hatched a bizarre plot to murder Harry Cohn by slipping into his office and firing a hidden revolver. She later said that she "almost found the perfect way of killing [Cohn] without getting caught." Arthur recounted this story matter-of-factly to friends on numerous occasions. "When she began telling it my mouth opened," said Roddy McDowall, "because I realized it was a definite plan. And it was quite reasonable in her mind and could have worked out."

When Frank Ross learned of her machinations he decided he had to take her away from Hollywood. The Rosses got in their car and headed north from Los Angeles toward San Francisco, stumbling on the oceanside colony of Carmel. Arthur was immediately captivated by the then picturesque, quiet community of talented young artists and writers. As Arthur marveled, it was "another world." What drew her attention most was a small clifftop cottage set on the westernmost, protruding tip of the village, with an unsurpassed view of the sea. As they were negotiating the treacherous curve on the cliff along the Point, as this spot was known, she told her husband to stop the car, that this was the house they were going to rent. Actually, they had not come looking to rent anything, but Arthur was hooked, and they negotiated a lease on the house known as "Driftwood," so named for the sturdy redwood lumber with which it was built in 1908.

Once ensconced in her new summer residence, Arthur set about calming her frazzled nerves. She spent most of her time in long walks along the beach, "not even thinking," as she said. "I was completely worn out, more mentally than physically. I'd made six pictures in a year, which are three too many—for me. The argument with the studio was, of course, nerve-racking to me. I was absolutely numb."

Ross soon returned to Los Angeles, where he had re-entered the movie business as an assistant to Hal Roach. When he left, Arthur's mother came to Carmel to keep her company. As Hannah Greene wrote to her sister Pearl that summer:

> Jean came here for a rest and wanted me here with her so—
> here I am.... We will go roaming one day Pearl—just now Jean
> is having quite a trial and I feel—as usual—that I should be
> near at such a time.

By January 1938, with Arthur still in Carmel, Hollywood columnist Sheilah Graham was reporting that the actress had decided to retire permanently from the screen. The story was probably a plant by Harry Cohn to draw out his star, for he desperately needed her back. He had just settled another bitter, protracted legal dispute—this one with Frank Capra over Columbia's false labeling of *If You Could Only Cook* as a Capra production. Now Capra wanted Arthur for his next project, the filming of George S. Kaufman and Moss Hart's Pulitzer Prize-winning play, *You Can't Take It With You.*

It was byzantine Hollywood politics that led to Arthur's reconciliation with Columbia. Assuming that his favorite actress was unavailable, Capra secured Warners' agreement to lend him Olivia de Havilland for the female lead in *You Can't Take It With You.* But after Capra maneuvered the Academy's first Irving Thalberg Award to Darryl Zanuck over Jack Warner's strong protest, Warner refused to deliver on de Havilland. With shooting scheduled to begin the next month, Capra turned his attention back to Arthur. He brokered a settlement between her and Columbia by persuading Harry Cohn to buy the Clifford Odets play *Golden Boy,* which

Capra would direct and in which Arthur would star in the role played by Frances Farmer on Broadway.

In March 1938, Columbia and Arthur officially ended their year-long legal battle by entering into a new three-year contract. It was a clear victory for the star. The contract allowed her to fulfill her obligations to Columbia with only two pictures a year, with the right to do one film a year at another studio. She also managed to negotiate an unusual "no publicity" clause that relieved her of any duty to participate in interviews or public appearances.

To the Hollywood press, this was an act of monumental hubris. The film media had been turning increasingly hostile toward Arthur ever since she began her one-woman boycott the previous year. Stories of her alleged temperamentalism were cropping up with regularity; according to one such tale, when she did not like a particular wig she had been given to wear, she tore it off, threw it on the floor and stomped on it. Another typical report was the following by *Photoplay* from the set of *You Can't Take It With You*:

> After the "cut" Jean Arthur sweeps by, snooty and unsmiling. Jean does not win our popularity contest in Hollywood, but maybe she doesn't want to be the life of the party. She looks very much the same after her year's holdout. Columbia used this grand part to lure her back again after her sulk about bad assignments. Still, she doesn't look a bit happy about it.

In truth Arthur didn't think much of her role as Alice Sycamore, the only normal member of the eccentric Vanderhof family headed by Lionel Barrymore. She saw the part as straight ingenue, the hardest thing for her to play, and a potential throwback to the kind of roles that nearly buried her career years earlier. But the film's theme of non-conformity appealed strongly to her. As Capra put it, the story was about "a happy-go-lucky family of rebels...living in perfect concord, finding happiness in individual expression: doing the things they had always *wanted* to do, even though they did them badly." Arthur likened their attitude to her own. "Don't let anyone tell you that you have to 'go the pace' in Hollywood," she advised newspaper readers. "There are lots of people like the Vanderhofs...really working and living in Hollywood. I'd like to be able to believe that I'm one of them."

With Capra directing and Robert Riskin supplying a suitably Capra-esque screenplay, *You Can't Take It With You* was destined to succeed. Exceeding expectations, it not only became Capra's biggest moneymaker for Columbia to that time, but also won Oscars for Best Picture and Best Director. Arthur could hardly have chosen a better vehicle for putting her back in the moviegoing public's mind.

Arthur's quietly sincere performance as a youthful bank stenographer is thoroughly convincing, notwithstanding that she was thirty-seven at the time. Conventional mugging would have dictated that she express constant embarrassment and apologies on behalf of her "screwball" family, but there is nothing stock in Arthur's Alice. Her impassioned courtroom speech near the end of the film in defense of Grandpa Vanderhof (Barrymore) is almost as effective as her similar monologue in *Mr. Deeds*. Best of all is the nightclub scene in which her blue-blood date unintentionally provokes her to scream in terror, then explains her outburst to the startled patrons by pointing to a non-existent scurry of mice. In the ensuing pandemonium, when most girls of the time would slink away, Arthur proudly struts out of the restaurant on her consort's arm, unaware of the "Nuts" sign he has pinned to the back of her cape.

Arthur's date in that scene was a relative newcomer named James Stewart, appearing in the first of his three films for Capra. Ann Miller later recalled that all the women in the cast developed a crush on the young actor ("I think even Jean Arthur," she ventured). Though Arthur preferred the quiet style of that other Capra hero, Gary Cooper, to the deliberate cuteness of the stammering Stewart, she respected the latter's talent. Stewart was even more impressed with his leading lady, later calling her "the finest actress I ever worked with. No one had her humor, her timing." *You Can't Take It With You* was far from either's best opportunity to display their respective abilities, but it helped establish them as the quintessential Capra couple.

As filming for *You Can't Take It With You* was being completed, Arthur expressed hope that she was learning to take things more in stride than she had before her year-long holdout. "This past year, I rather got in the habit of living each day for itself, not brooding about either yesterday or tomorrow. I learned how to relax—really relax, for the first time in my life," she said. She and Frank Ross had recently moved from Beverly Hills into a unique, modernistic three-story house high in the hills of Brentwood, complete with pool, terrace and garden. Though the Rosses continued to rent rather than own, Arthur spent much of her time furnishing their new residence and stocking it with books for evening reading. She was even talked into occasional visits to the nearby West Side Tennis Club where the picture crowd congregated.

Still, Arthur remained curiously frustrated from a professional standpoint. She insisted that her next film would not be screwball comedy, but rather something more substantial. Asked if she had a special ambition to do a particular part, she responded that she had "an actress's usual complex of wanting to play everything from Peter Pan to Joan of Arc." Her husband further explained that "Jean is not essentially a happy person, you know. She is not in any way a Polyanna. She is never satisfied with herself."

As 1938 began to draw to a close, however, Arthur suddenly found herself facing the acting opportunity of a lifetime. To her bitter disappointment, she did not win that opportunity, but nonetheless she did, in the great Hollywood year of 1939, score one of her greatest film successes. Having set out for old Atlanta, she instead ended up in contemporary Washington, D.C.

CHAPTER NINE

CONSOLATION PRIZES

*S*carlett O'Hara was not beautiful, according to the opening line of Margaret Mitchell's famous novel. But that disclaimer did nothing to diminish interest in the identity of the woman who would play her on the big screen. For Scarlett was endowed by her creator with qualities of charm, guile and resourcefulness unrivaled among American fictional heroines. Largely on the strength of Scarlett's fiery character, *Gone With the Wind* had become the best-loved novel of all time.

For David O. Selznick, who purchased the rights to the book in 1936, the search for the perfect Scarlett had turned from ponderous to methodical to urgent. Originally, he had toyed with casting a native Southerner like Tallulah Bankhead. Indeed, Georgia's Miriam Hopkins and Virginia's Margaret Sullavan were the early favorites among the readers and ladies clubs who flooded Selznick's office with letters of suggestion. But they were never seriously in contention, nor were Northern candidates Joan Crawford and Carole Lombard. Bette Davis and Katharine Hepburn were logical contenders, but their strong personalities alienated much of the potential audience. And therein lay the principal problem in casting Scarlett: the predetermined persona that any established actress would bring to the role.

By early 1937 Selznick concluded that what he needed was a complete newcomer to play Scarlett—someone without prior baggage who could be elevated to overnight stardom. To that end Selznick organized a nationwide talent search, sending assistants to fan throughout the country into hundreds of high schools, college drama departments and small community theaters. In Atlanta alone, 500 young and not-so-young belles turned out for auditions in one day. The press had a field day, and even Margaret Mitchell, traveling incognito, could not resist sneaking a peak at the festivities. But almost two years later, after nearly 1,500 interviews had been conducted and thirty actresses screen-tested, Selznick was no closer to finding his Scarlett than when he began.

In August 1938 Selznick signed his Rhett Butler, having struck a deal with his father-in-law, Louis B. Mayer, to secure Clark Gable's services from MGM. But Gable's contract specified that his shooting obligations were to commence no later than January 5, 1939, and that he would be available for only twenty weeks. As a result, the pressure intensified on Selznick to find a co-star and put an end to what had become a national obsession. In October, he wrote to Cukor that he was still "hoping against hope for that new girl," going so far as to proclaim that without her, the picture might be doomed to failure. In the meantime Selznick had narrowed the field of front-runners to a short list of five—including one amateur, Doris Jordan; two up-and-coming leading ladies, Paulette

Goddard and Loretta Young; and two clear superstars, the great Katharine Hepburn and...Jean Arthur.

Hepburn had been her friend Cukor's choice from the beginning, but her regal, almost sexless personality left Selznick cold, and Hollywood exhibitors had recently labeled her "box office poison." Although a tentative contract was drawn up, she fell out of the running by the end of November without having been tested.

Jean Arthur presented a more interesting possibility and a different kind of risk. Unlike almost any other major actress of the time, Arthur had few detractors among the moviegoing public, owing to her universally-likeable screen personality. She also had a recent record of box-office successes. But going with Arthur as Scarlett would have meant casting her wildly against type. Not since her forgotten Paramount days, in *The Saturday Night Kid* almost ten years earlier, had Arthur played a bitchy, conniving character, and even that had been an aberration.

But David Selznick had not forgotten Jean Arthur, nor the fascinating complex of emotions and intellect that underlay her piquant charm. Indeed, it must have been with a keen sense of irony that he now pondered awarding the most sought-after role in film history to a woman he had discovered, nurtured and romanced long before either of them climbed to the top of their industry.

Selznick began to entertain Arthur as a potential Scarlett as early as July 1938, possibly because he was then pursuing her two-time co-star Gary Cooper for the role of Rhett Butler. But even after he had acquired Gable, Selznick's interest in Arthur remained high, and a story was leaked to the press in late October, as a trial balloon, that the two of them had "reached a deal over long-distance telephone" and that she was to be signed as soon as Selznick returned from Bermuda, where he was re-writing the script. Two weeks later, no apparent opposition to her having emerged, Columbia issued a statement purportedly at her behest stating that she would not test for Scarlett because of Selznick's requirement that the chosen actress commit to two pictures a year for his production company. But this perfunctory denial of interest could not have fooled anyone, least of all Selznick, who kept Arthur on his short list. On November 18, downplaying the problem created by her identification with other roles, he wrote that it would be "silly" to rule her out on the basis of such pictures as *You Can't Take It With You* "without considering the limitations of opportunities."

Paulette Goddard seemed to be the front-runner through much of this period. She was hampered, though, by rumors that her live-in relationship with Charlie Chaplin was an unmarried one. She claimed otherwise, but was unable to prove it.

In the 1980 television movie *The Great Scarlett O'Hara War*, featuring Tony Curtis as Selznick, Chaplin introduces Goddard to Arthur (played by Vicki Belmonte) at a party for all the contenders, prompting a catty exchange between the two actresses. "I've been a fan of yours for years," Goddard says, a subtle dig at her rival's age. "I hope I can say the same about you some day," comes the tart response. Though the scene is apocryphal, Arthur's attributed remark was not entirely out of character. "It's the kind of thing she would've said," said her friend William Rothwell of Vassar's theater department. "She loved taking people down a peg."

On November 21, Arthur was still very much on Selznick's list of final candidates, to which had been added the name of Joan Bennett. But as always, Selznick continued to pray for "any new-girl possibility that may come along." Three weeks later, one finally did.

Vivien Leigh was a twenty-five-year-old English stage and screen actress with a passionate desire to play Scarlett O'Hara. Her chief claim to fame was her illicit romance with Laurence Olivier (somehow neither this, nor Leigh's having recently left her husband and young daughter, was viewed as disabling to her chances). Selznick had seen a couple of her British films but was not impressed. Leigh was as cunning as Scarlett, however, and when she visited Olivier in Hollywood in late 1938 during the filming of *Wuthering Heights*, she managed to acquaint herself with Olivier's American agent, who happened to be Selznick's brother Myron.

On the night of December 10, Leigh and Olivier accompanied Myron on a visit to the backlot of the Selznick Studio, where the burning of Atlanta was being shot. Legend has it that Myron Selznick stepped forward with Vivien, the towering flames lighting her face, and asked his brother to "meet Scarlett O'Hara." In fact Myron and his guests were late, arriving just as the last building had fallen. But David Selznick was clearly impressed, enough so that two days later, after Leigh gave a first reading for the part, he wrote of her to his wife: "Shhhh: she's the Scarlett dark horse, and looks damned good. (Not for anybody's ears but your own: it's narrowed down to Paulette, Jean Arthur, Joan Bennett and Vivien Leigh)."

Of those four, Arthur was the first to undergo a final round of pre-Christmas screen tests. She showed up in a foul mood, insisting on wearing a dress that she had specially commissioned from fashion designer Irene, who had recently outfitted her for *You Can't Take It With You.* Every other finalist tested in the costumes that were to be used in the film (Leigh later recalled that her dress was still warm from the previous body), but Arthur was going for her own look as Scarlett.

That Saturday, December 17, Selznick wrote his wife that Cukor had been "All day today with Jean Arthur, who has been no end of trouble (I look at her as though I had never known her before!), but who looks on the set as though she may be wonderful—although I have seen only a small part of one scene rehearsed." Joan Bennett's test followed, Goddard came back for further testing and Vivien Leigh went before the cameras, for the first time, on December 21 and 22. Now all the four of them could do was wait for Selznick's telephone call.

Christmas came and went, and still no word. Then on January 3, the New York *Journal & American* reported on "excellent authority" that Jean Arthur had been selected as Scarlett, with the announcement to be made the following day. The choice was "expected to meet with approval in the South," the paper stated. Reached for comment, Arthur insisted that she had not been notified, but added that "I wish it were true!"

It was not. As it turned out, Vivien Leigh had been told on Christmas Day that she had the part, although the formal public announcement was withheld until January 13. Bitterly disappointed, Arthur supposedly burned a copy of the screen test she had been given to keep. Frankly, it seems, she did give a damn.

It is easy in retrospect to say that only Vivien Leigh could have played Scarlett O'Hara. A comparison of the final screen tests, parts of which have survived, further confirms Selznick's wisdom: Joan Bennett lacks Leigh's spark and soul; Paulette Goddard is a bit tongue-in-cheek; and Jean Arthur is a little too old, a little too blonde. "Jean wasn't Scarlett," said her good friend Pete Ballard, also a close acquaintance of Vivien Leigh. "Scarlett was a pampered brat...all of a sudden the world collapsed around her and she had to learn to swim. And she swam. I don't think Jean ever learned to swim." Then there was her croaky voice, which in the screen test seems all wrong for the part, especially when she utters her version of "fiddle-de-dee" to Hattie ("Mammy") McDaniel.

"I can't believe he was seriously considering her," said Danny Selznick of his father's interest in Arthur for the part. "It's an indication of just how strongly he had felt about her. He was still carrying the residual of this romantic image he had formed of her."

Selznick's biographer David Thomson speculated that Arthur must have prevailed upon Selznick to let her test, to give her a chance "for old time's sake." Otherwise, he said, it would be inexplicable that the producer tested Arthur when he did. "By that late day he knew just what he was looking for, and she clearly wasn't it." No, everyone seems to agree, Jean Arthur could not have played Scarlett O'Hara.

Fiddle-de-dee, indeed. At least after 1934, Arthur managed to excel and appeal to audiences in virtually every film role she ever played, and the notion that she would not have found a way to do so as Scarlett O'Hara bears a heavy burden of proof. Moreover, the suggestion that Selznick's consideration of Arthur was for purely personal reasons does not withstand analysis; the producer was staking his whole career on *Gone With the Wind* and was not about to throw it away for the sake of misguided sentiment. No, Jean Arthur could have played Scarlett O'Hara— not as well as Vivien Leigh, to be sure, but well enough so that *Gone With the Wind* still would have been a major success.

Another blockbuster 1939 film in which Arthur did play the lead, Columbia's *Only Angels Have Wings*, merely proves that she could rise to any occasion. By many accounts Arthur was miscast as Brooklyn chorus girl Bonnie Lee, who falls in with a band of daredevil American mail fliers in South America. "A less convincing showgirl than Miss Arthur would be hard to find," said the New York *Times* on the film's May 11, 1939 premiere at Radio City Music Hall. But the *Post's* Howard Barnes spoke for the majority when he wrote that Arthur, "in a happily muted romantic role, is perfect."

Arthur spends the whole film hanging out with the boys, trying to prove she is one of them, wearing a mannish, wide-lapelled suit to improve her credentials. But all the while she is engaged in a cat-and-mouse game of courtship with co-star Cary Grant, himself playing against type as the hard-bitten, disillusioned head flier Geoff Carter.

Howard Hawks, that most male-oriented of filmmakers, produced and directed *Only Angels* from a story written from his own experiences as an aviator in Mexico. He later recounted that Arthur resisted his efforts to make her over into the sort of cool-sexy heroine he later created with Lauren Bacall. "She'd simply say, 'I can't do that kind of stuff,'" the director mused. Even to try, she explained to him, would upset her. "When the picture was over I said, 'Jean, I think you're the only person that I don't think I helped a bit,'" Hawks recalled many years later, even though he had to admit that she was "really good."

For her part, Arthur remembered that Hawks brought "a lot of excitement" to the set and that Grant "was making jokes all the time." "I loved sinking my head into Cary Grant's chest," she confessed to an interviewer years later. But privately Arthur came to despise Grant for what she considered his shameless attempts at upstaging her. "The scene would start out with the two of us talking to each other, and the next thing I knew he moved in front of me so I was out of the picture," she later told a friend. "He'd do that all the time."

Arthur had problems of a different sort with a shy young beauty who had the second female lead in the picture. For the part of Grant's ex-girlfriend, who shows up halfway through the picture, Harry Cohn had tabbed Rita Hayworth, a voluptuous redhead still looking for her first big break. She got it here, as the flame for whom Grant still carries a torch. Hayworth's passive, ultra-feminine style contrasts sharply, and unfavorably in Hawks's eyes, with the more straightforward and intelligent manner of Arthur's Bonnie, and Geoff comes to see this as well. But although Hayworth's spell over Grant is finally broken, her spell over audiences was cast in this film. And for the first time in almost five years, Harry Cohn had found himself a new female star.

There had been rumors that Arthur was unfriendly to Hayworth during filming, beginning when Arthur refused to stand next to the striking newcomer for publicity stills. "That beautiful girl and *me?*" she asked in exasperation. Then on the set, as Hayworth told her friend Paul Rosner years later, they shunned each other completely. Hayworth recalled that Arthur would do a scene, run off to her dressing room and lock herself in. Then Hayworth would do *her* scene, run back to her own dressing room, and lock *her*self in. Finally they bumped into each other on the last day of shooting. "You're shy," observed Arthur to the young newcomer. "You are too," Hayworth replied.

"Jean was very jealous of Rita Hayworth," recalled Arthur's friend Roddy McDowall. "She thought Rita was put in the film to make her look unattractive, and she hated Harry Cohn over that," he said. "Jean was obviously a woman who was very unsure of her attractiveness and the extent of her abilities. Yet she was so extraordinary in *Only Angels Have Wings*, she gave such a wonderful performance, that it's tough to see how she was that insecure." Many years later, Arthur admitted to McDowall that she had been overly paranoid about Hayworth and unfair to the young star as a result.

Rita Hayworth eventually displaced Arthur as queen of the Columbia lot, but she also inherited the title of Harry Cohn's chief whipping girl. Like Arthur before her and Kim Novak after her, Hayworth refused to bend to Cohn's will or to submit to his possessive, bullying tactics. All three actresses had introverted natures that did not respond well to the mogul's gruff manner, but it was Hayworth who suffered the special indignity of constantly having to ward off her boss's blatant sexual advances. Poor Rita even had to reject her own husband Eddie Judson's insistence that she sleep with Cohn as a means of boosting her career.

Arthur's husband never would have suggested any such thing to his wife, but Frank Ross did harbor notions of working in partnership with her someday. Ross had developed a knack for film production and by

March 1939 he had been promoted to vice president of Roach Studios. While Arthur was vying for Scarlett O'Hara, Ross had been engaged at Roach as associate producer on Lewis Milestone's filming of John Steinbeck's *Of Mice and Men*, which received an Oscar nomination for Best Picture in 1939.

Now that filmmaking was in his blood, it was only natural that Ross, who had acted as his wife's unofficial business manager for the past several years, should consider making that relationship official. Arthur, too, longed for a way to break free from the studio system, and she thought of forming an independent production company with her husband and playing the sorts of roles she always dreamed of: Joan of Arc, Eliza Doolittle from Shaw's *Pygmalion*, perhaps even Peter Pan.

But Arthur was tied to Columbia Pictures, and Harry Cohn had no intention of letting her go. On March 18, 1939, Louella Parsons reported that Cohn planned to keep his queen star busy over the next year with two new pictures. The second of these, a western called *Arizona*, was sure to be a hit; it was based on a story by Clarence Budington Kelland, the originator of *Mr. Deeds*, and was to be directed by Howard Hawks. First up, though, was a project that might not have attracted much attention except that it was to be Frank Capra's last film for Columbia Pictures. The story had been kicking around for two years as an unpublished screen treatment titled *The Gentleman from Montana*, about an idealistic young Westerner who becomes disillusioned after his appointment as a United States senator. Capra obtained the story by trading *Golden Boy* to director Rouben Mamoulian for it, which resulted in Arthur's casting in *Only Angels Have Wings*, rather than *Golden Boy* as originally planned, because Mamoulian preferred Barbara Stanwyck for his film.

For the female lead in *The Gentleman from Montana*, a cynical congressional secretary who instructs the young senator in the ways of Washington, Jean Arthur was Capra's first and only choice. Until January 1939 he was hoping to re-team her with Gary Cooper and reprise their chemistry from *Mr. Deeds*, to which the new story bore a strong resemblance (its working title, at times, was *Mr. Deeds Goes to Washington*). But Sam Goldwyn refused to loan out his biggest male star to another studio and two months later Capra's film had a new male lead, Jimmy Stewart, and a new title: *Mr. Smith Goes to Washington*.

Few Hollywood films have stamped themselves as deeply upon the American consciousness as this one; it is one of those movies that, when seen for the first time, creates the impression that somehow one has seen it before. As in most of Capra's greatest work, much in *Mr. Smith* is corny and manipulative, but a dark undercurrent of despair prevents the film from lapsing into mere flagwaving. The real message of *Mr. Smith* is that the forces of evil in America's political institutions are as powerful and entrenched as the forces of good, and that only through the latter's eternal vigilance can occasional, marginal progress be made. The film's own conflicting impulses were a product of the melding of the fundamentally conservative philosophy of its director, Capra, and the left-wing leanings of screenwriter Sidney Buchman, a Communist Party member who brilliantly adapted Lewis Foster's original story.

In the Capra/Buchman treatment, good is represented in the figure of Stewart's Jefferson Smith, a "Boy Ranger" leader who is unaware that his appointment to fill out the term of a deceased senator is the work of a political machine that expects him to serve as a rubber stamp for its graft. Smith's opposite number, with a heart as evil as Smith's is pure, is machine boss Jim Taylor, played by portly Edward Arnold, who practically came to define the role of the snarling, capitalist pig. This was his fourth film with Arthur, and he remained a favorite of hers for years for his gentlemanly manner off-screen.

Between the polar opposites of Stewart and Arnold in *Mr. Smith* were two other principal characters whose attitudes toward the democratic system were decidedly more ambivalent. Senator Joseph Paine, Smith's idol, was once an idealist whose presidential ambitions led him to sell out his principles to the powerful Taylor machine. Veteran character actor Claude Rains, with whom Arthur had once appeared on Broadway in *The Man Who Reclaimed His Head*, was cast in this role as the distinguished-looking orator whose eloquence masks a guilty conscience and weak stomach for the fraud he must perpetrate in order to continue Taylor's patronage.

Paine's secretary, known to everyone as Saunders, has come to learn the political ins-and-outs of Washington as well as he, and she has become equally jaded in the process. Though she constantly talks of quitting and going back home to Baltimore, Arthur's Saunders stays on because she needs the job "and a new suit of clothes." Paine has given her the assignment of watching over his junior colleague and keeping him away from anything that smacks of real politics. She protests that she "wasn't given a brain just to tell a Boy Ranger what time it is," but Paine promises her a bonus and "one of the biggest jobs in Washington" if his presidential hopes are realized (there is the slightest hint of a previous affair between the widower Paine and his secretary).

As in *Mr. Deeds*, Arthur's screen time in *Mr. Smith* is modest in comparison with that of her leading man, but again her role is the pivotal one in the film. She is both the agent of the unsuspecting hero's ultimate triumph and the buffer Capra has set up between the almost unbearably naive protagonist and the presumably more skeptical audience. For if the world-weary Saunders can be converted to Smith's cause, then we will be convinced as well.

In the beginning, we see Smith as Saunders does, as a hayseed whose wide eyes have failed to notice that he is nothing but an "honorary stooge," as the press has scornfully labeled him. When it begins to dawn on him that he is just taking up space in his new position, Smith hits upon the idea of introducing a bill to establish a national boys' camp in his home state. Saunders seeks to dampen Smith's enthusiasm by launching into a long explanation of the process of steering committees, calendars and everything else that conspires to inhibit a bill from becoming a law. But her smugness begins to break down, gradually, when Smith starts telling her of the campfires and lazy streams and snowdrifts back home, and of his late father's advice to try to see life as if one had just come out of a tunnel.

Soon after introducing his bill Smith is run out of the Senate, falsely accused by the unscrupulous Paine of trying to legislate for personal gain (in fact, Paine is trying to ram through a Taylor pork barrel project over the very land targeted by Smith for his boys' camp). By now Saunders is secretly on Smith's side, wondering aloud to her reporter friend Diz

Moore (Thomas Mitchell) "whether this Don Quixote hasn't got the jump on all of us" and whether it isn't "a curse to go through life wised-up like you and me." Then, in the most highly-praised acting sequence of her career, a long, one-take scene at the Press Club restaurant, she drunkenly reveals her growing fondness for Smith to the equally drunk Mitchell. Saunders is telling Mitchell how she felt the day she first escorted Smith to the Senate—like a mother sending her child off to school for the first time. She catches herself, and soberly exclaims, "Say—who started this?" On she rambles, alternating between tipsiness and seeming sobriety, at points talking wistfully of prairie grass and mountain streams and getting out of the tunnel she lives in, at other points decrying such talk as "sappy." Although she is in love with Stewart, she impetuously suggests to Mitchell, her long-time suitor, that the two of them get married that night and clear out of town (a proposal she later retracts).

"I defy any other actress to play that scene," Capra told biographer Joseph McBride years later. Howard Hawks likewise marveled that Arthur's marriage proposal to the disheveled Mitchell, when she was obviously in love with Jimmy Stewart, made this "one of the best love scenes that I've ever seen in a picture. That was a beautifully-done thing." Arthur modestly credited the script, commenting that "it's all there in the words." But she did allow that playing the scene took some skill on her part. "The trouble about a woman being drunk is you have to be careful not to go overboard because then it's not funny," she explained. "A man can be awfully funny when he's drunk but not a woman."

Mr. Smith Goes to Washington is best remembered for Stewart's famous filibuster at the end of the film. But the most moving scene in the movie is the immediately preceding one, where Saunders talks Smith out of quitting the Senate and urges him into battle. Smith sits sobbing at the Lincoln Memorial, where he has gone, baggage in hand, for one last look before leaving town that night. A soft prairie tune is playing in the film's background, while Smith sits at the base of a column, his head buried in his hands. Out of the shadows emerges Saunders, wearing a mannish hat and a knowing look on her face. She explains she had a hunch she would find him here and, smiling quietly, she sits on a suitcase beside him.

Wiping away his tears, Smith composes himself enough to tell her that she was right to tell him to go back home, that all the fancy words about high ideals carved on the city's monuments were a lot of "hooey" and "junk" put up there for "suckers like me" to read. She knows that he does not believe this, but he needs to be reminded of what he does believe. "You can't quit now, not you," she admonishes him. "You didn't just have faith in Paine or any other living man. You had faith in something bigger than that. You had plain decent everyday common rightness. And this country could use some of that—yeah, so could the whole cockeyed world—a lot of it."

On October 17, 1939—Jean Arthur's thirty-ninth birthday—*Mr. Smith Goes to Washington* had a celebrity preview at Washington's Constitution Hall, home of the conservative Daughters of the American Revolution. In attendance were 4,000 special guests, including members of Congress, the national press corps and several Supreme Court justices. Naturally, Arthur was a no-show.

Many members of the political establishment wished they had stayed home, too. Embarrassed and humiliated by the unflattering portrayal they had received, official Washington lashed back, calling the film an indictment, rather than a celebration, of American democracy (which was at least partly true). Senate Majority Leader Alban Barkley branded it "grotesque," Ambassador to England Joseph Kennedy claimed that the film would harm American prestige in Europe (where Hitler had just invaded Poland) and Senator James Byrnes of South Carolina pronounced it the type of picture totalitarian governments would like to show their subjects to demonstrate the corruption of democracy. Fortunately the critics and public strongly supported *Mr. Smith*, and it was nominated for eleven Academy Awards (second only to *Gone With the Wind's* thirteen nominations). And in 1942, defiant Parisians proved the opposite of Joe Kennedy's theorem: they chose *Mr. Smith* as the last English-language film to show before the Nazi ban on American and British films took effect.

Although Stewart, Rains and Harry Carey (who played the Senate President) were nominated for Oscars, Arthur was ignored by the

117

Academy, which now had overlooked every one of her performances. Arthur's friend Roddy McDowall, among many today, regards that as an unpardonable slight. Her roles in *Mr. Deeds* and *Mr. Smith*, for example, "aren't fantastic parts," he pointed out. "They are illuminated by a very particular individual talent. If a lot of other people had played them they would have been bland."

For her part, Arthur still was not entirely satisfied with the direction her career was following. "Being a stooge in pictures like the ones Frank Capra makes is wonderful, of course, and I'm happy to have such an opportunity," she said not long after *Mr. Smith*, "but I'd like to play a real role." One day she would need to appreciate that the kinds of roles she had been playing were as real, if not more so, than the ones to which she aspired.

CHAPTER TEN

THE PRINCESS AND

THE GOBLIN

*A*s Hollywood passed from the golden era of the thirties to a new decade, Jean Arthur stood as one of its most bankable commodities. Others may have had greater raw star power, but few in Hollywood could match Arthur's career, picture for picture. By all rights, Arthur's string of hits should have given her greater confidence in her work and worth. Instead, she became more insecure with each new success.

On the surface, at least, there was cause to believe that a new, more relaxed Jean Arthur was beginning to emerge. To "the amazement of all

Hollywood," as *Life* magazine put it, she allowed one of its photographers into her secluded Brentwood home in early 1940. Photographer Herbert Gehr found "a completely gracious woman, a happy wife, a charming hostess."

"Here is one of Hollywood's most livable homes," *Life* said of the nine-room, ranch-style house high in the hills above Hollywood. "The books in the library are well thumbed and look as if they had been read more than once. A Capehart radio-phonograph is stocked with Tchaikovsky, Brahms and Haydn albums."

Arthur was so taken with her Brentwood hideaway that when she decided to purchase the house at 13130 Boca de Canon Lane, she bought another one down the street for her father. Hubert Greene was once again estranged from his wife Hannah, who by this time was living in Carmel in the house Arthur had begun renting a couple of years earlier. When Hannah came to Los Angeles to visit her daughter and son-in-law she stayed with them, while her husband maintained his distance from a few doors away.

Gracious though Arthur may have been to *Life's* photographer, she could not bring herself to reveal anything truly intimate. "My personal life is my own business," she said pointedly. Other visitors found her no less elusive. When husband Frank entertained bridge and dinner guests, she often spent the entire evening curled up in a corner reading before heading off to bed early.

Her insecurities continued to spill over onto the shooting set. In Columbia's *Too Many Husbands* (1940), a tepid comedy adapted from a play by Somerset Maugham, her character was subjected to a tug-of-war between new husband Melvyn Douglas and first husband Fred MacMurray, who has returned after supposedly drowning years before. Off screen, she fretted constantly that she was not attractive enough to make a convincing object of their rivalry. MacMurray joked at one point that she needn't worry since they could shoot the next scene with an Indian blanket over her head. Furious, Arthur asked whether she really looked that bad, and burst into tears.

She could also make life difficult for those charged with her appearance before the camera. As Grace Huntley, a Columbia wardrobe worker, revealed:

> In a fitting room she's a regular female Simon Legree. She cracks the whip and drives you unmercifully. She wants every-thing done *right now*, is impatient in fittings and exacting in her requirements. She knows exactly what she wants, expects you to know, too, and is intolerant of mistakes. Arthur expects to be dressed as fast as a fireman and get results like Dietrich's. And if she doesn't she can be awfully frank in criticizing.

In May 1940, as Columbia's long-delayed *Arizona* went into produc-tion, Arthur was again worried about her appearance. She was especially terrified of how she might look alongside her leading man, an earnest young newcomer named William Holden, who was nearly twenty years her junior. When she met her co-star for the first time on location, she looked him over for a few seconds and walked away without a word, leaving the young man perplexed and upset.

Eventually they broke the ice and managed to generate a modicum of screen chemistry in this sprawling epic about the first woman settler in 1860s Tucson. *Arizona* had an authentic look and feel, having been shot in a specially constructed town about seventeen miles south of the actual city. But the story lacked enough excitement to sustain the film's two-hour plus length. "It sags under the weight of its own pretensions," said the New York *Times*.

Arthur's performance as the pioneering Phoebe Titus, while charming at times, lacks the conviction she brought to the role of Calamity Jane in *The Plainsman*. Perhaps this is because she reserved most of her passion for the cast's animals. She adopted a dozen or so stray dogs, several of them lame or blind, and kept them at the private guest ranch she had rented. For another forty mongrels that were selected from the local pound to appear in the movie, she collected sacks of groceries and hired veterinarians to look them over; often, late at night, she drove twenty miles from her ranch to the set to assure herself that they were properly being cared for. She had the cast pigs hosed down with kerosene to cure their skin diseases, and when she saw the goats with nothing to eat but cactus she ordered in tons of bales of hay (which they promptly ignored in favor of the cactus).

At the close of filming Arthur was frantically searching for a way to save the mongrel dogs, who were otherwise destined for the pound's gas chamber. Her solution was to sponsor a show in the lobby of the Santa Rita Hotel, at which the dogs were given away to Tucson's underprivileged Mexican children. With each dog given away went a three-year paid-up license, a new leash and collar and several months' worth of dog food, all courtesy of Jean Arthur.

Her timidity manifested itself again when *Arizona* premiered in Tucson in late 1940. On a day when she was expected for an appearance before a throng of Tucson citizens and dignitaries, Arthur stayed in and refused to answer her telephone. Columbia Vice President Nate Spingold found her at her ranch and managed to convince her to go to the auditorium where the Mayor of Tucson was waiting to present her an award. With some trepidation she waited as he began his speech about how honored everyone was by her presence. "And now," he said, "I present this copper plate to the Darling of Arizona—Miss Gene Autry!" At the Mayor's gaffe everyone burst out laughing, Arthur included, and her nervousness subsided.

The mediocrity of *Arizona*, and *Too Many Husbands* before it, finally led Frank Ross to form an independent production company as a means of getting his wife better roles. While Arthur was on location in Tucson, Ross and Broadway writer Norman Krasna decided to collaborate on a social comedy from a story Krasna had developed. Thus was born Frank Ross/Norman Krasna Productions.

The new company's maiden effort, *The Devil and Miss Jones*, was done under partnership with RKO. Krasna convinced veteran character actor Charles Coburn to play the gruff millionaire department store owner who poses as a shoe salesman in his own store to ferret out union malcontents, only to be reformed and humanized by his unsuspecting co-workers. Likeable Robert Cummings was enlisted as leading man, and Sam Wood, then in the prime of his career, was hired to direct.

Top-billed Arthur did her part to promote the project by agreeing, to everyone's astonishment, to pose for a publicity still in a sexy one-piece bathing suit. Though she still detested such cheesecake, the family finances were at stake this time and principle had to yield.

When it was released in April 1941, *The Devil and Miss Jones* reconfirmed Arthur's status as one of Hollywood's top comediennes. The picture really belonged to Coburn, who garnered a Best Supporting Actor Oscar nomination for his work. Wisely, Arthur would not permit the screenplay to be rewritten just to elevate her part. But she shone just the same and received her best reviews since *Mr. Smith Goes to Washington.* Unfortunately, the film's pro-union message did not serve it particularly well at the box office, dashing the lofty expectations of producer Ross. "It absolutely devastated him," said Zan Ross, his son from a later marriage.

Frank Ross was a curious study. Outwardly he was a social animal who enjoyed nightclubs and parties and mingling with the smart set. But at the same time he was extremely private and taciturn about his business and personal affairs. "A very closed-mouth type of person" who "didn't like small talk," his barber of fifty years, Lou Merino, said of him. "He was very articulate and verbose in most things, but on personal things you couldn't get a word out of him," said his friend and colleague Doug Morrow. And comedian Phil Silvers, who made one movie for Ross, called him "a man of wit and intellect, a serious writer who turned into a producer. I could not understand why he went into the movie business."

It was because Ross was a man with a mission. Within him burned the fires of political and spiritual idealism. A staunch liberal, he once offered to provide film credit to screenwriter Albert Maltz, one of the blacklisted "Hollywood Ten," when others said it would damage the producer's career. Ross would have gone through with the gesture, but Maltz, an old colleague, declined to put him in a difficult position. Said Ross's long-time secretary, Catharine Pace, "He was pretty upright in how he felt about the way he treated other people. He never was the kind of man who said he hated anybody."

Ross was also deeply religious. Though he did not practice the medical aspects of Christian Science, he was intellectually committed to the faith.

He shared the Christian Science concept of God as an impersonal, divine principle, a far cry from the anthropomorphic view of the Almighty as a changeable being who loves, hates and inflicts terrible suffering on his creatures. "God is good, God is love, God is honesty" was his belief, according to his son Zan. "There is no such thing as evil."

The films Frank Ross produced also tended toward spiritual and inspirational themes: *One Man's Way* (1964), a biography of Norman Vincent Peale; *The House I Live In* (1945), a short feature starring Frank Sinatra that promoted racial tolerance, and won Ross a special Academy Award; and most notably, the Biblical epic *The Robe* (1953). After buying the novel in 1942 when it was only half-written, Ross fought for more than ten years to bring it to the screen, turning down offers of millions for the movie rights because he wanted to produce it himself. Explaining that making money was not his first aim, he told Hedda Hopper that "if this picture can help people to be even a little better, as the book seems to have done in thousands of cases, I will have performed the greatest function I can ever perform as a producer." But he got rich from the film anyway. The first movie to be shot in CinemaScope, *The Robe* became the fourth-biggest money maker of the 1950s.

Frank Ross's wife shared his idealism and political liberalism, as well as his elevation of the spiritual over the material aspects of life. She never embraced Christian Science as he did; as she once explained, "I'm supposed to be a Christian Scientist but I can't be because I smoke and drink." Nevertheless, Arthur was keenly interested in the connection between mind and body, a central tenet of Christian Science thought. Her belief in the divinity of all of Nature also had much in common with Christian Science's vaguely pantheistic references to God as "All-in-all." And while neither a Christian nor a scientist, philosophically speaking, she searched for a theology that could reconcile science and religion, and settled on the theory of Creative Evolution, or vitalism, espoused by her hero Bernard Shaw and the French philosopher Henri Bergson. Less mechanistic than pure Darwinism, vitalism holds that God and Life are one and that, in Bergson's words, "creation, so conceived, is not a mystery; we experience it in ourselves when we act freely." Arthur once explained that "God must be a derivative of good somewhere way back. It's the magic of the world: How does a pine tree know how to be a pine tree, how does the maple learn to be a maple ? It's what is awe-inspiring. It's the greatest magic there is. It's what makes everything be alive."

Spiritual soulmates, Arthur and Ross appeared to have a thriving marriage. During the filming of *Arizona*, Ross frequently flew into Tucson from Los Angeles to be with his wife for the weekend, returning on the 5 a.m. Monday plane. "The lady always gets up and sees him off, so the Rosses must be getting along fine," wrote one movie beat reporter. Around the time *The Devil and Miss Jones* was being shot, Arthur showed up with her husband at a West Side Tennis Club costume party, where she uncharacteristically danced and wisecracked her way around as a circus ringmaster in high hat, tails and large black mustache. Then, in early 1942, Ross signed a deal with RKO to produce two more pictures over the next two years, one of them a vehicle for his wife. They were now established as full-fledged business, as well as marital, partners.

But in fact their relationship was crumbling. In the spring of 1944, Louella Parsons reported that the Rosses' marriage had been on the rocks for months. Arthur, the columnist revealed, had removed herself to New York while Ross worked in Hollywood night and day on the script for *The Robe*. In fact, by that time Ross had moved out of their house and into the one down the street inhabited by Hubert Greene. The marriage would linger on until 1949, but in name only.

Many years later, Arthur offered an explanation of what went wrong:

> For ten years we were very happy, each of us helping the other a great deal. But then our basic natures came through, and we had to go our different ways. The tragedy is that we stayed together for seven extra years before we got divorced—it is destructive for people to stay together when there is nothing productive left in the marriage. I feel that nothing went quite right for us in all those seven years.

An anonymously-quoted friend of the couple subscribed to the theory that it was their business relationship, not their "basic natures," that drove them apart. "Jean and Frank were always complete opposites—she loved solitude and symphony music, he loved parties, people and jazz—but they had an immensely happy marriage for a long time.... It was when his interests began to turn from strict management of Jean to movie making on his own that things went wrong."

Arthur's uncontested divorce action, filed in February 1949, painted a much darker picture of Frank Ross. Her complaint alleged "extreme cruelty"—which Ross denied—and in a written deposition she stated that "he was especially cold and indifferent to me." She continued:

> He was absent from home many, many times.... He would leave in the morning and say he wouldn't be home to dinner, and wouldn't come home until 3 or 4 in the morning.... He went skiing over week-ends, several times. Also to Palm Springs. And wouldn't take me with him. This took place over the last 5 years of our marriage on numerous occasions.

"I tried to make a comfortable homelife for us both," Arthur continued. "I wanted to make our marriage a success." But she alleged that Ross ignored her constant pleading and suggestions for a "reasonably constructive married life." And though he frequently asked her advice on business matters, she said, "After I gave it, he would argue and criticize me for long periods of time." His conduct and attitude, she concluded, "made it especially difficult for me to engage successfully in my professional activities.... I was extremely nervous and was constantly under tension. I worried and had many continuous sleepless nights."

For years afterward Arthur remained bitter toward Ross, casting him as the villain of the marriage. But by other accounts he could not have been the demon portrayed in Arthur's divorce filing. "My uncle was a very soft, caring person inside," recalled his niece, Wendy Ross. And his third wife, Joan Ross, who remained good friends with him even after their divorce in 1973, said, "If you were going to use a word to describe Frank Ross, there's one word that describes him completely, and that's a gentleman. He was also a Gentle Man."

The harshness of Arthur's divorce pleading undoubtedly was dictated by the relatively stringent matrimonial laws of the day. Indeed, the description Arthur gave of their final years together was clearly distorted in that, by her own calculation, the marriage was already effectively over when Ross began displaying his "cold and indifferent" attitude. The real question was what killed their relationship in the first place.

Arthur once told her friend Pete Ballard that her marriage had basically been a happy one until she discovered another woman's scarf in the glove compartment of her car. The scarf turned out to belong to a beautiful young actress named Joan Caulfield. A former model and cover girl, Caulfield landed a contract with Paramount in 1944 and went to Hollywood, where she played a number of demure, decorative leading ladies in a short, moderately successful film career. (In 1950 she was to marry Frank Ross, who had produced a couple of her films before turning her into a television situation comedienne. She starred in the Ross-produced series *My Favorite Husband* and *Sally* before they divorced in 1959.)

Although Ross began his affair with Caulfield while he was still married to Arthur, it could not have caused the marriage's demise. The Ross/Caulfield romance did not begin until 1945 at the earliest and was not in full flower until a couple years later, well after Ross's marriage to Arthur began to disintegrate. Arthur's scarf story notwithstanding, the "other woman" theory does not adequately explain her marital woes.

Was Arthur, perhaps, the one who first strayed? In her autobiography, Arthur's friend Mary Martin tells of attending a small dinner party with Arthur, Ross and Paramount story editor Richard Halliday shortly after Martin came to Hollywood in late 1939 under contract to Paramount. Martin was excited about meeting her idol Arthur for the first time, and equally anxious to strike up an acquaintance with Halliday, her date for the evening. But Arthur and Halliday ignored her and spent the entire dinner entranced in conversation with each other, then continued their talk for hours out on the balcony while Martin privately sulked.

But Richard Halliday posed no threat to Arthur's marriage; though not acknowledged at the time, the handsome young man was apparently bisexual. Notwithstanding, he soon married the young Miss Martin, whose career he managed for the next thirty years. The Hallidays and Rosses became both friends and neighbors, and when the Hallidays' first child, Heller, was born in late 1941, Jean Arthur became her godmother (along with Dame Judith Anderson), and Frank Ross her godfather.

Arthur and Martin grew particularly close and spent a great deal of time together. The two actresses shared an obsessive love for the character of Peter Pan and had "endless discussions," as Martin put it, about how to play the part, which both vowed to do some day. When the Rosses and Hallidays were invited to costume parties, the two wives always wanted to go as Peter Pan and called each other to claim first rights.

Just how close Arthur and Martin became, and the exact nature of their relationship, was to become a topic of Hollywood speculation for years. It was rumored within the film colony's inner sanctum that they were romantically involved. Private speculation was only encouraged by the fact that the two boyish-looking women began to resemble each other increasingly over time. As early as 1940, opposite Bing Crosby in *Rhythm on the River*, Martin appeared a virtual clone of her older friend. In 1943, reviewing Paramount's *True to Life*, James Agee wrote, "Mary Martin, I notice with some alarm, is playing Jean Arthur—a tendency even Miss Arthur must learn to curb." And when Arthur played in *Peter Pan* several years later, the New York *Post* commented that Arthur, "looking and sounding pleasantly like Mary Martin, is boyish and engaging."

Then there was the way that Martin seemed to follow so closely in Arthur's career footsteps. Arthur was Calamity Jane in the movies; Martin played Annie Oakley on stage. Arthur was Peter Pan on Broadway; then so was Mary Martin. Arthur took first stab at the Billie Dawn role in *Born Yesterday*, and Martin followed by playing the same role on television.

Hollywood gossips thought they had confirmation of all the rumors when, in late 1966, an obscure California publisher released a novel called *The Princess and the Goblin*. Written by first-time novelist Paul Rosner, the book was a thinly-veiled treatment of the alleged lesbian relationship between Jean Arthur and Mary Martin, and it became an instant source of underground conversation within the entertainment world. It tells the story of two women, Maureen Covillion and Josie Miller. Maureen (like Mary Martin) gains notice as a singer in New York revues, comes to Hollywood in the late thirties and returns to New York in the mid-forties to become the queen of the Broadway musical. While in Hollywood, Maureen falls in love with her female idol, Josie Miller, an enigmatic and publicity-shy star whose odd, cracked voice and deft comic talent playing secretaries and shopgirls have made her one of the world's top female film stars. Maureen achieves a similar level of stardom by borrowing and eventually usurping Josie's personality as her own. Meanwhile, Josie suffers an emotional breakdown as a result of their relationship and divorces her husband, a movie producer and her erstwhile career manager. After her divorce, Josie flees Hollywood to live out her life as a recluse by the ocean, making only a fleeting and abortive comeback attempt in the theater.

To anyone who asks, author Rosner frankly acknowledges what everyone who read the book assumed—that Maureen (the "Goblin") was intended to be Mary Martin, while Josie (the "Princess") was Jean Arthur. To people such as Hollywood writer George Eells, the book appeared to confirm the stories he had been hearing for years. Eells was a close friend of Martin's but never knew if the rumors about her and Arthur were true; when the book came out, he recalled, Hollywood's insiders told each other that it validated what they'd been saying all along.

There was just one problem—Rosner had made the whole thing up. "This was all my imagination," he confessed years later. Rosner had never met either Jean Arthur or Mary Martin and had no knowledge, when he wrote the book, of any affair between them. An avid fan of Arthur's films, he created the Josie Miller character based on his conception of what Jean Arthur was really like, while his inspiration for Maureen Covillion came from his observation that Mary Martin borrowed much of Arthur's personality in the course of building her own career. "I'd always wanted to do a book about one person assuming another person's identity and improving on it," Rosner said, and when he saw Mary Martin on Broadway as Peter Pan, it suddenly dawned on him how much she looked and acted like Jean Arthur.

Somewhat naively, Rosner did not realize that his principal characters would be instantly recognizable, and he was surprised to receive telephone calls and letters from people who simply assumed that he had written a genuine roman á clef. "I had no way of knowing when I wrote it that any of it was true," he insisted, adding that he never learned whether there was any substance to the rumors his book helped fuel. Although people expressed amazement about "how many things I hit," no one purporting to have any direct personal knowledge told him that Arthur and Martin had in fact had an affair.

Arthur never specifically acknowledged Rosner's book, but she did appear to allude to it, and to the rumors about her and Mary Martin, a couple of years after the book's publication. While teaching a drama course at Vassar College, Arthur had her students enact a scene from *The Children's Hour*, Lillian Hellman's play about a schoolgirl who accuses her two teachers of lesbianism. After the scene was completed, instead of critiquing the students' performances, Arthur drifted off into a discussion of how gossip can ruin people's lives. Visibly upset, she told the class that one has to be careful in life to avoid being subjected to malicious rumors.

For many years, *The Princess and the Goblin* remained the only published source of speculation about Arthur's sexual orientation. Then in 1992, Donald Spoto's *Blue Angel*, a biography of Marlene Dietrich, listed Arthur, along with Mary Martin, Janet Gaynor and a dozen other women from the fields of film, theater and literature, as members of "America's creative lesbian community." And in Boze Hadleigh's *Hollywood Lesbians*, a book comprising "ten interviews with sapphic women of Hollywood film," the author and several of his subjects treated Arthur's lesbianism, or at least bisexuality, as a given. For example, actress Marjorie Main (of "Ma and Pa Kettle" fame) appeared to accept the author's contention that it was "widely known in Hollywood in the 1930s and forties that actresses like Garbo or Jean Arthur, to name two, were lesbian." Comedienne Patsy Kelly asserted that Arthur and Mary Martin were members of "the sisterhood," as evidenced by their desire "to be Peter Pan...to be boys." And Agnes Moorehead made the following cryptic comments in reaction to

Hadleigh's listing of Arthur as among those Hollywood actresses who "have enjoyed lesbian or bi relationships":

> Let's suppose a biography is written of…Jean Arthur. She had her life, her work, a husband or two, no children, and different people thought different things about her. She was emotionally intricate. Most women are. Actresses, more so. An entire book could put much of Jean Arthur, and what she did and who she loved, into perspective. It would take an entire book, at least.

Although it is tempting to ascribe Arthur's fears and insecurities to a confused sexual identity, the evidence to support such a theory is inconclusive. As an older woman, Arthur frequently adopted the dress and appearance of a man, cropping her hair short in the manner of Peter Pan or Joan of Arc. But aside from Mary Martin, Arthur was never romantically linked to any well-known woman, and there is no proof that any of her relationships with lesser-known women over the years were of a sexual nature. Although she formed several close female relationships in later life, it seems plausible that the actress sought out these women for simple companionship.

Nor did Frank Ross attribute the breakup of his marriage to Arthur to any sexual ambiguity on her part. In conversations with several intimates, the producer implied that he and Arthur simply grew apart from each other over time. Although Ross (who was unequivocally heterosexual) might have been reluctant to admit that he had been married to a lesbian, it is unlikely that he would have remained wedded for long—certainly not seventeen years—to a woman he knew to be so.

Although Arthur would fall in love with at least one other man after Frank Ross, she evidently experienced no similar passions past the age of fifty. If anything, she grew distinctly asexual over time, as she revealed in a 1975 interview in which she listed sex as something she easily could live without. Indeed, as her friend and one-time agent Helen Harvey observed, precisely because Arthur's deepest passion in life was reserved for "her ideals" rather than for people, she seemed to be "the least likely candidate for any sort of deviation of that [sexual] kind." Another friend of many years acknowledged that Arthur may have had bisexual experiences at one time or another, but he emphasized that "I doubt if she had very much interest in any kind of romance." Frightened away from most intimate human contact, her mind "was in the sky most of the time," as this friend put it. "She wasn't very real," added Helen Harvey.

Arthur's close friend Roddy McDowall spoke about her in similar terms. "I know very little about her partnerships in life. I should imagine she wasn't an easy person to have as a partner because she was such an original, and so quixotic, and going her own way.

"It's very difficult to talk about Jean because lots of the words one uses sound derogatory and they're not," he added. "She was an original—I keep coming back to that word—and the emotions that she exhibited made one feel, even when she was functioning at her best, that she wouldn't be able to function the next day because she was this strange individual.... And I'm sure that as a young girl she was made enormous fun of and was made to feel like a freak."

Indeed, Jean Arthur's essential "strangeness" emerged early in life, before any issues of sexuality might have arisen. Perhaps the best clue to the origin of her oddities is contained in a set of divorce papers filed in 1942 in Monterey County, California by a nearly seventy-year-old woman against her seventy-eight-year-old husband, two days after their fifty-first anniversary. The woman's complaint alleged that:

> on or about the 1st day of June, 1909, at Jacksonville, Florida, said defendant left plaintiff with the intention of forever deserting her, without her consent and against her will, and has ever since remained separate and apart from her with the intention during all of such times to forever desert her...[that] for about twenty-three years, defendant has willfully neglected to provide for plaintiff any of the common necessaries of life, he having the ability at all of such times to do so, thus forcing plaintiff to obtain assistance from her relatives to procure for herself the common necessaries of life...during a considerable portion of said twenty-three years.

Among the children from this unhappy union was listed one Gladys G. Greene, then aged forty-one, who would have been eight years old at the time of her father's desertion. And on March 16, 1942, after more than fifty years of loveless marriage, a default judgment for divorce was granted to Johannah A. Greene against Hubert Sidney Greene. Two years later, the first, and most beloved, man in Jean Arthur's life would die, leaving his only daughter with memories of his mixed devotion.

* * *

The fiction of Paul Rosner perhaps holds a seed of truth:

"Josie."

The voice behind her was familiar but vague, as if heard through a long, clouded mustard corridor. Somehow she did not want to turn. The voice brought with it sorrow and serenity, turmoil and love.

"Josie," she heard again.

The little man stood above her. The skin was wrinkled, and all that lovely sandy hair was gone now.

…

"Oh, Daddy! Daddy!" She began to sob and pressed her face against his shoulder…. She wanted to say, "Oh, Daddy, Daddy, just sit there and let me look at you!" but she couldn't. She couldn't speak at all, because what she really wanted to say was too direct and incriminatory.

…

She ran to him, kneeling before him, and placed her fingers to his lips. "Oh Daddy, no! Please. Forgive me. I—I'm sorry. It's just that—. No, we won't speak of it anymore."

They were too much alike. Timid little birds who longed to be free and fly but who had no courage. Always dominated by larger, predatory birds.

CHAPTER ELEVEN

"I WANT TO LIVE IN THE SKY"

*D*uring the years of the Second World War Jean Arthur forged the apotheosis of her screen persona and cemented her reputation as one of the greatest of film comediennes. But no sooner did she reach the peak of her career than she turned her back on it, deciding, at age forty-three, to retire from active moviemaking.

She began the war years under suspension from Columbia for turning down at least four films in a row. But just after the attack on Pearl Harbor she was persuaded to make *The Talk of the Town*, in which she played a New England schoolteacher who rents a room in her country house to a distinguished Harvard law professor (Ronald Colman) at the same time she is harboring a radical fugitive from justice (Cary Grant). Co-written by Irwin Shaw and Sidney Buchman, *The Talk of the Town* was a curious mixture of slapstick comedy and political drama, the type of film Frank Capra might have made. But Capra was gone from Columbia, having severed all ties with Harry Cohn, and was off making war documentaries for the government. For *The Talk of the Town*, Cohn enlisted one of Hollywood's best and most versatile directors, George Stevens.

Like Arthur, Stevens had begun his career making silent westerns and slapstick comedies. He moved up quickly, from chief cameraman and gag writer for Hal Roach's Laurel and Hardy series to a director of comedy features at Universal. By age twenty-nine, he was a leading director at RKO. Beginning in 1934 and over the next several years he churned out a series of well-crafted comedies and light musicals, including *Alice Adams* (1935) and the Astaire/Rogers classic *Swing Time* (1936). In 1939 he made *Gunga Din*; then, after the expensive failure of *Vigil in the Night* (1940), Stevens was released by RKO and grabbed on the rebound by Harry Cohn. Wary of the Cohn's reputation for meddling, Stevens agreed to a three-picture deal with Columbia only after the studio head promised not to interfere with him.

As far as Arthur was concerned, any director who refused to have anything to do with Harry Cohn could not be all bad. She also took an instant liking to Stevens' directorial methods which, like her own acting style, were slow and methodical. Stevens was notoriously painstaking in his approach, shooting scenes from every possible angle so he could choose the best one in the cutting room. He spent hours meticulously setting the stage for the next scene, sometimes lapsing into long silences that left cast and crew in disbelief. But Arthur was not complaining; the director's dawdling gave her time to slide gently into her scenes, working off her nervous energy between takes. For her, Stevens had a soothing presence, "kind of like the best cup of coffee you ever had."

In *The Talk of the Town* Arthur shared top billing with Grant, their names placed just above Colman's in the credits. But she was a distant third in terms of pay. Grant received $106,250 to Colman's $100,000, while Arthur, still in Harry Cohn's doghouse, was cut back to $50,000.

Stevens reported little overt rivalry among the stars, except during the closing scene in which Arthur, following Grant down a Supreme Court corridor, drew laughter from the crew over her clowning. Grant, to whom such things mattered, thought she was trying to upstage him. Although the scene was written that way, Arthur made the most of her opportunity to exact a little revenge for Grant's one-upmanship tactics during *Only Angels Have Wings*.

As for Colman, already one of her favorite actors, Arthur gained nothing but additional respect. "I found out so many more things about him that were charming—of course, he is adorable—but he was so interesting and understanding. That became more appealing to me. I sat on the set once more and he recited 'If I Were King' for me—just for me."

Despite being laden with social significance, *The Talk of the Town* gave Arthur her best screwball comic opportunities since *Easy Living*. In a hilarious early scene, Arthur's character notices a picture of the fugitive Dilg (Grant) blazoned on the front page of the newspaper that Colman is reading at the breakfast table; until then, the law professor has been led to believe that Grant's character is merely the house gardener. With perfect timing, she races to the kitchen table, picks up the professor's plate of fried eggs and manages to "accidentally" slip them off the plate and over the picture, thus protecting Dilg's identity a little longer. "This is not your egg morning," she admonishes the startled Colman.

In another charming sequence, Arthur is standing in front of a full-length mirror, making faces at herself and performing a double impersonation of Veronica Lake and Katharine Hepburn that she improvised between takes. She takes a handful of her hair (which is longer than usual in this film), pulls it down and under her nose to make a mustache, and speaks into the mirror: "Lovely, lovely—*rah*lly lovely."

"Miss Arthur is charming, as usual, in her bewilderment," wrote Bosley Crowther in the New York *Times*. The *New Republic*'s Manny Farber observed that screwball comedy of this variety "depends on someone like Jean Arthur, who sums up in her person all the characters of these movies: she is both an ordinary girl with ordinary reactions and a scatterbrain." The *Herald Tribune*'s Howard Barnes found that Arthur's "consternation at finding herself in the middle with a couple of adoring suitors is so completely persuasive that she takes over the production time and again when the continuity gives her little support." And the Hartford *Times*'s reviewer termed her "a changed young woman from the Jean Arthur of *Mr. Deeds*" and "somewhat of a more finished actress."

In an interview in 1983, Frank Capra tried to explain Arthur's special gift for comedy. "When she did comedy she relaxed," he said. "She never thought about whether some line was funny.... She was just a natural." But Stevens, whom Arthur eventually came to regard as her favorite director, perceived her acting to be more deliberate. "When she works she gives everything that's in her, and she studies her roles more than most of the actresses I've known," he said. According to the director's son, George Stevens Jr., his father "felt that Jean Arthur was the greatest actress he had ever worked with. He thought she was 'true.'... When the humor came it was all that much funnier."

Ironically, Arthur "wasn't a basically funny woman," according to Roddy McDowall. "She had a wonderful sense of humor, but she was a serious woman. It was her view, her slant on things that was so amusing. She just had a particular view about how to be truthful in relation to material that was good.... Even in bad films, silly films that have no real content, she was always the central truth.... I think that's instinctual, you can't learn that."

The most direct insight into Arthur's personal craft came from the actress herself. She once told psychological counsellor Ned Hall that she would intensely study her character and work out everything in her mind scene by scene before she ever stepped in front of the camera. "Some people misinterpret my going to my dressing room between scenes instead of staying on the set, joking," she once said. "I know many people can joke one minute and go into a crying scene the next. They can change character instantly. I can't. I have to go into my dressing room after a scene, go over my lines, and build up the mood for the next scene." By this studied process, she managed to internalize her learning to such an extent that everything she did seemed natural and intuitive.

The Talk of the Town was nominated for five Academy Awards, including Best Picture. But Arthur was again overlooked in the balloting. Modern Oscar historians regard Arthur's repeated slightings as among the more egregious of the Academy's many errors of omission. In his 1990 book, *And The Winner Is...*, Emanuel Levy observed that Arthur "occupies a special position among the Academy's underestimated actresses," noting that at least three of her performances (in *Mr. Deeds*, *Mr. Smith* and *Shane*) should have been nominated but were not. More recently, in his provocative *Alternate Oscars*, film writer Danny Peary ventured that Arthur deserved several nominations (for *Mr. Deeds*, *Mr. Smith* and *Easy Living*), and at least one Best Actress award (for *The More the Merrier*).

Several factors conspired to cause Arthur's work to be overlooked so frequently by the Academy. For one thing, her roles most worthy of nomination were in comedies, and comediennes have fared especially poorly in Oscar competition (Myrna Loy, for example, was never even nominated). Furthermore, Arthur's two most clearly Oscar-caliber performances, in *Mr. Deeds* and *Mr. Smith*, were overshadowed by her leading men. Both Gary Cooper and Jimmy Stewart were strong contenders for Best Actor in their respective years, and although neither won, their overpowering characterizations probably caused Academy voters to overlook Arthur.

But the biggest factor Arthur had going against her in the annual Oscar sweepstakes was simple politics. In 1942, Hedda Hopper labeled her the "Least Popular Woman in Hollywood." The same year, the Hollywood Women's Press Club confirmed that opinion by bestowing upon her its annual "Sour Apple Award" for being the least cooperative actress in the business. The Academy voters, among whom Arthur had few friends, were aware of her reputation for being difficult, and although they had no love for Harry Cohn, it was considered bad form for a star to feud so openly and repeatedly with her employer. It is also unlikely that Cohn did much lobbying on Arthur's behalf or that he pressured Columbia personnel to support her with a block vote, the way studio heads typically achieved nominations for their stars.

And so, when Arthur finally did garner her first and only Oscar nomination, it was in spite of, rather than because of, Harry Cohn. In mid-1942 she fled to New York with Frank Ross for an extended stay, on suspension again from Columbia for having rejected more scripts. The two of them renewed their friendship with screenwriter Garson Kanin, who had recently been inducted into the Army and was stationed at Fort Monmouth, New Jersey. Barely subsisting on his Army pay, Kanin approached his friends with a business proposition: for $25,000, he would write a suitable script that Arthur could offer to Harry Cohn for free in place of the material she was being sent. Though skeptical, the Rosses invited Kanin to try his hand.

Within a few weeks Kanin befriended an Army bunkmate and budding writer named Robert W. Russell. After a weekend visit to wartime Washington, D.C., then in the throes of a severe housing shortage, Kanin and Russell developed a screenplay set in the nation's capital, tentatively titled *Two's a Crowd*, which they presented to Arthur and Ross. The couple was greatly impressed and gladly accepted the script.

Kanin called Harry Cohn to offer him a screenplay for nothing. Naturally, the mogul was suspicious, especially when he learned that it was being submitted on behalf of Jean Arthur. Over the phone to Kanin, whom he had never met, Cohn railed against his star actress, accusing her of not wanting to work, of existing only to aggravate him. But never one to pass on a bargain, he agreed to consider the script, even acceding to the one condition Kanin laid down—that Cohn sit and listen while Kanin read the screenplay to him aloud. Cohn laughed so hard at the opening scene that he immediately agreed to take the story, but Kanin forced the executive to sit through the rest of the reading. *Two's a Crowd* was to be turned into Jean Arthur's next vehicle, which Cohn retitled *The More the Merrier*.

Directed and produced by George Stevens from a screenplay credited to ~~Richard~~ *Robert* Russell, Richard Flournoy, Lewis R. Foster and Frank Ross, *The More the Merrier* was perhaps the greatest of all World War II movie comedies. It also provided Jean Arthur with what *Variety* called "undoubtedly the best screen role of her long Hollywood career." She plays Connie Milligan, a prim, pert government working girl in her late twenties, who is engaged to the dull Charles J. Pendergast, a successful agency bureaucrat played by Richard Gaines. Benjamin Dingle (Charles Coburn), the elderly retired millionaire to whom Connie, against her better judgment, has sublet half her apartment, decides early on that she deserves better than the lifeless Pendergast. The fatherly Dingle, whose motto is "Damn the torpedoes, full speed ahead!" surreptitiously sublets half of his space to Air Force Sergeant Joe Carter (Joel McCrea), a "high type, clean cut nice young fellow," and sets out to play matchmaker between Connie and Joe.

The rest of the movie follows the gradual but inevitable coupling of Connie and Joe, aided by the sly maneuverings of Dingle. His efforts reach fruition in the classic front stoop scene, justly regarded as among the sexiest comedy sequences ever filmed. Connie and Joe are walking home from dinner, alone for the first time, Pendergast having been detained by Dingle back at the restaurant where the four of them had met earlier that evening. Connie begins to pry for information about Joe's former girlfriends, but he is evasive. They reach the steps of their apartment and sit down, whereupon Joe, as McCrea later described it, begins "copping feels" while Connie half-heartedly resists (the scene was improvised, according to McCrea, when he and Arthur began playing around between takes to ease her nervous tension). As Joe continues to nuzzle her, Connie, practically gasping for air between words, gamely tries to switch the subject to her engagement to Mr. Pendergast. But eventually Connie embraces her fate, grabbing Joe's face in her hands and giving him a long, passionate kiss. Later that night, in a scene reminiscent of the Walls of Jericho sequence in *It Happened One Night*, McCrea proposes marriage from the bed in his room while Arthur, from her bed on the other side of the wall, tearfully accepts.

The chemistry between Arthur and McCrea, with whom she was working for the third time, has much to do with making *The More the Merrier* such a consummate romance. But the most arresting byplay is

that between Arthur and the sixty-five-year-old Coburn. Their relationship resembles that of father and daughter—or even grandfather and
granddaughter—the more so because they live together (even alone,
briefly, until McCrea shows up). On their first night alone in the apartment, Connie is in pigtails and pajamas, and Dingle in his bathrobe, while
she is setting out the morning schedule. With pencil and floor plan in
hand, she charts out their every move, minute by minute, so that they can
avoid bumping into each other in their tiny quarters ("At 7:01 I enter the
bathroom…by 7:05 you've started the coffee…. At 7:13 I put on my eggs
and I leave to finish dressing. Then you put on your shoes and take off my
eggs at 7:16…," etc.).

What makes the scene work so well are the contrasting reactions of the
two players. Arthur's Connie is completely earnest throughout her monologue, while Coburn's Dingle watches with amusement, his portly body
swaying and his hands gesticulating to and fro in response to each push
of her pencil.

There is also a suggestion here that what Dingle feels for Connie is the
mildest form of sexual attraction for a young woman. It is particularly
evident when Connie suggests that they leave the apartment separately
the next morning in order not to arouse any suspicions. Flattered as never
before, Coburn flashes a wide grin and thanks her for the unintended
compliment.

The vague sexual undertone to the Coburn/Arthur relationship helps
keep the movie from being overly cloying, and also sets the stage for the
arrival of McCrea. Whatever subconscious feelings Dingle has for Connie
can never be acted upon, so they are sublimated into the vicarious romance
that Dingle brokers between Connie and Joe.

The movie's ending explicitly caps off this theme. Connie and Joe have
returned to their upstairs apartment after a hastily arranged marriage
which they purportedly entered into only to avoid bringing scandal to
Pendergast. For a while it seems clear that the marriage will not be con-
summated, since Joe is off the next morning to Africa on a military
assignment and Connie lacks confidence that he will ever return to her.
They kiss goodbye and return to their respective rooms. But after several

minutes of talk, they notice that the Walls of Jericho separating their rooms have been torn down (Dingle has struck again), and they look at each other with sly glee. Satisfied that his work is done, Dingle walks upstairs, pins a "Mr. and Mrs. Sergeant Carter" nametag on their door and leads some elderly cohorts in a rousing chorus that ends the film:

> Damn the torpedoes, full speed ahead!
> Damn the torpedoes, full speed ahead!
> Damn the torpedoes, full speed ahead!

Oscar night, March 2, 1944, was marked by several firsts. The ceremony that year was moved to Grauman's Chinese Theatre and was the first to which the public was allowed to buy tickets. The awards were also the first to be broadcast by radio and the first to feature live entertainment. In a nod to the ongoing war, two hundred service personnel were given free passes and the lavish banquet was canceled.

Charles Coburn took home a deserved Best Supporting Actor award that night for his performance as Benjamin Dingle, the finest work of his long and distinguished career. *The More the Merrier* also earned nominations for Best Picture, Best Actress, Best Director, Best Screenplay and Best Original Story (the latter credited to Frank Ross and Robert Russell), but the top award went to *Casablanca*. The only clear injustice of the evening was in the Best Actress category. Young Jennifer Jones, David O. Selznick's latest discovery (and lover) won for her ethereal performance in *The Song of Bernadette*, beating out several more talented actresses including Arthur, Joan Fontaine and Ingrid Bergman (each of whom was also a present or former Selznick protégée).

Fellow losers Arthur and Fontaine repaired to a bar on Rodeo Drive with their husbands Frank Ross and Brian Aherne. As Fontaine later wrote in her memoirs, Arthur began to wax fatalistic over her battles with Harry Cohn, and professed admiration that Fontaine had taken up several hobbies (notably cooking) to distract her from her own similar contract struggles with Selznick. Fontaine offered to teach Arthur how to cook, and set up an appointment the next morning in her kitchen to glaze and decorate a whole salmon. But Arthur never showed.

Although she lost out in the Oscar competition, Arthur had finally received the recognition of her peers and was now at the height of her career. *The More the Merrier* stamped her as a star for a new era, the 1940s, during which the glamorous, independent female movie star of the thirties gave way to a more ordinary, home-style heroine. Arthur's own screen persona had undergone a subtle but definite shift in this direction over her past few films; no longer the cynical, wise-cracking idealist of *Mr. Deeds* or *Mr. Smith*, she had become the proverbial girl-next-door, albeit one with panache. Even when seen doing everyday things, like brushing her teeth in *The More the Merrier*, Arthur managed to project a personality that was both intriguing and irresistible.

Arthur's next film, another comedy entitled *A Lady Takes a Chance*, continued this trend, although not as successfully as *The More the Merrier*. More warm than funny, the movie tells the story of a New York City working girl who heads west on a sightseeing bus to broaden her horizons and ends up lassoing a rodeo performer played by John Wayne (in his first starring comic role). The film's best moments are the quiet ones between Arthur and Wayne, as when they lie side by side in a hay wagon talking of the respective merits of the horses they love. Even James Agee, normally no fan of Arthur's, acknowledged that the scenes between her and Wayne had "unusually frank erotic undertones" which placed the film "on the edge [of a] new kind of realistic sex comedy." The New York *Times* also found much to like, "largely because of Miss Arthur's pert little ways, her prim hesitations at the wrong times; her uncloying coyness. Quite gradually she has become one of Hollywood's delightful comediennes."

To counteract his leading lady's reputation as "the most criticized star in all Hollywood," as he put it, Wayne gave an extensive fan magazine interview in which he extolled her as an unassuming, intelligent and considerate woman who happened to suffer from an "inferiority complex." He overheard her at one point whisper to a man on the set, "Do you think Duke would mind coming to my dressing room to go over a scene with me?" evidencing a humility that stumped the young actor. Arthur later recalled that Wayne "was quite pleasant at the time," while confessing that had she known then of his arch-conservative politics she "would have shot him dead on the spot."

In reality, Arthur and Wayne saw very little of each other off the set. As usual, Arthur repaired immediately to her dressing room between scenes and, at day's end, to her cabin at the Courson guest ranch in nearby Palmdale. Mary Courson, who together with her husband hosted many celebrities at the ranch-hotel, remembered fifty years later that Arthur kept to herself the entire time while Wayne, who had a room there as well, was off chasing women (he used his cabin, she recalled, only to "change clothes"). The only time she saw them in the same place in public was one night at the ranch cafe when Arthur spent the whole evening dancing to a jukebox with a group of servicemen from nearby Edwards Air Force Base, then known as Muroc. Wayne claimed that Arthur was "on her feet in a minute" when the cadets asked her to dance, but Courson remembered it differently. The actress politely refused several such requests until Courson's husband firmly told her that she "simply *must* dance with the boys." Once prodded to the dance floor, she kept up an exuberant jitterbug, Courson recalled. Wayne found it so out of character that he termed it a "mirage."

Phil Silvers, who was fourth-billed in the film, recalled that Arthur had no friends on the set. He claimed he was the only person, besides her maid, who was allowed in her dressing room, because of his entertainment value. "We were worlds apart in background and interest, and I suppose that's why I amused her," he wrote in his autobiography. "I'd come every day and tell her the gossip of the day before—who slugged whom, who was under the table at Ciro's, who was at a benefit dinner he couldn't afford.... I invented and embroidered situations to make her smile."

Some years later Silvers discovered that Arthur's penchant for privacy had, if anything, increased. During a night on the town with her in New York, they changed tables three times to escape the stares and whispers of tourists. Halfway through supper, Arthur exploded at them. "You enjoy looking at the monkey?" she cried out. "Do you want me to hang from a chandelier by my toes?"

A Lady Takes a Chance was Arthur's last film done with her husband, who co-produced it with his brother Richard Ross for RKO. Needing to complete only one more film to finish her contract with Columbia, she rejected the studio's suggestion for something called *The Woman Doctor*. In an effort to change her mind, Harry Cohn traveled across the country in late 1943 to New York, where Arthur was staying because she believed the cold weather cleared her head. He found her nervous, tired and upset, complaining that the script gave her chills up and down her spine because it called for her to work with a cadaver. Despairing of ever being offered a good dramatic role by Columbia, she averred that "comedies are what I do best."

Unfortunately, the film that she and the studio finally agreed upon—*The Impatient Years*—could not make up its mind whether it was comedy or drama. Filmed in mid-1944 as one of the war's first "coming home" pictures, it told of a young soldier who returns to a bride he had known only four days before leaving for duty. The film was originally designed as a reunion of the stars of *The More the Merrier*, with Arthur as the young bride, Joel McCrea as her husband and Charles Coburn as the girl's father. But McCrea dropped out before shooting began and was replaced by a nondescript young actor named Lee Bowman who, at twenty-nine, was fourteen years Arthur's junior.

With McCrea's departure, Arthur had thought she would skip this film as well, but she changed her mind on the basis of Bowman's screen test. She made a serious misjudgment, for Bowman proved to be completely wooden, and totally inadequate as a substitute for McCrea. Arthur did her best with her role as the not-entirely-sympathetic young mother (*Photoplay* called her "still the best farceur in the business"), but the entire production suffered from the lack of chemistry between Arthur and her leading man. Even Coburn, who seems out of place this time as her father, could not rescue the film from its languidness.

The movie is notable for a single scene at the end. Impressed with her husband's tales of flying and his philosophical musing that life in the clouds was preferable to that down on earth, Arthur's prudish and domestic character realizes what she has been missing, and exclaims to him, "I just want to live in the sky!" It is a statement that, like the film's ambiguous title, could have served as a metaphor for Arthur's own mood at the time. For after she finished filming and her contract with Columbia was over at last, she elected not to sign with that or any other studio. Though the story that she ran around the Columbia lot shouting with joy at her freedom may be exaggerated, the feelings attributed to her were not. She quietly let it be known that she was retiring from filmmaking for the foreseeable future, manifesting her intentions by requesting that her entry be left out of the new edition of the Hollywood Player's Directory, an annual listing of active motion picture stars. Jean Arthur's impatient years were over; from now on she would lead a completely independent life, conforming to no one's demands but her own.

Part Two

LIFE IN THE SKY

CHAPTER TWELVE

STILLBORN

Gary Merrill was on his way to a Christmas party in New York
in 1945 when he learned that Garson Kanin was trying to reach him by
telephone from Boston. Merrill knew that Kanin was the author and
director of a new play then on a pre-Broadway tour, and that it had
received good reviews the week before in New Haven. But the young
actor suspected from the message that something might have gone wrong

with the show. When he returned the call that night, his suspicions (and hopes) were confirmed.

Kanin said cryptically that the production was having a few problems and asked Merrill if he could come to Boston to see it. Merrill flew up for the performance that Saturday night, and saw immediately that the romantic male lead was not up to the part; as Merrill later recalled, the actor practically had to be dragged across the stage by his leading lady. Kanin offered Merrill the job as the actor's replacement, subject to clearing it with the female lead.

After being introduced to Jean Arthur in her suite at Boston's Ritz Carlton hotel, Merrill could have sworn she said, "Well, at least he's got balls." He was struck by the frankness of this otherwise reticent woman, who encouraged him to hold out for as much money as he could extract from Kanin and producer Max Gordon. But sensing that the show was to be a hit, the out-of-work Merrill accepted a $300-a-week salary instead of the hoped-for $500, and two nights later, on New Year's Eve, found himself playing opposite one of Hollywood biggest names in one of the season's most eagerly anticipated Broadway offerings, *Born Yesterday*. It was to be their only performance together.

Max Gordon had not wanted to cast Jean Arthur in the role of Billie Dawn in the first place. The veteran producer of such Broadway hits as *My Sister Eileen*, *The Women* and *Roberta* had heard that she was aloof and difficult, and although he did not doubt her considerable talents, he feared that her reputed timidity was theatrically incorrect. "Next to her, it was said, Greta Garbo was both gregarious and positively garrulous," Gordon later recalled. "Many regarded Jean as a snob."

Nor was Arthur taken at first with the lead role. Ex-chorus girl Billie Dawn, the quintessential dumb blonde, is the mistress of a wealthy junk dealer who disparages her for her ignorance and hires a *New Republic* Washington correspondent to tutor her in politics and culture. Arthur was at home with the latter part of the play, in which the rough-edged bimbo blossoms into an educated young woman. But she was uncomfortable with the first act, which called for straight farce. "I suppose I'm a snob," she later said, echoing what Gordon had heard, "but I wanted to do something more ladylike."

The one person who was convinced that Jean Arthur was right for the part was Garson Kanin. In fact, Kanin wrote the play expressly with Arthur in mind, as he had similarly done with *The More the Merrier*. What's more, the play's villain—boorish Harry Brock—was based on Arthur's old nemesis, Harry Cohn. By allowing the Billie Dawn character to triumph over Brock, Kanin was giving Arthur the opportunity to vicariously conquer the hated Cohn. This prospect, along with the play's democratic-populist sentiments, enabled Kanin to talk Arthur into doing the project.

To combat Gordon's lingering skepticism, Kanin assured him that Arthur's detractors simply misunderstood her; she was shy, yes, and a little eccentric, but not difficult to work with. She had behaved perfectly well throughout *The More the Merrier*, Kanin reported; besides, he felt he could handle any problems with her that might arise. Reluctantly, Gordon acquiesced, and even gave in to Arthur's demands for a variety of perquisites beyond those customarily accorded to stars of her magnitude. In addition to a $2,500-a-week salary and a percentage of the gross, Arthur was given approval rights on the stage manager, press agent and any photographs released for promotional purposes; final say on billing; a personal chauffeur, maid and beautician; and a twenty-five percent investment in the play's profits. This last right was particularly significant, for the play was likely to be a hit and had an $80,000 advance sale in New York, unusually large for the time, mainly on the strength of Arthur's name. Acknowledging Arthur's contribution, Kanin's wife, Ruth Gordon, appeared at the rehearsals one day and thanked Arthur for the new mink coat she had just bought.

Almost from the beginning of rehearsals, though, producer Gordon's worst fears about the star were confirmed. Arthur immediately began objecting that some of the lines were unsavory and insisted they be stricken. Kanin usually responded with a compromise, rewriting some lines and scenes, and leaving others intact. Dissatisfied, Arthur showed her displeasure by reading her part in a bored monotone. At that point, recalled cast member Mary Laslo, "Gar would say, 'Okay, take five! Take ten!' They'd go into the dressing room, and maybe a half hour later they'd come back and there'd be a change made in the script." More than four decades later, Laslo could still recall Arthur explaining to her, "'You know, everything that I ever got in the movies, I had to fight for.'"

By the time of the December 20 opening in New Haven, Kanin was nearly beside himself over Arthur's antics. He was a victim, in Gordon's opinion, of not having really known his friend until he had to work with her in close quarters. Kanin was also struggling to rewrite the important third act, which he acknowledged needed much work. The reviews in New Haven, including those for Arthur, were encouraging, but immediately afterward the actress sent Kanin a note insisting on further significant changes and threatening to quit the production.

The positive notices continued after the opening in Boston on Christmas Day, but two days later Arthur complained of a sore throat and again talked of leaving the show. Gordon has written that he told Kanin, not for the first time, to let her quit, but Kanin urged him to be patient. "No one dared to tell her the plain truth—that her complaints were masks behind which she was trying to conceal her fears," Gordon recalled. Kanin has told an almost completely opposite story, claiming it was Gordon who, for box-office reasons, pressed to keep Arthur from resigning and required that changes be made to accommodate her.

When Gary Merrill arrived in Boston to take over the role of writer Paul Verrall, he instantly sided with Arthur. He learned that the actress had been promised a replacement before New Haven, as well as a new third act, yet neither had arrived. Merrill also felt that Kanin and his wife had not given Arthur the care and feeding she needed as an insecure actress who had been off the stage for more than a decade. In his view they risked losing someone with a quality he had seen only once before, in actress Laurette Taylor—"the ability to make an audience laugh and cry with the same line."

During the second act in Boston on the evening of New Year's Day, Arthur blacked out on stage. She missed about sixteen lines and was able to finish only after being pumped full of coffee and other stimulants during intermission. Back at Arthur's hotel room that night, Gordon found the actress surrounded by pitchers of heavy cream and bananas, under doctor's orders to eat as much as possible. She said she still planned to make the next day's matinee and had no intention of quitting.

The next morning, however, Arthur told Gordon she would not be able to go on until the Philadelphia opening the following week. She reported her doctor's findings that she had a viral infection of the throat and intestinal tract. Upset but unsurprised, Gordon quickly ordered the stage manager to prepare Mary Laslo, who was playing a manicurist, to take over. Though technically not an understudy, Laslo was the only option available because she happened to know all the lines.

When Gordon appeared on stage to tell the audience that Arthur would not be appearing, he offered refunds to anyone either then or after the first act, but surprisingly few people asked for their money back. About $65 was returned at the Wednesday matinee, $100 that night and $90 the next night. The show sold out for its final performances in Boston on Friday and Saturday, January 4 and 5. Laslo knew that she could be no more than a temporary replacement in the leading role, but she basked in her moment of glory. Forty years later, she remembered with tears of pride that the veteran cast was "not about to let me fail."

In the meantime, with a Philadelphia opening scheduled for January 7, the search was on for a permanent replacement in the not unlikely event that Arthur would not be back. Again at this point, Gordon's and Kanin's version of events differ, with each having taken credit for suggesting the new Billie Dawn. Gordon maintained that at his New York office the day before the Boston run ended, he interviewed a shrill-voiced Manhattan nightclub actress who had been recommended to him, realized immediately that she was "perfect" and sent her over to Kanin for a reading. But the playwright has claimed it was he who suggested the same woman to Gordon and convinced him to try her after the producer initially dismissed her as "that fat Jewish girl from The Revuers." The actress's biographers have since tended to adopt Gordon's account, but in either event it is clear that the departure of Jean Arthur led to the discovery of Judy Holliday.

The official end, for Arthur, came in Philadelphia's Warwick Hotel, where Gordon and Kanin were told by Dr. Clifford Barborka that she was suffering from low blood sugar and a worsening viral condition (although "nervous exhaustion" is how Kanin remembered the diagnosis). The physician said she was through with the show and that he was having her admitted indefinitely to Chicago's Passavant Hospital, where he regularly practiced.

Over the next few days, Judy Holliday engaged in round-the-clock rehearsals, aided herself by coffee and Dexadrine, in an effort to be ready for the postponed opening in Philadelphia on January 12. The play went on that night with Holliday and a new third act, opened to critical acclaim in New York on February 4 and ran for another three years with Holliday in the lead. Ironically, the 1950 movie version of the play, for which Holliday won a Best Actress Oscar, was produced by Harry Cohn, who probably did not even realize that the film's antagonist was modeled after him. The film established Holliday as Columbia's new comic queen, a title she held until her death from cancer in 1965 at age forty-three.

The real reasons for Arthur's leaving *Born Yesterday* remain obscure. The rumor at the time was that she felt overshadowed by acting newcomer Paul Douglas, whose portrayal of Harry Brock seemed to be garnering the best critical reviews during tryouts. As Mary Laslo recalled, "Everybody knew Jean Arthur's name, and nobody knew Paul Douglas. So Douglas got the notices and people just took Jean's work for granted because they were used to it. And I think that's what really made her lose heart.... I think that's why she 'took ill.'"

The contemporaneous reviews, however, provide little support for this theory. The New Haven *Register* was duly impressed with Douglas but no less so with Arthur; its critic wrote that she had

> not lost any of the tricks that have endeared her to a host of admirers. She modulates her cracked voice, she swings and sways in her own special way, she pouts and raises her eyebrows

for the right effects. As a comedienne, she continues in her
path as a first class entertainer.

The Boston *Herald* found Douglas "excellent in every respect," but
spent more time extolling Arthur:

> Jean Arthur's performance should give great pleasure alike to
> her huge screen public and to those who have never seen her
> before either on the stage or in pictures. Her style of acting is
> easy, natural and poised, her timing excellent, and she can
> throw away lines as well as drive them home.

While Arthur later acknowledged that she could not have given the
same performance that Judy Holliday did, doubtless she would have
achieved success in the role. "I heard that she was wonderful—not good—
wonderful," said Roddy McDowall. Mary Laslo also remembered that
Arthur "really was *lovely* in it. It's just that Judy had a different approach,
which was better for the part. She certainly didn't do a better job of *acting*
than Jean Arthur, not by a long shot."

To eradicate what they called the "vicious gossip and careless rumors"
about Arthur's departure, producer Gordon and playwright Kanin took
out an unusual advertisement in the February 2, 1946 New York *Times*
signed by them and by each cast member. It said that

> Jean rehearsed, worked and played to the limit of her physical
> capacity and beyond. Finally, on the considered advice of
> physicians retained by herself and the management, she left the
> Locust Street Theater, Philadelphia, for the Passavant
> Hospital, Chicago…. We have already conveyed to Jean our
> sincerest wishes for a speedy recovery. We repeat them here
> and now. And *loudly*.

While this could have been a heartfelt gesture by the show's managers,
it was more likely an effort to head off any further trouble with Arthur.
Arthur later asserted that after she became ill and it was clear the show
was going to be a hit with Judy Holliday, Gordon and Kanin came to her

and demanded that she give back her quarter share (which she did). In later years she told one close friend that Kanin was upset at the amount of control she had over the show, and set about to drive her from the production by withholding delivery of things she desperately wanted, such as a replacement for Merrill and a new third act. Though this particular charge seems dubious (surely Kanin did not want to lose the show's only box-office name), Arthur clearly felt frustrated with the situation. "There was such confusion, with changes being made continuously," she later said. "I know they do things that way in the theater sometimes, but I've got to have that play written down for me." Of the original Paul Verrall she explained simply, "I got no reaction from him at all.... If I had had Merrill from the beginning, I would have had some support." If Arthur was difficult in *Born Yesterday*, said Mary Laslo, it was because "she had a reason for being difficult."

There was another reason for her dispiritedness, however, to which she alluded but briefly in a 1972 interview. "It was a very hard time for me," she said. "My association with my husband was breaking up, and there was nobody I could turn to for help. I was so alone."

Roddy McDowall recalled Arthur implying to him that her troubles in *Born Yesterday* were connected to a deep emotional attachment she had to a doctor who had great influence over her. Arthur's close friend Nell Eurich said that after Frank Ross, one other man meant a great deal to her—a doctor in Chicago. Helen Harvey likewise remembered Arthur telling her that besides Frank Ross, there was another man with whom she fell madly in love but who let her down in time of need—someone who hinted that he might leave his wife for her but failed to do so. And Arthur told her friend Pete Ballard that Garson Kanin had the ability to "blackmail" her because he knew of an extra-marital affair she had been carrying on at the time of *Born Yesterday*. These fragments of information together suggest that Arthur may have been romantically involved with her doctor, Clifford Barborka.

Clifford Joseph Barborka, a nationally prominent diagnostician and gastroenterologist, was a doctor to the rich and famous, having treated the likes of Babe Ruth, Knute Rockne, Katharine Hepburn and Spencer

Tracy. But he was not fazed by either Hollywood or sports stars, preferring to view them simply as patients in need of help. A genuinely warm, caring man, his philosophy of medicine was to treat each patient like a person, not a number. His greatest loves were the cello and harp, the Chicago Bears, his Colorado summer ranch and his family—wife Bessie, to whom he was married for sixty years, and sons Clifford Jr. and Bill.

If there was anything between Arthur and Barborka it certainly was well hidden. More than twenty years after the doctor died in 1971 at age seventy-six, Bill Barborka could not recall his father ever talking about Jean Arthur or inviting her to their home. By contrast, other patient-stars, especially Hepburn, were frequent guests there. Nor could Bill Barborka shed any light on the suggestion that the relationship was more than that of doctor and patient. As he pointed out, his parents were nearly inseparable, having dated for eight years before their six decades of marriage. In all of those sixty years, Bill Barborka asserted, they never exchanged a cross word.

It also is significant that, in Barborka's words, his father's doctoring style was such that "he made you feel you were the only person on earth." For someone as insecure and self-conscious as Arthur, a professional relationship with a fatherly doctor figure, especially one who appeared to take such a personal interest in her welfare, might easily have led to an infatuation on her part. Her "illness" during *Born Yesterday* might then have been in reaction to feelings of unrequited love, or an effort to gain Barborka's attention, or both. Viewed in this light, Arthur's various statements about having been "let down" by a man around that time, of having fled the show out of an emotional attachment to him, were perfectly accurate indicators of her true feelings. They just failed to take account of reality.

The *Born Yesterday* debacle behind her, and with time and money on her hands, Arthur needed some new outlet for her energies and intellect. According to Warren Harris's biography of Cary Grant, she accepted an offer from Samuel Goldwyn to appear in *The Bishop's Wife* with Grant and David Niven, only to back out with a claim that she was pregnant. "You didn't just screw her—you screwed me!" Goldwyn reportedly fumed to Frank Ross. But besides its inherent implausibility, given Arthur's age at the time (forty-five) and the state of her relationship with Ross, this account suffers from a case of mistaken identity. In fact it was Teresa Wright, not Arthur, who was slotted for the female lead in *The Bishop's Wife* and had to withdraw due to pregnancy.

In truth, Arthur had no interest in making movies at this time; in the middle of rehearsals for *Born Yesterday*, she even turned down Frank Capra's offer of the Donna Reed part in *It's A Wonderful Life*. Instead, she was looking for something completely different. "All my life I've wanted to make enough money so I could stop and be a student for a while," she said. And so Jean Arthur, who never finished high school, decided it was time to go to college.

CHAPTER THIRTEEN

ADULT EDUCATION

"As a human being, she was something of a mystery," wrote theater critic Brooks Atkinson. "Only a few people penetrated the wall and air with which she surrounded herself. She probably lacked self-confidence."

"She glories in the fact that there is scarcely a woman on the stage about whom less is known," read the program to one of her most popular plays, *Peter Pan*. "She did not possess unlimited strength, and meeting people fatigued her, partly because of her genuine shyness, even among her friends," one of her intimates explained. Although publicity-shy in the extreme, she had a mischievous streak, and was described as pixieish, childlike, with a low, sweet voice.

Small wonder, then, that Maude Adams, the most renowned stage actress of the early twentieth century, should have become the idol of Jean Arthur. The quintessential performer of the plays of J.M. Barrie (*Quality Street, The Little Minister, What Every Woman Knows*), Adams became the original American Peter Pan in 1905 and played the role off and on for more than ten years. Reputedly Barrie told her that "the character came to my mind through you." In the summer of 1909 she played Joan of Arc in a spectacular outdoor production in Harvard Stadium, and she retired from the stage, in her mid-forties, after playing in Barrie's *A Kiss for Cinderella* in 1918. Never married (and notably indifferent to men), she lived as a virtual recluse until 1937, when she went to Stephens College, a women's school in Columbia, Missouri, to start a drama department.

Arthur had had a fascination with Maude Adams for many years. The two of them first met briefly in early 1939, after a lecture Adams gave at the Biltmore Hotel in Los Angeles. Arthur found the speech electric and inspiring, and was momentarily lifted from her depression over her contract woes with Columbia. She was so taken with the older woman that Arthur asked James Madison Wood, the President of Stephens and sponsor of the lecture, if he could arrange an audience with her the next day. The three of them did meet for lunch, where Arthur thanked the sixty-seven-year-old actress for what she had done for her.

Thus, it was no coincidence that when Arthur went looking for a college in the spring of 1947 she chose Stephens, where Maude Adams still taught. A small, private liberal arts school, Stephens was among the more fashionable women's colleges of the time. Wood, its personable president of thirty-five years and a leading proponent of higher education for women, had devised a curriculum specially tailored to the aspirations of the young, increasingly affluent, postwar American female. "Marriage and

162

the Family" was one innovative course that nearly every student took; another focused on consumer economics and comparative shopping. A strong theater department, headed by Adams, also attracted aspiring performers such as Tammy Grimes, a student in the early 1950s (Joan Crawford also briefly attended Stephens in 1921 and was befriended by President Wood).

Although Arthur had been drawn to Stephens because of Maude Adams, she did not go there to study acting. Instead, she concentrated on the humanities, taking courses in philosophy, psychology, sociology and biology. "I am particularly interested in the mental and spiritual phases of life," she said.

Arthur did not officially enroll at Stephens; instead, she attended classes as President Wood's special guest. Though some saw her college venture as a gimmick, the truth was that Arthur had been planning it almost from the day she dropped out of school in New York for a career in modeling. "I'd always thought, when I left high school, that I'd go back," she said, asking rhetorically, "Is there anything odd about wanting to learn about the world's history and peoples?" As she told the college newspaper:

> I would be content to spend the rest of my life studying here at
> Stephens because here I have the opportunity to get the things
> I have always wanted among such an amazing group of men-
> tally and physically healthy humans. I have worked all my life
> and have had to be content with philosophies and ideas of my
> own and now, at last I am gaining knowledge in an atmosphere
> where I can get the most and best from my studies.

In class, recalled Dorothy Martin, Arthur's sociology professor that spring term, Arthur was "very quiet," speaking "not often, always briefly." But she excelled in anything written, and was articulate in individual conferences, in which they discussed such novels of social significance as *The Grapes of Wrath*. "She was very humane in all her attitudes; she wanted everybody to have a chance in the world," Martin recalled of her celebrity student.

Outside the classroom, Arthur shied away from any close contact with her fellow students. Connie Schenck, then a freshman at Stephens and later a professor of foreign languages at the college, recalled that Arthur "never made any real effort to get to know the younger girls." Schenck remembered that it was exciting at first for all the students to see the actress walking through the halls in her blue jeans and pigtails, but the novelty soon wore off when Arthur consistently went her own way. "She was not mean to anyone," Schenck said. "She just was serious about wanting to study with the professors, and really didn't want to be noticed." Nevertheless, Dorothy Martin recalled that Arthur was well liked by the girls in class, who "related to her very well—more so than she to them."

To shield herself from the masses, Arthur originally took up residence at the Daniel Boone hotel, the best in town, but before long she was besieged by hordes of local newspapermen looking for interviews, and by University of Missouri boys eager to have her attend their fraternity parties. Shortly thereafter she moved into more private quarters in President Wood's home, where a number of students were also staying as a result of a housing shortage.

Maude Adams was also an occasional guest in Wood's home, but she and Arthur rarely talked. "Each respected the other's desire for privacy," said President Wood.

"There wasn't any real closeness as I felt I had to keep my place and I didn't bring up the subject of Peter Pan as I'd been told she wouldn't talk about it," Arthur told Hedda Hopper in 1965. Adams likewise kept her distance from Arthur, whom she did not recall from their meeting eight years earlier and with whose work she was unfamiliar (Adams had not attended a movie in years). In fact, Adams once complained to playwright William Inge that Arthur was making her uncomfortable by constantly staring at her. "Who is that woman, she's driving me crazy," Adams said, evidently unaware of the younger actress's reputation and her almost mystical attraction to the original American Peter Pan.

While at Stephens, Arthur also took the popular "Marriage and the Family" course to help her understand the cause of the failure of her marriage to Frank Ross. What she learned is unclear, for she later said the course helped her understand others' problems more than her own. She did make one cryptic statement, though, that revealed that she may have faulted herself, as much as Frank Ross, for the disintegration of their marriage. According to Nell Eurich, who was a student at Stephens in 1947 and later became acting president of the college, the actress said that the course led her to form an analogy between marriage and riding a bicycle: the key to both was keeping to the center of the road and steering clear of trouble off to the side.

Although Arthur had said she could spend the rest of her life studying at Stephens, she stayed only six weeks. She claimed that financial considerations prompted her to return to moviemaking, reluctantly, after a three-year absence. But the timing of her departure, just before final exams, suggests that fear of failure may have played a part in her decision. In any event, she signed a three-picture deal with her old studio, Paramount, and that May headed back to Hollywood. But to continue her studies, she invited three of her instructors to spend the summer as guest tutors in her home at Boca de Canon Lane in Brentwood.

More than forty years later, Dorothy Martin recalled it as a "delightful summer." She and Vera Washburne, Arthur's psychology professor, and Emma Spencer, who instructed the actress in tennis and swimming, were put up in a secluded three-bedroom guest house on the side of a high hill, from where Arthur took her lessons while sprawled on an outdoor cot. The three teachers took breakfast in the guest house, and lunch and dinner with Arthur in the main house. Occasionally they were joined by Frank Ross, from whom Arthur "might as well have been divorced," observed Dorothy Martin. She nevertheless recalled Ross as a pleasant, handsome man who arranged for his friend and fellow producer Milton Bren, who was soon to marry Claire Trevor, to take the three teachers, along with Arthur, on Bren's yacht to Catalina Island. But when Bren and Trevor, or other couples such as Danny and Sylvia Kaye, appeared as dinner guests, Ross would be elsewhere, usually with paramour Joan Caulfield.

Although she lacked formal schooling, Arthur possessed an inquisitive mind and a capacity for independent study. "She was a very eager, attentive student," Dorothy Martin recalled. "Any book I'd mention she'd send her chauffeur over to the [UCLA] university bookstore to pick up." While recognizing Arthur's interest as genuine, Martin also sensed that the actress was partly motivated by envy of her Princeton-educated husband.

Unquestionably genuine, in Martin's view, was Arthur's shyness and aversion to publicity. "She was very kind, but extremely private," the teacher recalled. On one occasion Martin happened to mention a story about Arthur that had appeared in the newspaper, and the actress "turned it right off; she was sort of annoyed." She never talked about anything so personal as her marriage or family.

Though distinctly un-starlike in private, Arthur did reveal, at least once, that she was not immune to the usual Hollywood pettiness. In discussing with Martin her upcoming film, *A Foreign Affair*, Arthur maintained that she, and not co-star Marlene Dietrich, should receive top billing. She got her wish, her name appearing above both Dietrich's and leading man John Lund's, as well as before the film's title, in the opening credits. It was just the beginning of her rivalry with the great German actress.

A Foreign Affair was a black comedy about the Allied military occupation of post-war Berlin, co-written and directed by Billy Wilder. Arthur plays Phoebe Frost, a prudish, bespectacled Iowa congresswoman and member of a committee conducting a fact-finding investigation into the morale and morals of the American occupation forces. Frost is gradually thawed out by a handsome officer (Lund), who wins her heart at the same time he is carrying on a secret affair with a basement nightclub singer and ex-Nazi (Dietrich) who is enjoying his protection. In Arthur's most memorable scene in the film, Phoebe, loosened by a few drinks, belts out "The Iowa Corn Song" at the underground Lorelei cafe and begins pursuing Lund without inhibition. The wholesome American ultimately bests the wanton German fraulein in the competition for Lund. But it was the exotic, glamorous Dietrich who won the battle for the critics' affections.

Not that Arthur's return to the screen after a four-year absence wasn't warmly greeted. Bosley Crowther of the New York *Times* commented that "Jean Arthur is beautifully droll," while *Variety* noted that she was "back in a top-flight characterization." *The New Yorker* responded with similar enthusiasm:

> Jean Arthur has a part similar to many she's had before—the ones in which she is required to go through three stages of personality. To begin with she is grimly moral, then she becomes mischievous, and finally she is mildly abandoned. The pattern may be simple but Miss Arthur knows how to follow it better than any other actress in Hollywood, and she is again quite satisfactory to watch as she proceeds along her familiar path.

Dietrich's path was not exactly an unfamiliar one for her, either. Her Erika von Schluetow is the proverbial woman with a tarnished past, and the sultry chansons she is given to perform—"Black Market," "Illusions" and "Ruins of Berlin"—were pure Marlene (all were written by her long-time composer Frederick Hollander, who brought her to fame with his "Falling in Love Again" in *The Blue Angel*). In truth Dietrich did little more than play herself in this film, but that inimitable self, which appeared wiser and more complex with the years, was enough to gain her the greater critical attention. She graced the cover of *Life* magazine, and was extolled by the *Times'* Crowther as the best and "most fascinating" aspect of the picture. Dietrich herself came to regard the film as one of her better efforts.

On its release, however, *A Foreign Affair* had as many detractors as admirers, mainly because of its controversial subject matter and Wilder's acerbic treatment of it. The film was unabashedly cynical about the Allies' black market operations and their sanctimonious attitude toward the conquered German people; at the Brandenburg gate, GIs swap candy bars for nylons to bestow upon their German mistresses and purchase girls outright with packs of cigarettes. Adding to the bleak atmosphere are the numerous background shots of bombed-out Berlin, which Wilder filmed on location with a small crew in the summer of 1947. The film was denounced on the floor of the House of Representatives and by the

Defense Department, and suffered at the box office. James Agee, hardly a prude, declared much of the film "in rotten taste."

Modern critics cannot seem to decide whether *A Foreign Affair* is a brilliant satire or a clumsy misfire. Nor are they agreed on the relative merits of the performances of Dietrich and Arthur. David Shipman called *A Foreign Affair* a "shining exception" to postwar Hollywood's tendency to avoid treating contemporary problems, and asserted that Arthur actually took the film from her German rival. But Andrew Sarris in 1987 called it a "disaster" for Arthur, finding her character "too patly based on screwball formulas of the more innocent '30s." Sarris and others have also taken umbrage at what they consider Wilder's unfair treatment of the innocent Arthur at the hands of the worldly Dietrich, who gets the better of their direct exchanges. "I see you do not believe in lipstick...and what a curious way to do your hair—or rather not to do it," Dietrich snarls in one encounter. Later, alone with Lund, Dietrich laughingly derides Arthur's Phoebe as a "funny little woman with a face like a kitchen door," a line that had to hurt Arthur, even if it was only make-believe.

Although the script inevitably glamorized the foreign chanteuse to the American's disadvantage, Arthur felt that Wilder stacked the deck in Marlene's favor more than was necessary. A native of Austria, Wilder spent his early filmmaking years in Berlin, where he befriended the young German actress. When they reunited to film *A Foreign Affair*, it was like old home week, the two of them constantly joking on the set and communicating in German with Hollander, who played the piano for Dietrich in the film. While Wilder visited Marlene in her dressing room, frequently to sample her German cooking, Arthur sulked, with growing jealousy, in her own quarters. She became convinced that Wilder was trying to sabotage her and that he was having an affair with Marlene (a "hallucination," the director later said). One midnight, Wilder recalled, Arthur showed up at his doorstep with Frank Ross, and with tears in her eyes accused the director of burning her close-ups in order to satisfy Dietrich's desire to make her co-star look bad. The flabbergasted Wilder took Arthur to the projection room the next day just to prove it wasn't true. In fact, he had to admit, Arthur was "simply wonderful" in her rushes, which was about the only thing that kept him from getting rid of her.

Arthur eventually made her peace with Wilder, though it took forty years. In 1988, after watching what she called "our film" on television the night before, she called Wilder and said that she "absolutely loved it." Arthur had already confessed to Roddy McDowall that she had been very unfair to her former director, and she used the occasion of her call to Wilder to apologize to him. She inquired whether, after four decades, they could still be friends. An amused Wilder responded affirmatively.

Arthur may have forgiven Wilder his real or imagined slights, but she never got over her dislike of Dietrich. The actress treated Arthur coolly or worse during the film's shooting, once commenting to Arthur that she must have had great courage to wear the shoulderless black gown that her character dons in order to catch Lund's attention (in the film itself, Dietrich's Erika brutally asks Phoebe if the gown is from Iowa and suggests that she has it on backwards). As a result of Dietrich's dismissive attitude toward her during *A Foreign Affair*, Arthur harbored a lifelong grudge against the fabled Blue Angel. In later years Arthur pressed her friend John Springer, who was also a confidant of Marlene, for details about the star's reclusive life in Paris. But the interest ran only one way. "I mentioned Jean to Marlene a couple of times," Springer said. "She couldn't have cared less."

Arthur's friend Pete Ballard also caught a glimpse of Arthur's antipathy toward her one-time co-star. He had been trying for some time in the 1970s, without success, to talk Arthur into writing her memoirs. One winter he flew out to Carmel to visit her and, after he walked in the door, Arthur yelled to him, "All right, there's your damn book!" On the table, Ballard found three pages of vitriol that Arthur had written on Marlene Dietrich. "She never once capitalized Dietrich's name," Ballard laughingly recalled. "Then I told her, 'Maybe you shouldn't write a book.'"

She never did.

CHAPTER FOURTEEN

TEMPORARY HELP

n 1941, German psychoanalyst Erich Fromm published his most important book, *Escape From Freedom*, which quickly won international acclaim for its psychological explanation of the rise of fascism. Fromm, who had fled Nazi Germany for America in 1933, asserted that Nazism was the result of men's inability to live with the freedom bestowed upon them by democratic capitalism. The submission to totalitarian authority, Fromm wrote, is one of two principal mechanisms by which modern man seeks to escape from the burden of freedom, and corresponding alienation, of contemporary civilization.

But it was the second type of escape mechanism—which Fromm termed "compulsive conforming"—that he viewed as the more prevalent one. And it was this concept that was to catch Jean Arthur's fancy and turn her into a lifelong, devoted follower of Erich Fromm. "To put it briefly," Fromm wrote:

> the individual ceases to be himself; he adopts entirely the kind of personality offered to him by cultural patterns; and he therefore becomes exactly as all others are and as they expect him to be.... The person who gives up his individual self and becomes an automaton, identical with millions of other automatons around him, need not feel alone and anxious any more. But the price he pays, however, is high; it is the loss of his self.

To Jean Arthur, a compulsive non-conformist, these words had a powerful resonance. When she read them, she felt they validated her entire philosophy of life. Dr. Fromm was someone she had to meet.

She found him in the summer of 1948, teaching at Bennington College, the small women's school in bucolic southern Vermont, where Arthur's ancestors had settled two centuries earlier. Founded in 1932 on the child-directed principles of John Dewey, Bennington was known for its progressive, inter-personal approach to higher education, and was considered eccentric for the degree of freedom it gave its students. It was thus a natural home for a free thinker like Fromm, who joined the faculty at Bennington in 1942 and began counseling students and others, as well as teaching a course in psychology. Among his patients over the years were such prominent personalities as actor Anthony Quinn, sociologist David Riesman (whose best-selling book, *The Lonely Crowd*, was an extension of Fromm's work)—and Jean Arthur.

Twice a week, in addition to attending Fromm's classes on an auditing basis, Arthur met with him to undergo formal psychoanalysis. Assisting him was Edward T. "Ned" Hall, a young anthropology instructor who later became the widely-read author of such books as *The Silent Language*. Hall found Arthur to be "a very human person" and "quite insightful," but "not particularly sure of herself." He was also surprised by her apparent modesty. "She was not impressed with her stature in the movies," he remembered. Although Hall could not recall (or felt ethically constrained not to reveal) the precise reason Arthur entered therapy, she later implied that the breakup of her marriage was the primary impetus. "If you become so frightened, so emotionally blinded that you don't even know you should get a divorce, then you have to have someone help you take the walls out of your mind," she explained.

Arthur remained in analysis with Fromm for about two years, following him to Mexico to continue her sessions when he went there briefly to teach. Afterward she described Fromm's counseling as

> the finest experience I ever had—the most constructive, in fact the only thing that makes sense. I've learned so much about myself, which means that I've learned about others too. I believe everyone should be analyzed. It should start when you're a young child, and then be repeated in your teens, and then again when you get over the Santa Claus idea of marriage and just want to die.

Although the substance of what transpired in their sessions can never be known, Fromm clearly urged his patient to celebrate, rather than apologize for, what others saw as her eccentricities. "His philosophy was very similar to hers, which was to be yourself," her friend Nell Eurich recalled. "She'd really lacked confidence, and he helped her to understand that she had every reason to have some." Arthur herself implied that Fromm had achieved some success on this score. "The greatest thing he did for me was teach me to laugh at myself," she said.

It is unlikely that Fromm spent any time exploring conventional Freudian themes with Arthur. Though originally trained in Freudian analytic methods, Fromm rejected Freud's view that human behavior is based purely on the satisfaction or frustration of biological instincts. A member of the so-called Neo-Freudian school, Fromm believed instead that social and cultural factors are the key to the understanding of human nature, and that interpersonal relationships are primarily responsible for the formation of character, including the development of neuroses.

Fromm did ask that Arthur probe her relationship with her parents and family, since she produced a short autobiography at his request that she kept for a time. A few years after writing it she showed it to her friend and agent Helen Harvey, who recalled it as being "nothing very revealing, which in itself is revealing." Arthur touched upon her mother in the auto-biography, but "it seemed as if the father almost didn't exist," Harvey recalled. Her impression from the piece was that Arthur "had been a troubled person all her life." Harvey said that she did not gain any insight into the source of Arthur's problems, "but I don't think she [Arthur] did, either."

Nell Eurich, who was closer to Arthur at the time, felt that Fromm's analysis in fact helped Arthur, but she added that "these things are always tentative. I'm sure it helped her to accept some things and express herself better; it certainly didn't make her satisfied with her life."

To whatever degree Fromm's treatment of her was a success, Arthur continued to worship him for the rest of her life. "She absolutely adored that man, his approach," according to Nell Eurich. Arthur consistently urged Fromm's succession of best-selling books upon her closest friends, long after he came to be derided by orthodox Freudians for his inatten-tiveness to clinical data, by political conservatives for his socialist ten-dencies ("a Marxist culture quack," *Time* called him) and by religious conservatives for his secular humanism.

While Fromm's views on the dangers of conformity may have helped Arthur see what was right with her, they were not capable of explaining what was wrong with her. Fromm frankly acknowledged that his approach was less concerned with individual than with "societal" neu-roses, and that the theories of other neo-Freudians, particularly those of his colleague Karen Horney, were better suited to dealing with individual neurotic anxiety.

Horney, the most important early feminist critic of Freud, began her career in Germany as a classically-trained Freudian analyst, then developed a more socio-cultural outlook after coming to America in the early thirties. She exerted a great deal of influence upon Fromm, as he did upon her (they were even lovers for a time), and some part of her thinking inevitably would have worked its way into Fromm's analysis of his patients, Jean Arthur included.

Horney's essential thesis was that all neuroses derive from the "basic anxiety" of childhood, and the child's attempts to cope with conflicting feelings of helplessness, fear and hostility generated out of uncaring or inadequate parenting. As a means of resolving these conflicts, the child adopts various character strategies, or "neurotic trends." She described these as falling into one of three principal categories: moving "towards," "against," or "away from" people. The first strategy is adopted by the "compliant" type, who seeks to win the affection of people out of a compulsive need to be loved. Those who move "against" people, by contrast, seek to win through intimidation. Arthur fit into neither of these categories, but rather into Horney's third category of the neurotic individual— the person who moves "away from" people. Like Ibsen's Peer Gynt, whose motto was "To thyself be enough," the detached type "hates regimentation. He never goes to the Zoo because he simply cannot stand seeing animals in a cage. He wants to do what he pleases when he pleases." Detached individuals avoid conformity for fear of "becoming submerged in the amorphous mass of human beings." They dislike gregariousness and social functions, crave privacy and prefer the pursuit of impersonal endeavors in the sphere of books, animals, art or nature. While noting that this same tendency may contribute to the development of the detached person's creative faculties, Horney cautioned that if the person who moves away from people is thrown into close contact with others, "he may readily go to pieces or to use the popular term, have a nervous breakdown."

Arthur's frequent bouts of stage fright, viewed in the context of Horney's theoretical system, had their source in what the psychologist called neurotic pride. To attain a sense of significance, the neurotic person creates in her mind an idealized image of herself, resulting in a drive for perfection and corresponding fear of failure when confronted with examinations, public performances or social gatherings. "Stage fright," while a good enough descriptive term for these fears, Horney wrote, "leaves out the fact that what constitutes failure for a given person is subjective. It may encompass all that falls short of glory and perfection.... A person is afraid of not performing as superbly as his exacting shoulds demand, and therefore fears that his pride will be hurt."

The theories of Alfred Adler, who exerted a strong influence upon both Horney and Fromm, provide yet further insight into Arthur's character and behavior. The founder of the Neo-Freudian movement, Adler believed that most neuroses result from failed efforts to compensate for the feelings of inferiority that every child develops based on such factors as birth order, gender or parental treatment (it was Adler who coined the term "inferiority complex"). All adult behavior, Adler posited, is "compensatory" in that it is marked by a striving for independence and significance—what he called "superiority." The neurotic individual either overcompensates for his feelings of inferiority by adopting unattainable "compensation ideals" (an example would be Joan of Arc), or by retreating into illness as a means of gaining a feeling of superiority. The person's illness is then made the excuse for her failure to attain the impossibly perfectionist goals she has set for herself.

Adler also described a more particular phenomenon he called the "masculine protest." He observed that women frequently feel themselves to be at a disadvantage in society due to cultural, not biological, factors (a point on which he disagreed with Freud). Women who suffer from gender envy, Adler theorized, may overcompensate for their perceived inferiority by developing an actual fear of the feminine role. Such was the case with Jean Arthur.

It may be recalled that Arthur felt "cheated" and "frustrated" by her sense that her older brothers led adventurous lives compared with hers, even though she was more competent and talented than any of them. She also noticed that her father, although a weaker person than her mother, seemed freer and happier. Less out of emulation than envy, then, Arthur developed a masculine way of thinking, and doing. She decided that she "was going to do things that were exciting, or at least interesting," and became a tomboy. She then selected a series of activist, accomplished female idols, from Mary Pickford to her Aunt Pearl Nelson; from Calamity Jane to Maude Adams to Joan of Arc. These women, Arthur's compensation ideals, all triumphed largely on their own, without the assistance of men.

In fact, Arthur's relations with men were mostly unsatisfactory all her life. For that, she mainly had her father to thank. As a young girl she had been devoted to Hubert Greene, preferring his winsome manner to that of her more pious mother. But with her father's increasingly errant ways, Gladys reverted to a more sympathetic and protective attitude toward her mother. It was one of the few positive ways she could relate to Hannah Greene.

While Arthur managed to work through her ambivalence toward her mother, she was less successful in her effort to win back, in her own mind, the father who had abandoned her. She originally turned to modeling, and then the movies, to gain his approval and adulation. But even as she came to attain success in those endeavors, the old feelings of insecurity resurrected themselves. Every time the movie cameras rolled—every time the still camera flashed—she was reminded, subconsciously, of her photographer father, whom she adored, but who constantly caused her to doubt his love and her worth every time he left her. The camera thus came to offer Jean Arthur both a symbolic opportunity and a risk: the chance to win her father's love and approval, but also the corresponding risk of incurring his rejection if she failed adequately to "pose." Her frequent bouts of nausea before film scenes, and her repeated illnesses during stage productions, were merely symptomatic of the feelings of anxiety that the camera engendered.

Both of Arthur's marriages can be viewed as part of her search for her missing father. She wed Julian Ancker—a photographer—for all of one day, but was unable to consummate the marriage. Her second husband, Frank Ross, was a Christian Scientist, and the man she thought her father should have been. But when that marriage failed, and her infatuation with Dr. Barborka ran its course, she literally gave up on men. A later student of hers described her as "generally down on the race."

On March 22, 1950, Jean Arthur and Frank Ross separately petitioned the Los Angeles Superior Court for a final decree of divorce, one year after the interlocutory decree that was granted to Arthur the previous March. Their petitions were filed just twenty-five minutes apart, but Arthur's was the first to be acted on by the county clerk. A day later, the clerk's office mailed Ross's petition back to his attorneys with an explanation that a decree had already been entered on behalf of his former wife.

Five weeks later, Ross would be married again, to his lover Joan Caulfield. Within that time Arthur, too, would embark on a new adventure designed to put her recent failures behind her and enable her to fulfill a lifelong dream.

CHAPTER FIFTEEN

GROWING YOUNG

"Who and what are you, Pan?"
"I'm youth, eternal youth, I'm the sun rising, I'm poets singing,
I'm the new world. I'm a little bird that has broken out of the
egg. I'm joy, joy, joy!"   —*Peter Pan*

I hate to admit it, but [Jean Arthur] *is* Peter Pan. She is youth,
joy, freedom, all the things Peter tells Captain Hook when
Hook asks, "Pan, who and what are you?"   —Mary Martin

*T*t had been almost seventeen years since *Peter Pan's* last appearance on Broadway when Peter Lawrence, a New York stage manager and
associate television producer in his late twenties, began his quest to produce a musical revival of the beloved J.M. Barrie work. Lawrence had
been mesmerized by the legendary Eva Le Galliene's performance when
he saw *Peter Pan* as a child, and when he heard, in late 1948, that Joan

Fontaine was anxious to re-create the role on Broadway he immediately set about to obtain the production rights.

After months of negotiation, Lawrence acquired an option for $2,500 from the Great Ormond Street Hospital for Sick and Crippled Children in London, to which Barrie had willed the rights to *Peter Pan*. The hospital was adamant that the work not be turned into a musical comedy, and Lawrence provided assurances that it would instead be a "play with music." He called his friend Leonard Bernstein, in great demand ever since the success of *On the Town* in 1944, to see if he would be interested in writing the score. Bernstein immediately said yes, explaining that it was the first time in five years that anyone had come to him with an idea involving something other than subways and skyscrapers. He enthusiastically began composing the music and lyrics, penning several new songs and revising some others that had been dropped from his earlier shows.

The next coup Lawrence scored was to line up veteran English character actor Boris Karloff for the role of the villainous Captain Hook. Though best known for his movie roles in *Frankenstein* and *The Mummy* in the early 1930s, Karloff was equally adept on stage. His rich English accent and courtly manner, cultivated by his training for the British diplomatic service, made him an ideal choice to play Pan's sworn enemy. His deep bass voice was also perfect for the two Gilbert and Sullivan-esque songs Bernstein wrote for Hook and his pirates, "Pirate Song" and "The Plank."

But almost a year after conceiving his idea Lawrence had yet to find a Peter. The rumor about Joan Fontaine's interest was just that, for she was still under contract to David Selznick. Lawrence considered Margaret Sullavan, Beatrice Lillie and dancer Vera Zorina for the part, and it was even suggested that Mickey Rooney or Gene Kelly be cast, despite the tradition of a female Peter. Through the Broadway grapevine Lawrence learned that Mary Martin was interested in playing the part, but she had only recently begun her run in Rodgers and Hammerstein's *South Pacific*. As Lawrence remembered it, Martin's "handlers," including the two famous songwriters and her husband, Richard Halliday, professed non-interest on her behalf, smugly assuming that the young producer would never get his project off the ground. But Lawrence knew that "Mary Martin was *dying* to do it."

By the fall of 1949, with all other options foreclosed, Lawrence was resigned to choosing Zorina. Despite his misgivings that she wasn't right for the part, Lawrence was tempted by a promise of financial backing from her husband, Columbia Records president Goddard Lieberson, and on October 19, 1949, it was announced that she had signed a contract to begin performances on Christmas Day. But the temperamental dancer began exhibiting increasingly difficult behavior and, when it became clear that the production would be delayed several months, she backed out, claiming other commitments. With his option set to expire in February, the frustrated producer's luck seemed to have run out.

Then one day Lawrence received a call from agent Maynard Morris, who said he had someone the producer would be very interested in for Peter, but that it had to be kept a secret. When Lawrence arrived at Morris's office near Bryant Park he was told that the agent's client was Jean Arthur. Lawrence had to admit that though her name had never crossed his mind before, she was a logical choice. Morris then surprised him by saying that Arthur already had her costume and wanted to audition. Before committing herself to the project, Arthur wanted to make certain that a nearly fifty-year-old woman could play a twelve-year-old boy. She hired out the Royale Theatre for a day, got into costume, recited a few lines and pranced about to a bit of Bernstein's music to the accompaniment of popular show pianist Trude Rittman. "It felt wonderful," Arthur reported. "I was at home on the stage for the first time in my life. Peter is my maturity."

The role was essentially Arthur's from that moment, subject to Lawrence's ability to obtain financing. To help on that front, Arthur promised to put up $25,000 of her own money, and performed at several backers' auditions with Bernstein. She and the composer became fast friends. He wrote the jaunty little "Shadow Dance" number for her, which she played over and over on a phonograph in her hotel room, working out her own choreography. Because Arthur could not sing, the tune contained no lyrics, and for that same reason Bernstein had to discard a love song,

"Dream With Me," that he wrote originally for *On the Town* and revised as a song for Peter.

Arthur's preparation for the role was relentless. At her suite in the Carlyle Hotel on Madison Avenue, where she took up residence two months before rehearsals began, she toiled eight hours a day to whip herself into physical shape. She worked with a fencing instructor on the art of swordsmanship, and with ballet master Edward Caton and Caton's teacher, Margaret Crasque, to learn how to move like a boy. She also enlisted the aid of yogi specialist Aladeo Fernandez, a self-described "zone therapy technician." Loren Hightower, who was to play one of the young Indians in *Peter Pan*, recalled Fernandez as a "miracle worker" with his hands who "kept half the dancers in New York on stage and worked fat off the muscles of very rich women."

Even before rehearsals for *Pan* began, Arthur would answer the door at the Carlyle dressed as a young boy, her hair cropped short, talking and moving with boyish mannerisms. Hightower's impression was that "the role was terribly important to her."

Just how important, she refused to say. One of the play's press representatives, Mary Ward, observed in a release that Arthur would not reveal how long she had wanted to play Peter Pan, for fear it would increase her embarrassment if her performance fell flat. But Ward noted that Arthur's desire went back at least as far as 1930, when a Hollywood fan magazine printed a full page picture of her in a Pan costume under the caption, "her favorite role." Arthur had also showed up dressed as Peter Pan at a late 1920s Paramount costume party, where studio players were supposed to attend as the characters they would most like to play. Unlike Arthur, none of the other guests, including Kay Francis (as Cleopatra), Claudette Colbert (Juliet) and Gary Cooper (Sydney Carton), ever got their wish.

Arthur "had very specific ideas about how Peter should look, and they were correct," reflected Barbara Baxley, her understudy in the play and a close friend thereafter. She balked at the neatly-tailored, sleeveless suede jacket and patched dungarees that designer Elizabeth Montgomery had drawn for her, and refused to try on the actual outfit when it was brought to her apartment—refused, in fact, to wear anything other than the costume

1

2

(1) Hubert Sidney Greene, Jean Arthur's father, c. 1900.   (2) Johannah ("Hannah") Greene, Arthur's mother, at age 28, c. 1900. "Like a Viking princess when she got mad," is how Arthur described her mother. (3) Arthur's maternal grandmother, Georgianna Nelson, started each morning with a shot of grain alcohol. (4) "Aunt Pearl" Nelson (on ladder), an early influence on Arthur, picking oranges with Arthur's mother Hannah in St. Augustine, Fla., 1914.

3

4

5

(5) Gladys Greene (Jean Arthur), about age three. (6) An early pose for her father's camera: Gladys Greene, around age eight. (7) Gladys, around age sixteen. (8) A doe-eyed brunette, c. 1919.

6

7

8

(9) The newly-christened Jean Arthur, in 1923, shortly before she headed to Hollywood.
(10) A western heroine, with Bob Custer in *A Man of Nerve* (1925).

9

10

11

(11) "A foghorn!" Arthur cried after the playback of her voice test with Paramount sound engineer Roy Pomeroy (right). But her voice proved to be her greatest asset in talking pictures. (12) With an inscription from "Gladys" to her grandmother Mary Greene, c. 1928.

12

The young
Paramount star,
c. 1928, as
photographed
by Eugene Robert
Richee. (courtesy
of Janet Letteron)
(13) As Oliver
Twist. (14) As her
favorite character,
Peter Pan, with
Wendy's thimble.

13

14

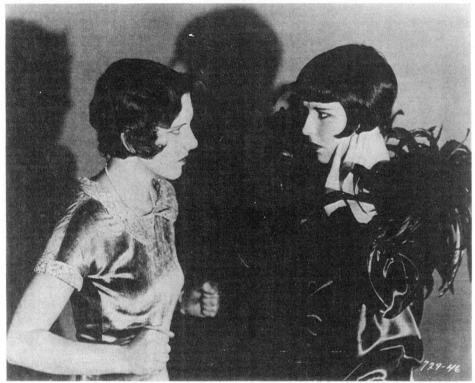

15

16

(15) Arthur (left) squares off against Louise Brooks in *The Canary Murder Case* (1929). (16) Arthur being tape measured by Phillips Holmes, with whom she fell in love during the filming of Paramount's *Stairs of Sand* (1929).

17

(17) Arthur as the adopted daughter of Warner Oland (right) in *The Mysterious Dr. Fu Manchu* (1929). (18) Arthur (second from left), with future husband Frank Ross Jr. (far left) on the set of *The Saturday Night Kid* (1929). Other cast members, from left to right: James Hall, Clara Bow, Eddie Dunn, Leone Lane.

18

19

(19) Arthur, striking a rare sultry pose, with Eric Linden in *The Past of Mary Holmes* (1933). (20) On Broadway, with Sam Jaffe, in *The Bride of Torozko* (1934).

20

21

(21) On the set of *Mr. Deeds Goes to Town* (1936) with Gary Cooper (left) and director Frank Capra.   (22)   Arthur and Charles Boyer in *History is Made at Night* (1937).

22

23

24

25

(23) Arthur's
parents, Hubert
and Hannah
Greene, outside
their home in
Hollywood,
c. 1936.
(24) Arthur and
husband Frank Ross,
in 1937, during
happy times.
(25) Arthur and
Ross in 1943, after
their marriage had
begun to crumble.

26

(26) Arthur looks on as Frank Capra cuts the 60th birthday cake for Lionel Barrymore (seated left) on the set of *You Can't Take It With You* (1938).   (27) Arthur casts a wary glance at Rita Hayworth, her rival for Cary Grant (center) in *Only Angels Have Wings* (1939).

27

28

(28) Arthur offers
words of inspiration
to Jimmy Stewart in
*Mr. Smith Goes to
Washington* (1939).
(29) With her dog
Pat, in 1939.

29

30

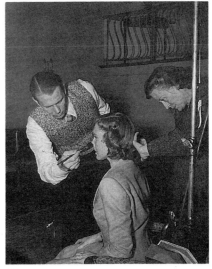

(30) Arthur at the premiere of *Arizona* (1940), in Tucson, flanked by Arizona Governor Robert Jones (left) and Arthur's long-time nemesis, Columbia Pictures studio boss Harry Cohn. (31) "A regular female Simon Legree in a fitting room." Arthur being powdered and curled for a scene in *Too Many Husbands* (1940).

31

(32) A rare cheesecake photo of Arthur, in a publicity pose for *The Devil and Miss Jones* (1941).

32

33

(33) With Charles Coburn (center) and Joel McCrea, in *The More the Merrier* (1943). (34) The camaraderie evident here during rehearsals for Garson Kanin's play *Born Yesterday* (1946) would not last long. Arthur is surrounded, from left to right, by Paul Douglas, Kanin and Richard E. Davis.

34

"Miracle of Entertainment"
—WALTER WINCHELL

PETER LAWRENCE and R. L. STEVENS
present

JEAN   BORIS
ARTHUR · KARLOFF

in J.M.BARRIE'S

PETER
PAN

MUSIC and LYRICS BY
LEONARD BERNSTEIN

Production Staged by JOHN BURRELL   Associate Director WENDY TOYE

Air-Conditioned · IMPERIAL Theatre, 249 W. 45th St., N.Y. 19

35

36

(35) Advertisement for *Peter Pan*, which opened April 24, 1950 on Broadway.   (36) Arthur and Marcia Henderson, as Wendy, in *Peter Pan*.

37

(37) Her final film: Arthur with Alan Ladd in *Shane* (1953).   (38) Arthur as Joan of Arc in the 1954 production of *Saint Joan*.

38

39

40

41

(39)   An aerial view of Arthur's home, "Driftwood," in Carmel, Calif., 1959. (40)   Arthur, flanked by Ron Harper (left) and Leonard J. Stone, during the short-lived 1966 television series, *The Jean Arthur Show*. (41)   Her final role: Arthur in rehearsal for the play *First Monday in October* (1975). (42)   Arthur on the eve of her 80th birthday in Carmel. She never knew that her friend Roddy McDowall had taken this photograph, as she thought he was just photographing one of her beloved cats.

42

she had designed herself. It was a simple, slightly shabby tunic—a jersey, really—with matching tights and flat moccasin shoes. She donned neither hat nor sword, so as to avoid any sort of elfin appearance. Her Pan was deliberately unkempt.

"Peter must look and walk and be like a boy; the more femininity you can hide, the better," said Barbara Baxley. "Jean was very careful about that. She never got cute. Being cute kills Peter Pan, kills the character. He had to be a straight-on person, a straight-on boy. In his victories, it's a stomping kind of victory. He's not smiling gaily."

By Christmas of 1949, Lawrence had lined up sufficient financing for what was to be a $110,000 production, expensive for its time. Roger L. Stevens, a rising young Broadway backer who would later head the Kennedy Center in Washington, signed on as co-producer after contributing $30,000 to the production, making him the largest single investor. Englishman John Burrell was hired to direct, having replaced Jerome Robbins as Lawrence's choice when it became clear that no musical extravaganza was in the offing. Also from England came choreographer Wendy Toye to serve as Burrell's assistant, and flying specialist Peter Foy to supply the aerial magic that is so essential to the play's appeal. Young Marcia Henderson, a recent drama school graduate making her New York debut as Wendy, and Peg Hillias, as Mrs. Darling, rounded out a cast that also included an assortment of pirates, mermaids, Indians and Lost Boys.

April 24, 1950, the opening night of *Peter Pan,* was the most important night of Jean Arthur's professional life to date. On that evening, she was to join Nina Boucicault, Gladys Cooper, Elsa Lanchester and Margaret Lockwood, among English actresses, and Americans Maude Adams, Marilyn Miller and Eva Le Gallienne as the latest in a list of women to bring Peter Pan to life on the stage. Everything that she was and aspired to be was at stake that night at Broadway's Imperial Theatre. But no one in the sellout crowd could have guessed the play's significance to Arthur from the enigmatic, four-sentence biography that appeared in the Playbills the ushers handed out that night:

> Miss Arthur is one of the best-known actresses on the
> American screen. Her present contract with Paramount

> Studios permits her to do plays and pictures independently of this studio. Her favorite picture of all time is *Mr. Smith Goes to Washington*. She feels the same way about *Peter Pan*, the play.

This was as much as Arthur would allow to be printed about her. At fifty-two words, it was a shorter sketch than the one for ten-year-old Charles Taylor, making his Broadway debut as Wendy's brother.

Despite a hefty advance sale, Peter Lawrence's *Peter Pan* had many strikes against it. The Barrie play was the product of a more innocent era, before the horror of two world wars and the invention of the atomic bomb, and many thought it would prove too whimsical for hardened modern audiences. It also arrived "cold" on Broadway, without having gone through the customary out-of-town tryouts, which Lawrence's budget would not allow. Finally, its star was seen as a moody, unreliable woman who had not appeared before a Broadway audience in sixteen years, and whose last stage outing had been a fiasco. When it was reported in December that Arthur was under consideration for the play's leading role, the New York *Herald Tribune* scoffed that it "sounds like a pipe dream."

All such concerns evaporated, however, the moment Jean Arthur flew in the window to Wendy's bedroom and announced herself as Peter Pan. Eschewing any temptation to be coy, Arthur played Peter as a cocky, matter-of-fact boy. Her straightforward style suited itself to the production, which emphasized the play's action and sped through the more sentimental moments, such as the Tinker Bell revival scene. "I remember the end of the first act," recalled Loren Hightower, "where Jean's standing on the rock and she says, 'to die must be an awfully great adventure.' That's her closing line, and it brings down the house. I don't know how she did it, but she was just brilliant."

When the curtain call came that night to tumultuous applause, Arthur found herself bewildered and speechless, hands locked behind her back. Uncomfortable just standing there, she dropped to her knees and crawled behind actor Norman Shelly, who played the dog Nana, and removed his costume head so that he could share in the adulation. Finally Boris

Karloff took her hand, stepped forward with her and declared to more applause, "I think I can say that Miss Arthur wishes to thank you." Later Arthur explained her feelings at the moment: "I just didn't know how to act, I didn't know what to do."

The next day, the critics left no doubt that they, too, had been won over by the opening night production. "A superb piece of theatrical illusion," wrote Howard Barnes in the New York *Herald Tribune*. "Still a thoroughly disarming stage entertainment, even for adults who imagine they have no time for anything except important things," observed John Chapman in the *Daily News*. "Although the world may have grown old and cynical, *Peter Pan* is still a thing of delight," crowed Brooks Atkinson in the *Times*.

But the most enthusiastic reaction—indeed the highest praise of her career—was reserved for Arthur. She was, as Atkinson affirmed,

> ideal as Peter. To a pleasant personality she has added the pleasantest kind of acting. When you think of how arch and maudlin the part might be in less scrupulous hands, you can appreciate the ease and simplicity of her performance. She is smiling without being coy and friendly without being patronizing. If there seems to be no acting at all in her performance it is because she is acting it superbly and has mastered the spirit and technique of the theater's most winning fairy story.

John Chapman of the *Daily News* similarly raved:

> I'm an old Maude Adams man—or was until last night, and now I'm an old Jean Arthur man and I feel much younger than I did three hours ago. Miss Arthur's Peter Pan is in all ways splendid—boyish and cocky, yet one to tug at the heartstrings.

Nor was it lost upon the critics that Arthur had overcome nearly everyone's doubts in regaining the pinnacle. "The choice of Miss Arthur for the title role may have seemed ill-advised when it was first announced," noted Howard Barnes, "but the actress is a perfect Peter. With shorn hair and an impish grin she flies through the air with the greatest of ease…. It is a bravura performance." Alluding more directly to her well-publicized disappearance from *Born Yesterday*, the critic for the New York *World Telegram & Sun* wrote:

> Not many people have had a bigger score to settle with any particular branch of their profession than Miss Arthur had in returning to the stage now. And nobody has ever met such a challenge more valiantly…. [Her] combining of the rowdy and the gentle in Peter reflects memorable understanding.

Along similar lines was the following review from the New York *Morning Telegraph*:

> It is Barrie's play, as it always was, but it is Miss Arthur's triumph today. In my book she never has had to demonstrate anything to anybody, but if she had to this superb, this completely flawless performance would have been the stunning and gigantic answer.

With notices like these, *Peter Pan* consistently played to packed houses. The nightly theatergoers were mostly adults, while two-thirds of the matinee audiences were made up of children under twelve. It was the demand of children, in fact, that forced the scheduling of a third matinee once school let out for the summer.

Arthur exited the theater immediately after each performance, in costume, so as not to be recognized as a woman. In this she followed the practice of Maude Adams. One day after leaving a matinee in street clothes, Adams was spotted by a little boy whose face dropped and looked like he had lost all faith in humanity. From then on, Adams always left the theater as Peter Pan.

Shortly after the play opened, Arthur reluctantly agreed to be interviewed by the New York *Times*. She explained that she had a long way to go before her performance would be to her liking ("No, not yet," she told a friend who wanted to bring his children to see the play), and she theorized that the production's surprising success had less to do with herself than with the times. "People are so desperate, they do want so much to get away from reality," she said. "There's so much negativism in the world. I think Barrie sensed it even then."

Arthur later described the message she thought Barrie had intended for the audience:

> Peter represents the youth in all of us—the freshness and originality of childhood before our parents and schoolteachers have pressed us into a mold. Barrie meant that we should not let that "genius of childhood" escape us—not let our neighbors and the man at the corner grocery store do our thinking for us. If I can get over the message that we should all try to be ourselves, to be free individuals, then I'm sure I'll have accomplished what Barrie wanted.

To fulfill her mission, Arthur hoped to make a long run of the play, perhaps even to take it on the road. "I want to make something really great out of this," she said.

But between her and greatness lay a brush with disaster. New York was suffering under a terrible heat wave that summer, and the eight-a-week performances were particularly taxing on the play's star, whose character was continually dashing and flying across the stage. By early August, an exhausted Arthur convinced herself that she needed a vacation.

At least that is what she told producer Lawrence. Informed of her request for four weeks off starting immediately, Lawrence replied that the show had just opened in April, that he did not have a name replacement for her and that the production could not afford such a blow to its commercial appeal so soon. But Arthur was adamant. "Hank is taking a vacation," she snapped, in reference to Henry Fonda, who was starring on Broadway in *Mister Roberts.* "Mary's taking a vacation," she added, pointing to her friend Mary Martin, still playing one street away at the Majestic Theater in *South Pacific.*

"I said to her, 'Mary's been in that show for two years,'" Lawrence recalled, but there was no use arguing with her. He told her he would be forced to speak to Actors' Equity, the theater players' union, about the matter.

To preserve his options, Lawrence began searching around for a possible star replacement. Among those he considered was Shirley Temple, who flew east with her mother to meet Lawrence for lunch at the St. Regis Hotel. "I didn't know if she could act her way out of a paper bag," Lawrence recalled, but he thought that by letting Arthur know someone was ready to take her place he might deter her from taking any precipitous action. Temple was in the audience one night that week, and as she wrote in her autobiography:

> [Arthur's] eyes kept sweeping the audience from the stage in a purposeful manner.... My phone was jangling as I reentered the hotel room.
>
> "Don't take Peter Pan away from me, please!" cried the voice, without introduction.
>
> "Stop. Who is this?" I interjected, guessing full well the identity.
>
> "You know who I am," the voice cried. "I'm Jean. I'm Peter Pan."
>
> Then she hung up.

Shirley Temple would not get the part, but not because Arthur failed to create an opening. At 4:30 p.m. on Friday, August 11, Arthur informed the play's management that she would not be going on that night, that she was tired and needed a rest. Lawrence told stage manager Mortimer Halpern to call twenty-three-year-old Barbara Baxley, who had replaced Anne Jackson as Arthur's understudy only days earlier. Forty years later, Baxley vividly recalled her summons:

> They called me and told me to get down to the theater immediately. I hadn't learned how to fence yet, and I hadn't learned Peter's little dance.... Marcia [Henderson, the play's Wendy] had to cut my hair that first night because we couldn't even find a barber. And so she just did an amateur home job of cutting. I learned the fencing moves with Boris Karloff and the dance that day.

Peter Foy and his crew hurriedly taught Baxley how to fly. "If you don't hit those marks you can break a rib," Foy cautioned. "As long as you put it that way, Peter, I'll hit the marks," she responded. Just before going on, she reminded stage manager Halpern that she had never rehearsed the climactic final scene. "We'll learn it at intermission," he said, and she did.

Over that weekend, rumors started swirling in the press as to why Arthur had gone AWOL. The star's withdrawal was officially attributed to laryngitis, but on August 14, the New York *Times* reported that she simply wanted to rest for a few weeks and was hoping to rejoin the play sometime after it moved to the St. James Theatre in September. "It's the most fun I've ever had in my life," she was quoted as saying.

That same weekend, a delegation of cast members, led by Norman Shelly, went to the Carlyle to try to talk Arthur out of leaving the show. "I told her that whatever her problems were, she had to see that many people's jobs were on the line, that there was a bigger issue at hand," he recalled. But she couldn't be persuaded.

Roger Stevens, with his $30,000 investment at stake, told Lawrence he had little choice but to give in to Arthur's demand for time off; although they might lose some business for a while, the production would be back to normal in another month. But Lawrence, the younger (and poorer) of the two men, was more in a mood to fight, and he decided to call Arthur's bluff. Under Actors' Equity rules, her contract could be canceled if she missed more than ten consecutive days of performances. Since Arthur had declared, prospectively, that she planned to be gone for at least that amount of time, Lawrence decided to bring to Equity a demand for cancellation of her contract. The handling of his request is recorded in the minutes of a special emergency meeting of Equity's Council, held on August 15, 1950:

> [The chairman] read a letter from Peter Lawrence requesting Council to take action re: cancellation of Jean Arthur's Run of Play contract with *Peter Pan* due to Miss Arthur's illness. She had submitted a doctor's certificate indicating an absence for the period of August 11 through at least August 28, this

absence exceeding the ten days minimum covered in the Run
of Play contracts; that in order to maintain the costly operation
of *Peter Pan* it will be necessary for Mr. Lawrence to engage a
star replacement for Miss Arthur on a Run of Play contract for
the New York engagement; that they are currently running the
show with an extremely capable but unknown understudy. Mr.
[Clarence] Derwent reported the result of a long conference
held with Miss Arthur the previous Sunday. A discussion
ensued, after which it was moved (by Mr. Clay) seconded and
carried, that the request be granted.

Lawrence's preemptive strike set off a public relations battle between
management and star. Arthur fired off the following telegram to Equity:

Have been informed of today's council action canceling my
contract with *Peter Pan* under ten-day clause. Feel such arbitrary
action grossly unjustified and unfair. I am due representation at
any meeting concerning action of such vital importance to my
entire career. My only representation at today's meeting was a
doctor's letter, the contents of which I had already withdrawn
in verbal agreement with the producers. I demand my side of
whatever disagreement there may be between me and *Peter Pan*
management be heard at an emergency meeting of council
before another actress is signed to succeed me. Will attend
emergency council meeting at any time it is called. Please wire.

Lawrence called a meeting after the show that night to explain the situation to the cast. "Like every producer he spoke in doubletalk, about his
investment in the show, and how, much as they'd like to make concessions
for personal reasons, they couldn't do that," remembered Loren
Hightower. In the course of the gathering Boris Karloff spoke up and
deplored Arthur's conduct. "It was rather sneering," Hightower said. "I
don't know the source of dissension between her and Karloff, but he didn't
like her. I won't say he made it obvious, but I was well aware of it, as I'm
sure everybody else was."

Before the gathering adjourned, Lawrence relayed Arthur's invitation to the cast to go up to the Carlyle and hear her side of the story. That night only the dancers went, because "by nature we're more liberal," Hightower laughed. "We're always kicked around during rehearsals and work harder physically than anyone. We see things in a different light. And besides, I was terribly fond of her, as were the other dancers. So we went."

When they arrived at the door about 11:30 that night and Arthur opened it, she "sort of smiled and said, 'I knew it would be you guys,'" Hightower remembered. Once they were inside she spoke almost in a whisper and said she had to watch what she said (which was little) because her lawyer was out of town, on a yacht off Nantucket, and couldn't be reached. Somehow she managed to find and drag him back from vacation the next day to battle by her side.

That next day, August 16, Lawrence moved swiftly to escalate the pressure, announcing that he was about to replace Arthur with veteran stage actress Betty Field. *Variety* reported that Field would sign a new contract, effective August 22, on the same terms as Arthur—ten percent of the gross against a $2,500-a-week guaranteed salary. The trade paper further reported that "several representatives of management and officials of Actors' Equity privately expressed bitter indignation" at Arthur's actions. "One Equity official," the article went on, "said it is time for the union to get tough on players who irresponsibly jeopardize the employment of fellow players."

Lawrence appeared resolute at this point, but two factors were working against him. For one, although he had Betty Field ready to step in as Arthur's replacement, he doubted that she had sufficient drawing power. More important, Lawrence was getting pressure from his co-producer Stevens to negotiate a truce with Arthur to avoid a costly legal battle. "You're fighting with my money," Lawrence remembered Stevens telling him.

And so a deal was cut. Long discussions between the producers and Arthur's lawyer, Morris Ernst, produced an agreement on August 18 by which Arthur would keep the role and return to the production a week later. She spent the time off on a lonely part of Long Island, in a beach cottage she had been escaping to on weekends that summer to avoid the crunch and heat of Manhattan. It was "just a simple cottage where you pump your own water," as she described it, where she could swim, fish, read and walk in perfect solitude.

When she returned to the play, Arthur called her understudy to her dressing room to offer her a check for a thousand dollars. Baxley said that she wouldn't feel right taking it, that just doing the part for two weeks had been pay enough. "She said, 'If you'd take this gift I'd personally feel a lot better about the whole thing,'" Baxley recalled. Eventually she took it because she needed the money.

Baxley also became close friends with Arthur, and remained so the rest of her life. "She was a person a young person could talk to, and really like. Because there wasn't a lot of bullshit in Jean. At all.... We were both terribly shy people. It wasn't easy for me to talk to other people, but I could really relate to her, and she to me."

After they got to know each other, Arthur invited the younger actress up to her apartment in the Carlyle, which Baxley called "the most beautiful apartment, I suppose, that I've ever been in. She did it in a kind of celadon green. So at sunset, everything would get this beautiful, misty fairy land green and lavenders, like a forest. She could easily have been an interior designer."

Forty years after her stand-in performance, Baxley defended Arthur's temporary absence, maintaining that the star had been physically "sick," not just tired. Lawrence disputed that diagnosis, recalling Arthur's having vividly discussed her need for a vacation, pure and simple. But to Norman Shelly, who led the unsuccessful delegation to talk her out of leaving the show when she did, the demand for a vacation was "just an excuse. Something was terribly wrong and upsetting her." He remembered that on the same night she abandoned the production, she took a telephone call at the theater and abruptly left. The reason, Shelly heard at the time, was that she was having financial problems with her ex-husband, Frank Ross, who was "trying to take her for a lot of dough." As Shelly recalled being told, "She was broken up by that and withdrew."

Certain evidence is at least consistent with that theory. In January 1950, RKO sued Frank Ross Productions for $1.8 million for Ross's failure to produce *The Robe* on schedule. It is therefore possible that Ross was attempting to take financial advantage of Arthur in order to salvage his beloved project.

Another story, related by a close friend of a musician connected with the production, has it that Arthur became distraught when a certain young woman (who is now long married) failed to reciprocate the actress's romantic overtures. But several other persons associated with Lawrence's play said they had never heard this rumor, and it remains just that.

Whatever the reason for Arthur's departure from the production, it seemed to disappear after her return. She continued in the play, without further incident, for the rest of its lengthy run. On November 17, 1950, Lawrence's production of *Peter Pan* had its 238th Broadway performance, breaking the record set by the original Maude Adams version of 1905-06. By the end of its New York run, on January 27, 1951, it had played 321 times, a record that would stand until Sandy Duncan assumed the role of Peter in the late 1970s.

On January 30, 1951, Lawrence's production went on tour, starting in Boston for two weeks, continuing on through several cities and arriving in Chicago for a turn at the Civic Opera House. There, after the April 14 performance, Arthur left the production to fulfill a contractual commitment to Paramount, which had given her exactly one year off to do *Peter Pan* and was now calling her back for a western to be directed by George Stevens. "They made her leave at the end of the year even though it was in the middle of the week," Lawrence recalled. She was replaced by Joan McCracken, a young ballet dancer best known as the "girl who falls down" from the dancing chorus of the original *Oklahoma!*

Had Arthur been able to stay with the touring company it undoubtedly would have continued to draw, but with her exit the production closed two weeks later in Minneapolis after a disappointing box office. By that time the play had grossed over $1 million and generated $100,000 in royalties for the London Children's Hospital, but it had managed to return just $65,000 to its backers, about two-thirds of the original investment. Lawrence tried taking his show on the road again in the fall with Veronica Lake in the title role and Lawrence Tibbett as Hook, but that tour quickly died from lack of interest.

Three years later, Mary Martin finally got her chance to play Peter Pan in the musical version of the play directed by Jerome Robbins. Though this particular *Pan* played Broadway for only 152 performances, less than half the number achieved by Lawrence's production, it has become the most popular and best-known version of Barrie's story. Much of that is due to Mary Martin's unique singing talent, and to the tuneful score, which proved more memorable than Bernstein's gentle, dreamy compositions. But the supreme durability of the Martin/Robbins musical is attributable, more than anything, to a single factor: television. On the night of March 7, 1955, more people saw *Peter Pan* than had seen all the thousands of previous stage performances of the play put together. The live program, broadcast on NBC "in living color," brought the play out of the red, and encore telecasts in 1956 and 1960, together with subsequent videotape airings, established this version as the one that most baby-boom children grew up with.

The Lawrence/Bernstein "fantasy with music" has never been performed anywhere since 1951. But those who were involved with the production insist that it was better than the Mary Martin play. "*Peter Pan* the way we did it didn't have the Jerry Robbins glitz, but it had another kind of quality," said Loren Hightower. As he explained it, the director John Burrell was English, as was assistant director Wendy Toye, and they fashioned the play in the tradition of the English pantomime, "which is a much simpler, sweeter, truer approach." Echoing this theme, Peter Lawrence maintained that for all its success, the Mary Martin version "destroyed the original," which was supposed to be "warm and charming."

Who was the better Peter Pan—Jean Arthur or Mary Martin? To Arthur's friends, the contest was not close. "There's no question Jean was better, and I saw them both," said Barbara Baxley. "Peter Pan doesn't sing and dance like a musical comedy star. Several whole generations have grown up with an incorrect impression." According to Nell Eurich, "Jean did it magnificently, it was unbelievable. She was much better than Mary

Martin; there was no comparison." The two stars had been good friends, Eurich noted, but were "never so close after Mary played it."

A more objective observer, and the only living member of the cast of both versions, is Norman Shelly. "Jean Arthur and Mary Martin were both good in their own way," he said. "Jean couldn't sing a song; Mary could tear up the place with a song. But there was more pathos in Jean's performance. She captured what some people say is the underside of Peter Pan."

Comparisons aside, Arthur left no doubt that *Peter Pan* was the high point of her career. "That was my happiest role and I think my finest acting," she said years later. "That role changed her life," confirmed Nell Eurich. "Everybody will say it. From then on, she began to wear her hair like Peter Pan, from then on she felt like Peter Pan. She lived that role."

For her next role, however, Arthur would do a complete turnaround, playing a woman closer in age to herself. For that very reason, she would not much like it, although everyone else would.

CHAPTER SIXTEEN

WESTERN SUNSET

Having begun her movie career in westerns, Jean Arthur chose to end it, in style, with what would become one of the classics of the genre. *Shane*, arguably the best of her eighty-nine films, was director George Stevens' attempt to create a new kind of "adult" western about real people and their problems. Set in 1889 Wyoming, *Shane* would contain no dashing cowboys, menacing Indians or lively dance hall girls.

The Old West was no more; as historian Frederick Jackson Turner declared, this period marked the closing of the frontier and the beginning of a new civilized era.

Part of Stevens' motivation for *Shane* was the wish to de-glamorize the weapon that played such a prominent role in earlier westerns. "Film and TV were full of guys with guns, everybody was bang bang banging with cap pistols," he later said. He saw the story of *Shane* as "a real put down of the heroic aspects of the six-shooter and the western legend.... I thought it was a good time to do that kind of a thing about this weapon, you know, not give it a sense of grace, but to show it for what it was—a destructive, violent instrument."

But *Shane* did not entirely eschew either romance or gunslinging, for Stevens was also looking to spin an American tale in the King Arthur tradition. The film's hero, a retired gunfighter, is a knight in shining white buckskin, with a mysterious, violent past. On his way to "one place or another, someplace I've never been," he stays only long enough to save the simple homesteaders by reluctantly resorting to the weapon he had sworn off using.

For the title role of the drifter Shane, Stevens chose Alan Ladd, whose career with Paramount as a laconic, tough-guy film noir hero was in a slump. Square-jawed Van Heflin was cast as homesteader Joe Starrett, and his wife Marian was played by Arthur, thus reuniting the former Broadway co-stars of *The Bride of Torozko*. The part of the Starretts' son, Joey, was given to nine-year-old child actor Brandon De Wilde, and it is through his eyes that much of the story of *Shane* is seen.

To enhance the mythological aspects of the story, Stevens chose to film on location in Jackson Hole, Wyoming, against the backdrop of the beautiful Grand Tetons. Shot entirely in Technicolor, the film begins in breathtaking fashion, with huge snow-capped mountains rising to the strains of lyrical music, as a lone rider on horseback is seen coming over a trail into the valley below. A farmer is swinging an axe against an old stump in front of his cabin, while a young boy is following a deer with a play rifle. Inside the cabin, a woman (Arthur) is singing (badly) to herself as she prepares dinner. The stage is set for the interruption of this family's earnest, but drab, existence by the enigmatic stranger.

To emphasize the stark lives of the homesteaders, Stevens had his crew construct a realistic frontier town five miles outside Jackson Hole. The cabins were built to specification and filled with period kitchenware. The general store sold nineteenth-century artifacts, and the mud in the town streets was real. Because the local cows were bigger and healthier than the ones that would have been there sixty years earlier, Stevens imported herds of scrawny Florida cattle more closely resembling Wyoming cattle of the 1890s.

Shooting on *Shane* began in the summer of 1951 and ran until mid-October. The principal players and production team were set up in twenty-five rented rooms in the best hotel in town, while fifty cabins housed the rest of the cast and crew. It was a close-knit bunch, and closest of all were the two leading men. Ladd and Heflin, who did not know each other before, became fast friends and remained like brothers for years afterward.

"The whole cast was most professional and great to work with," recalled Ben Johnson in 1990. The conviviality even contributed, indirectly, to the film's authenticity. As Elisha Cook Jr., who played the hot-headed home-steader Torrey, told an interviewer in 1985, "Nobody went to bed in *Shane*. We had two poker games, the small game and the big game. I'd play in the little one all night long, we'd go to work the next morning. It was no wonder we looked like hell, that was the way we should look."

As usual, though, Arthur remained aloof from her co-workers. She swam alone in forty-degree water each morning in a river near Jackson Hole, and spent most of her time with the cast's animals. She fell madly in love with a litter of pigs, favoring them with opulent lunches of cold cuts. Unfortunately one of the small piglets became sick from her generosity, and she refused to continue shooting until an ambulance was called and the piglet rushed to a veterinary hospital. The distraught actress would not return to the set until she received word from the doctors. Later, the production heads learned that the poor animal had died. Realizing that if they told Arthur the truth it might delay shooting indefinitely, they secured another piglet, passed it off as the actress's recovered friend, and she never knew the difference.

Arthur's best human friend during filming was young Brandon De Wilde, whom she adored. A terror on the set, Brandon's idea of fun was jumping up and down in the mud when others were near. Arthur picked up on the boy's mischievous spirit and began to egg him on. She urged him to make faces at Alan Ladd just before the two were about to play a tender scene together, or suggested that he ask for a drink of water or wander off somewhere when his scenes were called. Ironically, her character in the film spent much of her time scolding the young boy, who was almost as ill-behaved on screen as off.

When *Shane* wound up shooting on October 16, 1951, Ladd and his wife, Sue Carol, persuaded Arthur to join them in throwing a party for the 300-person cast and crew. As Ladd's biographer later wrote, "Even Jean Arthur was jubilant that afternoon." But Ladd himself would miss most of the party. Ever sensitive to his height (no more than five-foot-six), the actor stormed out after an anonymous prankster placed his canvas chair on a box to prop him up.

Everyone associated with *Shane* felt they had made a good picture, but it was another eighteen months before they saw the proof. Stevens spent so much time in the cutting room with the innumerable takes he had shot, and continued to run the budget so beyond expectations, that Paramount tried selling the film to Howard Hughes's RKO. When the deal failed to work out, Paramount ended up being stuck—to its eventual delight—with an instant classic and the third-highest grossing film of 1953.

Although Arthur's part in the film was relatively modest, opinions of her performance have grown greatly over the years. In a 1966 reappraisal of *Shane*, critic Alan Stanbrook wrote that the film was "the summit of her career, revealing her as an actress of unsuspected depth and subtlety." In particular, the unspoken love between her character and Ladd's Shane, largely overlooked by critics at first, has come to be recognized as one of the keys to the film. Their attraction is never acted upon, but it is clearly felt and expressed in their every glance and gesture. It is Marian Starrett who suggests that her husband invite the intriguing stranger to stay for supper the day he first appears, and when Shane compliments her on "an elegant dinner," she is silently embarrassed at having fallen so quickly for him. The next night, she cautions her son Joey, who idolizes their guest, not to "get to liking Shane too much" because "he'll be moving on one day." But the warning is really directed at herself. Hoping to stem her growing feelings, she embraces her husband and asks him to hold her. "Don't say anything, just hold me—tight," she says, burying her face in his.

What Marian actually falls in love with is the *idea* of Shane, who represents the possibility of escape from her monotonous life. Ironically, Shane himself is moving in the opposite direction, having laid down his guns in search of a more mundane vocation as Joe Starrett's farmhand.

In the penultimate scene, Arthur's strongest in the film, Starrett and Shane are fighting over which of them will go into town for a likely gunfight with cattleman Ryker and his hired killer, Wilson, memorably portrayed by Jack Palance. She pleads with both of the men she loves not to go. "You're both out of your senses," she cries. "This isn't worth a life, anybody's life. What are you fighting for—this *shack*, this little piece of ground and nothing but work, work, work. I'm sick of it." More heretical words about the glorified American West were never spoken on film, though their sentiments were probably shared by many who helped settle the brutal territory (including Arthur's grandparents).

Arthur's final moments in her final film were perhaps the most moving of her career. "Are you doing this just for me?" she asks Ladd, after he has knocked her husband unconscious with his gun, saving Starrett from near-certain death in a battle that only Shane is capable of fighting. "For you Marian, [for] Joe [and] little Joey," he answers. "Then we'll never see you again," she says resignedly to herself. "Please Shane," she says, extending a handshake, an emotionally wrenching gesture that somehow seems the only appropriate one at the moment. "Please," she repeats, then adds after a long pause, "take care of yourself."

After Shane has saddled up and headed into town, Joey calls out to Shane that he is sorry for having said that he hated him for knocking his father unconscious. But Arthur, with a distant, glassy look in her eyes, says softly, "He didn't hear you." This prompts the boy to chase after

Shane and eventually witness the climactic gun battle. Having slain the evil black knight, Shane rides off back into his mythic past, which he realizes he can never escape, as he knows there is "no living with a killing."

Brandon De Wilde and Jack Palance both received Oscar nominations for Best Supporting Actor for their work in *Shane*, and the film also garnered nominations for Best Picture, Best Color Cinematography and Best Screenplay. But with the exception of the cinematography award, *Shane* fell victim to a near-sweep by Columbia's *From Here to Eternity*.

Although Alan Ladd's role was the best of his career, he was not even nominated for an acting award. Studio politics undoubtedly contributed to the snub. By the time the votes were cast in the spring of 1954, Ladd was no longer under contract to Paramount, having accepted a more lucrative deal with Warner Brothers. His old studio, which had always treated the diminutive actor shabbily, elected to throw all its weight behind one of its new contract stars, William Holden, who received the Best Actor award for his performance in Billy Wilder's *Stalag 17*.

By this time Arthur, too, had terminated her relationship with Paramount, which eliminated whatever Oscar chances she might have had. After *Shane*, she was still committed to Paramount for two more pictures, for which she was to be paid about $400,000. But in 1952, after she had repeatedly turned down the scripts the studio offered her, Paramount decided to buy out the rest of the contract for $200,000. When 1954 rolled around, the studio made no effort to promote her for a deserved nomination for Best Supporting Actress, a prize won that year by Donna Reed in *From Here to Eternity*.

Arthur's performance in *Shane* might have led to other strong supporting roles had she been willing to continue her career as a character actress. But she did not enjoy the experience. "I didn't like it because I couldn't use any comedy bits in it at all—just had to act old and worn out," she told Hedda Hopper in 1965 (in fact, she looks to be in her mid-thirties in the film, not fifty-two). And so, just as she did two decades earlier, she left Hollywood altogether rather than stay on in supporting roles. Instead, she returned to the stage again, to play another child.

CHAPTER SEVENTEEN

MARTYRDOM

Unless Woman repudiates her womanliness, her duty to her husband, to her children, to society, to the law and to everyone but herself, she cannot emancipate herself. —George Bernard Shaw

I will never take a husband.... I do not want to be thought of as a woman. I will not dress as a woman. I do not care for the things women care for. —Shaw, *Saint Joan* (1923)

The fact that I did not marry George Bernard Shaw is the only real disappointment I've had. —Jean Arthur (1975)

Had Bernard Shaw ever met Jean Arthur, and had he not been forty-four years her senior, he might well have reciprocated her expression of sentiment. A showman in public, the private Shaw was a timid and prudish man whose forty-five-year marriage to his nurse, begun at the age of forty-three, remained unconsummated, and whose greatest romantic ardor was reserved for several actresses with whom he never progressed beyond the platonic stage. Shaw was drawn to, and could be drawn out by, women of intelligence who were capable of projecting their thoughts (and especially his) onto the stage. Mrs. Patrick Campbell, the Eliza Doolittle of his *Pygmalion* (1914), was one such woman; Jean Arthur, who always wanted to play the same part, fancied herself another.

More than any of her other intellectual heroes, Arthur regarded Shaw as her perfect soulmate. Paradoxical of thought, disdainful of convention, "G.B.S." dominated the early twentieth-century English stage, rivaled only by J.M. Barrie. Despite, or perhaps because of, the lack of sensuality in his own life, Shaw's plays focused on the relationship between the sexes, a relationship he constantly tried to de-mystify. "There is no such species in creation as 'Woman, lovely woman,' the woman being simply the female of the human species," he maintained. "To have one conception of humanity for the woman and another for the man, or one law for the woman and another for the man, or one artistic convention for woman and another for man, or, for the matter of that, a skirt for the woman and a pair of breeches for the man, is as unnatural, and in the long run as unworkable, as one law for the mare and another for the horse." Arthur's protest against the "tyranny of the 'ladylike'" in her article about Calamity Jane, wherein she championed dress reform and career independence, was simply her own expression of Shavianism.

Like Shaw, Arthur had first been enamored of Ibsen. The great Norwegian dramatist had focused on the problem of social passivity assigned to women in a male-oriented society, and on society's tendency to sacrifice to the majority will the freedom and individual expression of its most gifted members. Picking up on this theme, Shaw posited that humankind can be rescued only by those rare individuals he deemed to be of a higher evolutionary order. "The need for freedom of evolution," he wrote, "is the sole basis of toleration, the sole valid argument against Inquisitions and Censorships, the sole reason for not burning heretics and sending every eccentric person to the madhouse." As Arthur put it similarly in her Calamity Jane article, the gradual emancipation of women was achieved only through the pioneering efforts of such "freakish or plain ornery women" as Queen Elizabeth, Mary of Scotland, Catherine of Russia and, in the movies, Dietrich and Garbo. She might also have mentioned her namesake, Joan of Arc.

Inspired by the canonization of Joan in 1920, Shaw set out to dramatize his theory of Creative Evolution—the purposeful and persistent movement of human beings toward ever-higher forms of consciousness and intelligence. "I tell you that as long as I can conceive something better than myself I cannot be easy unless I am striving to bring it into existence or clearing the way for it," his Don Juan said in *Man and Superman* (1903), while in *Pygmalion*, Henry Higgins labors to perfect one particular sample of the race. In *Saint Joan* (1923), written when he was nearing seventy, Shaw related the story of a superior being who is killed precisely for her saintly qualities.

The androgynous Joan embodied Shaw's hope for the race, what he called the Life Force—the heroic spirit wending its way through individual human lives toward the eventual triumph of moral and intellectual passion over the more primal instincts of food and sex. Critics called it a cold, emotionless religion, just what one might expect from the priggish Shaw. But it was a religion to which Arthur enthusiastically subscribed. "They tell us we have three primitive needs—food, clothes and sex, and that's it. My God, I can live without any of it," she once said. "I could live on roots in the ground. There's more to us than that." The most important thing in life, she ventured, was "the need to expand and evolve," a particularly Shavian notion. "A tree overcomes and endures everything to be as beautiful as it can," she explained. "That's what we should do. Become as strong and beautiful as we can."

Arthur's fascination with Joan of Arc actually pre-dated Shaw's play. Even before *Saint Joan* had its world premiere in New York in December 1923, with Winifred Lenihan in the title role, Arthur adapted the Maid's name as her own, along with her short-haired bob. An artist friend of hers recalled her as a "fanatic" on the subject, as evidenced by her request that he paint her as Joan on horseback and in armor. Thus, had *Saint Joan* never been written, Arthur still would have wanted to portray the French heroine. But it was Shaw's Joan that Arthur most longed to play. "She always wanted to do *Saint Joan*," recalled her friend Nell Eurich. "Always, always, always."

Around the time of the 1954 Academy Awards, Arthur was close to joining a stage production of Ibsen's *The Master Builder*, in which she was to play Hilde Wangel, the impulsive heroine who dreams of castles in the air. By the summer, however, Arthur's newly-hired theatrical agent, Helen Harvey, introduced her to an up-and-coming Broadway producer named Robert Whitehead. "She came to me and said I'd very much like to do *Saint Joan*, would you consider producing it?" Whitehead recalled of their initial lunch meeting. He agreed that the play was due for a revival, having been the subject of only two major productions in the United States since 1923—the first in 1936, with Katherine Cornell as Joan, and then in 1951, with Uta Hagen in the title role.

Whitehead signed Arthur to a thirty-week, coast-to-coast tour that was to begin that September and end with a brief engagement on Broadway the following April. Among the veteran cast was Sam Jaffe (Arthur's co-star from *The Bride of Torozko*) as the Inquisitor; Hollywood villain George Macready as the Archbishop of Rheims; and British stage actor Wyndham Goldie as Joan's nemesis, the Earl of Warwick.

Rehearsals began in August in Wilmington, Delaware, under the direction of Harold Clurman, an acclaimed Broadway director who founded the influential Group Theatre with Cheryl Crawford and Lee Strasberg in 1931. Together with such talents as Clifford Odets, Stella Adler and Elia Kazan, Clurman helped develop a new American drama of contemporary realism, passion and radicalism. A product of New York's Lower East Side, Clurman was an arrogant and opinionated man not given to compromise. Brilliant and zealous about his work, he was, unfortunately, not the right director for Jean Arthur.

"They just couldn't get on," said Nell Eurich. Their problems began almost immediately, when Clurman tried to get Arthur to eliminate the famous catch in her voice. "Harold was being a purist; he thought no one in the Middle Ages would have such a voice," remembered John McLiam, who played Joan's defense attorney. Clurman suspected that Arthur's voice was a contrivance she could dispense with if she really wished, but as McLiam felt, "when you hire a star, you hire her 'catch' and all." Then the director began quarreling with her interpretation of the heroine. "He wanted her to play it like Ingrid Bergman, to be on one knee with the profile and everything," said Eurich, who attended several of the rehearsals. "She couldn't stand it, she saw the role as that of a peasant girl." In fact, Arthur was right. Shaw's Joan was neither a romantic heroine nor an unintelligible mystic but rather, as the playwright emphasized, "a sane and shrewd country girl of extraordinary strength of mind and hardihood of body…a thorough daughter of the soil in her peasantlike matter-of-factness and doggedness…."

"I could have had Harold Clurman fired; I had director approval in my contract," Arthur later said. "But I couldn't stand up to him. Before we began rehearsals, we had agreed on an interpretation of Joan, but afterward he forgot all about our agreement. He ordered me to stand on the stage and not to move, and then he directed the other actors to ignore me. 'Just recite the language' he'd say to me, 'and that will be enough.'"

"Clurman annihilated her, thinking that would bring out the best in her, and instead he just brought out the worst," recalled Arthur's agent, Helen Harvey. "He humiliated her in front of the company, belittled her, just destroyed any little self-confidence she had," she said. "Sometimes people think that's a good tactic. I was surprised he didn't realize how vulnerable she was. I think everybody else in the cast realized it."

The opening night audience in Wilmington gave Arthur an ovation at the curtain and the headline of the local paper's review declared that "Jean Arthur Is Saint Joan." But Clurman was not satisfied. "He was backstage sticking notes in front of her nose," said Barbara Baxley, who was in the audience that night. "His criticism was, 'Miss Arthur, you didn't tear up the confession right,'" Arthur later recalled, adding:

> Then I did something I had never done before. I got up, walked over to where Clurman was standing, and grabbed him by the lapels. And then I shook him and shook him and shook him—like a *thing*. "You *know* what you've done to me," I said. "You *know* you've ruined me, and you dare to stand here and talk about how I didn't tear up a piece of paper the right way!"

"Jean couldn't be bossed around," explained her friend Baxley. "If she thought they were right, she would accept it, and certainly do it. But if somebody asked her to do something that was wrong, wild horses couldn't get her to do it. The integrity was like granite."

But Clurman persisted in his fault-finding. In Washington, D.C., the second stop on the tour, Helen Harvey found the star miserable and unable to sleep. The reviews from the nation's capital were nevertheless promising, with the *Evening Star* pronouncing that Arthur was "Shaw's Joan," and the *Post* finding that she had "spirit and a sense of wonder," and was "on the verge of becoming a very splendid if belated Joan indeed." Only the *Daily News* was unimpressed, objecting that there was "no exaltation, no richness, no hint that here is a human being far beyond the common, a warrior saint."

Similar comments from the critics—to the effect that Arthur's Joan failed to project a mystical, otherworldly quality—were to repeat themselves as the tour continued, even if they did miss the point of Shaw's play. Typical was the following reaction from the Pittsburgh *Post-Gazette* on October 5: "The glow that Joan wears falls at times on Miss Arthur, yet only at times; the halo doesn't yet fit tightly enough." The Detroit *Free Press* complained that "at no point does she become transcendent," and the Columbus *Citizen-Journal* found that her performance "does not evoke the emotional response that it should."

But other reviewers found virtue in her restraint. The Cincinnati *Enquirer* praised her ability to convey "the essence of simplicity, foolhardy innocence and candor, inspired egotism and contrasting fear and courage of the country girl." The paper thought she displayed a "depth of characterization heretofore unknown of her." A week later, on November 2, the Columbus *Dispatch* carried the following glowing notice:

> Miss Arthur is the perfect embodiment of this audacious girl
> and plays her with a fine command of the technical means to
> set forth her audacity, her devastating sincerity and honesty,
> the elevation of vision and the complete insensitiveness to
> clerical and secular dialectic as opposed to just plain common

sense. Never does she permit purely literary or romantic pos-
turing or vocalization to intrude on the realism of her aptly
Shavian concept of the character.

"I'm a Clurman man myself, but I thought she was excellent and gave
a good interpretation," commented cast member John McLiam thirty-
five years later. "She played an earthy little girl. For her it worked. She's a
spunky little thing. She was convincing." And she was "getting better
every town we hit," McLiam added. Claude Rains was in the audience
opening night in Wilmington and told producer Whitehead he was quite
impressed, which "he wouldn't have said if he didn't mean it," Whitehead
noted. "She was never bad, she was always good," the producer added.

Being "good," however, was not enough for Arthur, certainly not in
this role. Nothing short of utter perfection and glory would suffice. The
critical reviews, along with Clurman's constant berating, had struck her
confidence a mortal blow.

After the last performance in Columbus on November 6, *Saint Joan*
was scheduled to begin a three-week run in Chicago on November 8. But
when they got there Arthur told Whitehead she was not feeling well.
"She said she just wanted to take a night or two off," recalled Whitehead,
who was rehearsing another play in Wilmington at the time. "I said
'Look, Jean, if you don't do it tonight you'll never come back.'"

Whitehead prevailed upon the rest of the cast and crew to speak to her,
and Arthur did show up at the Great Northern Theatre for the Monday
night opening. But half an hour before curtain time, with the audience
settling into its seats, Arthur left the theater, reportedly claiming she was
"too jittery and sick" to go on. Friends were quoted as saying that she was
suffering from a viral infection contracted the week before. Twenty minutes before opening a sign was placed on the box office window: "No
performance—Miss Arthur ill."

The next day, the right-wing McCormick paper, the Chicago
American, concocted a front-page story that said Arthur left the cast
because of a threatened picket by the American Legion to protest the
alleged presence of Communists among the cast. "If there are any

Communists in the cast, get them out of here. I'm sick, and they're not going to embarrass me," Arthur was alleged to have said upon exiting the theater. An earlier edition of the same paper that day, however, did not mention the Communist angle, instead reporting that Chicago doctor Manual Weiss concluded that she was suffering from exhaustion. "This woman needs rest," Weiss was quoted as saying.

That same day, Whitehead telephoned Arthur and asked her to call a press conference to deny that her non-appearance the night before had anything to do with alleged Communists. He was prepared to close the show, but not in the face of McCarthyism tactics. Arthur complied with his request and issued a statement to the effect that she resented any attacks on the integrity of the cast. She also stated that she looked forward to opening the following Monday after a week's rest.

Whitehead did not believe Arthur was really sick, but was convinced that she was simply afraid of Claudia Cassidy, the merciless Chicago *Tribune* drama critic. He told both Helen Harvey and Barbara Baxley (the latter was rehearsing with him in Wilmington at the time), to call Arthur in Chicago and urge her to drop her sickness excuse. But both women believed that their friend's illness, whatever its source, was genuine.

The matter came to a head the following Sunday, November 14, a day before the rescheduled opening. As Arthur later recalled it:

> I was exhausted—so sick that the lymph system had stopped
> working. The poison had settled in my body and there were
> huge swellings, like enormous eggs all around my middle. "You
> get on that stage," [Whitehead] said, "or we'll sue you." I went
> on stage, but in the middle of rehearsal, I began to sob hyster-
> ically and I couldn't stop. I was truly in great pain.

That afternoon, Dr. Weiss examined her, declared her to be "in a state of complete exhaustion" and ordered her to rest for at least a month, effec-tively canceling the tour. It was announced that the twenty-one members of the cast and the staff would return to New York. Arthur likewise boarded a plane for New York, without speaking to anyone in the production. "And that was the end of *Saint Joan*, the play I had wanted to do all my life," Arthur later said.

Whitehead was enraged at Arthur for having left without so much as a word to him or the others in the cast who were standing by for the opening, and years later he remained unremitting in his criticism of her. "I have nothing but total disregard for her as a worker and as a human being," he said. Arthur, he insisted, was unpleasant to the costume and makeup people, not the first time in her career such an accusation had been made. "As far as I was concerned she wasn't sick," Whitehead maintained, adding that "if a doctor explained it all to me I might have a feeling of remote sympathy."

Helen Harvey did have sympathy for Arthur, but it was not enough to save her friendship with the star. Harvey had been unable to go to Chicago due to other commitments, and she decided to remain neutral in a dispute between Arthur and Whitehead before Actors' Equity Council, the same group that had terminated Arthur's contract during *Peter Pan*. As a result, Arthur "cut me right off" and the two never spoke again. But she still had kind words for her one-time friend. "She had so many positive qualities, and she cared about decent things," Harvey said. "And yet she couldn't really cope with the world—even the world she chose to be in. Her ability to keep herself together and do it, block out whatever was bothering her, it didn't exist."

"Jean is not a bounce back type," her long-time friend Pete Ballard noted. "Like all purists, she keeps herself in a cocoon until it's time to come out and do something; it's the only protection she's got. You can be beaten down only so much [until] you learn to protect yourself, which is generally to withdraw, and that's what she does."

Arthur herself appeared to attribute her frequent stage-related illnesses to her fear of failure. "Fear can keep you from doing things," she acknowledged late in life. "I have the kind of body that breaks down under fear."

Nothing ever came of the Actors' Equity proceeding. According to Barbara Baxley, she went to her friend (and future husband) Donald Cook, who was on the Council, and explained to him that Arthur really had been sick, which helped avert any adverse action.

Real as Arthur's physical symptoms may have been, they undoubtedly had their origin in some psychological difficulty she was encountering at the time. "She just psychologically couldn't handle it any longer, and got sick," said Nell Eurich, who attributed Arthur's problems principally to her relentless battles with Clurman. Arthur was also jealous of the success Mary Martin was having with *Peter Pan*, which had opened on Broadway shortly after *Saint Joan* began its tour. And she was also extremely upset by a claim for back taxes filed by the Internal Revenue Service in the middle of the tour. The I.R.S. was claiming taxes and penalties against Arthur totaling $685,000 over a six-year period, from 1942-47, consisting of $235,000 in personal income tax claims and $445,000 in taxes due on the assets Arthur allegedly received from the liquidation of Frank Ross's movie production companies in 1942 and 1943. Arthur filed a denial to the charges, contending that the I.R.S. had made major errors in recomputing her personal income tax returns for the years in question, and had confused her income with her husband's. Eurich recalled that Ross had Arthur list herself as his companies' beneficial owner when they were dissolved, and "she didn't know what the hell she had signed." After some period of months, Eurich said, Ross "paid up," out of his substantial profits from *The Robe*.

Whatever the reasons for Arthur's illness during *Saint Joan*, the experience clearly shattered her. She felt she had failed her favorite heroine and, by extension, her beloved Shaw. "Every *bit* of me was committed to it," she later said. "When the show folded, I folded. I'd put everything into *Saint Joan*. There was nothing left.... I felt like the walking maimed." As Nell Eurich said, "That was a great upset, a real tragedy, from which I don't know that she ever got over."

CHAPTER EIGHTEEN

RESURRECTION

*T*he death of *Saint Joan* required Jean Arthur to resurrect herself, a task she began by occupying herself with everyday living. In January 1955 she took up residence at the weekend house of Nell Eurich in Sherman, Connecticut, where she worked busily—doing laundry, cooking, gardening and decorating. Arthur moved in about a month after the thirty-six-year-old Mrs. Eurich and the man she had recently married,

Alvin Eurich, the first president of the State University of New York, had bought the pre-Revolutionary War house. The actress was told she could do anything with the place that she wanted, except make structural changes, a caveat she promptly ignored. One weekend shortly after her friend moved in, Mrs. Eurich came up to the house from New York and found that the living room ceiling had been removed to make way for an open, beamed look. She became livid and told Arthur in clear language just what "structure" meant. To Eurich's great annoyance, Arthur wasn't the slightest bit apologetic, but simply responded, "Well, wait 'til you see the beams."

"I must say she made it extremely beautiful," Mrs. Eurich later confessed. "Everybody wanted to come see the place. She just spent full-time at it for a while, and it was therapeutic."

Arthur accompanied the Eurichs on vacation to Italy and Greece in the summer of 1955, then decided to return to Carmel, where she turned to the sea for comfort. She moved back into "Driftwood," the house overlooking the Pacific that she first rented in 1937 and bought immediately after World War II, when its long-time owner decided to sell. Hannah Greene, who had been living at Driftwood continuously for more than a decade by now, was there to greet her daughter's return, as was Don Greene, the perpetual drifter. With the death of Robert Greene from a heart attack in November 1955, at age 61, Don was now Arthur's only surviving brother.

Once back in Carmel, Arthur could be seen walking endlessly along the beach, head bowed, hands behind her, and alone—"always alone," according to one friend. She listened to classical music, read Keats and Shelley, and found a seclusion seldom achieved by a star of her magnitude since Garbo. "I have no TV, no radio, just a wonderful Hi-Fi," she boasted.

Despite her desire for solitude, Arthur managed to form close friendships with a small group of talented people from outside the entertainment world who respected her privacy and appreciated her impulsiveness. Among them were local artist Leslie Emery and his wife, Leora; Wynne Stilwell, wife of the deceased former general; and syndicated newspaper cartoonist Gus Arriola. Though never very social in Hollywood, Arthur eagerly participated in dinners and parties with her inner circle, provided she could be the center of attention. "The first night we ever met was at a party," recalled Arriola's wife, Frances, in 1990. "We were playing charades, Gus was down on the floor, depicting a salmon or something, and she was mad because he was outdoing her. Then, she couldn't get over him, she started walking around behind him, everything he'd do she'd try to do, too."

"We had a lot of fun, we loved her," said Gus Arriola, who nevertheless described Arthur as "very temperamental." Leslie Emery agreed, noting that "when she was in the right mood she was a delight, a joy to be with," but that occasionally "she'd just disappear, go into her house and not answer the phone."

Frequently, but unsuccessfully, Arthur tried to engage her friends in dramatic readings of Shaw and Ibsen, or in philosophical conversation about the latest person of intellect on whom she had become fixated, like scientist Linus Pauling. "She would tell us she was reading this person or that," recalled Gus Arriola, "but we were there for a good time, not a seminar. So we'd listen, and then we'd turn things around and start acting up. Pretty soon she'd forget it and want to do something physical, like make a human pyramid."

"She had the attention span of a four-year-old," added Frances Arriola. "She never stopped being Peter Pan." One night, Mrs. Arriola recalled, Arthur pulled out her *Peter Pan* scrapbook and "just completely changed. She just kept showing us pictures and she kept getting further and further out of it."

Said another of Arthur's close friends from that time, "I do not think of Jean as having her feet on the ground. She is a pixy, very imaginative, very bright and very impulsive." Leslie Emery likened her to "a seagull, just flying with the breeze, flowing with the currents." And from another friend: "I love her, she's a doll, but she's strictly her own person, nobody else's. Ever."

Much of Arthur's personality was reflected in Driftwood, a residence so distinctive that it was featured in *Architectural Digest*, *House and Garden* and other publications. Set on five lots, the 3,000-square-foot home actually consisted of two single-story buildings, the first a main living room and sleeping area, the other a kitchen and day room converted from an old greenhouse. The buildings were fronted by a landscaped Japanese-style garden and surrounded by a six-foot redwood wall designed to shield the house from the public road that formed a hairpin curve around the cliffpoint.

The large outdoor garden set the tone for the entire property. Meticulously designed by prominent landscape artist George Hoy, it alternated between ground covers of mossy Helxine, spiny Aloe and delicate Erodium. In one section of the garden was a bronze, flute-playing Pan; in another, some pewter penguins; and elsewhere, a Japanese stone lantern reflecting in a small pond. "It's the kind of garden that makes you want to whisper," said *House and Garden*. "What Jean wanted and achieved," one friend said, "was a sanctuary, a quiet place so necessary for well-being. There is serenity in her garden because everywhere there is something to contemplate—something green and growing, something timeless."

The interiors, which Arthur designed herself, had a feel of Oriental grace. Atop the Chinese modern furniture rested a laughing Japanese porcelain fisherman and grinning Buddha. Off the bedroom was an indoor garden room of ferns and subtropical plants. At one end of it were sliding shoji panels, while at the other end stood a statue of Kwan-on, the Zen goddess of mercy. "I love Japanese architecture for its purity and simplicity," Arthur explained. "You know, this house has a way of telling you what to do.... For example, the Kwan-on garden room was built as an exercise room and as a place where household plants could go for a rest. Ferns love it out there." So did Arthur, who often slept on the garden room deck, or even outdoors, on a simple Japanese bedroll.

Arthur's indoor decorating style also ran to eclecticism. Intermixed with the Oriental furnishings were several French pieces and objects, including carved mermaids and a hanging monkey, as well as some Italian furniture. In the living room hung two paintings that lent a mysterious air: one of a ghost ship in the fog and the other of fishing schooners putting out to sea. The focal point of the living room created a rustic touch: a large fireplace constructed of local volcanic rock with a tree trunk splayed on one side.

What inspired Arthur most, however, was her location. "Life by the sea is full of vitality," she once said. "For me that vitality is expressed in the trees, in the forms and shadows in the garden that often look like animal or human forms. You know, when I sit around the fire in the evening with friends, I'm always catching glimpses of faces in the stone and the firewood and the driftwood." As one visitor observed of the almost Wuthering Heights atmosphere, after dinner "everything conspires to hypnotize," from the beating rain on the windows to the crosswinds sweeping around the point to the rhythm of the surf coming through the living room floor.

"I couldn't live any place else in the world," Arthur put it simply. But in order to keep her private sanctuary, she had to engage in a public fight. For years, the State of California and Monterey County had been trying to buy from Arthur the beach property she owned east of her house, in order to re-route the hazardous curve around Driftwood and make for a wider, safer turn. When negotiations broke down in 1956, the county retaliated by placing all of Arthur's property on its Master Plan for acquisition as a state beach. Arthur protested the action and in January 1957 made a rare public appearance before the State Park Commission in San Francisco to plead her case. The Commission sided with her after concluding that the county was overreaching. "If they want a road, they can use their condemnation procedure and Miss Arthur can fight before the board of supervisors," Park Commissioner Charles Kasch said afterward. Weary of the battle, the county dropped its efforts to acquire Arthur's property.

Emboldened by her political victory, Arthur appeared before the county supervisors later in 1957 to present them with her own "Master Plan" for development of the Monterey Peninsula. Calling for preservation of the natural beauty of the area, she suggested that money earmarked for a proposed shopping center and freeway be diverted instead to development of the Monterey Bay waterfront. "I drove past the mouth of the Carmel Valley this morning," she said. "The grass was green and the cows were having their breakfast. When I think of this scene being marred by a concrete dirt highway twenty feet above the ground, and by a large shopping center, I think it will look like the Los Angeles area." Told by one supervisor that she was being "a little overdramatic this morning," Arthur replied, "That's because this has been steaming up in me for some time." She later told a newspaper reporter that the waterfront "could be made like the Lido near Venice" with "hotels and theaters which would attract concerts and performances." To clear the way for these developments, she suggested tearing down famed Cannery Row. But nothing came of her idea.

Following her uncharacteristic spurt of public activity, Arthur again retreated to her cherished solitude. When a reporter called on her in 1959 to ask for an interview, she met him at the door in faded blue jeans, a ragged sweatshirt and tennis shoes. After the reporter identified himself she replied, "Well, you just get on the other side of that fence. I don't mean to be impolite to you personally, but I'm out of the business and all I want to do is read and be let alone."

Shortly afterward Arthur was a little more alone. On December 4, 1959, Johannah Greene died at Driftwood at age 88. She had been bedridden for a couple of years as a result of a stroke and broken hip, during which time Arthur cared for her with the help of a maid and Arthur's Aunt Pearl, who made periodic visits. Arthur spent many hours reading her mother poetry, lavishing gifts upon her and generally displaying the warmth that eluded them much of their lives together. The night her mother died, Arthur turned up her hi-fi as high as it would go and turned on every light in the house. She had her cremated and her ashes cast out to sea, then arranged for the obituary in the local newspaper to state only that Johannah Greene was survived by a son, Donald Greene of Santa Cruz, and her daughter, Gladys Greene of Carmel.

For a time after Johannah Greene's death, Pearl Nelson (Goodall, by now) spent a great deal of time in Carmel keeping her niece company. But as was her habit with many of those closest to her, Arthur became estranged from the "dearest aunt in the world" when she felt crossed. Pearl decided to attend a Pioneer Day celebration in her native Billings,

Montana, rather than stay on in Carmel a few extra days, as the actress demanded. According to Pearl Goodall's son, Arthur, the two women never saw each other again.

Just as her mother and aunt passed from Arthur's life, however, another woman entered it who would become the greatest friend the actress ever had. Ellen Mastroianni was a forty-five-year old unmarried army nurse, and veteran of several World War II European field hospitals, when she moved to Carmel in 1956 to be stationed at nearby Fort Ord. One day two years later, she was outside calling after her dog when Jean Arthur happened to be visiting Mastroianni's next-door neighbor, Wynne Stilwell. "I had a little dachshund. Of course that's the catalyst for Jean, and that's how we met," Mastroianni later recalled. From that point on, and for more than thirty years until Arthur's death, the two women were virtually inseparable companions.

It was a classic case of opposites attracting. Where Arthur was whimsical, impulsive and other-worldly, Mastroianni was no-nonsense and down-to-earth. "Ellen is phlegmatic, and quiet and steady and practical, tends to get up and go to bed at the same time," said Nell Eurich. "She's very sensible. And sometimes she'd say Jean's crazy. They're quite different, and yet they're very good friends."

Ellen Mastroianni knew little about the movies or theater and was indifferent to celebrityhood. As a result, she treated Arthur without fanfare, and was able to convince the actress that Jean Arthur was someone with intrinsic appeal and value. Near the height of her career, in 1937, Arthur lamented that she had never had a close, intimate girlfriend in her life, a "chum" to whom she could confide her closest secrets. Now, nearing age sixty, she finally had one. With Ellen as her friend and confidante, Arthur gradually climbed out of the funk that had plagued her ever since the *Saint Joan* disaster. "Jean really owe[d] much of her life to Ellen," said Nell Eurich, perhaps the other best friend of Arthur's life.

Although Mastroianni was never officially Arthur's caretaker, at times she seemed to assume the role. For one thing, she was "the cook of the world," said Arthur's friend Pete Ballard. "And I'm sure if truth be known that's the basis for the friendship," he added laughingly. "Once in a while you felt Ellen was the cook, not the friend," said another mutual friend.

Another thing Mastroianni did for Arthur was get her out of the house. More of a social being, Mastroianni liked to attend parties, play tennis and be with people. Often the two of them threw parties themselves, cooking and rehearsing everything together the night before. Frances Arriola recalled that for one such gathering, thrown for some "sophisticated types" from San Francisco, Arthur gave orders to several of her Carmel friends to appear in particular types of jewelry. "You wear diamonds, you wear emeralds, you wear rubies," she told them. Just to be contrary, the women put on fake jewelry and, along with their husbands, donned yellow sweatshirts that read "Jean's Gym," a reference to the gymnastics exercises that Arthur often led her friends in at her home when they became bored with the conversation. The night of the party they walked into Arthur's home wearing the sweatshirts and carrying dumbbells and other athletic equipment. "We made our entrance, and there were all these people standing around with elegant clothes," Frances Arriola remembered. "Jean and Ellen both had on gorgeous blouses. We had their sweatshirts in a box. Jean let out a yell, pulled off her blouse in front of everyone, put on her sweatshirt and was absolutely as happy as a lark. It picked the party up because it was a very solemn affair."

With her private life as happy as it had been in years, Arthur had little interest in returning to show business. "There's no great temptation to come back because I'm living in one of the most beautiful places in the world. I'm alone except for loads of friends and three cats and a dog," she explained.

Periodically, though, rumors appeared in the press indicating that she was about to make a film comeback. Hedda Hopper reported in the spring of 1961 that Arthur had promised director Josh Logan she would play Aunt Kate in the film version of Moss Hart's autobiography, *Act One*, but the movie ended up being directed by Dore Schary and was made without her. A year later, producer Jerry Wald told the *Hollywood Reporter* he expected to sign Arthur for a role in the forthcoming film adaption of William Inge's play *Celebration*. But when it was released in 1963 as *The Stripper*, the part was played by Claire Trevor. It was later reported that

Arthur read the script and concluded the part was too serious for her.

The closest Arthur came to going through with a film comeback revolved around her interest in the Paul Gallico story *Mrs. 'Arris Goes to Paris*. In March 1962 she reportedly told the New York *Post* that she would eagerly chuck retirement if she could play the cockney charwoman. "On the second page I thought, 'This is me,'" she said. "By the third page, I knew I wanted only that role. It was right up my alley. Mrs. 'Arris and I were the same kind of people. We look at the brighter side of life, with a sense of fun, getting a hoot out of life. I thought she'd be as much fun to do as Peter Pan." By this time she had purchased an option on the story with a view toward producing the film version as a vehicle for herself, hoping to have it directed by George Stevens. But she inexplicably changed her mind and sold the rights to the project at a handsome profit.

One project, however, still held sway in the back of Arthur's mind; one idea still beckoned. As she gradually put behind her the tragedy it had brought her, Arthur began to entertain the notion of having another try at *Saint Joan*. Now past the age of sixty, Arthur could not realistically hope to play the Maid again on stage, but she considered other alternatives for becoming re-involved in the play. In 1963, purely by chance, such an opportunity presented itself.

Arthur was driving her brown Jaguar around the winding roads of Carmel near her house that year, recklessly as was her habit, when she happened to hit a car being driven by a friend of Travis Bogard, chairman of the drama department at the University of California at Berkeley. As a result of the minor accident, Arthur and Bogard were soon introduced at a faculty gathering on the Berkeley campus, at which they began to talk about collaborating on a play. Although Bogard mentioned several projects that his theater people had in the pipeline, Arthur wasn't interested in any of the department's suggestions, he recalled. For example, she hated Eugene O'Neill, finding him "so depressing." After a while, Bogard remembered, "it was very clear *Saint Joan* was going to be it."

The concept that developed was a concert reading by graduate students and faculty, to take place on a bare stage. The cast dispensed with traditional costumes, although Arthur wore a black leotard and a red leather uniform suggestive of Joan. According to a production note in the program, the intent of the staged reading was to "reveal what a play is to an actor in its later rehearsal period." Consistent with this premise, some of the cast had memorized its lines, while others read from a script.

At Arthur's insistence, her involvement with the production was to remain unannounced. She lived in a hotel near campus and plastered her windows with newspapers to keep herself hidden from view. As if to emphasize her anonymity, she showed up at the theater in work clothes and helped scrub out the restrooms. During rehearsals, she ducked her head down and averted her eyes from the audience.

Opening night was set for February 6, 1964, at the Durham Studio Theater in Dwinelle Hall. The posters around campus promoting the play contained no mention of Arthur's casting. But a day before the scheduled opening, a San Francisco newspaper columnist who'd gotten wind of her involvement revealed that she was to appear in the production, and "all hell broke loose," Bogard remembered. The small theater had only about 150 seats, and dozens of curiosity-seekers had to be turned away.

Arthur fled the theater afterward to avoid being photographed, but she made it through the play, and the reviews were splendid. Calling the reading "one of the highlights of the theatre season," the critic for the San Francisco *Chronicle* singled out Arthur for her "inspired naivete," adding that "she expresses defiance and sharp sensibility more deftly than inner pain, and one gets the impression of a much more dauntless Joan than usual, and fortunately, an exquisitely original one." The San Francisco *Examiner* remarked that "the mystic, the martyr, the saint and the innocent were missing," but "the earthy, intense, peasant girl was there." Of course, that a sixty-three-year-old actress could even approach capturing the essence of a teenager was remarkable enough.

Arthur stayed with the production for the limited run of ten performances, each of which sold out at twenty-five cents a ticket. The experience "provided a great sense of release for her," Bogard recalled. Although she was still tense after the first few nights, Bogard managed to keep her emotions in check. "I just roughed her up a bit," he said, explaining that he let her know when she was behaving childishly. She soon calmed down, took the newspapers out of her hotel window "and started to live like a human being again."

The only time Arthur lost her cool during the production was at a party at Bogard's house in the middle of the run. As Sidney Roger, a journalist and union activist who played two parts in the play, later recounted:

> It was a good party, everybody was drinking, getting a little loaded and having fun, and I mentioned to someone that I had just read a marvelous review in *The Nation* by Harold Clurman—and everybody in that room suddenly got quiet.... Everybody in the place seemed to realize that she had an absolute mad hatred for this guy. It was, I think, really quite inadvertent. And she suddenly turned to me and really called me some pretty foul names, and said, "How can you even mention his name?" And I was just stunned by this thing.... And even though we had several more performances, and we had a very important scene together (which we did very well together), she didn't talk to me after that.

While she may not have forgiven Roger his gaffe, Arthur later claimed to have forgiven Clurman. "I certainly don't think Clurman is an evil man; I'm sure he couldn't help what he did," she philosophized. Revealing that she had seen the director at a party some years after their contretemps, she said, "He looked so *nervous*. I'll bet he thought I was going to throw my plate of food in his face. Maybe I should have! But seriously, that's all in the past; I prefer thinking about the future."

It was, in large part, her success at Berkeley that enabled Arthur to wipe away the painful memories of that night in Chicago a decade earlier, when she abandoned *Saint Joan*. Berkeley, she boasted, was "a hit, the whole thing," which "overcame the horrible defeat I'd had playing the same role years ago." And "from that point," she said, "I began to get well.... Berkeley must have been the turning point for me."

As Travis Bogard observed, Arthur viewed the Berkeley *Saint Joan* production as "sort of a culmination of her theatrical career." But not the end. As Arthur reiterated, "I love Joan. I think she isn't finished with me yet." Having resurrected herself, the actress was now restless with Life after Acting, and ready to go back to town, even if that town was Hollywood.

CHAPTER NINETEEN

WASTELAND

*J*ean Arthur did not even own a television set when she got a call from Lucille Ball in 1964 suggesting that she make her television debut with a guest appearance on *The Lucy Show*. Ball, who had met Arthur thirty years earlier as a bit player in *The Whole Town's Talking*, was now the undisputed queen of the small screen, and her suggestion piqued Arthur's interest. "How often can you decorate a house?" asked

Ball, who told Arthur it was wrong to live in seclusion. While denying that she was a recluse or that she was bored with retirement, Arthur allowed that her creative juices were flowing again after her Berkeley *Saint Joan* experience. And though she had been terrified of the idea of appearing on television in its early days of live broadcasts, she was anxious now to give it a try.

By September, *Variety* was reporting that Arthur had agreed to return for a role in a *Lucy* episode and that a script was being written for her. When the script emerged, however, both actresses agreed that it was not right and the idea was shelved. But Ball allowed her new friend to sit in on some of the show's rehearsals to gain a feel for the medium, and Arthur liked what she saw. For the first time in her career, she hired a manager, with instructions to find her a suitable television project.

Within no time, savvy Hollywood agent Eddie Dukoff arranged a guest appearance for Arthur on the perennially popular series *Gunsmoke*. Arthur's friend Ellen Mastroianni reported that the actress was "petrified" as shooting was about to begin, and she declined to be interviewed beforehand. But when she reported for work on the set the first week of January 1965, she was on her best behavior. Director Joe Lewis described her as "delightful, harmonious," and cooperative, a professional of the type not seen since "the days of the great, great luminaries." She chatted easily with writer Hal Humphrey about how fast things were done on television, and she showed off to everyone on the set a diamond necklace she had bought for $25,000 on a splurge twenty years earlier.

Arthur's episode, entitled *Thursday's Child*, aired at 10 p.m. on Saturday, March 6, 1965. In a story adapted specifically for her, she played the mother of a rebellious young outlaw hiding out from a murder charge in a shack outside Dodge City. An old friend of Kitty (Amanda Blake), Arthur's character is introduced to Doc (Milburn Stone) before she goes to visit her son, whose wife is about to give birth. When complications develop, Doc is summoned to help, but the wife dies during childbirth. Arthur's embittered son tries to escape using the baby as a shield, and threatens to shoot Doc when he grabs the infant away. Rather than see her newborn grandson's safety jeopardized and an innocent man killed, Arthur shoots her errant son dead.

Arthur's guest appearance drew high ratings and critical plaudits. The *Hollywood Reporter* commented on the "subtle mutual attraction" between her Julie Blane and Milburn Stone's Doc, to whom regular stars Blake, James Arness and Ken Curtis (Festus) took a back seat. Arthur "proved she's the star she always was," the paper noted, adding that she did not at all look her age, then generally presumed to be fifty-six, not sixty-four:

> If time has taken its toll on Miss Arthur, it certainly wasn't noticeable on the screen; she looked as pert, pretty and youthful as ever, and it seemed almost impertinent to cast her in the role of an expectant grandmother. Her acting still has the flashing fire...and, though somewhat subdued, there was still the husky, cracked quality of vocal intonation that made her both provocative and irresistible.

Arthur was delighted with the results of her experiment. She claimed to have enjoyed filming so much she "didn't want to go home," and termed the cast and crew she had worked with "all angels." Television work, she proclaimed, was "a whole new life, a kind of opening of a door."

Eddie Dukoff made it clear that his client would continue her television career if the right series came along. As an interim project he tried to talk her into doing a few scenes from *Peter Pan*, but she preferred to wait for an opportunity to do *Saint Joan*. Then he came in contact with a man named Jay Richard Kennedy, who had an idea for a show he thought Arthur might like.

Kennedy was something of a mystery. A fifty-five-year-old novelist, songwriter, stockbroker and jack-of-all trades, his primary claim to fame was his authorship of the screenplay for *I'll Cry Tomorrow*, based on the autobiography of Lillian Roth. His notion was to star Arthur in a comedy series about a woman lawyer who, like Perry Mason, wins every case, but whose methods are less orthodox. Arthur eagerly signed onto the concept, which Kennedy peddled to Universal with the help of producer-director Richard Quine, off his recent success with Jack Lemmon in *How to Murder Your Wife*.

In October 1965, Universal Television and sponsor General Foods announced that they had completed negotiations for *Mother's Word is Law*, a half-hour comedy starring Jean Arthur to begin airing the following fall. By the time shooting for the pilot began in June, the series was re-titled *The Jean Arthur Show*, to capitalize on the star's perceived marquee value. Kennedy and Quine credited themselves as executive producers of the show and as co-authors, along with Johnny Keating, of the theme song, "Merry-Go-Round." Si Rose, who had been working on the just-canceled *McHale's Navy*, was hired as producer.

"Everybody was feeling great" about the series, Rose remembered. "General Foods was ecstatic," he said, for it believed it had scored a coup in affiliating itself with a reclusive movie legend. Indeed, Arthur was the first and only great screwball film comedienne to star in a prime time television comedy. As Si Rose thought at the time, "It was just awesome to be working with her."

The star herself could hardly contain her enthusiasm at first. She found her character—a flamboyant, eccentric, girl-woman—to be fresh and non-stereotyped, unlike the parts she had been offered so often by movie producers in recent years. "I didn't want to come back as a character actress," she said at the time. "I think that must be heartbreaking. I love to play comedy, and character parts couldn't be fun. I suppose I love being the big shot," she laughed.

Although she played a widow and mother, Arthur was to be the undisputed center of attraction. As Ron Harper, who played her son and law partner, Paul Marshall, observed, his character was "by the book, she was off the wall." Arthur explained happily that as Patricia Marshall, "I can do anything in a courtroom. I can cry, act, move feelings. In one case I represent a rooster living in Beverly Hills that crows every night. We're sort of making fun of the whole law procedure. I always win."

To accentuate her youthfulness, Arthur slimmed down at the Golden Door luxury spa in Southern California and donned a blonde wig for the show to cover her white, boyish bangs. She also voluntarily submitted to cosmetic surgery, which required operations on her face, hands and elbows. For much of her professional life Arthur had worn a veil in public, and covered her elbows with clothing, to help hide her age. But plastic surgery worked even better. "It took years off her, and lasted for a good long time," observed Ellen Mastroianni, who rented a house with Arthur that summer high in the hills of Laurel Canyon, about twenty minutes from the studio.

To stay in shape, Arthur swam laps in an unheated pool every morning before shooting. And to preserve her energy, she negotiated a special clause in her contract, unusual for its time, stipulating that she was not to work past 5:30 p.m. Ron Harper recalled that while Arthur was full of energy in the mornings, she tired noticeably as the day wore on.

As she had been during *Gunsmoke*, Arthur was cheerful and cooperative in the initial stages of shooting. "She was like Peter Pan, socially—dancing around, very ebullient," remembered Si Rose. And she did just about anything she was asked, he said. She submitted to publicity interviews in which she commented favorably on what she called the frantic pace of television work, even though privately she complained that there was "so much waiting between takes," Mastroianni revealed. "And my wardrobe!" Arthur exclaimed, of the elegant hats and satin coats designed for her by Nolan Miller, who later did the costuming for *Dynasty*, *Charlie's Angels* and numerous other television shows. "I never really cared much about clothes before," she said, "but these are so great I just love them. I guess I've undergone a metamorphosis."

Ron Harper, then a thirty-one-year old actor with two prior television series to his credit, had heard of Arthur's reputation for being difficult. But he didn't find it to be true. "We got along very well; she was wonderful," he said. He remembered that when he was first introduced to Arthur by Richard Quine as "your new son," she noticed that he had cut himself shaving and expressed concern. "I liked her right away," Harper said. She later had him over to her house to read scripts, once insisting that he bring his new German shepherd puppy inside despite his warning that the dog was completely untrained. The dog chased Arthur's elderly cat around the house until Harper thought the cat "would have a heart attack," then brought a beaded curtain crashing down, jumped in the indoor fish bowl and made a mess on the floor. "Jean said, 'Oh, don't worry. Isn't he cute, so energetic,'" recalled the actor, who sensed that

Arthur's friend Ellen was less amused because she would be the one who had to clean up.

Arthur and Harper also did several commercials for General Foods, and sang the "J-E-L-L-O" song for one of the sponsor's best-known products. "Her voice was lower than mine," Harper quipped.

As the September 12 debut approached, hopes for the heavily-promoted *Jean Arthur Show* were running high. Major articles on Arthur, based on the first interviews of any length she had given in sixteen years, appeared in the New York *Times* and *TV Guide*, a testament to Arthur's desire to see the show succeed. The network spent almost $300,000 on the pilot directed by Quine, which he shot more like a movie than a television show; he also planned to make each subsequent half-hour episode in the style of a continuing film to emulate the medium that had made her a star. And as a further attraction, the studio lined up several celebrity guest stars, including Mickey Rooney, Ray Bolger, George Kennedy and Wally Cox.

Although the show's 10 p.m. time slot was late—too late, thought Ron Harper, for a situation comedy—its placement carried certain advantages. CBS included it in its powerful Monday night lineup, preceding it with the third-and sixth-highest rated series of 1965, *The Lucy Show* and *The Andy Griffith Show*, and with a strong newcomer, *Family Affair*. The 10 p.m. competition, meanwhile, was only modest, consisting of two hour-long shows, both in their second year: NBC's *Run For Your Life* and ABC's *The Big Valley*, starring another Hollywood legend, Barbara Stanwyck. In the end, the success of *The Jean Arthur Show* would turn not on its schedule, but on its merits.

Unfortunately, it had none. The morning after the debut, the New York *Times* observed that "Jean Arthur, the actress who had so many comedy successes in films, encountered rougher going last night in the premiere of a series bearing her name on CBS.... The plot was far-fetched rather than funny, and Miss Arthur's part was virtually subordinate to that of Mickey Rooney." The *Times* was being charitable; the show was a total flop.

"The scripts were not funny at all," reflected Ron Harper years later. Despite the omnipresent laugh-track, "there were no boffo laughs," he said, explaining that the show was mostly built around the warmth between a mother and her son. Arthur, who in an effort to be fully supportive had kept any qualms about the series to herself before the premiere episode, later called the scripts "awful" and lamented her inability to make the producers alter the original concept. "We knew about the third show that I was playing straight man, and we tried to do something about it," she said. "But here is the other side—a bunch of fellows at Universal who have a budget. There wasn't anybody brave enough to say, 'Let's quit until we can find a way.'"

Part of the problem lay with the executive producers. Quine, though a talented film director, was seldom around after shooting the pilot, having gone off to Warner Bros. to direct *Hotel*. Kennedy, though he was always around, knew nothing of what he was doing. "Whenever anybody from other mediums comes to TV it's difficult," said Si Rose. For example, it was decided, against Rose's advice, that instead of airing the pilot segment first, the series would begin with an episode in which Mickey Rooney guest starred. "The big-wigs said it was to be Rooney because of star power," Rose said, but the problem was that "Rooney was so good that he upstaged [Arthur]."

After the opening reviews came out, Arthur lost her enthusiasm for the project. "From then on she was very tense, and felt kind of betrayed, like we had lulled her into a false sense of security," Rose recalled. She dropped her earlier cooperative attitude and began trying to take over the production. She rejected numerous script ideas, including one for a scene designed to recall her famous front-steps scene with Joel McCrea in *The More the Merrier*. "I'm not gonna do any of that stuff," Arthur told Rose. As she said of an earlier script she turned down, "They wanted me to fall in love with someone—at my age! I think it's disgusting. It's too soupy, too gooey. There's too much of that on the screen, anyway."

The Jean Arthur Show finished sixty-fifth out of ninety prime time series listed in Nielsen's first ratings survey of the fall season, proving that audiences thought as little of the program as did the critics. "Everything got difficult" after that point, Rose ruminated, as everyone began engaging in second-guessing and finger-pointing—"television at its worst." On October 13, 1966, barely a month after the series debut, CBS announced that it was being canceled and would be replaced on December 12 by *To Tell the Truth*. The final airing of *The Jean Arthur Show*, in the form of the pilot episode, ran on December 5.

In a post-mortem, Quine acknowledged it had been a mistake not to air the pilot first, which contained the show's establishing elements; as a result, he said, the series lost its continuity. But more fundamentally, he cited the show's inability to capitalize on Arthur's unique personality. "Unlike the sponsors, we were of the opinion that we should not have banana peels and cream pies on a show with Jean Arthur. She's not like Lucille Ball, who comes on and hits people in the mouth. She has developed a more subtle public image. Unfortunately, in many of the shows we compromised our aims." Picking up on Quine's comments, the New York *Times* attributed the show's hasty demise to the same reason that led ABC to axe *The Tammy Grimes Show* earlier that same fall, after only four weeks. Both shows, as the *Times* saw it, had fallen victim to the expectation by viewers that every female television comedy performer should be another Lucille Ball. While the initial plan behind their shows was to trade on the distinctive personae of Grimes and Arthur, the producers felt compelled to try to fit them into the Lucy formula.

"It was very difficult for Jean Arthur to recreate who she was," said Rose. "She wasn't the charming lady that audiences knew from the films." Whereas Arthur had an appealing air of vulnerability on the screen, even when playing strong, independent women, her television character was styled as domineering and indefatigable. Her Patricia Marshall was an urbane Calamity Jane, but untempered by the sweetness, the tentativeness—the femininity, even—that Arthur brought to that and similar roles.

While Roddy McDowall thought that some part of Arthur's originality shone through in her television show ("there's no way to prevent it; you'd have to have a sledgehammer"), he analyzed the problem as simply that "they wanted her to be funny and Jean Arthur wasn't somebody who was funny." Her comic style flowed instead from "that peculiar, wonderful honesty from her peculiar point of view." McDowall had only recently befriended Arthur after she sent him a fan letter for his performance as the Dauphin in a Hallmark Hall of Fame production of *Saint Joan* with

Genevieve Bujold. "The letter said, 'If you'd been my Dauphin perhaps we'd still be running,'" he recalled. "I was bowled over." He then visited her during shooting of her television show, and was struck by how utterly unhappy he found her. "It was very painful to watch her stress, to see her crying," he said.

Arthur herself turned philosophical over the show's failure, which she attributed to the inherent limitations of the medium. "There are no writers on TV; and the directors are nothing at all," she ventured a few years later. "'Walk in the door,'" my director kept saying to me, 'turn right, face the camera and start talking.' Finally, I said, 'Look, if you say that to me one more time, I'll knock your teeth out.'"

"It was very heartbreaking to know that there is an establishment that you can't move, that won't listen, that won't do anything," she continued. "They understand but they don't care. They do a deal with an actor, writers and a director and that's it no matter how it goes. The pilot is always the best because that's what they sell to Jello or whoever puts up the money. And that's all you ever see of the scripts."

On the announcement of the show's cancellation, Arthur expressed some willingness to try another television series if she were given authority over production matters. But it was a perfunctory statement, for she knew that she was through with Hollywood for the last time. She also knew where she belonged. "I'm going back to Carmel," she declared. "I have a beautiful house up there and I've got four cats that I am lonesome for. And I also have a big Thanksgiving party coming up."

CHAPTER TWENTY

FREAKING OUT

A few weeks after Arthur's Thanksgiving party in Carmel, another gathering up the coast in San Francisco attracted considerably greater attention. On January 14, 1967, thousands of young people congregated there for the first "Human Be-In," designed to advertise the emerging counterculture. They burned incense, dropped acid and passed out flowers, listened to Allen Ginsberg chant Hindu phrases and heard Timothy Leary advise them to "Turn on...tune in...and drop out." They reveled in their psychedelia, trashed the Establishment and exchanged vows to "Make Love, Not War." The Year of the Hippie had officially begun, and Jean Arthur, erstwhile heroine of Capracorn, was destined to play her part in it.

Early that year Arthur had become restless spiritually, a feeling that coincided with the suicide of her brother Don. At 6:50 a.m. on April 4, 1967, seventy-seven-year-old Don Hubert Greene's life ended in a bathtub at the Carmel Convalescent Center, a local nursing home. The death certificate description of injury was "Elderly despondent man slashed his wrists." The newspaper reported that he left "no known survivors"; but a younger sister, whom he had once known as Gladys, quietly arranged for his cremation and burial at sea.

Around this time, out of curiosity, Arthur paid a visit to the nearby Carmelite Sisters Monastery, where the prioress was known to have been a former movie magazine writer. Mother (now Sister) Francisca, the former Kay Hardy, had worked for *Modern Screen* for several years in the 1940s until she tired of the lifestyle and joined the Red Cross, then left society altogether to become a cloistered nun. She had never met Jean Arthur in Hollywood, but knew of her reputation as a shy, insecure actress who "cried easily if things didn't go just right." She also knew that Arthur's mother was a Christian Science practitioner, from which she assumed that the daughter had similar religious leanings. But the woman she greeted at the monastery in 1967 could not be so easily pigeonholed.

The two of them strolled around the grounds, quietly exchanging beliefs, politely begging to differ at times. "You could see this free-spirited woman who didn't feel she could be bound by any particular religious group," recalled Sister Francisca:

> She had a great relationship with an almighty being, but it wasn't particularly a person, it was more like nature. I said it's even more interesting to know the creator of all this nature, but she didn't take that in too well. She said that was very interesting, but I was entitled to my opinion and she hers.... It was all very cordial and gracious, no contentiousness at all.

Sister Francisca recalled sensing that Arthur's somewhat shapeless religious thought stemmed from a psychological need for freedom:

> She felt this constriction at times which bound her down and made it impossible for her to function. The concept of nature was so unbinding, so all-embracing, she could lose herself and feel really at home in this awareness of everything that was powerful and loving and good all around her. It didn't restrict her in any way.

Given her aversion to authority, Arthur was unusually intrigued by her hostess's totally restricted lifestyle. She expressed wonder that anyone could willingly stay "locked up like this," the prioress recalled.

Arthur was also fascinated by a book she was shown about a little-known French saint, Thérèse of Lisieux, a late nineteenth-century nun for whom the Carmel monastery's chapel was named. Thérèse, who died in 1897 at age twenty-five, was canonized in 1925 in recognition of her life of virtue in the face of great physical suffering. But what caught Arthur's attention was a picture of the young woman, at age twenty-one, as Joan of Arc in a play presented by her convent. "She said she could tell just by looking at this woman that she understood Joan of Arc," Sister Francisca remembered. "She felt a real kinship with Thérèse."

Although Arthur promised to return to the monastery to visit sometime, this was the last time Sister Francisca saw her. The sister kept in touch by calling, sending birthday cards and books, but her cloistered status prevented her from paying any personal visits. More than twenty years later, though, she remembered their brief encounter with great fondness.

Back in civilization, in June 1967, the Monterey Pop Festival was playing just across the bay from Arthur's Driftwood. The nation was on the verge of the Summer of Love. "What came next," writes historian William Manchester, was a nightmare for tens of thousands of mothers and fathers…. The parents of the late 1960s could not grasp that the country had become so prosperous that it could afford to support tramps, or that their own children would want to be among the tramps.

Back in New York at this time, a young, mild-mannered writer named Richard Chandler was completing work on a play that would ply this theme of generational conflict and in the process, he hoped, capture the Zeitgeist of the sixties youth explosion. It concerned a middle-aged spinster from Illinois who, sent to Greenwich Village to retrieve her wayward niece from a group of hippies, ends up falling in with them and having her consciousness raised. From the working title of *A New Person*, the play eventually emerged, in catchier terms, as *The Freaking Out of Stephanie Blake*.

Chandler's idea was for the play to have the "same fluidity" as the young characters appearing in it. The "New Generation," Chandler wrote, is "always on the move; they never sit still for a second…. They are as much at home in a smoky coffee house, protesting on a street corner and dancing under the new strobe lighting as their parents are in their suburban home and the local country club. The new generation 'goes where the action is' and that is home to them."

Chandler sought for his play "a freedom to move wherever the kids took me without being burdened by heavy sets…. Because of these requirements, I devised the idea of using what I have probably inaccurately labeled 'screens,'" which were movable backdrops for projecting slides of Washington Square, the East Village and Park Avenue. They varied in size from those large enough to capture an entire protest to one "small enough to project a single flower."

Pop-rock composer Jeff Barry was commissioned to write seven numbers for the play, to be performed by live musicians on a revolving bandstand. A line from one of the songs, "The Younger Generation," pretty much summed up the play's message: "We of the younger generation are gonna see you through. So don't be afraid, we'll clean up the mess you made."

Meanwhile, Chandler was trying to figure out how to finance his

burgeoning project, which eventually cost nearly $300,000 to produce—
expensive by Broadway standards of the day. For the answer he turned to
the woman for whom he had been working as a right-hand assistant,
bookkeeper and general office boy for several years. Cheryl Crawford,
then sixty-four, was a Broadway legend, having been casting director for
the Theatre Guild in 1930 and, along with Jean Arthur's old nemesis,
Harold Clurman, a founding member of the Group Theatre the following
year. She produced numerous successful plays in the forties and fifties,
including *One Touch of Venus* (starring Mary Martin), *Brigadoon* and *Sweet
Bird of Youth*, but recently she had suffered a series of failures and was
perceived as having fallen behind the times. *Stephanie Blake*, a play for the
sixties, held the promise of a rejuvenated career, and Crawford agreed to
finance the production.

When it came to casting the title role, Crawford thought immediately
of a contemporary whose own career was in even greater need of repair.
Although Crawford was aware of Jean Arthur's problematic theatrical
history, she also knew, as she wrote later in her autobiography, that
Arthur was "very right for the part," which called for an old-fashioned
but independent-minded woman who was free-spirited at heart. In the
spring of 1967, Crawford placed a call to Carmel.

"If you fell in love with a play, would you do it on Broadway?" Crawford
inquired, to which the response was "send me a script." After receiving
and reading the first scene of *Stephanie Blake*, Jean Arthur was in love
with it. "Most of the plays people send me are about the past," she said.
"This one is about today, and I believe in what it's saying." As she explained when she accepted the part, "I didn't want to do any of the formula
plays, which are boring to me, because we are in a great evolutionary and
revolutionary period."

Before Crawford would accept Arthur, however, she obtained assurance
from the star that her withdrawals were, in Crawford's words, "a thing of
the past." Chandler had his doubts, too, but they were put to rest before
Arthur signed for the title role. "When she tried television last year everyone reported she had been most cooperative," he reasoned. "I spent two
and a half weeks with her when she came here [to New York] for talks

before the production of *Stephanie Blake*, and she really wanted to work."

And so it was with great expectations that Jean Arthur arrived in New York in early August 1967, with Ellen Mastroianni, a month before rehearsals were to begin. As if to emphasize her break with the past, she took up residence this time not at the Carlyle, her Upper East Side home during *Peter Pan*, but at the Hampshire House overlooking Central Park South, not far from the theater where she would be playing. From her suite, she practiced a drum solo that (despite Arthur's lack of musical talent) was inserted in the play for her.

A few days after Arthur's arrival, theatrical attorney Carl Schaeffer joined Cheryl Crawford as co-producer of the play, and John Hancock, a twenty-eight-year-old wunderkind from Pittsburgh, was hired to direct. Hancock, who had made a reputation for himself in regional theater, was concerned that the play had overly sanitized the hippie world in an effort to go commercial. "You can't portray it in all its drug-infested reality," he acknowledged, "but you can't quite make it this prophylactic either." Nevertheless, he thought the show had merit, and to imbue the cast with a sense of authenticity, he had them attend some local discotheques to soak up the atmosphere. Arthur found one such establishment, Cheetah, particularly conducive to her research: "It's a beautiful place," she reported. "After the first five minutes, I forget the noise and just feel it. I could almost fall asleep there."

There were those in the cast, however, who needed no instruction in the ways of the new world. Several of the twenty-eight players were amateurs already familiar with the flower child scene, at least one of whom was advertised as a "real life hippie." Jim Fouratt, a young colleague of Abbie Hoffman, had organized Central Park's Be-In earlier that year, and most recently had been in the news for eating and burning money in the gallery of the New York Stock Exchange. He was running a communications company in the East Village, producing mimeographed local newsletters and love manifestoes, when he was plucked for a part in the play.

The rest of the cast included a number of people who, although unknown at the time, later attained a measure of fame on television. Franklin Cover, who played Hamilton Reed, father of the runaway niece,

Blake, was to take part in television's first interracial marriage in *The Jeffersons*. William Devane, cast as a hippie named "Motherball," starred in the series *Falcon Crest*. The play also featured two women who achieved pop-cult status as characters in television commercials: Jan Miner, who played Nancy Reed, the girl's mother, was later better known as Madge the Manicurist, while Dena Dietrich, cast in a variety of small parts in the play, became the "Mother Nature" it was not nice to fool.

The only name in the show at the time, however, and the person on whose shoulders the entire production rested, was Jean Arthur. It was her care and feeding that counted, and it was she whom the play's management would be watching for any signs of trouble. It did not take long for the trouble to start.

"It started the very first day of rehearsal," remembered Franklin Cover. "Miss Arthur really would not go through a scene without stopping— would not get ahold of something and work with it, making mistakes... and just get through it." Arthur would constantly "break the take," stopping every few minutes, "thinking we could start the cameras again," Cover recalled. "So that way, you never got a run at the scene."

"We'd go into the scene," he continued, "and then she would stop and say: 'I just *love* the way you ate those peanuts! That's hilarious!' And then the director would say, 'Well, could we start from the top again, Miss Arthur?'"

As she did so frequently in the past, Arthur began complaining about the script. She loved what she had previously read, which was Act One. In it, Aunt Stephanie, a registered Republican, is sent by Blake Reed's distraught parents to a cockroach-infested hotel in the Village where their daughter is living with her hippie friends. Horrified at first by all the filth, LSD and free love, Stephanie moves in to keep a closer watch over Blake, then gradually undergoes a metamorphosis that only begins to become visible near the end of the first act, when she declares: "Do you realize we had *no business* in the Dominican Republic? I think we should apologize to those people!"

In the second act, however, which was not yet written when Arthur signed for the role, the play degenerated into a mess of slapstick and sermonizing. As Arthur later told it, "During rehearsals we kept getting new scenes every day, and you wouldn't believe how stupid they were. They *couldn't* have been written by the same person who wrote that first scene." They had been, of course, but Chandler could not seem to make the second act meet the promise of the first. Most of the rewrites, in fact, were changes for the worse; one of them set up a forced romance between Arthur and an aging radical played by Sidney Lanier, an Episcopal minister and cousin of playwright Tennessee Williams.

As time went on, the show's expenses began to mount, forcing Chandler to sink much of his own money into the production. He was becoming too emotionally wrapped up in the effort, and it was starting to show. But his was not the only increasingly erratic behavior.

When a photographer crashed a private cast party before the previews, Arthur hid under a table and refused to move until he left. As the production was pushing toward opening night, with rehearsals scheduled to continue to midnight, she would announce at 9:30 that she was tired and was going home, leaving the rest of the cast to stumble through the complicated scenes with an understudy. Then, in the spirit of the season, she began wearing a series of Halloween masks as she left rehearsals for her limousine back to the Hampshire House. The explanation Cover received from others in the cast was that Arthur was afraid her fans would recognize and mob her. But as Cover observed for himself, "There were no 'fans' out there waiting for her—there was no one waiting for her."

The first public preview of *Stephanie Blake* was to be on October 9. It was postponed a day, ostensibly because the stagehands and technicians needed more time to install the complicated production. On October 10 there was no preview, but an explanation in the New York *Times*: John Hancock had resigned as director "because of what he termed a disagreement with the author, Richard Chandler." Cheryl Crawford herself took over the direction, for all of a day, followed by the hiring of Michael Kahn, another young director with a reputation for talent developed off Broadway. The first of several previews was moved to October 30, and opening night, previously set for October 30, was rescheduled to November 4. Because of the additional rehearsal time this entailed, and to keep the show afloat, Arthur agreed to contribute $25,000 of her own money to the production.

By this time, the show was clearly tottering. New scenes and lines kept coming, scenery was literally falling down on people's heads, stagehands were wandering on and off duty as they pleased. The only constant was the heavy smell of marijuana burning nightly during rehearsals.

On October 30, 1967, *Stephanie Blake* began previews at the Eugene O'Neill Theatre. Author William Goldman, sitting in the audience that night, later wrote that "rarely ha[d] sadistic expectation been so high." The sadists were not to be disappointed. A few moments after the curtain rose, Jean Arthur's entrance—her first appearance on Broadway in sixteen years—was botched by a failure to answer her knock at the door, which she then had to open herself. The cast stumbled its way through the rest of the play until curtain calls, when the turntable sets started going haywire and the curtain nearly fell upon Arthur's head. "You should have let it hit you, Jean," somebody yelled.

Arthur later recalled that the audience was actually "cringing" during the previews. "Then my voice began going; I'd start to speak and nothing but a squeak would come out. I was so terrified of making a fool of myself." Mary Martin, then starring on Broadway in *I Do! I Do!* saw one preview and told Arthur that it was no good, which surely added to her friend's doubts about the show.

On Wednesday, November 2, *Stephanie Blake* was set for another preview, this one a matinee. The full-house audience that afternoon included many elderly grandmother types clustered among the front rows to obtain a better view of the woman they recalled fondly from their moviegoing years. To help them interpret the happenings on stage, they would find in their Playbills a "Glossary of Hippy Terms," including "Freaking Out" ("Freeing one's mind from the ordinary or mundane frame of reference"); "Blow Your Mind" ("Expand the consciousness of your thoughts, usually with the aid of drugs or narcotics"); "crash" ("to fall asleep"); "split" ("to leave or depart"); and assorted others such as "a drag," "a trip," "cop out," "Do Your Thing," "joint" and "turned on."

After the audience settled into its seats, the curtain rose again, followed by a knock at the door. This time they got it right: Nancy Reed yelled to husband Hamilton, who was mixing a martini in their Park Avenue penthouse, "That must be Stephanie!" Jan Miner then walked to the door, opened it to Jean Arthur and exclaimed with open arms, "Stephanie!"

But instead of embracing Jan Miner's welcoming arms, as called for by the script, Arthur ducked under them and headed straight for the footlights. Franklin Cover uttered his line, "Come in, Stephanie," to which she replied, "Just a minute, Frank, I want to talk to the audience." When she got to the footlights, she knelt down and started talking directly to the ladies in the front rows.

"This play and these people," she began, "are dearer to me than life itself. But I just can't go on." Cheryl Crawford, standing at the back of the theater, yelled out, "Try!" The matinee ladies gasped. Franklin Cover stood frozen in position, staring at Arthur with an astounded look on his face, all the while continuing to hold the cocktail shaker above his shoulder while he mixed his martinis.

"The atmosphere was poisonous, toxic," recalled Barton Heyman. "Suddenly she started going off into the wings and pulling people onto the stage, saying, 'This is so and so, he's a wonderful actor,'" he recalled. "She sort of became like the stage manager in *Our Town*."

Cheryl Crawford was beside herself. Before Arthur finished her impromptu monologue, which went on for several minutes, Crawford found herself screaming, "You will go on! You *will* play the play!" Arthur was momentarily stunned, then regained her composure and appealed to the audience for sympathy. "I'm told I must go on," she said, "and I'm going to because I believe in the show. But if something happens...." They started all over again. Arthur went back behind the penthouse door to make her re-entrance. "At that point I didn't know what play it was," remembered Franklin Cover. "I really thought, 'where am I?'" At least one onlooker had enough: Neil Simon, who had just purchased the theater and came to see how his first tenants were doing, turned from where he was standing at the back of the auditorium and quietly walked out.

Somehow the play proceeded apace, but to little end. Arthur warned the audience that her voice was failing and that if they should see her putting her hand to her mouth and dropping something in, not to worry—it would only be a cough drop. She did so several times during the play, prompting wild applause each time from the audience, and she spoke through the performance in a virtual whisper. When she walked off the stage at the end, she was waving her hands in the air and saying an eerie "good bye," to no one in particular. "She sort of floated out," recalled Barton Heyman, who was sitting by the stage door, "and that was the last I saw of her."

This being a Wednesday matinee, the cast was due back at the theater a few hours later for the evening performance. Cheryl Crawford met them backstage to report that Arthur had fled the theater and locked herself in her hotel room. Before the audience could be turned away it had filled up the theater, requiring Crawford to appear before them to announce the cancellation of that night's preview.

But Cheryl Crawford was not ready to give up. The next day, still unable to reach Arthur by phone, she sent a telegram stating that "your failure to appear at rehearsal this afternoon and at performances tonight and tomorrow will necessitate the closing of the play...with an estimated loss of $250,000." In return, she received a telegram from Arthur's manager, Eddie Dukoff, saying that Dr. Gershon Loesser had her under strong sedation for fear that she might suffer a "nervous breakdown." Dukoff cited Arthur's prior $25,000 contribution to the play as evidence that she still wanted to continue with it. "She's just sick about it," he reported, adding that if she carried out her doctor's orders not to talk for seventy-two hours, she might yet make Saturday's opening. On Friday night, Crawford was quoted as saying she hoped something could be done in the next few days to salvage the production.

She knew better than that. The following night the premiere was canceled, and on Tuesday, November 7, 1967, the New York *Post* pronounced the play dead. "So much for *Stephanie Blake*, on which I lost more money than I care to think about," wrote Crawford in her memoirs. She lost even more money when it was discovered that for years Chandler had been forging his name on checks to himself while working in her office.

Those who were involved with the production of *Stephanie Blake* hold differing views as to who was chiefly to blame, besides the most obvious target, the star who quit. "The problem was the author," said the original director, John Hancock. "He was not only the producer but he also wanted to direct. Chandler was interested in the casting of types and amateurs: he wanted real hippies and real musicians. I love casting amateurs because they can sometimes give you something wonderful, but only in one or two parts. What we [had was] a group of non-actors, and it goes so slowly; they don't know what they're doing, they won't remember what they did yesterday...."

Franklin Cover, on the other hand, thought that Hancock—young, without Broadway experience but with a tremendous ego—was the wrong person to direct the play. "He felt he had all the answers, and he didn't," Cover said, recalling the experience after nearly three decades. For example, Hancock insisted that Cover and his wife go to a disco, as the others in the cast had done, even though, as Cover pointed out, he was playing Blake's father and wasn't supposed to know anything about such places. "It was just ghastly," he remembered. "I stayed for five minutes and left."

"I think we got off on the wrong foot with Hancock," said Cover. "What we needed was a hard-nosed Broadway professional, somebody like George Abbott, to get this thing in some kind of form and perspective. And then it might have gone.... Because the tragedy was, the show did have merit." Dena Dietrich similarly believed that the play had some potential but that it "sort of got off track when it got all involved with Day-Glo lighting and smoky nightclubs, that sort of thing."

Barton Heyman, however, was convinced that there was nothing worth salvaging. "Nobody could have saved that pot of shit," he maintained. "It was an attempt at co-opting the whole San Francisco counterculture scene. The writing was pap, the circumstances all strained and obvious. It was watered down—a sort of 'aunt knows best.' The whole production was ersatz."

The one thing upon which all agreed was that *Stephanie Blake* was, in a perverse sense, a play for the ages. "The weirdest experience I ever had," recalled Franklin Cover. "A one in a million experience," Dena Dietrich agreed. "Most of us in the production felt that it was inconceivable that this kind of thing could happen," she continued, in reference to Arthur's sudden departure. "I felt sorry for her, but more for us who were left out of work."

Nevertheless, Dietrich, for one, found a silver lining in the play's demise. "I dined out on it for weeks," she laughed. "Everywhere people were inviting me out to hear the story." She even ran into Arthur about a month after the play closed, at a dinner party in Connecticut thrown by Jan Miner, Arthur's closest friend from the cast. The whole incident was "just glossed over" that night, Dietrich recalled.

Perhaps it was fitting, anyway, that *Stephanie Blake* closed just as the Summer of Love faded into the fall of 1967. "Hippiedom would survive in one form or another," wrote historian Manchester, "but the movement as it had been known that year was doomed. All that was lacking was a final curtain." That came, in his view, on the night of October 8, 1967, the day before the curtain was originally scheduled to rise on *Stephanie Blake*. Linda Rae Fitzpatrick, the eighteen-year-old daughter of a wealthy Connecticut couple, was found beaten to death that night in a tenement on New York's Lower East Side, the victim of a brutal gang rape. She supposedly went to Greenwich Village with her parents' blessing to be among artists, not hippies; as it turned out, she took up with some East Village drug addicts who could not even mourn her death. "The chick wasn't anything to us," one of them was quoted as saying.

With the horror of this story fresh in their minds, Broadway audiences might have been put off by *Stephanie Blake's* reverential, rose-colored treatment of its subject had the play lasted long enough to be seen. In the final scene, after Blake has left the Village and agreed to return to Vassar College, Stephanie hears the sound of tambourines, finger cymbals and bongo drums in the background off stage, then suddenly has a revelation. "Go back!" she tells her niece, advising her not to listen to her parents and instead to return to her friends in the Village. She must go back, Stephanie explains, because they are involved in "the biggest revolution of them all." Meanwhile, Stephanie announces, she is going back to Illinois to look up her hawkish Republican friend, Senator Everett Dirksen, to "fill him in on some things," after which she plans to "wear flowers in my hair," the play's closing line.

Ironically, though she did not yet know it, Jean Arthur's next stop would be the same Vassar College that the newly "enlightened" Stephanie Blake was telling her niece to forgo. After a hiatus of nearly twenty years, Arthur was going back to college, only this time as teacher, not student. But what could she teach, having repeatedly broken the first rule of show business, that one must always go on?

CHAPTER TWENTY-ONE

MISCASTING

After the disaster of *Stephanie Blake*, Nell Eurich, the new dean of faculty at Vassar, suggested to her friend that she might like to try her hand at teaching in the school's drama department. Arthur embraced the idea of becoming associated with as prestigious an academic institution as Vassar, which was regarded as a haven for affluent, intellectually gifted, independent-minded young women.

249

In the spring of 1968, Professor William Rothwell agreed to let Arthur observe his introductory freshman acting course. She quickly moved to Poughkeepsie, New York, and settled into a small apartment in Alumnae House, a Tudor-style complex just across the street from campus.

For her first couple of terms, Arthur sat in Rothwell's class, often in the back, commenting when asked about the scenes the students enacted. Occasionally she came to the front of the room for a practical demonstration.

Joanne Gates, a freshman in the fall of 1968, remembered Arthur was "reserved and hesitant at first, but when she committed herself to speak up, it was very heartfelt, very moving." One subject about which she was particularly passionate was *Saint Joan*. After some classroom readings from the play, Arthur picked out Ms. Gates as a potential Joan, and even had her over to her apartment for some dramatic tutoring.

For most of the young women in Rothwell's class, Arthur was the first famous person with whom they had come in close contact. But none of them knew who she was, at least until their parents told them. "My parents were just astounded and excited that Jean Arthur was my teacher," recalled Carolyn Pines. "That got a lot of mileage." After a campus screening of *Mr. Smith Goes to Washington* that Arthur attended, the students began to realize with whom they were associating. "All of a sudden it hit them like a ton of bricks," remembered Rothwell.

Arthur herself did little to encourage any such adulation. She refused to allow the school to advertise her presence, and she seldom spoke, in class, of her Hollywood days. She befriended few of the faculty, and as one professor put it, she let it be known they should regard her as "just Jean Arthur, a person." Or occasionally someone else altogether. At one early faculty party that Rothwell persuaded her to attend at his home, she was accosted by a local society woman who demanded to meet her and would not wait for Rothwell's introduction. "I am Millicent Heatherington Dodge," the woman announced in pompous tones (her real name was something similarly pretentious, Rothwell recalled). After a moment of silence, Arthur croaked, "I'm Martha Washington."

In the fall of 1969, Arthur was paired as a team teacher of introductory drama with Clint Atkinson, a charismatic young actor-director beginning his first year at Vassar. At first the two of them hit it off, as Atkinson, who was more dynamic and innovative than most members of the drama department, appealed to Arthur's playful spirit. "She behaved beautifully to me," recalled Atkinson, who found her to be "charming company." She also came to respect his talent, particularly his direction of the August Strindberg play, *Miss Julie*, which starred a young drama major named Meryl Streep. Then in her junior year, and in her first major part, Streep electrified the audience with her performance and "emerged with the true presence that stayed with her," recalled fellow student Georgia Buchanan Morse. Arthur watched one of Streep's rehearsals with Atkinson and remarked with awe that it was "just like watching a movie star," as if she had never been one herself.

As a result of *Miss Julie*, Clint Atkinson became "the toast of the campus," recalled Robyn Reeves Travers, a freshman in that 1969-70 year. "Everybody was dropping dead over him," she said. But left behind in all the hoopla was Atkinson's co-teacher, Jean Arthur, setting the stage for a rivalry that would eventually destroy their friendship.

At the same time Atkinson was directing *Miss Julie*, Arthur was trying to put together her own production of William Saroyan's *The Beautiful People*, a sweet fantasy about a whimsical fifteen-year-old boy. But students found the play too "corny," recalled Robyn Travers, a feeling many of them had about Arthur's own demonstrative style. "Jean had a way of making everything come out the same. Everything had a pixie-like, sort of *Mr. Smith Goes To Washington* quality," said Joan Bogden. "The things she had done on film seemed rather dated to us. The gee-whiz Americana was out of favor in 1969." Given a choice between what they perceived as Arthur's highly theatrical, histrionic acting style and the more fashionable, naturalistic method taught by Atkinson, most of the drama majors opted for the latter. Arthur kept her students rehearsing the Saroyan play for weeks on end, but the project was plagued by lack of interest and by Arthur's inability to find a suitable actress for the young-boy lead. "Finally I said to her, 'Jean, I have a funny feeling you don't want to direct the play, you want to play the little boy,'" Atkinson recalled, which she admitted was the case. She took over the part in classroom rehearsals, but the production never did come off.

After a time, a split developed at Vassar between the more serious, ambitious drama majors, who gravitated to Atkinson's productions (the "in crowd," Robyn Travers called them), and those who went with Arthur "because she was a sweet lady." Included in the latter group was Travers' roommate, Marcy Kelly, who got to know Arthur as well as any student at Vassar. As Kelly recalled, "there was a whole cadre of people who were certain they were Broadway bound," who cast their lot with Clint Atkinson and tended to discount Arthur. Others, among whom Kelly counted herself, were simply looking for a way of avoiding freshman English and "were not interested in auditioning for Joe Papp." This more sympathetic group of students was willing to accept Arthur for what she was, while recognizing precisely what she was not, which was a drama teacher.

"As a teacher, it was difficult for her," William Rothwell recalled. "She was very good at criticism; she could put her finger on exactly what was wrong with the interpretation of the role, and then she would show them how she thought it should be done. But the problem was that she could not elicit from the student a performance on her own."

Arthur Ward, a Poughkeepsie-area antiques dealer who befriended the actress, found her a charming, opinionated woman with "exquisite taste," but thought "a cog was missing someplace" as far as teaching went. "I don't think she knew what she was doing, and I don't think she thought so, either," he said.

"Well I don't think there are any rules," Arthur explained of her teaching method. "I feel that getting caught up in rules thinking instead of being really all in the part is not good for students." She also freely admitted that she could only teach by doing. "I somehow know how to read every part in the plays. And that's how I help the students. I can tell when things look right on a stage…I don't know how I know. I must have absorbed something along the way."

Arthur "didn't particularly think of acting as a skill that can be learned," explained Marcy Kelly. "She thought of it as a talent." Whereas Clint

Atkinson was out to "academically examine what it takes to be a thespian," Arthur was more interested in finding good actresses and doing what she could to enhance their innate abilities. "She thought you either have talent or you don't, and if you have it, then the question is how to nurture and promote it. She wasn't going to spend a lot of time re-running the scene with the untalented girls."

Kelly thought that Atkinson was dismissive of Arthur in class because of her lack of academic orientation. "She felt cut off and ignored by him," the former student recalled. "She was a spunky person in some ways, but she was not assertive, and she wasn't going to contradict him or try to get her words in edgewise." Atkinson recalled simply that "I did all the work and she listened." She became jealous of him, he said, and convinced herself that he was somehow trying to use her to further his own career. Eventually she stopped talking to him altogether, and began calling him the "Cro-Magnon Man," even in his presence at faculty meetings. "She could be very trying," Atkinson remembered, though without any rancor.

Marcy Kelly instead found the actress to be "fun, neat—a very chatty lady." The two of them had dinner together once a week for two straight semesters, often speeding all over the rural roads of upstate New York in Arthur's tortoiseshell-finish Jaguar. As Kelly recalled, "I was eighteen or nineteen and here was this famous or quasi-famous person who had stories about Clark Gable and enough money to go out to dinner. It was a kick."

But the young woman also found something very sad about her older friend. The actress seemed to regard herself as a failure, and was looking to Vassar more for nurturing than as a professional opportunity. "Some of us had the feeling she was sent there by her psychologist to take care of herself," one student remembered. Added Marcy Kelly: "She wasn't particularly interested in being a great teacher; she was looking for something useful to do. I liked her a lot at the time, but I always felt sorry for her."

"It was sort of pitiful," remembered Robyn Travers. "She felt very persecuted and very ostracized by the drama department, which she was. They didn't treat her with dignity, which is a horrible thing."

As Arthur's tenure at Vassar wore on, the students, too, grew less tolerant of her shortcomings. "I felt shortchanged by her class, which was a total waste in many ways," said Carolyn Pines, a freshman in Arthur's acting class in the fall of 1970. "She was not a very focused or effective teacher." As Pines recalled, when Arthur would "stop trying to teach and just relax and tell stories, then it was fascinating." Consequently, the students tried every way they could to force Arthur out of her teaching mode. "We really egged her on a lot and gave her a difficult time," she confessed. Arthur, in turn, was frustrated at the inability of her supposedly-bright Vassar students to comprehend what she was getting at. "How can you be so dumb when you're so smart?" was her frequent rhetorical query.

Nevertheless, Arthur professed to enjoy the repartee. "I love the students," she said. "You know they communicate and I've learned to communicate much more with them than with adults. Students like to talk about things that really matter—about the world and what we're going to do about it."

At times, Arthur gave up on trying to teach her students anything about acting and instead turned her class into a seminar on nature appreciation. One beautiful autumn day she announced they were going outside to look at some trees. "So they all went out and they looked at the trees for half an hour," recalled William Rothwell. "She said to them, 'I just want you to remember this.'"

Another time, Rothwell recalled, Arthur lectured her students on the importance of even the smallest forms of life. "She told them, 'If you see a little animal dead on the side of the road, you should get out of the car, take a tissue and wrap the animal up, and you should lay it reverently up on the grass and then go on. But don't just drive by the animal—give it the respect it deserves.'"

A world view so idiosyncratic as Arthur's could not fail to leave an impression on even the most cynical of her students. While agreeing that she was ineffective as a teacher, Arthur's former students remember her as a distinctive personality they were glad to have known. She wore her hair with short, grayish bangs, cut like Gertrude Stein's, and she was never seen around campus in anything but pants. "My impression of her was Peter Pan," said one former student, Nancy Barber. Even when Arthur was teaching a serious acting scene, "it was still Peter Pan when she got up and demonstrated it," Barber said. "She was very childlike in her mannerisms, and completely optimistic about what she did."

Although Vassar was known as a bastion of liberalism and tolerance, its geographical isolation prevented it from becoming a political battleground in the late sixties and early seventies. As a result, Arthur had no occasion to take sides in any of the great student protests of the day. Nevertheless, she was "very supportive of students" in their questioning of the establishment, recalled Marcy Kelly. If an issue was important to a student Arthur encouraged action, be it a boycott or a draft dodge. According to Kelly, the genesis of this attitude was "humanitarian rather than political."

To the extent Arthur had political thoughts, they tilted heavily leftward (Shaw and Fromm, her two greatest intellectual heroes, were both committed socialists). "The wrong people are running the country," she said shortly after Richard Nixon began his second term as president in 1972. "You only have to look at their brutal faces to know that. But there are people who have the right answers—Ralph Nader, Buckminster Fuller, Dick Gregory, Loren Eiseley—and one day people are going to listen to them. The best thing that can happen is for kids to get together and talk and plan."

Long before it became fashionable, Arthur was also an environmentalist. "What are they doing to the Earth today?" she asked in 1966, when the first Earth Day was still four years off. "Killing it, smothering it! Soon there won't be anything. I feel like wrapping my arms around the little bit I have and protecting it forever."

"So many people don't see the birds and the water, the trees and the bugs," she complained. "If they see bugs, they just want to squash them. They're not curious."

Eventually Arthur came to think the same thing of her colleagues at Vassar. As William Rothwell recalled:

> She wanted to be part of a group who would discuss all sorts of wonderful "ideas"—new thoughts, new ways of looking at life—and she didn't find it. Well, you're not apt to find it in an academic atmosphere, anyway. A lot of people don't like to talk shop. They teach philosophy, you go to a party with them, they don't want to talk about philosophy. They want to talk about

having their car fixed, or something similar. And I think she
was disappointed in that.

In early 1972, after Arthur had spent four years at Vassar, she and the
school decided they'd had enough of each other. "I'm very grateful to
Vassar for giving me the chance to prove that I have something to contribute to young people," she said. "But I'm lonely here. The faculty is
quite conservative, and I can count the teachers with whom I have some
communications on my hands and still have some fingers left over. I'm
ready for something different now, I'm ready for some excitement."

She made it clear, though, that a return to acting was not what she had
in mind. She had just turned down the role of Steve McQueen's mother,
later played by Ida Lupino, in Sam Peckinpah's *Junior Bonner*, as well as
the part of the lady missionary in producer Ross Hunter's musical remake
of *Lost Horizon*.

Nor was Arthur interested in becoming an object of the nostalgia craze
that was sweeping the country in the early seventies, much of it focused
on the Hollywood films and stars of the thirties. Shortly before announcing her departure from Vassar, she dipped her toe into the nostalgia
boomlet, accepting an invitation to pay tribute to Frank Capra at the
USA Film Festival at Southern Methodist University in Dallas. Agent
John Springer, who was handling publicity for the festival, recalled his
efforts to coax her into attending: "For about a week she would say to me,
'I'd love to but I can't, I can't. I think I will, but…I just can't face it,' etc."

Face it she did, eventually, but with extreme reluctance. "We got there
on a Friday," John Springer remembered. "There were all kinds of parties.
Peter Bogdanovich was beside himself, so excited about meeting her. But
she wouldn't come out of her hotel room the whole weekend. Finally on
Monday the first of the Capra movies were to be shown as matinees,
mostly with students attending. So Frank and Mrs. Capra and I talked
her into coming to that first screening, which was *Mr. Deeds*."

Springer and Arthur sat in the back row of the auditorium with Capra
and his wife. Springer recalled that

> as they turned down the lights, the reaction was beyond belief.
> These kids were applauding everything, just adoring the

movie. At the end of the movie, Frank went onstage and thanked them for their reaction. He said how he wished Gary Cooper could have been there. Thunderous applause. Then he said, "And that marvelous Jean Arthur!…" And they cheered. He said, "I've got to tell you something you don't know. Jean Arthur is here in the back row with my wife and John Springer!"

At that point, Arthur sank down in her seat. After another thunderous ovation, the audience cheered her into going onstage with Capra. "She could barely speak," Springer said, "but whatever she said they cheered her. Well she suddenly realized they adored her and she could relate to young people. She couldn't relate to authority figures but she could relate to these kids."

"Jean was the star of the whole week," Springer recalled. "They virtually carried her around on their shoulders. And she loved the experience. She just came to life." She attended each of the other Capra movies, including *Mr. Smith* and *You Can't Take It With You*, and "was up on stage before Frank was."

"It was just the most fun I've ever had," Arthur said afterward. "It was so wonderful being with Frank again; I wish we could go on a road show together, showing his movies and talking to the people." She marveled at meeting Andy Warhol, whom she called "so darling, so naive" for encouraging her to work in movies again. "Oh, and that little boy from *Love Story* was there, too," she said, referring to Ryan O'Neal. "He seems very charming, very modest."

But Arthur's foray into the world of fan appreciation proved short-lived. Back in Poughkeepsie after the Dallas festival, Arthur called Springer for advice about an invitation she had received from New York's Town Hall for a public tribute. Springer encouraged her and took the idea a step further, suggesting to the Town Hall that it sponsor a series of appearances by great actresses of the thirties who had been neglected over the years. His notion was to present Arthur, Myrna Loy and Sylvia Sidney separately in a format that called for an hour of the star's film clips, followed by an informal question and answer session. The Town Hall agreed to the concept.

"That week I ran into Bette Davis at a party and I said I was going to do this," Springer recalled. "'I wanna do it too,'" she said. "I told her, 'Bette, nobody can ever say you were neglected.'" She said she wanted to do it anyway, "'as long as that Crawford isn't in it,'" Springer related.

"So it became something else; it became 'Legendary Ladies,'" Springer said. "We announced it as Bette, Sylvia, Myrna and Jean." But then Arthur got cold feet. "She called several times, said 'I can't sleep, can't do it, couldn't possibly,'" Springer recounted. "I finally realized that indeed she couldn't, that it was psychologically impossible." Joan Crawford, who had been bugging Springer to add her to the group, was announced as Arthur's replacement. "I explained to Bette that they wouldn't be on the same stage," Springer said. "She said, 'Ok, as long as I'm first.'"

What Arthur really wanted at this point, she explained, was a chance to develop her directorial skills. At Vassar, she had directed a few small-scale productions but had been denied access to the main stage in Avery Hall. "I want to teach and to direct all over the world. I *hunger* for that," she said when she left Vassar. "And one of these days I *will* direct. I'll find the right actress, and I'll direct her in *Saint Joan.*"

An off-chance remark by her friend Art Ward led to Arthur's next experiment in education. Ward's brother, Robert, happened to be the president of the North Carolina School of the Arts, a unique state-sponsored school in Winston-Salem offering a coordinated program of professional and academic training for both high school and college students. After briefly considering Southern Methodist University in Dallas and Smith College in Massachusetts, Arthur accepted Bob Ward's offer to join the drama faculty at the North Carolina school beginning in the fall of 1972.

Ward realized that Arthur had not been comfortable at Vassar, but he thought it was because its drama department was too academic for the actress's taste. The North Carolina school, by contrast, featured artists-in-residence among its faculty, and so offered Arthur a better opportunity for hands-on teaching. But as Ward soon concluded, Arthur "really didn't have the ability to convey what she knew to others," nor "any ability to mix in as everyone else did." Faculty colleague Pauline Koner, a dancer-choreographer who occasionally socialized with Arthur, confirmed that the actress "really didn't fit into the complex of a school" because she "couldn't codify what she did so it could be taught."

If anything, the students she encountered in North Carolina had even less regard for her teaching talents than the students at Vassar. "She really wasn't a teacher," said Beverly Petty, who took Arthur's acting class as a sophomore in the fall of 1972. Petty became a teacher's pet and occasionally chauffeured Arthur around in the actress's Jaguar. "She kind of adopted one other guy and myself and didn't really pay much attention to the other kids," Petty remembered.

Another student, Sandra Lavalle, recalled that Arthur gave people their lines and expected them to repeat them *her* way, "otherwise it was wrong." She was "difficult because she just wanted to do everything," Lavalle added. "I just don't think she had the patience."

"By this time she was a rather bitter woman," added Petty. "She could treat people very badly. She'd dismiss them and say ugly things about them, like 'you'll never work, just look at that tooth, it's a horrible tooth.' You just didn't tell students that."

Part of the problem, Petty thought, was that her fellow drama students tended to take themselves too seriously. "We had no sense of humor," she said. By contrast, Arthur "had a wonderful sense of humor, when she wasn't being crabby or unhappy."

Partway through the semester, the entire class went to the head of the drama department and said they wanted out. Only four students of the original dozen or so remained with Arthur; Beverly Petty stayed, she said, because the dean promised her any teacher she wanted "for the rest of my life." But whatever Arthur's deficiencies as a teacher, "she was not an evil woman," Petty insisted. "She was eccentric enough and sad enough, but she was an interesting lady. When she was charming she was charming, and when she wasn't we just cut out."

Arthur's only real friend in Winston-Salem was Pete Ballard, a costume designer who taught high school English on the academic side of the arts school. "My feeling is Jean was blackballed by the whole drama department," he said. As Ballard saw it:

> They never knew what they had. She didn't have a regular class. It was more ad-hoc.... They wound up letting her do a little one-act play, *Sneaky Fitch*, a melodrama that she chose to do. It was silly and nonsense but the kids did it. And that let her feel she was doing something. But everybody just sort of cast her off. At that point they began to spread rumors that she was a kook. And simply blackballed her with the students.

"It was an awkward situation," Ballard said. "I think the reason she came down here was to be able to do *Saint Joan*, to direct it the way she wanted it. I think somebody either told her, 'Of course you can do it,' or she was hoping to spring this on them. They should have done it here, except I don't think we had the caliber of student at that time. We were still in the hippie period, and a lot of the kids who came here just came as outcasts."

Sandra Lavalle, a theater major and college junior when she took Arthur's class, did not think of herself as an outcast; later a marketing executive for HBO, she called the school "a great opportunity for me." She welcomed the chance to study under Jean Arthur at first, and despite Arthur's insistence on doing everything her way, Lavalle found her "exciting to work with." But she made the unpardonable sin of leaving a workshop production of *Saint Joan*, for which Arthur had chosen her as the lead. "I was told by the theater department to forget this, that I should go into some other show," she recalled. Arthur cast another lead after Lavalle dropped out, but her *Saint Joan* never got off the ground.

After that, Arthur refused to speak to Lavalle. "I was not loyal, I was an ungrateful person," was Arthur's attitude, Lavalle recalled. Around campus, Arthur began referring to her former Joan ruefully as "that girl."

"By Christmas break when she went back to Carmel, I think she had pretty much decided, that's it," said Ballard. "I think it was I who talked her into staying. I said, 'Ok, don't go run away from this one, you agreed to be here for a year....' So after Christmas she came back and pretty much sat home in her apartment all day playing with the cats rather than go to school because there wasn't much for her to do."

Ignored by her peers, unappreciated by her students, Arthur began turning increasingly to alcohol for comfort. For years she had been a heavy drinker, preferring to sip from a mug of vodka while people around her were having tea or coffee. "She had to have a drink to sort of smooth the edges," explained one of her Carmel friends. "It would make her easier to be around; it broke down some of these idiosyncrasies. But she never got roaring drunk. I never saw her impossible."

At North Carolina, however, Arthur occasionally did become impossible. "You couldn't talk to her when she was drinking," recalled Lavalle. "She was drinking quite a lot." Pauline Koner confirmed that Arthur "did like her liquor, more than she should have." Arthur was "a very lonely person" at this point, Koner added.

By the time of her run-in with the Winston-Salem police over the dog/trespassing incident in April 1973 (inspired by her drinking, according to her accusers), Arthur had already decided that that semester at North Carolina would be her last. Of the brouhaha, in retrospect, Bob Ward said simply that "the school was embarrassed, the police department was embarrassed." His friend Weston Hatfield, who served as Arthur's lawyer in the matter, told Ward that if he "could get Jean to pick up stakes and get out of town," no further action would be taken against her. But she needed no encouragement to leave; by the end of May she was back in Carmel, licking her wounds.

That summer, Merv Griffin invited her to appear on his television show with Frank Capra. To the amazement of everyone, she agreed to make this the occasion for her first-ever talk show appearance. Realizing that surely she would be quizzed about the dog incident, Pete Ballard cautioned her that she "shouldn't get nasty about it" because she was still on probation. He flew out to Los Angeles to accompany Arthur and Ellen Mastroianni to the Griffin set. "She was brilliant," Ballard proudly recalled. "The first thing he asked about was the dog, and she handled it beautifully; she didn't even mention Winston-Salem."

Arthur sat on her hands throughout Griffin's interview, explaining that she'd been working in the garden and that they were dirty; more likely she was afraid they would give away her age. Otherwise she was relaxed and witty, particularly in answering Griffin's inquiries about her views on the then-raging Watergate scandal. "If you really want to get on Mr. Nixon, I can let myself go," she said, volunteering that she would like to be put on his famed Enemies List as a "guest of honor." But she added that such bravery did not come easily to her. As she confessed to Griffin, "I had more courage on the screen."

Her ill-fated teaching career now behind her, Arthur was hoping to muster some of that courage for another foray into the world of acting. As she approached the age of seventy-five, Arthur found herself making one last attempt to finish her career on a winning note.

CHAPTER TWENTY-TWO
FINAL APPEAL

Six years before Sandra Day O'Connor became the first female member of the United States Supreme Court, playwrights Jerome Lawrence and Robert E. Lee anticipated the event with a fictional stage comedy about a conservative woman jurist who ascends to the highest court in the land, then finds herself in a battle of the sexes with a crotchety liberal justice modeled after William O. Douglas. Lawrence, who planned to direct the play, had already cast the woman and was looking around for an older leading man to star with her. He placed a call to his old friend Melvyn Douglas, who had played the Clarence Darrow character in Lawrence and Lee's most famous play, *Inherit the Wind*. The seventy-four-year-old Douglas explained that he was in ill health and was not sure he was up to the project. As an inducement, Lawrence threw out the name of Douglas's prospective leading lady, a woman with whom the actor had co-starred in the film *Too Many Husbands* in 1940.

"How would you feel about working with Jean Arthur?" Lawrence inquired of his friend.

"Oh Christ no!" Douglas immediately responded.

Thus were the beginnings of *First Monday in October*.

By mid-August of 1975, it was announced that Jean Arthur and Melvyn Douglas would star in the Lawrence and Lee play, scheduled to open on October 17 that year at the Cleveland Play House. The occasion would mark the sixtieth anniversary of the theater. After a month's test run in Cleveland, the play was to move on to the Kennedy Center in Washington, D.C., and then to Broadway.

Lawrence had written *First Monday* with Arthur in mind. He had befriended the actress when she was at Vassar, as a result of her interest in *The Night Thoreau Spent in Jail*. "She wrote me and said, 'I want to meet you,'" recalled Lawrence, who invited her to visit him at his house in Malibu the next time she was on the West Coast. In the summer of 1974, the year after she left North Carolina, she came to Lawrence's oceanside house "and we got to be great, great friends," the playwright said. "I really liked and admired her."

Lawrence described for Arthur the play he was writing with her in mind for the female lead, but she was noncommittal. Undeterred, he continued writing. The following summer, he showed the near-finished product to Pete Ballard, who accepted the author's summons to Malibu to broker a deal with Arthur. Ballard was favorably impressed with what he read. "He didn't have an end to it yet, but it was a damn good script," Ballard said, "and he'd written it so Jean didn't have a lot to do physically. An easy play, and fun." Then Lawrence had Arthur to his house in Malibu again, where the two of them sat reading the play on the author's patio, feet up, facing the Pacific Ocean. Arthur loved the play and said she would do it "wherever, whenever," Lawrence recalled. "She was perfect for the part."

Lawrence was aware of Arthur's history of stage dropouts, having been warned by both Garson Kanin and Cheryl Crawford that she would never stay with the play. But based on his friendship with the actress, and his conviction that she was a natural for the part, Lawrence decided to "take a chance." His partner was similarly inclined. At a party shortly after Arthur's casting in First Monday was announced, author Lee and his wife ran into their journalist friend George Eells and told him that Arthur would not falter, that it "was not going to happen this time," Eells remembered. "People were so beguiled by those early performances," Eells said. "They all believed they were going to save her."

To get the seventy-four-year-old actress ready for the part that summer in Carmel, Pete Ballard put her on a rigorous schedule, helping her with her lines and tutoring her in basic constitutional law. "She worked like a dog, and in three weeks she was perfect," he said. Then Lawrence called to say Melvyn Douglas had agreed to do the part, which greatly excited Arthur, who was unaware of his qualms about her. A crusty veteran, Douglas was as perfect for his part as Arthur was for hers. His politics were also acceptable to Arthur, who had already rejected the idea of Jimmy Stewart as her leading man because of his increasingly pronounced conservativism. Arthur especially admired Douglas's wife, Helen Gahagan, a liberal Democratic congresswoman who lost a bitter Senate contest in 1950 to a young Richard Nixon.

When Pete Ballard left Carmel to return to North Carolina, Arthur checked into the Golden Door to whip herself into physical shape. She also cut down on her drinking, turning away cocktails at a coming-out party at Lawrence's in late August with the explanation that she was allowed only one drink a day and that she'd had her one. "She was ready,"

Pete Ballard recalled. "She was Joan of Arc on her little white horse, in her golden armor, all ready to hit the boards."

When Arthur and Lawrence headed to Cleveland in September to begin rehearsals, Ballard told each of them that if they ran into any problems, they should call him and he would fly in from Winston-Salem to lend his assistance. But in the month of rehearsals that began September 16, Ballard heard nothing. He called Ellen Mastroianni, who had remained in Carmel as Arthur had asked, and inquired, "What do we hear from Cleveland?" Arthur's closest friend reported that she hadn't heard anything.

But all was far from quiet on the Cleveland front. After being set up in a new apartment complex in downtown Cleveland, Arthur began complaining about the accommodations. "She was very fussy about the food," Lawrence recalled. "There wasn't room service in a place like that so we had to have kids in the cast run out and get her her meals. She would scream about it." Then rehearsals began, and Lawrence and Arthur began arguing over her costume. "She said, 'I won't wear a dress, I want to wear pants all the way through,'" Lawrence remembered. "I said, 'You can't, this is about the first woman on the Supreme Court, you don't turn her immediately into a man.' And she said, 'I can't wear a dress.'"

Arthur never did accede to the pleas of her director, or those of costume designer Estelle Painter, that she put on a dress. Instead she wore pantsuits and other items from her personal wardrobe. "We all felt it wasn't appropriate for the character, but it was appropriate for her to be comfortable," Painter recalled.

Indeed, the play's cast members, mostly drawn from the Play House's close-knit resident company, went out of their way to make Arthur feel at home. "We tried to give her her space," said Eugene Hare, who played one of the justices. She remained stand-offish, once telling cast member Earl Keyes to stop bringing her roses for her dressing room and to "leave them in the garden where they belong." But occasionally she allowed herself to be drawn out. Cast member Robert Snook, who thought her unapproachable at first, found her charming once he came to know her. "I just took the bull by the horns and invited her to dinner one night," he said. She came to his apartment, along with Mel Douglas and Lawrence, and expressed fascination with Snook's library, going through every book he had and wanting to discuss the fine points of each. "She sat on the floor all night and played with my two schnauzers," Snook recalled. "The talk was bright and fun." But as far as he knew, no one else in the cast ever socialized with the reticent actress.

Besides her fights with Lawrence over food and costumes, Arthur was having misgivings during rehearsals about her leading man. Everyone else adored Mel Douglas, who, in contrast to Arthur, was a model of compatibility. "An absolute gentleman," said Eugene Hare, who served as Douglas's personal assistant for the play. "This man should have written a book on how an actor should behave." Hare recalled once being asked by Douglas to find some cigarettes for him, and "you'd have thought he'd asked me to murder someone." He also happened to be, in the view of everyone, wonderful in the role.

Except that he had trouble remembering his lines. This infuriated his leading lady, who had made a point of being fully prepared from day one. Douglas had arrived in Cleveland, according to what Arthur later told Pete Ballard, "not well at all, living on pills," having learned none of his lines. "She said he only had half a stomach, he was taking all those damn pills, he wasn't even ready," Pete Ballard said. Arthur also told Ellen Mastroianni that Douglas arrived at rehearsals late and had "no discipline."

But for everyone else, Douglas's rendition of the role more than made up for any such shortcomings. "Mel Douglas's performance was itself worth the price of admission," thought Allan Leatherman, who played the second male lead, an Everyman character. "He'd blow a line and say the hell with *that* and go on and hit the next one even better," Leatherman said.

For all her problems, Arthur survived the rehearsal period. And while she was not the cast favorite that Mel Douglas was, she held her own with him on stage. Director Lawrence felt she was good in rehearsals, especially in her first big encounter with Douglas over women's rights. After he has repeatedly called her "Madam Jus-*tess*," she finally shoots back, "Would you call a female governor a gover-*ness*?" She also was excellent,

Lawrence thought, in the Senate confirmation scene, in which she declared that justice has no gender, and reacted angrily to being called a "lady" by the lawmakers. "I'm a woman. An 'ex-girl,'" her character pointed out. "What has sex got to do with being a judge? Somebody with the capacity to bear children is gifted, not crippled."

Lawrence and Lee remained optimistic about the production, as did Cleveland's theater community, which quickly turned the entire run into an advance sellout. A gala black tie party was arranged for opening night to coincide with the sixtieth anniversary of the Play House, which also happened to be Arthur's seventy-fifth birthday. To celebrate the occasion, Robert Snook baked two birthday cakes and brought them to the theater that evening, expecting to continue the party after the formal affair concluded. But Arthur would attend no parties that night.

"On opening night she was very down," Lawrence recalled. "She didn't give a performance at all, she kind of walked through it." Out-of-town producers and critics were disappointed at what they had flown in to see; one of them was Herman Shumlin, who had staged *The Bride of Torozko* when Arthur starred in it in 1934, and who had gone on to direct numerous Broadway plays, including *Inherit the Wind*. Shumlin was interested in bringing *First Monday* to New York until he saw Arthur's performance, which "appalled" him, Lawrence recalled. *Time* magazine found the play a "draggy, flaccid, unconvincing brief," and laid much of the blame at Arthur's doorstep. She "still has the raspy little girl's voice that people remember…and a spunky air of perennial optimism," *Time*'s reviewer wrote. "But the stage has never been her home, and it is not now." The Cleveland daily papers, influenced by civic pride, were much more positive, with the *Press* terming Arthur "excellent in a role that is not so showy as it might be," and the *Plain Dealer* calling her, along with Douglas, "disarming and enchanting." But the Chagrin Valley *Times*, a small suburban weekly, voted with the out-of-towners. It called Arthur's performance "totally emotionless," and her stage movements "totally unnatural," as if she were "concerned only with the quality of the squeak in her voice."

"It wasn't fair to have that opening night performance reviewed," Lawrence said. "Because she was better." She did improve over the next several performances, but it was too late; her confidence was gone. During the show on October 29, the eleventh of the run, Arthur appeared weak and coughed throughout her performance. The next morning she checked herself into the Cleveland Clinic, where doctors found her to be suffering from a viral infection, the same affliction that drove her from several previous plays. She told the show's publicity man that she was not going on that night, but she did not bother to inform Lawrence, which infuriated the director.

Rather than cancel the evening's performance, Lawrence pressed Dee Hoty, one of the Play House's apprentice actresses, into service. The barely twenty-year-old woman was not technically Arthur's understudy; her main job had been to serve as the star's driver and errand girl. But she did know most of the lines, having filled in during rehearsals when Arthur was too tired to continue. Over the course of the day Hoty learned the rest of the play, and she made it through the performance that night, crying like a baby through the curtain call after Mel Douglas kissed her. It was the first big break for an actress who went on to a successful Broadway career. Her Play House colleagues might have predicted her success; as Eugene Hare remembered, "when we were backstage the night Dee took over, we all said to each other, 'Oh *that's* what it means, *that's* what the scene was about. Dee made sense out of the play I think for the first time."

But Dee Hoty was too young for the part, and union rules required that she be replaced by a member of Actors' Equity after a few more performances. Edith Owen, a resident character actress, came in and finished the play, which closed on November 17 after a four-week run. The production did not make it to Broadway.

After her no-show on October 30, Arthur spent another week in the hospital. On November 7 she officially withdrew for good and caught a plane to California. She said no good-byes. *Variety* reported that it was at least the fourth time she had pulled out of a legitimate stage production "for physical or possibly emotional reasons."

While Arthur never told her friend Pete Ballard exactly what her version of events was, he gathered that she had expected Lawrence to spend more time rewriting the play, which needed much work. Eventually, she became disenchanted when the changes were never made—the same objection she voiced about *Born Yesterday* and *Stephanie Blake*. "He never got around to it because he was busy directing, and Jerry's just not a director," Ballard theorized. "This was auld lang syne Ohio, and Jean never understood this. So Jerry became the villain."

Two years later, Lawrence managed to resurrect *First Monday* in a revised version starring Henry Fonda and Jane Alexander. The play enjoyed great success at the Kennedy Center in Washington, D.C., and later on Broadway. "We did some major rewriting and made it much better," Lawrence explained. Eventually it was turned into a movie with Walter Matthau and Jill Clayburgh that opened shortly after Sandra Day O'Connor's nomination.

"When the play got to D.C. it was just a sensation," Lawrence recalled. All the Supreme Court justices came to see it, and William O. Douglas, who had retired the week before the Cleveland production was staged, threw a cast party at the Court's principal conference room, where no similar event had ever been held. "Warren Burger came three times and kept raving about it," Lawrence said. "It was a great, great experience and I'm sorry that Jean Arthur missed it, because if she had behaved she would have gone on and done it and it would have been one of the triumphs of her career."

Lawrence, an author first and director second, once thought that a director who wasn't as emotionally involved in the play as he was might have handled it better. But his friend Garson Kanin assured him that no one could have made a difference, and the Play House cast tended to agree. "Jerry handled her with kid gloves because we were told that we wouldn't keep her for the run," said Allan Leatherman. "She just lacked self-confidence at the end. It was a pity."

"It was the other end of the rainbow, I guess," said Earl Keyes, who found a very different person from the one he remembered from Arthur's films forty years before. "My God, is this the young heroic gal who was afraid of nobody?" he asked himself upon seeing the diminutive actress for the first time in person. As for her leaving the show, he attributed it to "probably a very deep-seated psychological thing."

Earl Keyes was right: Jean Arthur's departure from *First Monday* was inevitable, a reaction that had its source in some psychological wellspring that was tapped every time she appeared on stage after securing fame as a movie star. It sprang not only from a lack of confidence, but from a positive desire she could not control—a desire to escape from responsibility and (reversing her hero Erich Fromm's phrase) to escape to freedom.

Even after deserting his family when he was forty-six years old, Hubert Greene never stopped loving them. Indeed, he kept coming back to them, to be near if not with them, because he could not stay away long from those he loved. But he could not stay with them for long, either, for ultimately freedom meant more to Hubert Greene than did love. Love carried with it too much responsibility, too much of the thing that Hubert Greene sought to escape when he went west to become a cowboy.

Though she disdained stardom, Jean Arthur had loved being an actress, had cherished her favorite roles, had never stopped loving the feeling that acting brought to her. Even as she feared the camera, and the stage, for the risk of failure they posed, she kept coming back to them for the opportunity they offered to win back, at some subconscious level, the fatherly love she had come to doubt. But she also kept abandoning her career, kept leaving plays that she ostensibly loved, kept seeking her freedom from the challenges and responsibilities that acting imposed. This pattern of escape, learned from her father, was the real reason Jean Arthur continually shrank from giving performances that her audiences undoubtedly would have embraced. For her, too, freedom was more important than love.

From her father, Arthur also learned that escape was possible, at least periodically, through alcohol, and that animals could effectively substitute for people as an object of love. But beyond this, she extended her pattern of escape to a broad-based retreat from the real and personal, which she found dull and conformist, toward the imagined and whimsical. "The only people who lead dull lives are the unimaginative ones," she once said.

Jean Arthur

Louella Parsons thought Arthur's aversion to conformity was the real explanation for her idiosyncrasies. An experienced observer of the acting personality, Parsons didn't buy the conventional wisdom that Arthur suffered from an inferiority complex. "No, I never believed that Jean Arthur suffered from any kind of a complex," Parsons said, "unless you want to call doing exactly what you want, at exactly the time you feel like doing it, a 'complex.'"

As Arthur similarly explained just before the opening of *First Monday*, in one of the last interviews she ever gave, "You have one life, you do what you want to do. Some people like to do what everybody else does—go to parties and talk about nothing. I don't happen to." The "only real reason for living," she said, "is doing what you want to do, or trying to, anyway." For the remaining years of her life, Arthur would keep on doing just what she wanted—or trying to, anyway.

272

CHAPTER TWENTY-THREE

FINAL YEARS

*P*utting Driftwood up for sale was not the way Arthur wanted to begin the rest of her life, but she had no choice; she was running out of money. A financial advisor in Chicago with investment discretion had dissipated much of her wealth over the years, and she knew she would never work again. Nothing was left to do but sell her beloved home.

The house she bought for $20,000 in 1946 was now worth nearly half a million dollars, a hefty nest egg for a seventy-five-year-old woman. But her new financial advisor, a local banker named Peter Wright, saw a problem: if she were to trade down for a smaller and less expensive residence, as she planned, Arthur would face a prohibitive capital gains tax that would wipe out much of her profit. So Wright worked out a deal whereby she would sell Driftwood and use the proceeds to buy a new house, which she would turn around and sell at a bargain price to a pair of charities. Wright selected the Robert Louis Stevenson School in Pebble Beach, and the Monterey Institute for International Studies, neither of which had any particular connection to Arthur except as willing participants in the arrangement. Under the deal, Arthur could live in the new house the rest of her life, the charities would each inherit half of the house on her death and she would pay only a nominal capital gains tax.

Now all she needed was to find the house. She spotted a candidate one evening in 1977 during an after-dinner walk with Pete Ballard, who was visiting from North Carolina. It was a small, one-story bungalow at 2313 Bayview Avenue, a couple of blocks west of the Point and about a minute's walk from Ellen Mastroianni's home. The "For Sale" sign that Arthur spied would have been easy to miss, as the house was nearly hidden from view by an overgrown cover of green foliage on the front fence, giving it the feel of a small private hideaway.

Unable to sleep that night, Arthur roused Ballard from bed at 4 a.m., grabbed a flashlight and dragged him along to take another look at the house. Undaunted by his reminder that she'd already been arrested for trespassing once before, Arthur led Ballard on a tour of the property and declared, emphatically, "that's the house." She stayed up the rest of the night and bought it the next morning, for $165,000.

Soon thereafter, Driftwood had a buyer, a doctor from Salinas who paid $450,000. Doris Day had come to see the property earlier, but Arthur stopped her at the gate and told her that because of the delicate ground covering the house was not suitable for dogs, which she knew Day owned in droves. "This is a house for cats," Arthur explained. "If you want dogs, go up to Carmel Valley, buy ten acres and grow all the dogs you want."

It did not take Arthur long to make the transition to her new residence.

"This was a whole new decoration project for her," recalled Pete Ballard. Remarkably, she was able to fit almost all her belongings into it. She added an English garden in the front yard and an Oriental one in the back, and decorated everything inside in the color of spider-web gray. The ocean view out the back window, though less spectacular than Driftwood's, was still impressive. "It was marvelous the way she sort of mentally got out of one house and into the other," said Pete Ballard.

Once settled in, Arthur rarely ventured out. She continued to drive her Jaguar around the tortuous roads of Carmel, but she gave up driving around 1980 when she suffered a blowout at the top of a steep grade just as she was beginning to head down the hill. Frightened by the experience, from then on she had Ellen Mastroianni and others drive her wherever she wanted to go.

Arthur still "smoked like hell and drank too much," said her financial advisor Wright, but eventually she gave up cigarettes and cut down on her drinking. With Wright's help she had straightened herself out financially as well; in addition to the proceeds from her sale of Driftwood, she received about $60,000 a year from a combination of actors' pensions, Social Security and an annuity she had purchased years before. "She wasn't as well off as she should have been" because her mind had always been strictly "on artistic things," said her realtor, Bruce Jones. But she had enough to live on.

What she did, mostly, was tend to her gardens, her cats and her intellect. Her reading often centered on a subject that had long concerned her—the tension between science and religion. As she observed as early as 1948, between her stints at Stephens and Bennington Colleges, "Some scientists have scoffed at religion; some churchmen have fought the teachings of science. We need both." Accordingly, she sought out thinkers who attempted to reconcile modern scientific humanism with old-style Christian ethics. She discovered the historian Arnold Toynbee, who expressed hope that a merger of the world's great religions might rescue what he called the "post-Christian century," and she avidly read Christian existentialist Paul Tillich, who longed for a religion without myths. Her love for Shaw, the great exponent of Creative Evolution, led her to Pierre

Teilhard de Chardin, the Jesuit theologian and paleontologist, who believed, as did Shaw, that the salvation of mankind lay in the development of a community of higher intelligence and consciousness (symbolized, for Chardin, in Christ, as Joan of Arc embodied the same idea for Shaw). She also embraced anthropologist Loren Eiseley, whose modern interpretation of Darwin sounded positively Arthurian. Man, he wrote, is only "one of the many appearances of the thing called life, not its perfect image, for life is multitudinous and emergent in the stream of time."

These men believed, as did Arthur, that individual creativity is the source of all human progress. They also shared with her a certain impatience—a disgust, even—with human beings as they are, and a vague, idealized yearning for what humans might become, biologically speaking, in the future. It was as if they felt they were born a million years too soon.

Another Arthur favorite was the liberal editor of the *Saturday Review*, Norman Cousins, a long-time champion of nuclear controls and world government who became even better known in the late 1970s as an advocate of the physical healing powers of the mind. His views struck a responsive chord in Arthur, whose Christian Science upbringing, as well as her repeated stage illnesses, gave her an appreciation for the connection between mind and body. When Cousins wrote, in his best-selling book *Anatomy of an Illness* (1979), that Americans were "becoming a nation of pill-grabbers and hypochondriacs, escalating the slightest ache into a searing ordeal," Arthur could not help but see herself in that mirror. She corresponded with Cousins for a time, and rarely saw a doctor the rest of her life (although she never rejected medicine as a matter of principle).

One thing about which she remained dogmatic, though, was her past: she wanted nothing to do with it. She refused to sign autographs, sit for photographs or answer fan mail (her attitude, however, did not prevent her from writing a fan letter to the actor Christopher Reeve, on whom she developed a school-girl crush; flabbergasted, but flattered, the *Superman* star obliged her by sending an autographed picture and a personal note). When distant relatives, such as second and third cousins, looked her up in Carmel they were unceremoniously turned away from the doorstep. Even cherished memories were not immune. One night shortly before moving from Driftwood, Arthur threw her costume from *Peter Pan* in the fire. She was "paranoid about being in somebody's collection," her friend Pete Ballard explained. "She wasn't interested in museums."

When the American Film Institute honored Frank Capra with its Life Achievement Award in the spring of 1982, practically all the major living stars Capra had directed, including Bette Davis, Claudette Colbert, Jimmy Stewart and Donna Reed, showed up to pay tribute. But not Jean Arthur. "She's just a hermit," Capra told Tom Shales of the Washington *Post*. "She doesn't do very well in crowds, and she doesn't do very well with people, and she doesn't do very well with life," the director said on another occasion, "but she does very well as an actress."

It was to Capra, however, as well as to the advent of the videocassette recorder, that Arthur owed her rediscovery by many thousands of people who were unfamiliar with her work. She had never ceased being revered by younger filmmakers and movie buffs; as filmographer Buck Rainey wrote in 1984, "Arthur, more than any other contemporary actress, excepting Garbo, is considered a legend among fans." But it was not until the VCR revolution of the 1980s that Arthur became a recognizable star again to general audiences. Among the first videocassettes released for home viewing was Capra's *It's a Wonderful Life*, which helped spark a renewed interest in Capra's other classic films—including *Mr. Deeds Goes to Town*, *You Can't Take It With You* and *Mr. Smith Goes to Washington*. And when moviegoers sought out these Capra films, inevitably they stumbled upon the director's "favorite actress," Jean Arthur.

In an early scene from the 1984 comedy, *Irreconcilable Differences*, Ryan O'Neal, playing a budding young filmmaker whose everyday speech is peppered with references to old movies, turns tenderly to girlfriend Shelley Long in bed and tells her that he sees in her "exactly what Jimmy Stewart saw in Jean Arthur...[in] *Mr. Smith Goes to Washington*." Audiences knew just what O'Neal meant, or at least they knew where they could go to find out. America's "forgotten actress," as one journalist called her on the occasion of her birthday in 1985, was suddenly showing up everywhere on video. In addition to the Capra films, she could readily be seen in such classics as *The Plainsman*, *Only Angels Have Wings*, *The*

Devil and Miss Jones, The More the Merrier and *Shane*. And her list of leading men was the equal of any Hollywood actress, before or since: Jimmy Stewart, Gary Cooper, Cary Grant, Charles Boyer, William Powell, Ronald Colman, John Wayne, Ray Milland, William Holden, Joel McCrea and Alan Ladd.

In 1985, Arthur appeared prominently in George Stevens Jr.'s documentary tribute to his father, *George Stevens: A Filmmaker's Journey*. Although she declined to follow other Stevens colleagues who appeared on camera to offer anecdotes, Arthur's film clips were as impressive as anyone's. "She doesn't have to sell her work because each generation discovers her unique talents for themselves," Michael Blowen of the Boston *Globe* observed a few months later. "She left us with a legacy not of publicity and fluff but of style and substance," he wrote. "She is an exception to the stereotype of Hollywood as a factory where stars were stamped out on thin tin. She was, and remains, an original."

Roddy McDowall, who felt the same way about her, did what he could to promote her legacy, telling interviewers that this or that appealing actress of the moment—Annie Potts, for example—reminded him of Jean Arthur. An irrepressible chronicler of the careers of his many friends, Roddy dutifully taped Arthur's movies whenever they appeared on television and created a personal library for her (to which she paid scant attention). He thought it a crime that she was never honored with life achievement awards or special Oscars like those given to so many of her contemporaries, and he joined a small but vocal chorus of film lovers who perennially advocated that Arthur be given some such tribute. "Of course, she wouldn't have shown up, and it was well known that she wouldn't have shown up," he lamented.

Next to Roddy McDowall, the most influential advocate of Arthur's cause was Dr. Ralph Wolfe, an English professor at Bowling Green State University in Ohio and curator of the university's Gish Film Theater. Wolfe was vacationing in Carmel in 1984 when he decided to seek out the reclusive actress, who had long been one of his favorites. At the time, he was rehearsing for the grandfather role in a community theater production of *You Can't Take It With You*, and he was determined to have her sign his play program. After promptly answering his knock at her door on Bayview, Arthur explained that she did not give autographs. As Wolfe later wrote:

> I replied by saying that I understood and appreciated her position. I then told her how much I liked her film work and that we used *Shane* in our literature and film class at [Bowling Green]. Her interest piqued by this remark, she immediately said in that inimitable voice, "Let's sit in the garden and talk." We then had an hour's conversation in which I shared my enthusiasm for her work and she recalled her experiences in making films.

During the course of their conversation, Arthur casually remarked that she intended to burn all of her memorabilia, a bare-bones collection of albums containing publicity stills from a few of her movies, newspaper reviews of her earliest stage appearances and a scrapbook of photos and other mementoes from *Peter Pan*. She included in her "to burn" list a few treasured photographs of her mother, father and brothers, as she had no relatives to inherit them. Dr. Wolfe immediately offered Bowling Green as a haven for her effects, which she eventually agreed to donate to the college after her death.

Ralph Wolfe was to become the unofficial president of an Arthur admiration society headquartered at Bowling Green. In 1987, he presented a retrospective showing of fifteen of her films, and the following year he persuaded the university board of trustees to confer upon her the honorary degree of Doctor of Performing Arts, which he presented to her personally in Carmel (in appreciation, she autographed a picture of herself for both Wolfe and the university). Wolfe also encouraged a student acquaintance, Steven Bauer, to write a laudatory commentary on her work, which was published in Bowling Green's *Journal of Popular Film & Television*. Bauer, too, gained Arthur's friendship over the course of several pilgrimages he made to Carmel.

Ralph Wolfe and Steve Bauer were among the few new acquaintances Arthur allowed into her life in the 1980s. But there was one old acquaintance who suddenly reappeared.

❧

After divorcing Joan Caulfield in 1959, Frank Ross continued to produce movies, but none of them approached the success he achieved with *The Robe*. He married beauty pageant winner Joan Bradshaw, with whom he had a son, Zan, in 1970, but they later divorced. In 1973 he produced his final film, *Maurie*, one of the less successful sports tragedy tearjerkers of the period.

Financially well-off, Ross retired to a comfortable high-rise condominium on Wilshire Boulevard in Los Angeles. But he became more private and withdrawn. "Frank was very taciturn," said Doug Morrow, his friend and co-producer of *Maurie*. "He stayed to himself quite a bit in later years," confirmed his long-time secretary, Catharine Pace.

Then around 1982, Frank Ross had a crazy idea. He had not seen Jean Arthur in person since their divorce in 1949; what if he were to look her up now? He placed a call to Carmel and asked his former wife if he could come visit. To his amazement, and even more to hers, she said yes.

"The son of a bitch is coming up," she told Pete Ballard, who asked her if she had lost her mind. "She said 'no, he's just getting nostalgic and he's getting old, and he said of all his wives he loved me best,'" Ballard recalled.

"For years she had *nothing* good to say about him," remembered Frances Arriola. She and her husband, Gus, warned Arthur that she should be nice to Ross when he came up, but the actress expressed doubt that she could be. Nevertheless, when he showed up and took her to dinner, she managed to act civilized enough so that he planned to make another visit.

Not long after, Ross came calling again, this time with his twelve-year-old son Zan. Arthur took an immediate liking to the boy, showering him with candy and gifts. But by the end of his next visit, Zan was driving her crazy. "Don't bring the kid again," she told Ross. But later she changed her mind and allowed Zan to return, after which they came to enjoy each other's company. The three of them got together five or six times a year, usually with Ellen Mastroianni, for dinner one night and lunch the next day.

"Frank was a nice, friendly chap, very pleasant," said Mastroianni. "He was always smiling, never saw him angry. He got a little boring, though, would tell you pretty much the same stories."

"My father loved to tell all the old stories about old Hollywood," Zan Ross recalled of their get-togethers with Arthur. If Arthur was the subject of any of his reminiscences, she would begin slowly slouching down in her chair, then more and more until, by the end of the story, she was practically on the floor. She "did it for laughs," according to Zan, who thought her "a very funny person."

All of her friends agreed with that assessment. "She's one of the wittiest people I've known," said Mastroianni. "Not in terms of jokes. She doesn't tell jokes. She never gets it. It's really in terms of the way she says things, how she expresses herself."

"You couldn't live with her and not laugh all the time," said Nell Eurich. "She's fun to talk to, no doubt about it," echoed Barbara Baxley.

Ross clearly looked forward to his visits to his former wife. "Give me a good haircut, I'm going up to see Jean," he would tell his barber, Lou Merino. Ross was also genuinely interested in Arthur's well-being. He helped her secure some actors' pension money to which she was entitled but had never pursued. He had his lawyers look over the manner in which Peter Wright was handling her finances, and pronounced himself satisfied. He called her at least once a month to see how she was doing.

Arthur's attitude toward Ross during this period was more difficult to gauge. Outwardly she was inclined to forgive, if not forget, whatever transgressions she had charged him with. She sparred with him, good-naturedly, as if it were a game. "I've never seen anyone be able to talk to my uncle like Jean could," recalled Wendy Ross, Frank's niece. "He had a little bit of a shell around him, and Jean was able to say things to him that none of us would dare say."

But in conversation with friends, Arthur often belittled her ex-husband. For one thing, she complained that his visits were becoming tedious. "'He's so *boring*,' she'd say," remembered Frances Arriola. For several years Arthur refused even to introduce the Arriolas to her former husband, explaining that they would find him too dull. Finally they went to dinner together in Carmel, found him to be charming and told Arthur so. But then the actress "started telling terrible stories about their life together," Mrs. Arriola recalled, as if Arthur were trying to make sure her friends understood where she thought the blame for her failed marriage lay.

Barbara Baxley, who'd listened to plenty of Frank Ross-bashing over the years, recognized that time had not erased the sting of failure Arthur felt over her marriage. In an autobiography she was working on at the time of her death in 1990, Baxley wrote the following passage concerning her friend, whom she likened to her mother:

> [I]n some areas Jean and Mama are a lot alike. As "women" I suppose they each failed. Well at least Mama had two kids. But where men were concerned they did fail. Or more to my way of thinking the men failed them. I guess they were too raucous, independent and vital.

Arthur's decision not to become a mother was a mystery to many of her friends. Until Frank Ross confided in his son Zan, only the actress and her husband knew that she was unable to have children. Whether this caused her great disappointment is unknown, as it was one of the many personal issues she never discussed. Still, she certainly could have adopted if she had wanted to. In fact, when she was thirty-six she said that she'd "thought of children a lot of late. I'd like to have twins and then, a couple of years later, more twins." Then in 1939, asked if she regretted not having children, she responded, "Yes, I'm sorry I haven't five."

However, others who knew her well were not surprised by her choice. "She never talked about not having children, and I never asked," said Ellen Mastroianni. "I guess they just didn't fit into her life when she was able to have them." Gus Arriola thought she eschewed children because she "would have regarded them as competitors." Barbara Baxley felt that Arthur "didn't need them the way some women do. She had enough stimulation from elsewhere—her work, her books, her animals."

Perhaps related to her choice, Arthur appeared to have something against playing mothers. With the exception of *The Most Precious Thing in Life* in 1934, she never appeared on film in a maternal role until *The*

Impatient Years, in 1944, after which she retired from making movies. She played a mother again in *Shane*, but she did not enjoy the part and she made it her last one in film. She turned down numerous movie offers in the years following, once explaining, "I don't want to play 'mamas.'"

None of her stage appearances, either, featured her in a mother role. This was true even of the plays she appeared in after the age of sixty. In *The Freaking Out of Stephanie Blake*, she played a spinster, and in *First Monday in October*, a childless widow. Questioned about that status, her character indignantly asks a Senate panel, "Does the Constitution say a Supreme Court Justice has to be a mother?"

Although her television series cast her as a widowed mother, lawyer Patricia Marshall's eccentricities tended to obscure her maternal characteristics. But beyond that was something else that Arthur's television son, Ron Harper, found curious. As he recalled, she did not like him calling her "mom" or "mother" in rehearsals for the show; there was "something sensitive to her in that," he said. As a result, the scripts were rewritten so that he always referred to her as "Mrs. M."

If Frank Ross was telling his son Zan the truth about Jean Arthur's infertility, it might explain her strong aversion to playing maternal characters. But Ross may have been shading the truth; he may have really meant that his wife *would* not have children, not that she *could* not. If that was the case, she had much in common with the little girl who, as Karen Horney put it, "is half afraid of experiencing this mysterious and dreadful event in the future and at the same time is half afraid she may never have the opportunity to experience it," and therefore "escapes these uneasy feelings...by flight into a desired or imagined masculine role." This flight from the female role is exacerbated, Horney pointed out, when the girl's early love for her father fails "due to disappointments in the father, or due to guilt feelings toward the mother." One way or another, it was what happened to Gladys Greene that prevented Jean Arthur from having children.

Since the first flowering of screwball comedy in the 1930s, interest in the genre had never completely disappeared. But periodically there have been especially strong flourishes of nostalgia for this uniquely American art form and its stars. The early 1970s was one such period, and the late 1980s was another. And with these, necessarily, came renewed focus on the unique contributions of Jean Arthur to romantic comedy. "No one was more closely identified with the screwball comedy than Jean Arthur," wrote James Harvey, whose 1987 book *Romantic Comedy* devoted an entire chapter to Arthur's place in the genre. Ed Sikov, in his *Screwball* (1989), opined that no other actress appeared in more classic romantic comedies than Arthur had. And in *The Runaway Bride* (1990), Elizabeth Kendall wrote, in a chapter entitled "Capra and Arthur," that in *Mr. Deeds* Arthur gave "what may be the most complete and thought-out performance of any of Capra's romantic-comedy heroines." With notices such as these, Arthur was firmly re-established among the pantheon of screwball actresses, such as Loy, Lombard, Colbert and Stanwyck, who were more familiar to the modern public.

Though she continued to turn down interview requests ("Quite frankly, I'd rather have my throat slit," she told one beseecher), she publicly surfaced for select friends and colleagues. In early 1988 she taped a greeting for a Frank Capra film series shown at the Museum of Modern Art in New York, saying she wished she "could have it to do over again." That same year she called Jimmy Stewart, with whom she had not spoken in years, to say she was sorry for not attending a tribute to him at a film festival in nearby Monterey. And in early 1989 she startled Roddy McDowall by letting him publish a couple of his recent photographs of her in his celebrity picture book, *Double Exposure: Take Two*. The photographs, which showed her smiling brightly, wearing short white bangs, a button sweater and straight-leg pants, were the first of her to be published in more than twenty years.

But she never got to appreciate them. On May 25, 1989, Arthur fell and broke her hip, suffered a stroke that caused significant brain damage, and was left an invalid. Thus began a long, inexorable decline that continued for another two years.

Her loyal companion, Ellen Mastroianni, tended to her constantly, supervising a pair of nurses hired to provide twenty-four-hour care. "She's helped me before and now I'm helping her," her friend explained. Mastroianni administered the meals, paid the bills and handled the mail, which included at least one fan letter a day, sometimes as many as half a dozen, from young film buffs as far away as Germany and Estonia. She monitored the visitors and telephone calls, which gradually reduced themselves to Arthur's closest friends. "She's just a helpless invalid," Mastroianni said a year after the stroke. "She doesn't know the time of day." When informed in February 1990 that Frank Ross had died (of complications following brain surgery), all that Arthur could manage was a feeble "Oh."

In August 1990, over the course of several hours of interviews, the seventy-nine-year-old Mastroianni spoke both lovingly and candidly of her friend of more than thirty years, who was then eighty-nine:

> I think people had a misconception of what she was like. They always thought of her as stand-offish, not wanting to be bothered with people. In its own way it's true enough. She didn't let many people see what she was really like. So there was no way they could know that she was just a pleasant, intelligent woman who was friendly enough and cheerful and very witty.

Asked what was going on inside her friend, Mastroianni gave a long pause. "I think," she hesitated, "she sometimes had an inferiority complex. I think that's true. I don't know why, you know she accomplished so much from humble beginnings." Echoing what Arthur herself once said, her friend ventured that she had turned to acting to become "somebody else."

One question Mastroianni had no difficulty in answering, though it was contrary to the answer provided by most of Arthur's other close friends, was whether the actress had been a happy person. "Oh, I think so," she responded almost instantaneously.

> Yes indeed. She was very philosophical. She wasn't given to moods, depression. I never saw her depressed. No, no. She was happy. She had a lot of stuff going on inside that you didn't

realize was going on. And she had a lot of inner resources that made her happy. She read a lot. She loved classical music. She still listens to it a little bit today. It seems to somehow distract her a little bit, put her in a different frame of mind. Once in a while you see her smiling while she's listening to it. So I would say she was essentially a happy person. That was my impression of her.

This happiness flowed despite what Mastroianni acknowledged was Arthur's general aversion to people. "She just didn't like people around that much. She's essentially a loner. She likes people around when she wants them around. She didn't need a lot of people to make her happy. That's the only way to be if you can achieve it."

Among the inner resources supporting Arthur's peace of mind was her personal pantheistic creed. "She loved all kinds of life," remarked Mastroianni. "Any kind of life, anything that had life, birds and animals and plants. That's where she got her happiness from." To Arthur, God and life were one, moving freely through a universe of unending creation.

The loss of freedom that Arthur sustained as a result of her stroke was more painful than any physical suffering she had to endure. Mastroianni recalled Arthur telling her, in a lucid moment, that "she never wanted it to be this way." Her friend thus took care to ensure that the actress was not denied her dignity. "I'd like to show you her house but I'm not gonna let you see Jean," she told the author of this book in Carmel in 1990. "I want you to remember Jean as you see her in pictures. If you see her it might confuse you."

In June 1991, the expense of round-the-clock care forced Arthur to move to a nursing home, the Carmel Convalescent Hospital, where her brother Don had committed suicide in 1967. She would seek a similar end, though by a more passive route. She so hated her confinement that she just stopped eating and "wanted to die," said Peter Wright. "She gave up finally," confirmed Mastroianni. Roddy McDowall visited Arthur there but found her hard to recognize. "She had drifted so by then," he recalled.

On June 19, 1991, at 3:20 a.m., Jean Arthur died at the age of ninety. The cause of death was listed as heart failure. In accordance with her wishes, no funeral service was held. As planned, she was cremated and her ashes scattered at sea by Mastroianni off Carmel Point, where Arthur had buried her mother and oldest brother before her.

By her will, last revised in 1978, she left her entire estate to Peter Wright; had he predeceased her, it would have gone to the Humane Society of the United States in Washington, D.C. Ellen Mastroianni, another obvious candidate for inheritance, had often told Arthur she didn't need the money. In the end, the value of the estate turned out to be only about $20,000.

In a twist of fate that went largely unnoticed, Arthur's death was preceded by only a few hours by that of Joan Caulfield, who succumbed to cancer at age sixty-four on the evening of June 18 in Los Angeles. Their obituaries appeared on the same page of many newspapers, often side by side, without mentioning that both had been married to Frank Ross. The coincidence did not escape Ross's third wife, Joan; as Zan Ross later quipped, his mother laid low for a while after hearing the news.

Although Arthur had not appeared in a movie in more than forty years, the press reaction to her death was substantial and worldwide. Her passing was reported on national network news, in *Time, Newsweek, U.S. News & World Report*, and in lengthy obituaries in the *Times*es of New York, Los Angeles and London. *Variety* devoted an entire page to the woman it called "an enigmatic and often rebellious figure in Hollywood and in the theater." Film critic and author Leonard Maltin, reporting her death on *Entertainment Tonight* with a showing of several film clips, told viewers, "You deserve to discover Jean Arthur." Jimmy Stewart, advised of his one-time leading lady's death, called her "a very rare and special talent."

Britain's David Shipman, among the world's foremost film historians and a long-time admirer of Arthur's work, was especially perceptive in his obituary:

> The underlying characteristic of her playing, no matter what
> the role, was that the world was a funny place, but not fun. Her

comic genius was founded in a combination of fear, sadness and sweetness: her eyes flashed in indignation, flooded in dismay or blinked in disbelief; her lips quivered when confronted with injustice; but she could also assume a bold assurance of being believed no matter how blatantly she was lying.

She spoke with great individuality, as they all did: but we may note that she, like [Margaret] Sullavan, like Judy Garland, like Audrey Hepburn, had the ability to turn every other statement into a question, as though afraid of being certain about anything.

Charles Champlin, the long-time film critic of the Los Angeles *Times*, was equally insightful in his assessment:

No other actress in the Hollywood galaxy was even remotely like Jean Arthur…. she was a kind of educational force in a way that neither she nor Capra nor anyone else may have thought about consciously. Perhaps to her own generation, but certainly to those of us who were coming on stream a bit later, she was a revelation.

To at least one teen-ager in a small town (though I'm sure we were a multitude), Jean Arthur suggested strongly that the ideal woman could be—ought to be—judged by her spirit as well as her beauty…. The notion of the woman as a friend and confidante, as well as someone you courted and were nuts about, someone whose true beauty was internal rather than external, became a full-blown possibility as we watched Jean Arthur.

She was nothing so banal as the girl next door, which always hints of a placid demureness, golden and empty. This was a woman of spirit, smart, free, loyal, resilient, loving, not quite tomboyish despite Calamity Jane, but someone who knew a run batted in from a run. (I speak as a teen-ager, remembering.)

… So we are left with her rich legacy of indelible performances, from Ford to "Deeds" to "Shane." And we are left as well with renewed gratitude that she shaped our dreams and, it may even be, our lives.

Of Arthur's contributions to feminism, Ellen Mastroianni spoke as convincingly as the actress could have for herself. "She lived it," Mastroianni said. "She's not a flag-waver. She wouldn't go out and demonstrate or anything like that. But she believed it. Her life is living proof of that."

Indeed, Arthur's life and career paralleled the progression of women's freedom over the century that she spanned. A "Christy Girl" model before the First World War, she was a flapper-ingenue in silent films in the twenties, a populist symbol of female survival in the Depression thirties and a star of international magnitude during the war-torn forties, when she became one of the first film actresses to produce her own vehicles. Having secured her place in cinema history, she spent nearly four decades reading, thinking and studying what pleased her, occasionally foraying out into the world of theater, television or academia, often without success, but always on her own terms. Timid in the extreme, she paradoxically summoned the courage to resist the gravitational pull of human convention. She was a Capra heroine in the movies, but in life she was finally, and most profoundly, a Shavian heroine.

"There was nothing superficial about her," said Mastroianni. It was an observation not so easily applied to Arthur's acting contemporaries. Unlike so many of them, she became more, rather than less, interesting the deeper one probed.

"I wish she'd been the kind of person who would write; I think she'd have been a marvelous writer," Mastroianni added. "Jean never kept a diary. Never put a thing on paper. In all the years I've gotten two or three letters from her."

Of course, Arthur had no more interest writing down her thoughts for the whole world to read than she had in being written or talked about. She was an exception to her idol Shaw's dictum that "An American has no sense of privacy. He does not know what it means." As Arthur had said of Hollywood, "I hated the place—not the work, but the lack of privacy, those terrible, prying fan magazine writers and all the surrounding exploitation."

Asked late in life what advice she would give to young people in the acting profession, Arthur replied that she would give none. "That would be sticking my nose in somebody else's business," she said. "Influencing their lives. And I think everybody has to find their own way."

ACKNOWLEDGMENTS

Of Arthur's friends, two deserve mention above all others. Pete Ballard was a constant source of information, leads and encouragement. He provided many introductions, helped interpret what others were telling me and commented on portions of the text, always constructively.

Ellen Mastroianni, Arthur's closest friend and her neighbor of more than thirty years, agreed to an interview for the very first time and sat patiently (with her cat Joe) for several hours of questions. She provided details of Arthur's life not previously revealed and allowed me into the actress's house to view scrapbooks and photographs. "Ellen, that wonderful Ellen," as Roddy McDowall calls her, is owed a debt of gratitude beyond anything I can repay.

Other close friends of Arthur who were interviewed about her for the first time included Nell Eurich, the late Barbara Baxley, and Carmel friends Leslie Emery and Gus and Frances Arriola. Additional Carmel-area acquaintances who spoke to me included Bruce Jones, Jean Zion, Peter Wright, Hugh Hannon, Sister Francisca (Kay Hardy), Cordner Nelson, Michael Whitcomb and Dale Hale.

I was extremely fortunate to track down most of Arthur's surviving family members, none of whom had been interviewed before about their reclusive relative. Art and Miriam Goodall spoke lovingly of Art's adoptive mother, Pearl Nelson, who was Jean Arthur's favorite aunt, and of Arthur's mother Johannah Nelson, Pearl's half-sister. The Goodalls generously provided me with numerous family photographs and with private letters from both Arthur and her mother. Also among the Nelson clan, Myrl Wyman and Vivian Linster were most helpful in providing both anecdotes and family photos. Other Nelson family members who furnished valuable information included Beatrice Gregg, John D. Nelson, Joyce Ruby (daughter of Myrl Wyman), Thelma Wexberg, Doug Foster, Muriel Nelson, Jimmie Nelson and Susie Breese Blair. Special thanks also to genealogist Marcia Luther.

Ella Greene was instrumental in putting me in touch with living descendants of Arthur's father, Hubert Greene. Other Greene family members who were especially helpful were Mary (Greene) Fraenckel, Barbara (Tanis) Fetzer, Janet Letteron, Ferdinand "Bill" Greene and Abbott Lowell Cummings. Thanks also to Greene relatives Leonard Longe, William Wernecke, Ann Parta, Mary Thorne and Carlie Coolidge (Mrs. Gomer) Richards.

Roddy McDowall's comments on Arthur's life and work were especially perceptive. Publicist John Springer gladly recounted stories from his friendship with Arthur, as did theatrical agent Helen Harvey.

Actors and actresses who appeared in films with Arthur and shared their insights with me included Ann Doran, the late Ben Johnson, Charles Lane and the late Lionel Stander. Film studio personnel I interviewed were the late director Richard Thorpe; the late Paramount assistant director Arthur Jacobson; Paramount publicist Teet Carle; and Columbia sound technician Edward Bernds.

Among the theater personnel I spoke to were producer Peter Lawrence (*Peter Pan*); producer Robert Whitehead (*Saint Joan*); playwright-director Jerome Lawrence (*First Monday in October*); and Travis Bogard, head of the Drama Department at the University of California at Berkeley.

Theater performers interviewed included Arthur's fellow cast members Mary Laslo (*Born Yesterday*); Barbara Baxley, Loren Hightower and Norman Shelly (*Peter Pan*); the late John McLiam (*Saint Joan*); the late Sidney Roger (*Saint Joan*, University of California at Berkeley production); Franklin Cover, Dena Dietrich and Barton Heyman (*The Freaking Out of Stephanie Blake*); and Eugene Hare, Allan Leatherman, Earl Keyes and Robert Snook (*First Monday in October*). I also spoke to *First Monday*'s costume designer, Estelle Painter.

Ron Harper, Arthur's co-star from *The Jean Arthur Show*, and Si Rose, who produced the show, generously shared their memories of that unsuccessful venture.

I was able to speak to several sources at each of the four colleges which Arthur attended or at which she taught.

Stephens College: faculty members Dorothy Martin and Albert Delmez; student Connie Schenck; and Registrar Bobbie Burk and Mary Wilkerson in Public Relations.

Bennington College: faculty member Edward T. ("Ned") Hall and student Letitia (Evans) Frank. Thanks also to Rebecca Stickney and David Scribner.

Vassar College: faculty members William Rothwell, Thadius Gesek and Clint Atkinson; students Nancy Barber, Joan Bogden, Diana Chace, Suzanne Palmer Dougan, Dana Kilbourn Fairbank, Joanne Gates, Marcy Kelly, Georgia Buchanan Morse, Rosalie Blooston Mosier, Carolyn Pines, Ruth Freeman Swaine and Robyn Reeves Travers. Thanks also to Genevieve Kenny and John Kurten, and to Arthur's friend from her Vassar tenure, Arthur Ward.

North Carolina School of the Arts: Chancellor Robert Ward; faculty members Pauline Koner and Leslie Hunt; and students Sandra Lavalle, Beverly Petty and Cathleen Lindsay Moulds.

I am grateful to Kevin and Zan Ross for sharing their memories of their father, Frank Ross. Joan Ross, Zan's mother and Frank Ross's third wife, was also most helpful, as was Wendy Ross, the daughter of Frank Ross's brother Richard. I also wish to thank Frank Ross's long-time friend and colleague Doug Morrow; Ross's long-time secretary Catharine Pace; and his barber of fifty years, Lou Merino.

Danny Selznick talked with great animation and insight concerning his father David O. Selznick's love affair with Arthur in the late 1920s. William Barborka spoke with love and conviction about his late father, Dr. Clifford Barborka. Paul Rosner, author of the designedly fictional (but possibly truthful?) account of Arthur's affair with Mary Martin, *The Princess and the Goblin*, could not have been more patient and helpful in explaining the derivation of that work.

Other individuals who deserve to be thanked for their help include Steve Bauer, David Chierichetti, Mary Courson, Nancy Easterbrook, the late George Eells, George Furth, Eve Golden, Larry Hart, Eleanor (Harris) Howard, Larry Imber, George Katchmer, Richard Lamparski, George Osan, Mrs. Charles Osan, Mary Ann Palumbo, James Robert Parish, Arthur Pierce, Paul Plamondon, William McDowall, Buck Rainey, Joe Savage, David Stenn, David Thomson, Ed Wyatt and Ralph Wolfe.

In addition to the individuals I interviewed, many institutions rendered invaluable assistance in my research.

New York City: New York Public Library (particularly the Library for the Performing Arts at Lincoln Center); Department of Municipal Archives; Museum of the City of New York; New York Historical Society; U.S. Bureau of the Census; New York Regional Office.

New York State: Plattsburgh Public Library; Schenectady Public Library; Howe School in Schenectady (Mrs. Levy); Southampton (Long Island) Public Library.

Portland, Maine: Portland Public Schools; Portland Public Library; Family History Center of the Church of Jesus Christ of Latter Day Saints.

Montana: Montana Historical Society, Helena (Dave Walter); Billings Public Library; Clerk of District Court, Yellowstone County (Billings).

Los Angeles: Los Angeles Public Library (particularly the History and Genealogy Department); Academy of Motion Picture Arts and Sciences, Margaret Herrick Library; American Film Institute, Louis B. Mayer Library; University of California, Los Angeles, Theater Arts Library; University of Southern California, Doheny Library; Los Angeles Superior Court; Los Angeles County Recorder's Office.

Carmel: Harrison Memorial Library; First Church of Christ, Science.

Also in California: Monterey County Clerk, Office of the Recorder; San Francisco Public Library; Riverside Public Library.

I also wish to thank Elizabeth Weitzman, who edited the final manuscript; Nancy Davidson, Andrea Meyer and Saïd Sayrafiezadeh, who handled the design and layout; and my publisher, Mel Zerman, at Limelight.

BIBLIOGRAPHY

BOOKS

Allen, Frederick Lewis. *Only Yesterday*. New York: Harper & Row, 1931.

Ansbacher, Heinz L., and Rowena R. Ansbacher, eds. *The Individual Psychology of Alfred Adler*. New York: Basic Books, 1956.

Atkinson, Brooks. *Broadway*. New York: Macmillan, 1970.

Banner, Leslie. *A Passionate Preference: The Story of the North Carolina School of the Arts*. Winston-Salem, N.C.: North Carolina School of the Arts Foundation, 1987.

Behlmer, Rudy, ed. *Memo from David O. Selznick*. New York: Viking, 1972.

Black, Shirley Temple. *Child Star*. New York: McGraw-Hill, 1988.

Brockway, Thomas P. *Bennington College: In the Beginning*. Bennington, Vt.: Bennington College Press, 1981.

Brooks, Louise. *Lulu in Hollywood*. New York: Alfred A. Knopf, 1982.

Brown, J.A.C. *Freud and the Post-Freudians*. Baltimore: Penguin, 1964.

Capra, Frank. *The Name Above the Title*. New York: Macmillan, 1971.

Carey, Gary. *Judy Holliday*. New York: Seaview Books, 1982.

Clarke, John, trans. *Story of a Soul: The Autobiography of St. Thérèse of Lisieux*. Washington, D.C.: Institute of Carmelite Studies, 1976.

Crawford, Cheryl. *One Naked Individual: My Fifty Years in the Theater*. Indianapolis/New York: Bobbs-Merrill, 1977.

DeMille, Cecil B. *Autobiography of Cecil B. DeMille*. Englewood Cliffs, N.J.: Prentice-Hall, 1959.

Dick, Bernard F., ed. *Columbia Pictures: Portrait of a Studio*. Lexington, Ky.: University Press of Kentucky, 1992.

Dooley, Roger. *From Scarface to Scarlett*. New York: Harcourt Brace Jovanovitch, 1981.

Eames, John D. *The Paramount Story*. New York: Crown, 1985.

Edmonds, I.G., and Reiko Mimura. *Paramount Pictures and the People Who Made Them*. San Diego: A.S. Barnes, 1980.

Ford, Dan. *Pappy: The Life of John Ford*. Englewood Cliffs, N.J.: Prentice-Hall, 1979.

Fenin, George, and William K. Everson. *The Western*. New York: Bonanza Books, 1962.

Finch, Christopher. *Gone Hollywood*. Garden City, New York: Doubleday, 1979.

Finler, Joel W. *The Hollywood Story*. New York: Crown, 1988.

Fontaine, Joan. *No Bed of Roses*. New York: William Morrow, 1978.

Fromm, Erich. *Escape From Freedom*. 1941. Reprint. New York: Avon, 1969.

_____. *The Art of Loving*. New York: Harper & Row, 1956.

Gabler, Neal. *An Empire of Their Own*. New York: Crown, 1988.

Goldman, William. *The Season*. New York: Harcourt Brace & World, 1969.

Gordon, Max. *Max Gordon Presents*. New York: Bernard Geis Associates, 1963.

Greene, Walter A., and Ella Greene. *A Greene Family History*. Schenectady, New York, 1981.

Hadleigh, Boze. *Hollywood Lesbians*. New York: Barricade Books, 1994.

Hale, Sharon Lee. *A Tribute to Yesterday*. Santa Cruz, Calif.: Valley Publishers, 1980.

Hanson, Bruce K. *The Peter Pan Chronicles*. New York: Birch Lane Press, 1993.

Harris, Warren G. *Gable & Lombard*. New York: Simon & Schuster, 1974.

_____. *Cary Grant: A Touch of Elegance*. New York: Doubleday, 1987.

Harvey, James. *Romantic Comedy*. New York: Alfred A. Knopf, 1987.

Haskell, Molly. *From Reverence to Rape*. New York: Holt, Rinehart and Winston, 1974.

Haver, Ronald. *David O. Selznick's Hollywood*. New York: Alfred A. Knopf, 1980.

Hirschhorn, Clive. *The Columbia Story*. New York: Crown, 1990.

Holroyd, Michael. *Bernard Shaw: The Search for Love*. New York: Random House, 1988.

_____. *Bernard Shaw: The Pursuit of Power*. New York: Random House, 1989.

Holtzman, Will. *Judy Holliday*. New York: G.P. Putnam's Sons, 1982.

Horney, Karen. *The Neurotic Personality of Our Time*. New York: W.W. Norton, 1937.

_____. *New Ways in Psychoanalysis*. New York: W.W. Norton, 1939.

_____. *Our Inner Conflicts*. New York: W.W. Norton, 1945.

_____. *Neurosis and Human Growth*. New York: W.W. Norton, 1950.

_____. *Feminine Psychology*. New York: W.W. Norton, 1967.

Kanin, Garson. *Hollywood*. New York: Viking Press, 1974.

Kendall, Elizabeth. *The Runaway Bride*. New York: Alfred A. Knopf, 1990.

Kobal, John. *Rita Hayworth*. New York: W.W. Norton, 1977.

_____. *People Will Talk*. New York: Alfred A. Knopf, 1986.

Kotsilibas-Davis, James, and Myrna Loy. *Myrna Loy: Being and Becoming*. New York: Alfred A. Knopf, 1987.

Lahue, Kalton C. *Winners of the West: The Sagebrush Heroes of the Silent Screen*. Cranbury, N.J.: A.S. Barnes, 1970.

LaMance, Lora S. *The Greene Family and its Branches*. New York: Mayflower, 1904.

Lambert, Gavin. *Norma Shearer*. New York: Alfred A. Knopf, 1990.

Larkin, Rochelle. *Hail Columbia*. New Rochelle, N.Y.: Arlington House, 1975.

Leaming, Barbara. *If This Was Happiness: A Biography of Rita Hayworth*. New York: Viking Penguin, 1989.

Levant, Oscar. *The Memoirs of an Amnesiac*. New York: G.P. Putnam's Sons, 1965.

Levy, Emanuel. *And The Winner Is...* New York: Continuum, 1990.

Linet, Beverly. *Ladd: The Life, The Legend, The Legacy of Alan Ladd*. New York: Arbor House, 1979.

Manchester, William. *The Glory and the Dream*. Boston: Little, Brown, 1974.

Martin, Mary. *My Heart Belongs*. New York: William Morrow, 1976.

McBride, Joseph. *Hawks on Hawks*. Berkeley: University of California Press, 1982.

_____. *Frank Capra: The Catastrophe of Success*. New York: Simon & Schuster, 1992.

McDowall, Roddy. *Double Exposure: Take Two*. New York: William Morrow, 1989.

Merrill, Gary. *Bette, Rita, and the Rest of My Life*. Augusta, Maine: Lance Tapley, 1988.

Meyer, Susan E. *James Montgomery Flagg*. New York: Watson-Guptill Publications, 1974.

Morella, Joe, and Edward Z. Epstein. *The It Girl: The Incredible Story of Clara Bow*. New York: Delacorte Press, 1976.

_____. *Rita: The Life of Rita Hayworth*. New York: Delacorte Press, 1983.

Paris, Barry. *Louise Brooks*. New York: Alfred A. Knopf, 1989.

Peary, Danny. *Alternate Oscars*. New York: Dell, 1993.

Pierce, Arthur, and Douglas Swarthout. *Jean Arthur: A Bio-Bibliography*. Westport, Conn.: Greenwood Press, 1990.

Quirk, Lawrence J. *Norma*. New York: St. Martin's Press, 1988.

Ragan, David. *Who's Who in Hollywood, 1900-1976*. New Rochelle, N.Y.: Arlington House, 1977.

Rainey, Buck. *Heroes of the Range*. Metuchen, N.J.: Scarecrow Press, 1987.

Rivadue, Barry. *Mary Martin: A Bio-Bibliography*. Westport, Conn.: Greenwood Press, 1991.

Robbins, Phyllis. *Maude Adams: An Intimate Portrait*. New York: G.P. Putnam's Sons, 1956.

Robinson, Edward G., with Leonard Spigelgass. *All My Yesterdays*. New York: Hawthorn Books, 1973.

Rosen, Marjorie. *Popcorn Venus: Women, Movies and the American Dream*. New York: Avon, 1973.

Rosner, Paul. *The Princess and the Goblin*. Los Angeles: The Sherbourne Press, 1966.

Schatz, Thomas. *The Genius of the System*. New York: Pantheon, 1988.

Scherle, Victor, and William Turner Levy. *The Complete Films of Frank Capra*. Secaucus, N.J.: Citadel Press, 1977.

Schickel, Richard. *The Men Who Made the Movies*. New York: Atheneum, 1975.

Schulberg, Budd. *Moving Pictures*. New York: Stein & Day, 1981.

Selznick, Irene Mayer. *A Private View*. New York: Alfred A. Knopf, 1983.

Sennett, Ted. *Lunatics and Lovers*. New Rochelle, N.Y.: Arlington House, 1973.

Shaw, George Bernard. "The Quintessence of Ibsenism." In *Bernard Shaw, MajorCritical Essays*. 1891. Reprint, with an introduction by Michael Holroyd, New York: Penguin, 1986.

Shipman, David. *The Story of Cinema*. New York: St. Martin's Press, 1982.

_____. *Movie Talk*. London: Bloomsbury, 1988.

Sikov, Edward K. *Screwball*. New York: Crown, 1989.

Silvers, Phil, with Robert Saffron. *This Laugh Is on Me*. Englewood Cliffs, N.J.: Prentice-Hall, 1973.

Spoto, Donald. *Blue Angel*. New York: Doubleday, 1992.

Springer, John, and Jack Hamilton. *They Had Faces Then*. Secaucus, N.J.: Citadel Press, 1974.

Stenn, David. *Clara Bow: Runnin' Wild*. New York: Doubleday, 1988.

Swindell, Larry. *Screwball: The Life of Carole Lombard*. New York: William Morrow, 1973.

_____. *Gary Cooper: The Last Hero*. New York: Doubleday, 1980.

_____. *Charles Boyer, The Reluctant Lover*. Garden City, N.Y.: Doubleday, 1983.

Thomas, Bob. *King Cohn*. New York: G.P. Putnam's Sons, 1967.

_____. *Selznick*. New York: Doubleday, 1970.

Thomson, David. *Showman: The Life of David O. Selznick*. New York: Alfred A. Knopf, 1992.

_____. *A Biographical Dictionary of Film*. New York: Alfred A. Knopf, 1994.

Walker, Joseph, and Juanita Walker. *The Light on Her Face*. Hollywood: The ASC Press, 1984.

Wansell, Geoffrey. *Haunted Idol: The Story of the Real Cary Grant*. New York: William Morrow, 1984.

Weintraub, Stanley, ed. *The Portable Bernard Shaw*. New York: Viking Penguin, 1986.

Whitcomb, Michael, and Kelly Steele (illus.). *Carmel: The Architectural Spirit*. Carmel, Cal.: Ridgewood Press, 1978.

Wilkie, Jane. *Confessions of an Ex-Fan Magazine Writer*. Garden City, N.Y.: Doubleday, 1981.

Wray, Fay. *On the Other Hand*. New York: St. Martin's Press, 1989.

Yochelson, Bonnie. *Alfred Cheney Johnston: Women of Talent and Beauty, 1917-30*. Malvern, Pa.: Charles Isaacs Photographs, 1987.

Zolotow, Maurice. *Billy Wilder in Hollywood*. New York: G.P. Putnam's Sons, 1977.

Zukor, Adolph, with Dale Kramer. *The Public Is Never Wrong*. New York: G.P. Putnam's Sons, 1953.

SELECTED ARTICLES

"*Architectural Digest* Visits: Jean Arthur." *Architectural Digest*, May-June 1976.

Arthur, Jean. "Who Wants to Be a Lady?" *Screen and Radio Weekly*, September 20, 1936.

Broughton, Diane. "The Things in Jean Arthur's Doghouse." Los Angeles *Times*, March 30, 1975.

Calhoun, Dorothy. "The Girl Nobody Envies." *Motion Picture*, July 1928.

Champlin, Charles. "An Appreciation: Jean Arthur's Legacy of Indelible Performances." Los Angeles *Times*, June 21, 1991.

Condon, Frank. "Leave the Lady Be." *Collier's*, July 27, 1940.

DeRoos, Robert. "It's Back to Carmel...for Now." *TV Guide*, November 26, 1966.

Flatley, Guy. "From Mr. Deeds Goes to Town to Miss Arthur Goes to Vassar." New York *Times*, May 14, 1972.

Fletcher, Adele Whitely. "The Only Authorized Story of Jean Arthur's Life and Love." *Screen Guide*, March 1937.

_____. "Hidden Heritage." *Photoplay*, August 1937.

Goldbeck, Elisabeth. "Where Are the Breaks?" *Motion Picture*, May 1931.

Harris, Eleanor. "The Actress Nobody Knows." *Collier's*, October 7, 1950.

Kerr, Martha. "Jean Explains Miss Arthur." *Modern Screen*, May 1937.

"Life Goes Calling on Seclusive Jean Arthur in Her California Home." *Life*, March 11, 1940.

Pettit, George. "Now You'll Understand Jean Arthur." *Photoplay*, February 1937.

Rainey, Buck. "Buck Rainey's Filmographies." *Classic Images*, March-April, 1984.

Ryan, Don. "Jean Arthur Charms Men." *Photoplay*, December 1935.

Service, Faith. "Is Jean Arthur Really Unhappy?" *Modern Screen*, December 1938.

Springer, John, A. Bressan and M. Moran. "Great Star as Great Lady." *Interview*, June 1972.

Stone, Judy. "Jean Arthur: Still After Laughter." New York *Times*, September 11, 1966.

Stuart, Margaret. "Did She Steal Clara's Picture?" *Photoplay*, February 1930.

"The Very Personal Garden of Jean Arthur." *House and Garden*, July 1970.

Vermilye, Jerry. "Jean Arthur." *Films in Review*, June-July 1966.

Wolfe, Ralph Haven. "For Jean Arthur: An Appreciation." *Journal of Popular Film & Television*, Spring 1989.

OTHER SOURCES

Chandler, Richard. *The Freaking Out of Stephanie Blake*. Script Nos. 4416, 7118. 1967. New York Public Library for the Performing Arts, Billy Rose Theatre Collection.

Chierichetti, David. *Mitchell Leisen Oral History*. Transcript. American Film Institute, Los Angeles, 1970.

Christian Science: A Sourcebook of Contemporary Materials. Boston: The Christian Science Publishing Society, 1990.

Lawrence, Jerome and Robert E. Lee. *First Monday in October*. Revised version, New York: Samuel French, 1978.

Lee, Rowland V. *The Adventures of a Movie Director*. Unpublished manuscript. American Film Institute, Los Angeles, 1971.

Shaw, George Bernard. *Saint Joan*. 1923. Reprint, under the editorial supervision of Dan H. Laurence, New York: Penguin, 1986.

Stevens, George, Jr., prod. and dir. *George Stevens: A Filmmaker's Journey*. 1984.

NOTES

"To JO" denotes interview with author.

The following interviews, when credited in text, are not referenced in these notes: Dorothy Martin, September 21, 1989; Barton Heyman, September 21, 1989; John McLiam, September 28, 1989; William Rothwell, October 13, 1989; Mary Laslo, October 18, 1989; Arthur Ballard, October 28-29, 1989; Franklin Cover, October 1989; Jerome Lawrence, November 5, 1989; Ron Harper, January 9, 1990; Barbara Baxley, January 13, 1990; Nell Eurich, January 27, 1990; Teet Carle, January 27, 1990; Arthur Jacobson, January 28, 1990; Dena Dietrich, March 12, 1990; Pauline Koner, March 22, 1990; Ellen Mastroianni, August 20-25, 1990; Gus and Frances Arriola, August 22, 1990; Sister Francisca (Kay Hardy), August 23, 1990; Loren Hightower, July 2, 1991; Peter Wright, January 21, 1993; John Springer, January 26, 1993; Robert Whitehead, February 4, 1993; Roddy McDowall, March 8, 1993; Daniel Selznick, March 8, 1993; Travis Bogard, March 9, 1993; Paul Rosner, March 10, 1993; George Eells, March 22, 1993; Helen Harvey, April 14, 1993; Norman Shelly, April 14, 1993; Peter Lawrence, July 2, 1993; Ann Doran, July 7, 1993; Wendy Ross, January 3, 1994; Leslie Emery, January 3, 1994; Joan Ross, January 7, 1994; Zan Ross, January 9, 1994; Si Rose, January 9, 1994; Eugene Hare, January 19, 1994; Sandra Lavalle, January 20, 1994; Clint Atkinson, January 21, 1994; Robyn Reeves Travers, January 21, 1994; Beverly Petty, January 23, 1994; Marcy Kelly, February 19, 1994.

PROLOGUE
THE AMERICAN GARBO

Page

1   "Next to Garbo": "*Life* Goes Calling on Seclusive Jean Arthur in her California Home," *Life*, March 11, 1940, p. 59.

"most fascinating": Eleanor Harris, "The Actress Nobody Knows," *Collier's*, October 7, 1950, p. 22.

"hardest-to-understand": Sheilah Graham, Chicago *Daily News*, December 7, 1940.

"I really hadn't learned": Louella O. Parsons, "The Disappearing Jean Arthur," *Cosmopolitan*, May 5, 1953, p. 6.

2   "my favorite actress": Frank Capra, *The Name Above the Title* (New York: Macmillan, 1971), p. 184.

"this mysteriousness": Parsons, "The Disappearing Jean Arthur," p. 7.

"Every movie star": Larry Swindell, *Charles Boyer, the Reluctant Lover* (Garden City, New York: Doubleday, 1983), pp. 116-117.

Page

2   "When she's not": Harris, "The Actress Nobody Knows," p. 22.

"She really wants": Dee Lowrance, "Genuine Jean," *Every Week Magazine*, October 10, 1943.

3   "If people": Frank Condon, "Leave the Lady Be," *Collier's*, July 27, 1940, p. 50.

"it wasn't an act": Capra, *The Name Above the Title*, p. 184.

4   "butter": David Shipman, *The Story of Cinema* (New York: St. Martin's Press, 1982), p. 325.

"grated": Edward G. Robinson (with Leonard Spigelgass), *All My Yesterdays* (New York: Hawthorn Books, 1973), p. 156.

"low, husky": Capra, *The Name Above the Title*, p. 184.

"if Harlow": James Harvey, *Romantic Comedy* (New York: Alfred A. Knopf, 1987), p. 357.

5   "I am not": Martha Kerr, "Jean Explains Miss Arthur," *Modern Screen*, May 1937, pp. 35, 86.

6   "It means nonconformity": Judy Stone, "Jean Arthur: Still After Laughter," New York *Times*, September 11, 1966.

"If you can": New York *Herald Tribune*, September 18, 1950.

"people who aren't free": New York *Daily Mirror*, June 12, 1950.

"She was a nonconformist": Stone, "Jean Arthur: Still After Laughter."

7   "It's hardly fair": George Pettit, "Now You'll Understand Jean Arthur," *Photoplay*, February 1937, p. 96.

"men have always": Guy Flatley, "When Jean Arthur Was the Gem of Columbia's Ocean," New York *Times*, January 28, 1977.

women of the thirties: Marjorie Rosen, *Popcorn Venus: Women, Movies and the American Dream* (New York: Avon, 1973), p. 142.

"I don't know": William Glover, Associated Press, November 2, 1975.

CHAPTER ONE
ANIMAL INSTINCTS

11   The principal sources for this chapter are the author's interviews with Arthur "Pete" Ballard on October 28-29, 1989 and Weston Hatfield on January 6, 1990, as well as newspaper accounts of Jean Arthur's brush with the law in Winston-Salem, North Carolina. Bill Gilkeson's article on Arthur's trespassing trial in the April 12, 1973 Winston-Salem *Journal* was particularly helpful.

Page

17 "But for the fact": Glover, Associated Press, November 2, 1975.

"Animals have": Harris, "The Actress Nobody Knows," p. 80.

"When I'm walking": Diane Broughton, "The Things in Jean Arthur's Doghouse," Los Angeles *Times*, March 30, 1975, Calendar section, p. 29.

"I wouldn't have": Katharine Hartley, "She Didn't Take It With Her," *Screen Book*, October 1938, p. 60.

"I've never been": Duncan Theron, "Jean Arthur's New Setup," *Motion Picture*, August 1938, p. 53.

"I guess": Guy Flatley, "From Mr. Deeds Goes to Town to Miss Arthur Goes to Vassar," New York *Times*, May 14, 1972, p. 11.

CHAPTER TWO
HIDDEN HERITAGE

20 "charming": Eleanor Howard to JO, January 4, 1990.

"The scene": Elizabeth Kendall, *The Runaway Bride* (New York: Alfred A. Knopf, 1990), p. 126.

21 Greene's roots: Walter Anson Greene and Ella Greene, *A Greene Family History* (Schenectady, New York, 1981); Lora S. LaMance, *The Greene Family and its Branches* (New York, Mayflower, 1904).

22 "What do you want?": Ferdinand Greene to JO, October 9, 1989.

23 Greene paraded his horse: Ferdinand Greene to JO, May 27, 1990.

The family history of Hans P. Nelson and Georgianna Nelson, Jean Arthur's maternal grandparents, is drawn from genealogical research provided by Marcia Luther (letter to JO, August 7, 1991), and Vivian Linster (letter to JO, November 4, 1991); U.S. Census records 1880, 1900, 1910 and 1920; Billings, Montana City Directories; and the author's interviews with Nelson family members, including Vivian Linster (October 2, 1991); Beatrice Gregg (August 20, 1991 and June 16, 1992); Arthur and Miriam Goodall (October 1, 1991 and June 14, 1992); John W. Nelson (October 10, 1991 and May 10, 1992); Thelma Wexberg (April 27, 1992); Myrl Wyman and her daughter, Joyce Ruby (April 28, 1992); Muriel Nelson (June 18, 1992); James Nelson (June 16, 1992); and Susie Breese Blair (October 11, 1992).

24 "house and sign painting": 1884 Montana Regional Directory.

Page
24 "profligacy": Complaint filed in District Court, Seventh Judicial District of State of Montana, Yellowstone County, *Georgi[a]na Nelson vs. H.P. Nelson*, dated August 4, 1906, and decree of divorce of same date.

"widowed": U.S. Census 1900; Billings City Directories 1907, 1912, 1916.

"real Norwegian trouper": Vivian Linster to JO, October 2, 1991.

"liked to control": Beatrice Gregg to JO, August 20, 1991.

25 "Like a Viking princess": Broughton, "The Things in Jean Arthur's Doghouse," Calendar section, p. 28.

"humorist": Ferdinand Greene to JO, October 9, 1989.

Don Greene: The death certificate for Don Hubert Greene lists his birth date as January 15, 1890, six months before the July 7, 1890 marriage between Hubert and Johannah Greene. In later years, Mrs. Greene listed her date of marriage as January 13, 1890, which would have been two days before her oldest son's birth. U.S. Census records from 1900 and 1910 also understate Don Greene's age by one year, probably part of an effort by his parents to disguise his out-of-wedlock birth.

26 October 17, 1900: Although no birth certificate for Gladys Greene could be located, the date and place of her birth are confirmed by several sources. Her school records from Portland, Maine for the 1912-13 school year list her "certified date of birth" as October 17, 1900, and her place of birth as Plattsburgh, New York. Jean Arthur's death certificate also lists her birthdate as October 17, 1900, and the state of birth as New York. These facts are consistent with information reported in the 1910 and 1920 U.S. Census, and were further confirmed by Ellen Mastroianni.

Arthur's true date and place of birth were never correctly identified together in print during her lifetime. Fan magazine writer Adele Whitely Fletcher uncovered the Plattsburgh connection in 1937, as reported in "Hidden Heritage," *Photoplay*, August 1937, but the article mistakenly reported Arthur's year of birth as 1908.

CHAPTER THREE
UNCERTAIN BEGINNINGS

27 "leaders": advertisements in Plattsburgh *Republican*, October-November 1900.

28 "It seemed": Pettit, "Now You'll Understand Jean Arthur," p. 96.

"It was like": Don Ryan, "Jean Arthur Charms Men," *Photoplay*, December 1935, pp. 44, 120.

"I've never had": Kerr, "Jean Explains Miss Arthur," p. 86.

Page

29   "thought she was better": Leonard Longe to JO, October 9, 1989.

"When are you": Broughton, "The Things in Jean Arthur's Doghouse," Calendar section, p. 28.

"very venturesome": Mary (Greene) Fraenckel to JO, October 8, 1989.

"was born": William Wernecke to JO, October 23, 1989.

"GLADYS9": Walter Greene and Ella Greene, *A Greene Family History*, p. 115.

"proper people": Mary Fraenckel to JO, October 8, 1989.

30   "I've come away": Abbott Lowell Cummings to JO, October 9, 1989.

"He was a great one": Ferdinand Greene to JO, October 9, 1989.

31   "On a hunting trip": Harris, "The Actress Nobody Knows," p. 78.

32   "Mary Pickford": Katharine Hartley, "Play Truth or Consequences with Jean Arthur," *Photoplay*, February 1939, p. 14.

33   "very timid girl": George Osan to JO, March 11, 1990.

34   "get husbands": Dorothy Calhoun, "The Girl Nobody Envies," *Motion Picture*, July 1928, p. 71.

"I knew that": Pettit, "Now You'll Understand Jean Arthur," p. 96.

"change in family circumstances": Paramount Pictures studio biography, January 1931.

"family financial reverses": Paramount Pictures pressbook, *Young Eagles*, 1930.

returning cousin: Doug Foster to JO, April 28, 1992.

Albert Greene: his death remains something of a mystery. His mother later maintained that he was "killed in the World War at the age of approximately twenty-three years." (divorce complaint, *Johannah A. Greene vs. Hubert Sidney Greene*, Superior Court of the State of California, in and for the County of Monterey, No. 21743, filed January 15, 1942). Yet federal census records, as well as the Portland, Maine City Directory, show him married and living in Portland as late as 1920, when he was twenty-five. The 1921 Portland directory indicates that he and his wife, Mildred, had recently moved to New York. There is no record of his death in either the New York City or Portland death records from that period, or in World War I military service records (most of which have been destroyed by fire).

Several of Jean Arthur's friends and relatives recall her saying that Albert died a young man. Most likely his death resulted from some war-related injury, allowing his mother to later claim he was a casualty of the conflict.

Page

35 "They asked me": Jerry Vermilye, "Jean Arthur," *Films in Review*, June-July 1966, p. 329.

36 "Norma Shearer gained": Ibid., p. 330.

"outstanding personality": Dora Albert, "Jean Arthur—When," *Modern Screen*, October 1937, p. 78.

"selected by": *Classic*, October 1923, p. 43.

CHAPTER FOUR
SUFFERING IN SILENTS

40 "I was the spark": David Shipman, *Movie Talk* (London: Bloomsbury, 1988), p. 150.

"one of the most": Press Kit for *Cameo Kirby*, 1923.

41 "There wasn't a spark": Ryan, "Jean Arthur Charms Men," p. 44.

"I thought": Calhoun, "The Girl Nobody Envies," p. 103.

"I almost forgot": Ibid.

42 "inferiority complex": Whitney Williams, "Jean Arthur Defeats Her Jinx," *Screen Book*, June 1936, p. 20.

"So I stayed": Calhoun, "The Girl Nobody Envies," p. 103.

"One of the 'stars'": Ibid., p. 71.

"a pretty girl": *Motion Picture News*, quoted in Vermilye, "Jean Arthur," p. 346.

"I like to act": Baltimore *Sun Post*, December 26, 1943.

43 "beautiful, charming": Richard Thorpe to JO, September 22, 1989.

44 "is daintily played": *Motion Picture News*, circa 1926.

"not only": *Motion Picture News*, circa 1925.

"ok": *Variety*, October 27, 1926.

"serves to bring": *Exhibitors' Daily*, quoted in Vermilye, "Jean Arthur," p. 331.

45 "diet of spinach": Pettit, "Now You'll Understand Jean Arthur," p. 96.

"My mother says": Calhoun, "The Girl Nobody Envies," p. 71.

"the appeal of Jean Arthur": New York *Times*, July 19, 1927.

"With everybody": *Variety*, July 20, 1927.

Page

46 "It would have been": Calhoun, "The Girl Nobody Envies," p. 103.

"I want my break": Ibid., p. 107.

47 "Without sound effects": *Variety*, June 27, 1928.

"a brilliant forerunner": Boston *Traveler*, July 28, 1928.

"Dix and June Arthur": *Variety*, June 27, 1928.

"one of the most": *Screenland*, October 1928.

CHAPTER FIVE
FALLEN STARLET

51 "a continuous supply": *Film Daily Yearbook*, 1929.

"not going to talk": Joe Morella and Edward Z. Epstein, *The It Girl: The Incredible Story of Clara Bow* (New York: Delacorte Press, 1976), p. 156.

52 "a foghorn": Adolph Zukor, *The Public is Never Wrong* (New York: G.P. Putnam's Sons, 1953), p. 256.

53 "I was a very poor actress": Ben Maddox, "Jean Arthur Left Films—Became a Star," *Motion Picture*, December 1935, p. 72.

54 "Please write": Jean Arthur letter to David O. Selznick [undated], quoted in David Thomson, *Showman: The Life of David O. Selznick* (New York: Alfred A. Knopf, 1992), p. 85.

"the terms": Thomson, *Showman*, p. 85.

"with a young actress": Budd Schulberg, *Moving Pictures* (New York: Stein & Day, 1981), p. 306.

Arthur there some nights: Thomson, *Showman*, pp. 86-87.

"heard David Selznick's voice": Fay Wray, *On the Other Hand* (New York: St. Martin's Press, 1989), p. 97.

55 "desperately didn't want": Irene Mayer Selznick, *A Private View* (New York: Alfred A. Knopf, 1983), p. 117.

"only brain": Arthur Ballard to JO, October 28, 1989.

"someone who could understand": Sonia Lee, "'Don't Want Anything Too Much'— Jean Arthur," *Motion Picture*, August 1936, pp. 38, 67.

56 "Julian dreamed": Flatley, "Miss Arthur Goes to Vassar," p. 11.

Page
56 "You should have heard": Ibid.

obtained an annulment: Adele Whitely Fletcher, "Hidden Heritage," *Photoplay*, August 1937, pp. 31, 90.

"I'd marry a man": Albert, "Jean Arthur—When," p. 79.

57 "There was nothing": Harris, "The Actress Nobody Knows," p. 78.

58 "Jean Arthur makes": *Variety*, July 24, 1929.

"Miss Arthur has": New York *Herald Tribune*, July 22, 1929.

"Jean Arthur was": Rowland V. Lee, *The Adventures of a Movie Director* (American Film Institute, Los Angeles, 1971, unpublished manuscript).

60 "Jean Arthur probably leads": Paramount Pictures biography, January 1931.

"a negative personality": Margaret Stuart, "Did She Steal Clara's Picture?" *Photoplay*, February 1930, pp. 43, 92.

"She has been": Ibid., p. 93.

61 "were it not": New York *Times*, November 16, 1929.

"She was so generous": David Stenn, *Clara Bow: Runnin' Wild* (New York: Doubleday, 1988), pp. 178-179.

"a good looking girl": *Variety*, December 11, 1929.

"my first personal film": Ronald Haver, *David O. Selznick's Hollywood* (New York: Alfred A. Knopf, 1980), p. 60.

62 "a girl in whose": Selznick, *A Private View*, p. 117.

"Oh, lost ecstasy": Thomson, *Showman*, p. 95.

"brief little thing": Daniel Selznick to JO, March 8, 1993.

"Heavens": John Springer, A. Bressan and M. Moran, "Great Star as Great Lady," *Interview*, June 1972, pp. 22-23.

63 "The success story": Elisabeth Goldbeck, "Where Are the Breaks?" *Motion Picture*, May 1931, p. 76.

64 "There just aren't": Ibid.

"Mary Brian": Maddox, "Jean Arthur Left Films," p. 72.

"So far as the studio": Ibid.

65 how Ross met Arthur: David Stenn to JO, January 26, 1990.

"I was to go East": *Movieland*, July 1943, p. 30.

Page

65 by "accident": Lee, "'Don't Want Anything Too Much,'" p. 67.

66 "Playing those": Maddox, "Jean Arthur Left Films," p. 73.

CHAPTER SIX
BROADWAY REVIVAL

69 "numb": Dickson Morley, "A Thousand Teachers," *Silver Screen*, February 1936, p. 63.

"Miss Arthur": New York *World Telegram*, April 14, 1932.

"dryly witty": New York *Sun*, April 14, 1932.

"not only charming": New York *Post*, April 14, 1932.

"If 'grapevine' reports": Los Angeles *Herald-Examiner*, October 13, 1932.

70 "endowed": New York *Herald Tribune*, September 9, 1932.

"personable young actress": New York *Post*, September 9, 1932.

"her voice": New York *Times*, September 9, 1932.

"better than usual": New York *Times*, May 1, 1933.

"looks wonderful": Johannah Greene letter to Pearl Goodall, January 1, 1933.

71 "Twice this season": New York *Herald Tribune*, May 28, 1933.

"tedious": New York *Times*, May 10, 1933.

"very attractive": Southampton *Press*, August 3, 1933.

"I don't think": Ryan, "Jean Arthur Charms Men," p. 119.

"I learned": Lee, "'Don't Want Anything Too Much'" p. 38.

72 "a fair girl": New York *Herald Tribune*, October 20, 1933.

"natural": New York *American*, October 20, 1933.

"the chief pleasure": New York *Post*, October 20, 1933.

"When Jean Arthur": New York *Times*, October 20, 1933.

"temperament": *Variety*, December 12, 1933.

73 "the happiest years": John Springer and Jack Hamilton, *They Had Faces Then* (Secaucus, N.J.: Citadel Press, 1974), p. 13.

74 "I'm staying": Adele Whitely Fletcher, "The Only Authorized Story of Jean Arthur's Life and Love," *Screen Guide*, March 1937, p. 47.

CHAPTER SEVEN
GOING TO TOWN

Page

75 son of a bitch: Bob Thomas, *King Cohn* (New York: G.P. Putnam's Sons, 1967), p. xix.

"sadistic son of a bitch": Ibid., p. xviii.

76 "it only proves": Ibid., pp. xvii-xviii.

"He believed": Garson Kanin, *Hollywood* (New York: Viking Press, 1974), p. 184.

77 "brilliant": New York *Herald Tribune*, May 5, 1934.

78 "Some of our": Lee, "Don't Want Anything Too Much," p. 67.

79 "ineffectual": New York *Post*, September 14, 1934.

"may still be": New York *Times*, September 14, 1934.

80 "a new, peculiarly American": Roger Dooley, *From Scarface to Scarlett* (New York: Harcourt Brace Jovanovitch, 1981), p. 38.

81 "Second in unusualness": *Variety*, March 6, 1935.

82 "They were handsome": Robinson, *All My Yesterdays*, p. 156.

"He's got this handkerchief": Springer, "Great Star," p. 22.

"tendency for melancholia": New York *Herald Tribune*, December 28, 1935.

83 "had to *say* something": Capra, *The Name Above the Title*, p. 185.

84 "Who's the girl?": Ibid., p. 184.

"offbeat quiet love scene": Ibid.

"cuckoo": Ibid.

"Great voice?": Ibid.

86 "When I was crying": Springer, "Great Star," p. 23.

"Some actresses": Michael Blowen, "Jean Arthur at 80: A Legend Made of Style and Substance, Not Publicity," Chicago *Tribune*, October 20, 1985.

"delightful woman": Charles Lane to JO, January 25, 1990.

"real pro": Lionel Stander to JO, September 6, 1989.

"kind of an unhappy girl": Edward Bernds to JO, June 24, 1991.

"Never have I seen": Capra, *The Name Above the Title*, p. 184.

Page

86 "She stalled": Joseph McBride, *The Catastrophe of Success* (New York: Simon & Schuster, 1992), p. 343.

87 "Now I look": Springer, "Great Star," p. 23.

CHAPTER EIGHT
MAKING HISTORY

90 "Finally I decided": Lowrance, "Genuine Jean."

"our happiness": Maud Cheatham, "Give Her a Break," *Screenland*, June 1939, p. 95.

91 "verily": Morley, "A Thousand Teachers," p. 24.

"You don't see": Ibid.

tennis club appearance: Carolyn Somers Hoyt, "The Girl's a Natural!" *Movie Mirror*, September 1936, p. 48.

"Believe me": Faith Service, "Is Jean Arthur Really Unhappy?" *Modern Screen*, December 1938, p. 42.

"I can't seem": Kerr, "Jean Explains Miss Arthur," pp. 35, 86.

"How can anyone": Lewis Funke, "Portrait of a Press Shy Peter Pan," New York *Times*, May 7, 1950.

turned away a writer: James Reid, "The Strange Case of Jean Arthur," *Modern Screen*, August 1940, p. 82.

92 "Jean doesn't want": Ibid.

"With Garbo talking": Ted Towne, "Calamity Jean," *Movie Classic*, January 1937, p. 31.

"I like to think": Kerr, "Jean Explains Miss Arthur," p. 87.

met only once: Arthur Ballard to JO, October 28, 1989.

93 "Disdaining the cries": New York *Times*, May 28, 1936.

94 "taking some liberties": Cecil B. DeMille, *Autobiography of Cecil B. DeMille* (Englewood Cliffs, N.J.: Prentice-Hall, 1959), p. 350.

"He wouldn't let me": Ted Towne, "Calamity Jean," p. 85.

"He never went up": Springer, "Great Star," p. 23.

"I can't remember": McBride, *The Catastrophe of Success*, p. 345.

"If I had married him": Arthur Ballard to JO, October 29, 1989.

Page

95   "brief, laconic": DeMille, *Autobiography*, p. 350.

"peaches and cream" portrayal: Montana Newspaper Association, Insert Series, August 2, 1937.

"What I like": This and subsequent quotations from Jean Arthur, "Who Wants to Be a Lady?" *Screen and Radio Weekly*, September 20, 1936.

97   "But in their scenes": Swindell, *Charles Boyer: The Reluctant Lover*, p. 117.

"Jean Arthur will zoom": *Film Daily*, March 8, 1937.

98   "I told them": New York *Daily News*, June 9, 1937.

"We took the curse off": David Chierichetti, *Mitchell Leisen Oral History* (American Film Institute, Los Angeles, 1970).

99   "fabulous sense": Ibid.

"special talent": Harvey, *Romantic Comedy*, p. 352.

100   "almost found": Flatley, "Miss Arthur Goes to Vassar," p. 11.

"another world": Theron, "Jean Arthur's New Setup," p. 53.

101   "not even thinking": Prince, "Is Jean Arthur Really Unhappy?" p. 42.

"Jean came here": Johannah Greene letter to Pearl and Archie Goodall, c. August 1937.

byzantine Hollywood politics: McBride, *The Catastrophe of Success*, pp. 385-386.

102   "After the 'cut'": *Photoplay*, August 1938.

"happy-go-lucky family": Capra, *The Name Above the Title*, p. 240.

"Don't let anyone": Jean Arthur, New York *Daily Mirror*, August 25, 1938.

103   "even Jean Arthur": .Quoted in "James Stewart: Hometown Hero," Arts & Entertainment Network's *Biography* (1993).

"the finest actress": San Francisco *Chronicle*, April 2, 1989.

104   "This past year": Theron, "Jean Arthur's New Setup," p. 53.

"an actress's usual complex": Service, "Is Jean Arthur Really Unhappy?" p. 42.

"Jean is not": Ibid.

CHAPTER NINE
CONSOLATION PRIZES

Page

106 "hoping against hope": Rudy Behlmer, ed., *Memo from David O. Selznick* (New York: Viking, 1972), p. 168.

107 "reached a deal": New York *Journal & American*, October 26, 1938.

Columbia statement: New York *Journal & American*, November 10, 1938.

108 "silly": Behlmer, *Memo From David O. Selznick*, p. 172.

"any new-girl": Ibid., p. 175.

109 "Shhhh": Ibid., p. 180.

"All day today": Ibid., p. 181.

burned her screen test: Ronald Haver, *David O. Selznick's Hollywood*, p. 260.

110 "By that late day": David Thomson to JO, March 8, 1993.

"less convincing showgirl": New York *Times*, May 12, 1939.

111 "happily muted": New York *Post*, May 12, 1939.

"She'd simply say": Joseph McBride, *Hawks on Hawks* (Berkeley: University of California Press, 1982), p. 98.

"When the picture": Harvey, *Romantic Comedy*, p. 354.

"really good": John Kobal, *People Will Talk* (New York: Alfred A. Knopf, 1986), p. 493.

"a lot of excitement": Springer, "Great Star," p. 23.

"I loved sinking": Flatley, "Miss Arthur Goes to Vassar," p. 11.

"The scene": William Rothwell to JO, October 13, 1989.

112 "That beautiful girl": Joe Morella and Edward Z. Epstein, *Rita: The Life of Rita Hayworth* (New York: Delacorte Press, 1983), p. 41.

"You're shy": Paul Rosner to JO, March 10, 1993.

116 "I defy": McBride, *The Catastrophe of Success*, p. 417.

"one of the best": Richard Schickel, *The Men Who Made the Movies* (New York: Atheneum, 1975), pp. 105-106.

"it's all there": Springer, "Great Star," p. 23.

118 "Being a stooge": Marian Rhea, "The Private World of Jean Arthur," *Movie Mirror*, June 1940, p. 87.

CHAPTER TEN
THE PRINCESS AND THE GOBLIN

Page

119 "amazement of all Hollywood": this and subsequent quotations concerning Arthur's home are taken from *Life*, "*Life* Goes Calling on Seclusive Jean Arthur in her California Home," March 11, 1940, pp. 59-62.

120 "My personal life": Ibid., p. 59.

burst into tears: Sister Francisca (Kay Hardy) to JO, August 24, 1990.

121 "In a fitting room": W.F. French, "What Hollywood Thinks of Jean Arthur," *Photoplay*, September 1942, p. 49.

"It sags": New York *Times*, February 7, 1941.

123 "very closed-mouth type": Lou Merino to JO, August 11, 1990.

"He was very articulate": Doug Morrow to JO, August 9, 1990.

"man of wit": Phil Silvers (with Robert Saffron), *This Laugh Is on Me* (Englewood Cliffs, N.J.: Prentice-Hall, 1973), p. 121.

"He was pretty upright": Catharine Pace to JO, January 7, 1994.

124 "if this picture": Hedda Hopper, Baltimore *Sun*, November 19, 1944.

"I'm supposed to be": Robert DeRoos, "It's Back to Carmel...for Now," *TV Guide*, November 26, 1966, p. 14.

"creation": Henri Bergson, *Creative Evolution* (New York: Holt, 1911), p. 248.

125 "God must be": Stone, "Jean Arthur: Still After Laughter."

"The lady always": Condon, "Leave the Lady Be," p. 50.

marriage on the rocks: Louella Parsons, "The Art of Being Arthur," *Photoplay Combined with Movie Mirror*, May 1944, p. 30.

"For ten years": Harris, "The Actress Nobody Knows," p. 18.

126 "Jean and Frank": Ibid.

"He was especially cold": this and subsequent quotations taken from *Gladys Greene Ross vs. Frank J. Ross Jr.*, No. S.M.D. 6645, Superior Court of the State of California in and for the County of Los Angeles, Deposition Taken Out of the State of California on Written Interrogatories.

127 small dinner party: Mary Martin, *My Heart Belongs* (New York: William Morrow, 1976), pp. 93-94.

Page

128   "endless discussions": Ibid., p. 202.

"Mary Martin, I notice": James Agee, *The Nation*, October 8, 1943.

"looking and sounding": New York *Post*, April 25, 1950.

130   *The Children's Hour*: Marcy Kelly to JO, February 19, 1994.

"America's creative lesbian community": Donald Spoto, *Blue Angel* (New York: Doubleday, 1992), p. 105.

"ten interviews with": Boze Hadleigh, *Hollywood Lesbians* (New York: Barricade Books, 1994).

Marjorie Main: Ibid., p. 44.

Patsy Kelly: Ibid., p. 62.

Agnes Moorehead: Ibid., pp. 192-193.

131   could live without sex: Broughton, "The Things in Jean Arthur's Doghouse," Calendar section, p. 30.

132   "I doubt if she had": Leslie Emery to JO, January 3, 1994.

Divorce complaint: *Johannah A. Greene vs. Hubert Sidney Greene*, Superior Court of the State of California, in and for the County of Monterey, No. 21743, filed January 15, 1942.

133   "'Josie'": Paul Rosner, *The Princess and the Goblin* (Los Angeles: The Sherbourne Press, 1966), pp. 343-345.

CHAPTER ELEVEN
"I WANT TO LIVE IN THE SKY"

136   "kind of like": "W," unidentified clipping, October 22-29, 1982.

137   "I found out": Springer, "Great Star," p. 23.

"Miss Arthur is charming": New York *Times*, August 28, 1942.

138   "depends on": *New Republic*, September 21, 1942.

"consternation": New York *Herald Tribune*, August 28, 1942.

"a changed young woman": Hartford *Times*, August 29, 1942.

"When she did comedy": Blowen, "Jean Arthur at 80: A Legend Made of Style and Substance, Not Publicity."

Page

138 "When she works": Parsons, "The Disappearing Jean Arthur," p. 7.

his father "felt": San Francisco *Chronicle*, April 2, 1989.

told counsellor Ned Hall: Edward ("Ned") Hall to JO, February 23, 1990.

"Some people misinterpret": Theron, "Jean Arthur's New Setup," p. 53.

139 "occupies": Emanuel Levy, *And the Winner Is...* (New York: Continuum, 1990), p. 211.

deserved several nominations: Danny Peary, *Alternate Oscars* (New York: Dell, 1993), p. 73.

"Least Popular Woman": Hedda Hopper, "My Own Super-Superlative Awards for 1941," *Photoplay Combined with Movie Mirror*, March 1942, p. 42.

140 Garson Kanin screenplay: The principal sources for this account are Kanin's *Hollywood* and Thomas's *King Cohn*.

141 "undoubtedly the best": *Variety*, April 7, 1943.

"copping feels": Interview in *George Stevens: A Filmmaker's Journey* (George Stevens Jr., Prod. and Dir., 1984).

144 "unusually frank": James Agee, *The Nation*, October 8, 1943.

"largely because": New York *Times*, September 16, 1943.

"inferiority complex": John Wayne (as told to Jack Holland), "Jean Arthur As I Know Her," *Screenland*, July 1943, p. 84.

145 "would have shot him": Flatley, "Miss Arthur Goes to Vassar," p. 11.

only to "change clothes": Mary Courson to JO, May 4, 1993.

"on her feet": Wayne, "Jean Arthur As I Know Her," p. 85.

"We were worlds apart": Silvers, *This Laugh is on Me*, p. 121.

"You enjoy": Ibid., p. 122.

146 work with a cadaver: Parsons, "The Art of Being Arthur," p. 98.

"comedies": Ibid.

"still the best farceur": *Photoplay Combined with Movie Mirror*, November 1944, pp. 22-23.

CHAPTER TWELVE
STILLBORN

Page

151   Gary Merrill: the following account is taken from Chapter 4 of Merrill's *Bette, Rita, and the Rest of My Life* (Augusta, Maine: Lance Tapley, 1988).

152   "Next to her": Max Gordon, *Max Gordon Presents* (New York: Bernard Geis Associates, 1963), p. 276.

153   "I suppose I'm a snob": Flatley, "Miss Arthur Goes to Vassar," p. 11.

new mink coat: Arthur Ballard to JO, October 28, 1989.

154   "No one dared": Gordon, *Max Gordon Presents*, p. 277.

completely opposite story: Kanin, *Hollywood*, pp. 322-323.

"the ability": Merrill, *Bette, Rita, and the Rest of My Life*, pp. 75-76.

155   pitchers of heavy cream: Gordon, *Max Gordon Presents*, p. 278.

The next morning: Ibid., pp. 278-279.

realized she was "perfect": Ibid., p. 279.

156   "that fat Jewish girl": Kanin, *Hollywood*, p. 324.

the actress's biographers: Will Holtzman, *Judy Holliday* (New York: G.P. Putnam's Sons, 1982), p. 113; Gary Carey, *Judy Holliday, An Intimate Life Story* (New York: Seaview Books, 1982), pp. 74-78.

"nervous exhaustion": Kanin, *Hollywood*, p. 323.

"not lost any": New Haven *Register*, December 21, 1945.

157   "Jean Arthur's performance": Boston *Herald*, December 26, 1945.

Arthur later acknowledged: Flatley, "Miss Arthur Goes to Vassar," p. 11.

"vicious gossip": New York *Times*, February 2, 1946.

Gordon and Kanin demanded: Flatley, "Miss Arthur Goes to Vassar," p. 11.

158   Kanin upset at amount of her control: Barbara Baxley to JO, January 13, 1990.

"There was such": Flatley, "Miss Arthur Goes to Vassar," p. 11.

"I got no reaction": Ibid.

"It was a very hard time": Ibid.

159   Bill Barborka: William Barborka to JO, May 25, 1993.

Page

159 "You didn't just screw her": Warren G. Harris, *Cary Grant, A Touch of Elegance* (New York: Doubleday, 1987), pp. 142-143.

160 Teresa Wright: Berg, *Goldwyn*, p. 424.

"All my life": New York *Times*, June 20, 1991.

CHAPTER THIRTEEN
ADULT EDUCATION

161 "As a human being": Brooks Atkinson, *Broadway* (New York: Macmillan, 1970), p. 27.

"She glories": *Peter Pan* program, Empire Theater, November 6, 1905.

162 "She did not possess": Phyllis Robbins, *Maude Adams: An Intimate Portrait* (New York: G.P. Putnam's Sons, 1956), p. 215.

"the character": Ibid., pp. 89-90.

163 "I am particularly interested": Hedda Hopper, "Perfection is Her Goal," Chicago *Tribune*, July 4, 1948.

"I'd always thought": Harris, "The Actress Nobody Knows," p. 78.

"I would be content": Leslie Powen, "Jean Arthur, 'The *Plainsman's* Calamity Jane,' Visits Stephens to Study Until Graduation," *The Stephens Life*, April 11, 1947.

164 "never made any real effort": Connie Schenck to JO, September 27, 1989.

"Each respected": Harris, "The Actress Nobody Knows," p. 78.

"There wasn't any": Hedda Hopper, "Acting Bug Bites Jean Arthur Again," Los Angeles *Times*, February 28, 1965.

"Who is that woman": Paul Rosner to JO, March 10, 1993.

165 helped her understand others' problems: Hopper, "Perfection is Her Goal," Chicago *Tribune*, July 4, 1948.

167 "Jean Arthur is": New York *Times*, July 1, 1948.

"top-flight characterization": *Variety*, June 16, 1948.

"Jean Arthur has": *New Yorker*, July 10, 1948.

"most fascinating": New York *Times*, July 1, 1948.

168 "in rotten taste": James Agee, *The Nation*, July 13, 1948.

Page
168 "shining exception": Shipman, *The Story of Cinema*, p. 729; see also p. 686.

a "disaster" for Arthur: Andrew Sarris, *The Village Voice*, September 1, 1987.

a "hallucination": Roddy McDowall, *Double Exposure: Take Two* (New York: William Morrow, 1989), p. 54.

the flabbergasted Wilder: Maurice Zolotow, *Billy Wilder in Hollywood* (New York: G.P. Putnam's Sons, 1977), p. 250.

"simply wonderful": McDowall, *Double Exposure: Take Two*, p. 54.

169 "absolutely loved it": Ibid., p. 55.

CHAPTER FOURTEEN
TEMPORARY HELP

172 "the individual ceases": Erich Fromm, *Escape From Freedom* (1941; reprint, New York: Avon, 1969), pp. 208-209.

173 "very human person": Edward ("Ned") Hall to JO, February 23, 1990.

"If you become": Flatley, "Miss Arthur Goes to Vassar," p. 11.

"finest experience": Harris, "The Actress Nobody Knows," p. 22.

"The greatest thing": Flatley, "Miss Arthur Goes to Vassar," p. 11.

175 "basic anxiety": Horney first used this term (which she sometimes referred to as the "Basic Conflict") in *The Neurotic Personality of Our Time* (New York: W.W. Norton, 1937). The thesis was elaborated upon in *New Ways In Psychoanalysis* (New York: W.W. Norton, 1939); *Our Inner Conflicts* (New York: W.W. Norton, 1945); and *Neurosis and Human Growth* (New York: W.W. Norton, 1950).

"neurotic trends": Horney's categorizations are most explicitly developed in *Our Inner Conflicts*, Chs. 3-5.

"hates regimentation": Horney, *Neurosis and Human Growth*, p. 274.

fear of "becoming submerged": Horney, *Our Inner Conflicts*, p. 93.

"he may readily": Ibid., p. 90.

176 "Stage fright": Horney, *Neurosis and Human Growth*, pp. 100-101.

Alfred Adler: A good overview of Adler's thought can be found in Heinz L. Ansbacher and Rowena R. Ansbacher, eds., *The Individual Psychology of Alfred Adler* (New York: Basic Books, 1977), and in J.A.C. Brown, *Freud and the Post-Freudians* (Baltimore: Penguin, 1964), pp. 38-41.

Page
176 "cheated": Pettit, "Now You'll Understand Jean Arthur," p. 96.

"was going to do": Ibid.

177 "generally down": Marcy Kelly to JO, February 19, 1994.

178 petitions were filed: Los Angeles *Examiner*, March 23, 1950.

decree already entered: Los Angeles *Times*, March 23, 1950.

CHAPTER FIFTEEN
GROWING YOUNG

179 "Who and what": J.M. Barrie, *Peter Pan* (New York: Charles Scribner's Sons, 1911).

"I hate to admit it": Martin, *My Heart Belongs*, p. 202.

181 "Mary Martin was *dying* to do it": Peter Lawrence to JO, July 3, 1993.

"It felt wonderful": New York *Herald Tribune*, September 18, 1950.

184 "sounds like": New York *Herald Tribune*, December 15, 1949.

185 "I think": Lewis Funke, "Portrait of a Press Shy Peter Pan," New York *Times*, May 7, 1950.

"superb piece": New York *Herald Tribune*, April 25, 1950.

"thoroughly disarming": New York *Daily News*, April 25, 1950.

"Although the world": New York *Times*, April 25, 1950.

"an old Maude Adams man": New York *Daily News*, April 25, 1950.

"The choice of Miss Arthur": New York *Herald Tribune*, April 25, 1950.

186 "Not many people": New York *World Telegram & Sun*, April 25, 1950.

"It is Barrie's play": New York *Morning Telegraph*, April 25, 1950.

"People are": Funke, "Portrait of a Press Shy Peter Pan."

187 "Peter represents": Harris, "The Actress Nobody Knows," p. 79.

"I want to make": New York *Times*, May 7, 1950.

"Hank is taking": Peter Lawrence to JO, July 2, 1993.

188 "[Arthur's] eyes": Shirley Temple Black, *Child Star* (New York: McGraw-Hill, 1988), p. 468.

189 "If you don't": Barbara Baxley, unpublished memoirs.

Page

189 "It's the most fun": New York *Times*, August 14, 1950.

190 "Have been informed": The text of Arthur's telegram is reprinted in the New York *Times*, August 16, 1950.

191 "several representatives": *Variety*, August 16, 1950.

192 "just a simple cottage": Washington *Post*, September 26, 1954.

"If you'd take this gift": Baxley, unpublished memoirs.

193 RKO suit: New York *Times*, January 13, 1950.

195 "my happiest role": New York *Post*, March 15, 1962.

CHAPTER SIXTEEN
WESTERN SUNSET

198 "Film and TV": Interview in *George Stevens: A Filmmaker's Journey*.

199 "The whole cast": Ben Johnson, letter to JO, February 1990.

"Nobody went to bed": Washington *Post*, November 3, 1985.

200 secured another piglet: Roddy McDowall to JO, March 8, 1993.

"Even Jean Arthur": Beverly Linet, *Ladd: The Life, The Legend, The Legacy of Alan Ladd* (New York: Arbor House, 1979), p. 151.

"the summit": Alan Stanbrook, *Films and Filming*, May 1966, p. 38.

202 "I didn't like it": Hopper, "Acting Bug Bites Jean Arthur Again," Los Angeles *Times*, February 28, 1965.

CHAPTER SEVENTEEN
MARTYRDOM

203 "Unless Woman": "The Quintessence of Ibsenism," in *Bernard Shaw, Major Critical Essays* (1891; reprint, New York: Penguin, 1986), p. 61.

"I will never": George Bernard Shaw, *Saint Joan* (1923; reprint, under the editorial supervision of Dan H. Laurence, New York: Penguin, 1986), p. 83.

"The fact": Flatley, "Miss Arthur Goes to Vassar," p. 11.

204 "There is no": Shaw, *Major Critical Essays*, pp. 154-155.

"The need for freedom": Ibid., p. 147.

"freakish or plain": Arthur, "Who Wants to Be a Lady?"

Page

205 "They tell us": Broughton, "The Things in Jean Arthur's Doghouse," Calendar section, p. 30.

"fanatic": Leslie Emery to JO, January 3, 1994.

207 "sane and shrewd": Shaw, *Saint Joan*, preface.

"I could have": Flatley, "Miss Arthur Goes to Vassar," p. 11.

"His criticism": Ibid.

208 "Shaw's Joan": Washington *Star*, September 21, 1954.

"spirit": Washington *Post*, September 21, 1954.

"no exaltation": Washington *Daily News*, September 21, 1954.

"The glow": Pittsburgh *Post-Gazette*, October 5, 1954.

"at no point": Detroit *Free Press*, October 12, 1954.

"does not evoke": Columbus *Citizen-Journal*, November 2, 1954.

"essence of simplicity": Cincinnati *Enquirer*, October 26, 1954.

"Miss Arthur is": Columbus *Dispatch*, November 2, 1954.

209 "too jittery": Associated Press, November 8, 1954.

"No performance": Chicago *American*, November 9, 1954.

"If there are any Communists": Ibid.

210 "I was exhausted": Flatley, "Miss Arthur Goes to Vassar," p. 11.

"in a state": Associated Press, November 14, 1954.

211 "And that was": Flatley, "Miss Arthur Goes to Vassar," p. 11.

"Fear can keep you": Broughton, "The Things in Jean Arthur's Doghouse," Calendar section, pp. 28-29.

212 I.R.S. claim: Associated Press, September 30, 1954; New York *Times*, October 1, 1954.

filed a denial: New York *Times*, October 1, 1954.

"Every *bit* of me": *Photoplay*, December 1966.

CHAPTER EIGHTEEN
RESURRECTION

Page
214 "always alone": New York *Morning Telegraph*, September 2, 1959.

"I have no TV": DeRoos, "It's Back to Carmel...for Now," p. 12.

215 "I do not": Ibid., p. 13.

"I love her": *Photoplay*, December 1966.

216 "It's the kind of garden": "The Very Personal Garden of Jean Arthur," *House and Garden*, July 1970, p. 71.

"What Jean wanted": Ibid.

"I love Japanese architecture": "*Architectural Digest* Visits: Jean Arthur," *Architectural Digest*, May-June 1976, p. 58.

217 "Life by the sea": Ibid.

"everything conspires": Broughton, "The Things in Jean Arthur's Doghouse," Calendar section, p. 29.

"I couldn't live": Hopper, "Acting Bug Bites Jean Arthur Again."

"If they want": Monterey *Peninsula Herald*, January 18, 1957.

"I drove past": Monterey *Peninsula Herald*, 1957.

218 "could be made": Ibid.

"Well, you just": New York *Morning Telegraph*, September 2, 1959.

219 never saw each other again: Arthur Goodall to JO, October 1, 1991.

220 "There's no great": New York *Post*, March 15, 1962.

221 Arthur read the script: Ibid.

"On the second page": Ibid.

222 "one of the highlights": San Francisco *Chronicle*, February 8, 1964.

"the mystic": San Francisco *Examiner*, February 8, 1964.

223 "It was a good party": Arthur Pierce and Douglas Swarthout, *Jean Arthur: A Bio-Bibliography* (Westport, Conn.: Greenwood Press, 1990), p. 82.

"I certainly don't": Flatley, "Miss Arthur Goes to Vassar," p. 11.

"a hit": *Photoplay*, December 1966.

Page

223 which "overcame": DeRoos, "It's Back to Carmel…for Now," p. 14.

"from that point": *Photoplay*, December 1966.

224 "I love Joan": Stone, "Jean Arthur: Still After Laughter."

CHAPTER NINETEEN
WASTELAND

225 "How often": New York *World Journal Tribune*, *TV Magazine*, September 18-24, 1966.

226 script was being written: *Variety*, September 25, 1966.

"petrified": DeRoos, "It's Back to Carmel…for Now," p. 14.

"delightful": New York *Morning Telegraph*, January 8, 1965.

227 "proved she's the star": *Hollywood Reporter*, March 6, 1965.

"If time": *Hollywood Reporter*, March 8, 1965.

"didn't want to go home": Hopper, "Acting Bug Bites Jean Arthur."

228 "I didn't want to come back": Stone, "Jean Arthur: Still After Laughter."

"I can do anything": Ibid.

229 "And my wardrobe!": Los Angeles *Times*, *TV Times*, September 18-24, 1966.

230 "Jean Arthur, the actress": New York *Times*, September 13, 1966.

231 "We knew": DeRoos, "It's Back to Carmel…for Now," p. 14.

"They wanted": Stone, "Jean Arthur: Still After Laughter."

232 "Unlike the sponsors": New York *Times*, November 20, 1966.

233 "There are no": Flatley, "Miss Arthur Goes to Vassar," p. 11.

"It was very heartbreaking": Springer, "Great Star," p. 23.

"I'm going back": DeRoos, "It's Back to Carmel…For Now," p. 12.

CHAPTER TWENTY
FREAKING OUT

236 "no known survivors": Monterey *Peninsula Herald*, April 4, 1967.

237 "What came next": William Manchester, *The Glory and the Dream* (Boston: Little, Brown, 1974), p. 1115.

Page

238 "New Generation": Script No. 4416, on file at New York Public Library for the Performing Arts, Billy Rose Theatre Collection.

239 "very right": Cheryl Crawford, *One Naked Individual: My Fifty Years in the Theater* (Indianapolis/New York: Bobbs-Merrill, 1977), p. 258.

"If you fell": New York *Times*, May 14, 1972.

"Most of the plays": New York *Times*, September 9, 1967.

"I didn't want": New York *Times*, May 9, 1967.

"thing of the past": Crawford, *One Naked Individual*, p. 258.

"When she tried": New York *Times*, November 26, 1967.

240 "You can't portray": William Goldman, *The Season* (New York: Harcourt Brace & World, 1969), p. 177.

"It's a beautiful place": New York *Times*, September 9, 1967.

242 "During rehearsals": Flatley, "Miss Arthur Goes to Vassar," p. 11.

243 "rarely ha[d]": Goldman, *The Season*, p. 180.

"Then my voice": Flatley, Miss Arthur Goes to Vassar, p. 30.

244 "This play": Barton Heyman to JO, September 21, 1989.

"You will go on!": Crawford, *One Naked Individual*, p. 258.

"I'm told I": New York *Post*, November 3, 1967.

245 "your failure": New York *Times*, November 4, 1967.

"nervous breakdown": Ibid.

"She's just sick": New York *Post*, November 3, 1967.

"So much for *Stephanie Blake*": Crawford, *One Naked Individual*, p. 258.

forging his name: Ibid., p. 260.

246 "The problem": Goldman, *The Season*, p. 179.

247 "Hippiedom": Manchester, *The Glory and the Dream*, p. 1117.

"The chick": Ibid.

CHAPTER TWENTY-ONE
MISCASTING

Page

250 "reserved and hesitant": Joanne Gates to JO, January 14, 1994.

"My parents": Carolyn Pines to JO, January 23, 1994.

"just Jean Arthur": Thadeus Gesek to JO, January 14, 1994.

251 "emerged with": Georgia Buchanan Morse to JO, January 21, 1994.

"Jean had": Joanne Bogden to JO, January 23, 1994.

252 "exquisite taste": Arthur Ward to JO, December 20, 1993.

"Well I don't": Springer, "Great Star," p. 22.

253 "I felt shortchanged": Carolyn Pines to JO, January 23, 1994.

254 "I love the students": Springer, "Great Star," p. 22.

"My impression": Nancy Barber to JO, January 23, 1994.

255 "The wrong people": Flatley, "Miss Arthur Goes to Vassar," p. 30.

"What are they doing": *Photoplay*, December 1966.

"So many people": New York *Times*, September 11, 1972.

256 "I'm very grateful": Flatley, "Miss Arthur Goes to Vassar," p. 30.

257 "It was just": Ibid., p. 11.

258 "I want to teach": Ibid., p. 30.

"really didn't have": Robert Ward to JO, December 20, 1993.

261 "She had to have": Gus Arriola to JO, August 22, 1990.

"school was embarrassed": Robert Ward to JO, December 20, 1993.

CHAPTER TWENTY-TWO
FINAL APPEAL

264 "Oh Christ no!": Jerome Lawrence to JO, November 5, 1989.

266 "We all felt": Estelle Painter to JO, January 14, 1994.

"leave them": Earl Keyes to JO, April 6, 1994.

"I just took": Robert Snook to JO, January 9, 1994.

Page

267 "Mel Douglas's performance": Allan Leatherman to JO, January 7, 1994.

268 "draggy, flaccid": *Time*, November 3, 1975.

"excellent": Cleveland *Press*, October 18, 1975.

"disarming and enchanting": Cleveland *Plain Dealer*, October 18, 1975.

"totally emotionless": Chagrin Valley *Times*, October 23, 1975.

269 fourth time she pulled out: *Variety*, November 12, 1975.

270 "Jerry handled": Allan Leatherman to JO, January 7, 1994.

"it was the other": Earl Keyes to JO, April 6, 1994.

271 "The only people": Pettit, "Now You'll Understand Jean Arthur."

272 "No, I never": Parsons, "The Art of Being Arthur."

"You have one life": Glover, Associated Press, November 2, 1975.

"only real reason": New York *Times*, June 20, 1991.

CHAPTER TWENTY-THREE
FINAL YEARS

274 "that's the house": Arthur Ballard to JO, October 28, 1989.

"This is a house": Ibid.

275 "She wasn't": Bruce Jones to JO, April 22, 1993.

"Some scientists": Hopper, "Perfection is Her Goal," Chicago *Tribune*, July 4, 1948.

276 "one of the many": quoted in *Current Biography*, 1960.

277 "She's just a hermit": Washington *Post*, April 2, 1982.

"She doesn't do very well" Schickel, *The Men Who Made the Movies*, p. 76.

"Arthur, more than": Buck Rainey, "Buck Rainey's Filmographies," *Classic Images*, March 1984, p. 18.

"forgotten actress": Blowen, "Jean Arthur at 80: A Legend Made of Style and Substance, Not Publicity."

278 "She doesn't have to": Ibid.

279 "I replied": Ralph Haven Wolfe, "For Jean Arthur: An Appreciation," *Journal of Popular Film & Television*, Vol. 17, No. 1, Spring 1989, p. 24.

Page

280 "Frank was very taciturn": Doug Morrow to JO, August 9, 1990.

"He stayed to himself": Catharine Pace to JO, January 7, 1994.

281 "Give me": Lou Merino to JO, August 11, 1990.

282 Frank Ross confided: Zan Ross to JO, January 19, 1994.

"thought of children": Kerr, "Jean Explains Miss Arthur," *Modern Screen*, May 1937.

"Yes, I'm sorry": Hartley, "Play Truth or Consequences with Jean Arthur," p. 14.

283 "I don't want": *Variety*, August 25, 1966.

"is half afraid": Karen Horney, *Feminine Psychology* (New York: W.W. Norton, 1967), p. 129.

"due to disappointments": Ibid., p. 79.

284 "No one was": Harvey, *Romantic Comedy*, p. 351.

"what may be": Kendall, *The Runaway Bride*, p. 132.

"Quite frankly": Angela Fox-Dunn, "Jean Arthur: A Shy and Lonely Recluse at 87," *The Globe*, August 23, 1988.

285 "She's just": Ellen Mastroianni to JO, May 30, 1990.

286 "she never wanted": Ibid.

287 "an enigmatic": *Variety*, June 24, 1991.

"very rare": Los Angeles *Times*, June 20, 1991.

"The underlying": David Shipman, *The Independent*, June 21, 1991.

288 "No other actress": Charles Champlin, Los Angeles *Times*, June 21, 1991 (Copyright, 1991, Los Angeles *Times*. Reprinted by permission).

289 "An American has": George Bernard Shaw, speech in New York City, April 11, 1933, quoted in John Barlett, ed., *Familiar Quotations*, 14th ed. (Boston: Little, Brown, 1968), p. 838.

290 "I hated the place": Associated Press Interview, 1966.

"That would be": Glover, Associated Press, November 2, 1975.

FILMOGRAPHY

Films are listed in order of release. Where conventional reference sources indicate a release date different from that indicated in the first published review by a major newspaper, the release date indicated in the review has been selected.

Major cast members are listed, to the extent possible, in the order in which they appeared in actual onscreen credits. Other cast and production credits are selectively listed.

SILENT

1. *Somebody Lied* (Fox, Oct. 14, 1923), 2 reels. Directors: Stephen Roberts and Bryan Foy.
   Cast: Ken Maynard, Jean Arthur.

2. *Cameo Kirby* (Fox, Oct. 21, 1923), 7 reels. Director: John Ford; Scenario: Robert N. Lee; Based on the play "Cameo Kirby," by Booth Tarkington and Harry Leon Wilson; Photography: George Schneiderman.
   Cast: John Gilbert, Gertrude Olmstead, Alan Hale, Eric Mayne, William E. Lawrence, Richard Tucker, Phillips Smalley, Jack McDonald, Jean Arthur, Eugenie Ford.

3. *The Temple of Venus* (Fox, Oct. 29, 1923), 7 reels. Director: Henry Otto; Scenario and Story: Henry Otto and Catherine Carr; Photography: Joe August.
   Cast: William Walling, Mary Philbin and Jean Arthur as an unbilled extra among "1,000 West Coast Beauties."

4. *Spring Fever* (Fox, Dec. 30, 1923), 2 reels. Director: Archie Mayo.
   Cast: Al St. John, Jean Arthur.

5. *Case Dismissed* (Universal, May 13, 1924), 1 reel. Director: Slim Summerville.
   Cast: Slim Summerville, Jean Arthur, Bobbie Dunn.

6. *The Powerful Eye* (Universal, May 23, 1924), 2 reels. Director: Ernst Laemmle; Story: Earle Wayland Bowman.
   Cast: Pete Morrison, Jean Arthur, Olin Francis.

7. *Biff Bang Buddy* (Approved Pictures/Weiss Brothers Artclass Pictures, Sept. 15, 1924), 5 reels. Director: Frank L. Inghram [pseudonym for Richard Thorpe]; Story: Reginald C. Barker; Photography: Irving Ries.
   Cast: Buddy Roosevelt, Jean Arthur.

8. *Fast and Fearless* (Action Pictures/Weiss Brothers Artclass Pictures, Sept. 15, 1924), 5 reels. Director: Richard Thorpe; Photography: Irving Ries.
   Cast: Buffalo Bill Jr., Jean Arthur.

9. *Bringin' Home the Bacon* (Action Pictures/Weiss Brothers Artclass Pictures, Nov. 15, 1924), 5 reels. Director: Richard Thorpe; Story: Christopher B. Booth.
   Cast: Buffalo Bill Jr., Jean Arthur.

10. *Thundering Romance* (Action Pictures/Weiss Brothers Artclass Pictures, Dec. 15,

1924), 5 reels. Director: Richard Thorpe; Story: Ned Nye; Photography: Ray Ries.
Cast: Buffalo Bill Jr., Jean Arthur.

11. *Travelin' Fast* (Anchor Film Distributors, Dec. 30, 1924), 5 reels.
    Cast: Jack Perrin, Jean Arthur.

12. *Seven Chances* (Buster Keaton Productions/Metro Goldwyn Distributing Co., March 16, 1925), 6 reels. Director: Buster Keaton; Scenario: Jean Havez, Clyde Bruckman and Joseph A. Mitchell; Story: Roi Cooper Megrue; Photography: Elgin Lessley and Byron Houck.
    Cast: Buster Keaton, T. Roy Barnes, Snitz Edwards, Ruth Dwyer, Frankie Raymond, Jean Arthur.

13. *Drug Store Cowboy* (Independent Pictures, June 1, 1925), 5 reels. Director: Park Frame.
    Cast: Franklyn Farnum, Robert Walker, Jean Arthur.

14. *The Fighting Smile* (Independent Pictures, Aug. 4, 1925), 5 reels. Director: Jay Marchant; Photography: Harry J. Brown.
    Cast: Bill Cody, Jean Arthur.

15. *Tearin' Loose* (Action Pictures/Weiss Brothers Artclass Pictures, Sept. 4, 1925), 5 reels. Director: Richard Thorpe; Photography: William Marshall.
    Cast: Wally Wales, Jean Arthur.

16. *A Man of Nerve* (R-C Pictures/FBO, Sept. 20, 1925), 5 reels. Director: Louis W. Chaudet; Story: John Harold Hamlin; Photography: Allen Davey.
    Cast: Bob Custer, Jean Arthur.

17. *Hurricane Horseman* (Action Pictures/Weiss Brothers Artclass Pictures, Oct. 14, 1925), 5 reels. Director: Robert Eddy; Scenario: A.E. Serrao and Katherine Fanning.
    Cast: Wally Wales, Jean Arthur.

18. *Thundering Through* (Action Pictures/Weiss Brothers Artclass Pictures, Dec. 13, 1925), 5 reels. Director: Fred Bain; Scenario: Barr Cross.
    Cast: Buddy Roosevelt, Jean Arthur.

19. *Under Fire* (Clifford S. Elfelt Productions/Davis Distributing Division, Jan. 1, 1926), 5 reels. Director: Clifford S. Elfelt; Story: Captain Charles King.
    Cast: Bill Patton, Jean Arthur.

20. *Roaring Rider* (Action Pictures/Weiss Brothers Artclass Pictures, Jan. 2, 1926), 5 reels. Director: Richard Thorpe; Screenplay: Reginald C. Barker..
    Cast: Wally Wales, Jean Arthur.

21. *Born to Battle* (R-C Pictures/FBO, Jan. 24, 1926), 5 reels. Director: Robert DeLacy; Story and Scenario: William E. Wing; Photography: David Smith and Harold Wenstrom.
    Cast: Tom Tyler, Jean Arthur, Frankie Darro.

22. *The Fighting Cheat* (Action Pictures/Weiss Brothers Artclass Pictures, Feb. 11, 1926), 5 reels. Director: Richard Thorpe; Scenario: Betty Burbridge.
    Cast: Wally Wales, Jean Arthur.

23. *Eight Cylinder Bull* (Fox, April 11, 1926), 2 reels. Director: Jack Leys; Story: Walter Ruben and Sydney Lanfield.
Cast: Harold Austin, Ralph Sipperly, Jean Arthur.

24. *The Mad Racer* (Fox, April 18, 1926), 2 reels. Director: Ben Stoloff; Story: Richard Harding Davis.
Cast: Jean Arthur, Earle Foxe.

25. *Riding Rivals* (Action Pictures/Weiss Brothers Artclass Pictures, May 2, 1926), 5 reels. Director: Richard Thorpe; Screenplay: Betty Burbridge.
Cast: Wally Wales, Jean Arthur.

26. *Double Daring* (Action Pictures/Weiss Brothers Artclass Pictures, June 11, 1926), 5 reels. Director: Richard Thorpe; Story: Betty Burbridge.
Cast: Wally Wales, J.P. Lockney, Jean Arthur.

27. *Lightning Bill* (Goodwill Pictures, June 29, 1926), 5 reels. Director: Louis W. Chaudet.
Cast: Bill Bailey, Jean Arthur.

28. *Twisted Triggers* (Action Pictures/Associated Exhibitors, July 11, 1926), 5 reels. Director: Richard Thorpe; Story: Tommy Gray; Photography: Ray Ries.
Cast: Wally Wales, Jean Arthur.

29. *The Cowboy* Cop (R-C Pictures/FBO, July 11, 1926), 5 reels. Director: Robert DeLacy; Story: Frank Richardson Pierce; Photography: John Leezer.
Cast: Tom Tyler, Jean Arthur, Frankie Darro.

30. *The College Boob* (R-C Pictures/Harry Garson Productions/FBO, Aug. 15, 1926), 6 reels. Director: Harry Garson; Story: Jack Casey; Photography: James Brown.
Cast: Lefty Flynn, Jean Arthur.

31. *The Block Signal* (Gotham Productions/Lumas Film Corp., Sept. 15, 1926), 6 reels. Director: Frank O'Connor; Story: F. Oakley Crawford; Photography: Ray June.
Cast: Ralph Lewis, Jean Arthur.

32. *Husband Hunters* (Tiffany Productions, Jan. 15, 1927), 6 reels. Director: John G. Adolphi; Story: Douglas Bronston; Photography: Joseph A. Dubray and Stephen Norton.
Cast: Mae Busch, Charles Delaney, Jean Arthur.

33. *Hello! Lafayette!* (a/k/a *Lafayette, Where Are We?*) (Fox, Jan. 16, 1927), 2 reels. Directors, Max Gold and Al Davis; Story: Gene Ford and Henry Johnson.
Cast: Ernie Shields, Harry Woods, Jean Arthur.

34. *The Broken Gate* (Tiffany Productions, Feb. 15, 1927), 6 reels. Director: James C. McKay; Based on the novel "The Broken Gate," by Emerson Hough; Photography: Joseph A. Dubray and Stephen Norton.
Cast: Dorothy Phillips, William Collier Jr., Jean Arthur, Phillips Smalley, Florence Turner.

35. *Bigger and Better Blondes* (Pathé, April 11, 1927), 2 reels. Director: James Parrott; Producer: Hal Roach.
Cast: Charley Chase, Mario Carillo, Jean Arthur.

36. *Horse Shoes* (Monty Banks Enterprises, Pathé Exchange, April 17, 1927), 6 reels. Director: Clyde Bruckman; Scenario and Story: Monty Banks and Charles Horan; Photography: James Diamond.
Cast: Monty Banks, Ernie Wood, Henry Barrows, John Elliott, Jean Arthur.

37. *The Poor Nut* (Jess Smith Productions/First National Pictures, July 19, 1927), 7 reels. Director: Richard Wallace; Screenplay and Continuity, Paul Schofield; Based on the play "The Poor Nut," by J.C. Nugent and Elliott Nugent; Photography: David Kesson.
Cast: Jack Mulhall, Charlie Murray, Jean Arthur, Jane Winton.

38. *The Masked Menace* (Pathé, Nov. 6, 1927), 10 chapter serial. Director: Arch Heath; Story: Clarence Budington Kelland.
Cast: Larry Kent, Jean Arthur.

39. *Flying Luck* (Monty Banks Enterprises/Pathé Exchange, Dec. 4, 1927), 7 reels. Director: Herman C. Raymaker; Story: Charles Horan and Monty Banks; Photography: James Diamond.
Cast: Monty Banks, Jean Arthur.

40. *Wallflowers* (FBO, Feb. 16, 1928), 7 reels. Director: Leo Meehan; Based on the novel "Wallflowers," by Temple Bailey; Photography: Allen Siegler.
Cast: Hugh Trevor, Mabel Julienne Scott, Charles Stevenson, Jean Arthur.

SOUND EFFECTS ONLY (NO DIALOGUE)

41. *Warming Up* (Paramount, July 15, 1928), 8 reels (sound and silent versions). Director: Fred Newmeyer; Adaptation and Screenplay: Ray Harris; Story: Sam Mintz; Photography: Edward Cronjager.
Cast: Richard Dix, Jean Arthur, Claude King, Philo McCullough, Billy Kent Schaefer, Roscoe Karns, James Dugan, Mike Donlin.

42. *Brotherly Love* (MGM, Oct. 13, 1928), 7 reels (sound and silent versions). Director: Charles F. Reisner; Scenario: Earl Baldwin and Lew Lipton; Story: Patterson Margoni; Photography: Henry Sharp; Sets: Cedric Gibbons.
Cast: Karl Dane, George K. Arthur, Jean Arthur.

43. *Sins of the Fathers* (Paramount, Dec. 29, 1928), 10 reels (sound and silent versions). Director: Ludwig Berger; Adaptation: E. Lloyd Sheldon; Story: Norman Burnstine; Photography: Victor Milner.
Cast: Emil Jannings, Ruth Chatterton, Barry Norton, Jean Arthur, ZaSu Pitts, Dawn O'Day [Anne Shirley].

SOUND

44. *The Canary Murder Case* (Paramount, March 9, 1929), sound version 82 minutes (also released in silent version). Director: Malcolm St. Clair (reshot for sound by Frank

Tuttle); Screenplay: Florence Ryerson and Albert S. Le Vino; Based on the novel "The Canary Murder Case," by S.S. Van Dine; Photography: Harry Fischbeck.
Cast: William Powell, James Hall, Louise Brooks, Jean Arthur, Gustav von Seyffertitz, Charles Lane, E.H. Calvert, Eugene Pallette, Ned Sparks.

45. *Stairs of Sand* (Paramount, June 8, 1929), 6 reels. Director: Otto Brower; Adaptation: Agnes Brand Leahy, Sam Mintz and J. Walter Ruben; Based on the novel "Stairs of Sand," by Zane Grey; Photography: Rex Wimpy.
Cast: Wallace Beery, Jean Arthur, Phillips Holmes, Fred Kohler.

46. *The Mysterious Dr. Fu Manchu* (Paramount, July 21, 1929), Sound version 81 minutes (also released in silent version). Director: Rowland V. Lee; Screenplay: Florence Ryerson and Lloyd Corrigan; Based on the novel "The Insidious Dr. Fu Manchu," by Sax Rohmer; Photography: Harry Fischbeck.
Cast: Warner Oland, Neil Hamilton, Jean Arthur, O.P. Heggie.

47. *The Greene Murder Case* (Paramount, Aug. 9, 1929), Sound version 71 minutes (also released in silent version). Director: Frank Tuttle; Screenplay: Louise Long; Adaptation: Bartlett Cormack; Based on the novel "The Greene Murder Case," by S.S. Van Dine; Photography: Henry Gerrard.
Cast: William Powell, Florence Eldridge, Ullrich Haupt, Jean Arthur, Eugene Pallette, E.H. Calvert.

48. *The Saturday Night Kid* (Paramount, Nov. 15, 1929), sound version 65 minutes (also released in silent version). Director: Edward Sutherland; Screenplay: Ethel Doherty; Based on the play "Love 'em and Leave 'em," by George Abbott and John V.A. Weaver; Photography: Harry Fischbeck.
Cast: Clara Bow, Jean Arthur, James Hall, Edna May Oliver, Charles Sellon, Ethel Wales, Hyman Meyer, Eddie Dunn, Leone Lane, Jean Harlow, Frank Ross, Irving Bacon.

49. *Half Way to Heaven* (Paramount, Dec. 6, 1929), sound version 66 minutes (also released in silent version). Director: George Abbott; Adaptation: George Abbott; Based on the novel "Here Comes the Bandwagon," by Henry Leyford Gates; Photography: Alfred Gilks and Charles Lang.
Cast: Charles "Buddy" Rogers, Jean Arthur, Paul Lukas, Oscar Apfel, Irving Bacon.

50. *Street of Chance* (Paramount, Jan. 31, 1930), sound version 76 minutes (also released in silent version). Director: John Cromwell; Scenario: Howard Estabrook; Story: Oliver H.P. Garrett; Photography: Charles Lang.
Cast: William Powell, Kay Francis, Regis Toomey, Jean Arthur.

51. *Young Eagles* (Paramount, March 21, 1930), sound version 72 minutes (also released in silent version). Director: William Wellman; Scenario: Grover Jones and William Slavens McNutt; Story: Elliott White Springs; Photography: Archie Stout.
Cast: Charles "Buddy" Rogers, Jean Arthur, Paul Lukas, Stuart Erwin, Virginia Bruce, Gordon DeMain, James Finlayson, Frank Ross.

52. *Paramount on Parade* (Paramount, April 19, 1930), 102 minutes. Directors: Dorothy Arzner, Otto Brower, Edmund Goulding, Victor Heerman, Edwin H. Knopf, Rowland V. Lee, Ernst Lubitsch, Lothar Mendes, Victor Shertzinger, Edward Sutherland, Frank Tuttle; Photography: Harry Fischbeck and Victor Milner.
Cast: Iris Adrian, Richard Arlen, Jean Arthur, Mischa Auer, William Austin, George Bancroft, Clara Bow, Evelyn Brent, Mary Brian, Clive Brook, Virginia Bruce, Nancy Carroll, Ruth Chatterton, Maurice Chevalier, Gary Cooper, Cecil Cunningham, Leon Errol, Stuart Erwin, Stanley Fields, Henry Fink, Kay Francis, Skeets Gallagher, Edmund Goulding, Harry Green, Mitzi Green, James Hall, Phillips Holmes, Helen Kane, Dennis King, Abe Lyman and his Band, Fredric March, Nino Martini, Mitzi Mayfair, the Marion Morgan Dancers, David Newell, Jack Oakie, Warner Oland, Zelma O'Neal, Eugene Pallette, Joan Peers, Jack Pennick, William Powell, Charles "Buddy" Rogers, Lillian Roth, Rolfe Sedan, Stanley Smith, Fay Wray.

53. *The Return of Dr. Fu Manchu* (Paramount, May 2, 1930), 73 minutes. Director: Rowland V. Lee; Screenplay: Florence Ryerson and Lloyd Corrigan; Based on the novel "The Return of Dr. Fu Manchu," by Sax Rohmer; Photography: Archie J. Stout.
Cast: Warner Oland, O.P. Heggie, Jean Arthur, Neil Hamilton.

54. *Danger Lights* (RKO, Aug. 21, 1930), 73 minutes (later released in Wide Screen version, 87 minutes). Director: George B. Seitz; Story and Adaptation: James Ashmore Creelman; Photography: Karl Struss and John Boyle.
Cast: Louis Wolheim, Robert Armstrong, Jean Arthur.

55. *The Silver Horde* (RKO, Oct. 24, 1930), 75 minutes. Director: George Archainbaud; Adaptation: Wallace Smith; Based on the novel "The Silver Horde," by Rex Beach; Photography: Leo Tover.
Cast: Evelyn Brent, Louis Wolheim, Joel McCrea, Raymond Hatton, Jean Arthur, Blanche Sweet.

56. *The Gang Buster* (Paramount, Jan. 23, 1931), 65 minutes. Director: Edward Sutherland; Scenario and Story: Percy Heath; Photography: Harry Fischbeck.
Cast: Jack Oakie, Jean Arthur, William Boyd, Wynne Gibson.

57. *Virtuous Husband* (Universal, May 7, 1931), 75 minutes. Director: Vin Moore; Screenplay: Dale Van Every; Adaptation: Edward Luddy and C. Jerome Horwin; Based on the play "Apron Strings," by Dorrance Davis; Photography: Jerome Ash.
Cast: Elliott Nugent, Jean Arthur, Betty Compson, J.C. Nugent, Alison Skipworth.

58. *The Lawyer's Secret* (Paramount, May 29, 1931), 65 minutes. Directors: Louis Gasnier and Max Marcin; Screenplay: Lloyd Corrigan and Max Marcin; Story: James Hilary Finn; Photography: Arthur Todd.
Cast: Clive Brook, Charles Rogers, Richard Arlen, Fay Wray, Jean Arthur.

59. *Ex-Bad Boy* (Universal, July 15, 1931), 76 minutes. Director: Vin Moore; Scenario: Dale Van Every; Based on the play "The Whole Town's Talking," by Anita Loos and John Emerson; Photography: Jerome Ash.
Cast: Robert Armstrong, Jean Arthur, Jason Robards, Lola Lane, George Brent.

60. *The Past of Mary Holmes* (RKO, April 28, 1933), 70 minutes. Directors: Harlan Thompson and Slavko Vorkapich; Adaptation: Marion Dix and Edward J. Doherty; Story: Rex Beach; Photography: Charles Rosher.

Cast: Helen McKellar, Eric Linden, Jean Arthur.

61. *Get That Venus* (Starmark Productions/Regent Pictures, Production June-July 1933 (no general U.S. release)), 6 reels. Director: Grover Lee; Adaptation: Val Valentine; Story: Gerald Villiers Stuart; Photography: Nick Rogalli and Marcel Picard.

Cast: Ernest Truex, Jean Arthur, Harry Davenport.

62. *Whirlpool* (Columbia, May 4, 1934), 73 minutes. Director: Roy William Neill; Screenplay: Dorothy Howell and Ethel Hill; Story: Howard Emmett Rogers; Photography: Benjamin Kline.

Cast: Jack Holt, Jean Arthur, Donald Cook, Allen Jenkins, Lila Lee, Ward Bond.

63. *The Defense Rests* (Columbia, Aug. 15, 1934), 70 minutes. Director: Lambert Hillyer; Screenplay and Story: Jo Swerling; Photography: Joseph August.

Cast: Jack Holt, Jean Arthur, Nat Pendleton, Donald Meek.

64. *The Most Precious Thing in Life* (Columbia, Nov. 19, 1934), 68 minutes. Director: Lambert Hillyer; Screenplay: Ethel Hill and Dore Schary; Story: Travis Ingham; Photography: John Stumar.

Cast: Richard Cromwell, Jean Arthur, Donald Cook, Anita Louise, Mary Forbes, Jane Darwell, Ward Bond.

65. *The Whole Town's Talking* (Columbia, Feb. 28, 1935), 93 minutes. Director: John Ford; Screenplay: Jo Swerling and Robert Riskin; Story: W.R. Burnett; Photography: Joseph August.

Cast: Edward G. Robinson, Jean Arthur, Arthur Hohl, James Donlan, Arthur Byron, Wallace Ford, Donald Meek, Edward Brophy, Paul Harvey, Lucille Ball.

66. *Party Wire* (Columbia, May 16, 1935), 69 minutes. Director: Erle C. Kenton; Screenplay: Ethel Hill and John Howard Lawson; Based on the novel "Party Wire," by Bruce Manning; Photography: Al Siegler.

Cast: Jean Arthur, Victor Jory, Helen Lowell, Robert Allen, Charley Grapewin.

67. *Public Hero # 1* (MGM, June 7, 1935), 91 minutes. Director: J. Walter Ruben; Screenplay: Wells Root; Story: J. Walter Ruben and Wells Root; Photography: Gregg Toland; Art Direction: Cedric Gibbons.

Cast: Lionel Barrymore, Jean Arthur, Chester Morris, Joseph Calleia.

68. *Diamond Jim* (Universal, Aug. 23, 1935), 93 minutes. Director: Edward Sutherland; Screenplay: Preston Sturges; Based on the book "Diamond Jim," by Parker Morell; Adaptation: Doris Malloy and Harry Clork; Photography: George Robinson; Art Direction: Charles D. Hall.

Cast: Edward Arnold, Jean Arthur, Binnie Barnes, Cesar Romero, Eric Blore, William Demarest.

69. *The Public Menace* (Columbia, Sept. 23, 1935), 73 minutes. Director: Erle C. Kenton; Screenplay and Story: Ethel Hill and Lionel Houser; Photography: Henry Freulich. **Cast:** Jean Arthur, George Murphy, Douglass Dumbrille, Victor Kilian.

70. *If You Could Only Cook* (Columbia, Dec. 25, 1935), 72 minutes. Director: William Seiter; Screenplay: Howard J. Green and Gertrude Purcell; Story: F. Hugh Herbert; Photography: John Stumar; Art Direction: Stephen Goosson; Costumes: Samuel Lange. **Cast:** Herbert Marshall, Jean Arthur, Leo Carrillo, Lionel Stander, Frieda Inescourt.

71. *Mr. Deeds Goes to Town* (Columbia, April 16, 1936), 118 minutes. Director: Frank Capra; Screenplay: Robert Riskin; Story: Clarence Budington Kelland; Photography: Joseph Walker; Art Direction: Stephen Goosson; Costumes: Samuel Lange; Producer: Frank Capra.
   Cast: Gary Cooper, Jean Arthur, George Bancroft, Lionel Stander, Douglass Dumbrille, Raymond Walburn, H.B. Warner, Ruth Donnelly, Walter Catlett, John Wray, Emma Dunn, Charles Lane, Ann Doran.

72. *The Ex-Mrs. Bradford* (RKO, May 27, 1936), 80 minutes. Director: Stephen Roberts; Screenplay: Anthony Veiller; Story: James Edward Grant; Photography: J. Roy Hunt; Art Direction: Van Nest Polglase; Gowns: Bernard Newman.
   Cast: William Powell, Jean Arthur, James Gleason, Eric Blore, Robert Armstrong, Lila Lee, Grant Mitchell, Ralph Morgan.

73. *Adventure in Manhattan* (Columbia, Oct. 22, 1936), 73 minutes. Director: Edward Ludwig; Screenplay: Sidney Buchman, Harry Sauber and Jack Kirkland; Story: Joseph Krumgold (suggested by May Edington's "Purple and Fine Linen"); Photography: Henry Freulich; Art Direction: Stephen Goosson; Gowns: Bernard Newman.
   Cast: Jean Arthur, Joel McCrea, Reginald Owen, Thomas Mitchell, Victor Kilian.

74. *More Than a Secretary* (Columbia, Dec. 10, 1936), 77 minutes. Director: Alfred E. Green; Screenplay: Dale Van Every and Lynn Starling; Story: Ethel Hill and Aben Kandel (based on story by Matt Taylor); Photography: Henry Freulich.
   Cast: Jean Arthur, George Brent, Lionel Stander, Ruth Donnelly, Reginald Denny, Dorothea Kent.

75. *The Plainsman* (Paramount, Jan. 13, 1937), 115 minutes. Director: Cecil B. DeMille; Screenplay: Waldemar Young, Harold Lamb and Lynn Riggs; Adaptation: Jeanie Macpherson; Photography: Victor Milner; Art Direction: Hans Dreier and Roland Anderson; Costumes: Natalie Visart, Dwight Franklin and Joe DeYong; Producer: Cecil B. DeMille.
   Cast: Gary Cooper, Jean Arthur, James Ellison, Charles Bickford, Helen Burgess, Porter Hall, Paul Harvey, Victor Varconi, John Miljan, Frank McGlynn Sr., Granville Bates, Frank Albertson, Anthony Quinn, George "Gabby" Hayes.

76. *History Is Made at Night* (United Artists, March 27, 1937), 97 minutes. Director: Frank Borzage; Screenplay: Gene Towne and Graham Baker; Photography: David Abel; Special Technical Effects: James Basevi; Art Direction: Alexander Toluboff;

Musical Direction: Alfred Newman; Costumes: Bernard Newman; Producer: Walter Wanger.

Cast: Charles Boyer, Jean Arthur, Leo Carrillo, Colin Clive, Ivan Lebedeff.

77. *Easy Living* (Paramount, July 7, 1937), 88 minutes. Director: Mitchell Leisen; Screenplay: Preston Sturges; Story: Vera Caspary; Photography: Ted Tetzlaff; Art Direction: Hans Dreier and Ernst Fegte; Costumes: Travis Banton; Producer: Arthur Hornblow Jr.

Cast: Jean Arthur, Edward Arnold, Ray Milland, Louis Alberni, Mary Nash, Franklin Pangborn, William Demarest.

78. *You Can't Take It With You* (Columbia, Sept. 1, 1938), 126 minutes. Director: Frank Capra; Screenplay: Robert Riskin; Based on the play "You Can't Take It With You," by George S. Kaufman and Moss Hart; Photography: Joseph Walker; Musical Score: Dimitri Tiomkin; Art Direction: Stephen Goosson; Jean Arthur's Gowns: Bernard Newman and Irene; Producer: Frank Capra.

Cast: Jean Arthur, Lionel Barrymore, James Stewart, Edward Arnold, Mischa Auer, Ann Miller, Spring Byington, Samuel S. Hinds, Donald Meek, H.B. Warner, Halliwell Hobbes, Dub Taylor, Mary Forbes, Lillian Yarbo, Eddie Anderson, Charles Lane, Harry Davenport.

79. *Only Angels Have Wings* (Columbia, May 11, 1939), 121 minutes. Director: Howard Hawks; Screenplay: Jules Furthman; Story: Howard Hawks; Photography: Joseph Walker and Elmer Dyer; Special Effects: Roy Davidson; Music: Dimitri Tiomkin; Art Direction: Lionel Banks; Costumes: Kalloch; Producer: Howard Hawks.

Cast: Cary Grant, Jean Arthur, Richard Barthelmess, Rita Hayworth, Thomas Mitchell, Allyn Joslyn, Sig Rumann, Victor Kilian, John Carroll, Donald Barry, Noah Beery Jr.

80. *Mr. Smith Goes to Washington* (Columbia, Oct. 19, 1939), 130 minutes. Director: Frank Capra; Screenplay: Sidney Buchman; Story: Lewis R. Foster; Photography: Joseph Walker; Musical Score: Dimitri Tiomkin; Art Direction: Lionel Banks; Gowns: Kalloch; Producer: Frank Capra.

Cast: Jean Arthur, James Stewart, Claude Rains, Edward Arnold, Guy Kibbee, Thomas Mitchell, Eugene Pallette, Beulah Bondi, H.B. Warner, Harry Carey, Astrid Allwyn, Ruth Donnelly, Grant Mitchell, Porter Hall, Charles Lane, William Demarest.

81. *Too Many Husbands* (Columbia, March 7, 1940), 84 minutes. Director: Wesley Ruggles; Screenplay: Claude Binyon; Based on the play "Home and Beauty," by W. Somerset Maugham; Photography: Joseph Walker; Music: Frederick Hollander; Art Direction: Lionel Banks; Producer: Wesley Ruggles.

Cast: Jean Arthur, Fred MacMurray, Melvyn Douglas, Harry Davenport, Melville Cooper, Edgar Buchanan.

82. *Arizona* (Columbia, Feb. 6, 1941), 127 minutes. Director: Wesley Ruggles; Screenplay: Claude Binyon; Based on the novel "Arizona," by Clarence Budington Kelland; Directors of Photography: Joseph Walker (Interiors), Harry Hallenberger and Fayte

Browne (Exteriors); Music: Victor Young; Art Direction: Lionel Banks; Jean Arthur's Costumes: Kalloch; Producer: Wesley Ruggles.

Cast: Jean Arthur, William Holden, Warren William, Porter Hall, Edgar Buchanan, Paul Harvey, George Chandler, Regis Toomey.

83. *The Devil and Miss Jones* (RKO, April 11, 1941), 92 minutes. Director: Sam Wood; Screenplay: Norman Krasna; Photography: Harry Stradling; Music Direction: Roy Webb; Art Direction: Van Nest Polglase; Jean Arthur's Clothes: Irene; Producer: Frank Ross.

Cast: Jean Arthur, Robert Cummings, Charles Coburn, Edmund Gwenn, Spring Byington, S.Z. Sakall, William Demarest, Walter Kingsfield, Montagu Love, Florence Bates.

84. *The Talk of the Town* (Columbia, Aug. 20, 1942), 118 minutes. Director: George Stevens; Screenplay: Irwin Shaw and Sidney Buchman; Adaptation: Dale Van Every; Story: Sidney Harmon; Director of Photography: Ted Tetzlaff; Music: Frederick Hollander; Art Direction: Lionel Banks; Gowns: Irene; Producer: George Stevens.

Cast: Cary Grant, Jean Arthur, Ronald Colman, Edgar Buchanan, Glenda Farrell, Charles Dingle, Emma Dunn, Rex Ingram, Leonid Kinskey, Tom Tyler, Don Beddoe, Frank M. Thomas, Lloyd Bridges.

85. *The More the Merrier* (Columbia, May 13, 1943), 104 minutes. Director: George Stevens; Screenplay: Robert Russell, Frank Ross, Richard Flournoy and Lewis R. Foster; Story: Robert Russell and Frank Ross; Director of Photography: Ted Tetzlaff; Music: Leigh Harline; Song, "The Torpedo Song," by Henry Myers; Art Direction: Lionel Banks; Producer: George Stevens.

Cast: Jean Arthur, Joel McCrea, Charles Coburn, Richard Gaines, Bruce Bennett, Frank Sully, Don Douglas, Cyde Fillmore, Stanley Clements, Grady Sutton, Ann Savage, Sugar Geise, Don Barclay, Ann Doran, Mary Treen.

86. *A Lady Takes a Chance* (RKO, Aug. 19, 1943), 86 minutes. Director: William Seiter; Screenplay: Robert Ardrey; Story: Jo Swerling; Director of Photography: Frank Redman; Music: Roy Webb; Art Direction: Albert S. D'Agostino and Alfred Herman; Gowns: Edward Stevenson; Producer: Frank Ross.

Cast: Jean Arthur, John Wayne, Charles Winninger, Phil Silvers, Mary Field, Don Costello, John Philliber, Grady Sutton, Grant Withers, Hans Conreid.

87. *The Impatient Years* (Columbia, Sept. 7, 1944), 91 minutes. Director: Irving Cummings; Screenplay: Virginia Van Upp; Photography: Joseph Walker; Producer: Irving Cummings.

Cast: Jean Arthur, Lee Bowman, Charles Coburn, Edgar Buchanan, Charley Grapewin, Phil Brown, Harry Davenport, Jane Darwell.

88. *A Foreign Affair* (Paramount, June 30, 1948), 116 minutes. Director: Billy Wilder; Screenplay: Charles Brackett, Billy Wilder and Richard Breen; Adaptation: Robert Harari; Story: David Shaw; Director of Photography: Charles Lang Jr.; Musical

Score: Frederick Hollander; Art Direction: Hans Dreier and Walter Tyler; Costumes: Edith Head; Producer: Charles Brackett.

Cast: Jean Arthur, Marlene Dietrich, John Lund, Millard Mitchell, Peter Von Zerneck, Stanley Prager, Gordon Jones.

89. *Shane* (Paramount, April 23, 1953), 118 minutes. Director: George Stevens; Screenplay: A.B. Guthrie Jr.; Based on the novel "Shane," by Jack Shaeffer; Photography: Loyal Griggs; Musical Score: Victor Young; Art Direction: Hal Pereira and Walter Tyler; Costumes: Edith Head; Producer: George Stevens.

Cast: Alan Ladd, Jean Arthur, Van Heflin, Brandon De Wilde, Walter Jack Palance, Ben Johnson, Edgar Buchanan, Emile Meyer, Elisha Cook Jr., Ellen Corby, Nancy Kulp.

STAGE APPEARANCES

1. *Spring Song* (Opened December 11, 1930 at the Pasadena Community Playhouse, Pasadena, California. Closed December 20 after a limited engagement).
A revival of the drama by Bella Spewack. Director: Gilmore Brown.
Cast: Vera Gordon, Nadje Gordon, Jean Arthur, Morris Strassberg, Franklin Provo.

2. *Lysistrata* (Opened January 24, 1932, at the Riviera Theatre, New York City. Closed March 6, 1932 at the Westchester County Centre, Mount Vernon, New York, after a limited area tour).
An adaptation of Aristophanes' drama by Gilbert Seldes. Presented by Chamberlain Brown.
Cast: Thais Lawton, Ethel Wilson, Jean Arthur, Fay Marbe, Sydney Greenstreet.

3. *Foreign Affairs* (Opened April 13, 1932 at the Avon Theatre, New York City. Closed after 23 performances).
A comedy by Paul Hervey Fox and George Tilton. Staged by Lester Fuller; Producers: Lester Fuller and Ben F. Kamsler.
Cast: Henry Hull, Dorothy Gish, Edouard La Roche, Osgood Perkins, Jean Arthur, J. Edward Bromberg, Carl Benton Reid.

4. *The Road to Rome* (Opened July 2, 1932 at the Red Bank Auditorium, Red Bank, New Jersey. Closed July 9 after a limited engagement).
A revival of the comedy by Robert E. Sherwood. Staged by William A. Brady Jr.; Producers: Benjamin Hoagland and William A. Brady Jr.
Cast: Alice Brady, McKay Morris, Jean Arthur, Jessie Ralph.

5. *Let Us Be Gay* (Opened July 11, 1932 at the Red Bank Auditorium, Red Bank, New Jersey. Closed July 16 after a limited engagement).
A revival of the comedy by Rachel Crothers. Staged by William A. Brady Jr.; Producers: Benjamin Hoagland and William A. Brady Jr.
Cast: Alice Brady, Jean Arthur, McKay Morris, Jean Adair, Ross Alexander.

6. *Coquette* (Opened July 18, 1932 at the Red Bank Auditorium, Red Bank, New Jersey. Closed July 23 after a limited engagement).
A revival of the play by George Abbott and Ann Preston Bridgers. Staged by William A. Brady Jr.; Producers: Benjamin Hoagland and William A. Brady Jr.
Cast: Aleta Freel, Jean Arthur, McKay Morris, Ross Alexander, Benjamin Hoagland, Robert Barrett, Gavin Muir, Jean Adair.

7. *The Man Who Reclaimed His Head* (Opened September 8, 1932 at the Broadhurst Theatre, New York City. Closed after 28 performances).
A melodrama by Jean Bart. Staged by Herbert J. Biderman; Producers: Arthur Hammerstein and L. Lawrence Weber.
Cast (in order of appearance): Richard Barrows, Romaine Callender, Claude Rains, Evelyn Eaton, Carleton Young, Janet Rathbun, Emily Lowry, Paul Wilson, Allen

Nourse, Jean Arthur, Stuart Casey, C. Ellsworth Smith, Paul Wilson, Lionel Braham, Dennie Moone, Lucille Lortel, Alexander Cross, Marshall Hale, Kay Miller, Marjorie Dalton, Mona Moray, Ray Harper, James J. Coyle, Richard Bowlen.

8. *$25 an Hour* (Opened May 10, 1933 at the Masque Theatre, New York City. Closed after 22 performances).
A comedy by Gladys Ungar and Leyla Georgie. Staged by Thomas Mitchell; Producers: Alfred E. Aarons and Thomas Mitchell.
Cast (in order of appearance): Natalie Browning, Catherine Field, Helena Rapport, Georges Metaxa, Stanley Harrison, James E. Lightfoot, Cyrena Smith, Ralph Sanford, Olga Baclanova, Jean Arthur, Paul Huber.

9. *Perhaps We Are* (Opened August 1, 1933 at Parrish Memorial Hall in Southampton, Long Island, New York. Closed August 5 after a limited engagement).
A comedy by Paul Osborn. Director: H.C. Potter; Setting: Mary Merrill.
Cast: Esther Dale, Jean Arthur, Granville Bates, Josephine Brown, John Hoysradt, Ernest Woodward.

10. *The Curtain Rises* (Opened October 19, 1933 at the Vanderbilt Theatre, New York City. Closed after 61 performances).
A comedy by Oskar Rempel [pseudonym for Benjamin M. Kaye]. Staged by Ernest Truex; Producers: Morris Green and Frank McCoy.
Cast (in order of appearance): Helen Salinger, Millicent Hanley, G. Albert Smith, Jean Arthur, Bertram Thorn, Kenneth Harlan, Donald Foster.

11. *The Bride of Torozko* (Opened September 13, 1934 at Henry Miller's Theatre, New York City. Closed after 12 performances).
A play by Otto Indig. Staged by Herman Shumlin; Producers: Gilbert Miller and Herman Shumlin.
Cast (in order of appearance): Francis Pierlot, Don Costello, Lionel Stander, Victor Kilian, Sam Jaffe, Van Heflin, Jean Arthur, Rose Keane, Frank Verigun, Harry M. Cooke, Genevieve Belasco.

12. *Born Yesterday* (Pre-Broadway tryout opened December 20, 1945 at the Shubert Theatre, New Haven, Connecticut. Arthur's last performance on January 1, 1946 in Boston).
A play by Garson Kanin. Director: Garson Kanin; Producer: Max Gordon.
Cast (in order of appearance): Ellen Hall, Richard E. Davis, Frank Otto, William Harmon, Rex King, Paul Douglas, Carroll Ashburn, Jean Arthur, Otto Hulett, David M. Pardoll, Mary Laslo, Milton Williams, Larry Oliver, Mona Burns, C.L. Burke.

13. *Peter Pan* (Opened April 24, 1950 at the Imperial Theatre, New York City. Moved to the St. James Theatre on October 3. Final New York performance on January 27, 1951 after 321 performances. Began tour January 30 at the Boston Opera House. Arthur's last performance April 14, 1951 at the Chicago Civic Opera House).
A revival of the play by J.M. Barrie. Staged by John Burrell and Wendy Toye;

Producers: Peter Lawrence and R.L. Stevens; Music and Lyrics: Leonard Bernstein; Scenery and Lighting: Ralph Alswang; Costumes: Motley; Musical Conductor: Ben Steinberg; Orchestrations: Hershy Kay; Musical Arrangements: Trude Rittman.

Cast (in order of appearance): Norman Shelly, Peg Hillias, Jack Dimond, Marcia Henderson, Boris Karloff, Jean Arthur, Gloria Patrice, Lee Barnett, Richard Knox, Philip Hepburn, Charles Brill, Edward Benjamin, Buzzy Martin, David Kurlan, Joe E. Marks, Will Scholz, Nehemiah Persoff, Harry Allen, John Dennis, William Marshall, Vincent Beck, Ronnie Aul, Kenneth Davis, Norman De Joie, Loren Hightower, Jay Riley, William Sumner, Stephanie Augustine, Eleanor Winter.

14. *Saint Joan* (Pre-Broadway tour opened September 17, 1954 at the Wilmington Playhouse, Wilmington, Delaware. Arthur's last performance on November 6 at the Hartman Theatre in Columbus, Ohio).

A revival of the drama by George Bernard Shaw. Directed by Harold Clurman; Producers: Robert Whitehead and the Producer's Theatre; Scenery: Mordecai Gorelik.

Cast (in order of appearance): Paul Ballantyne, Robert Van Hooten, Jean Arthur, John McLiam, George Macready, Howard Fischer, Milton Carney, George Lloyd, Lou Polan, Paul Richards, Carol Gustafson, Larry Ward, David Post, Wyndham Goldie, Robert Goodier, Frank Silvera, Richard Striker, Sam Jaffe, Philip Huston, Norman Roland.

15. *Saint Joan* (Opened February 6, 1964 at the Durham Studio Theater, University of California at Berkeley. Closed February 15 after a limited engagement).

A concert reading of the drama by George Bernard Shaw. Director: Robert W. Goldsby; Setting and Costumes: Henry May.

Cast: Jean Arthur, John Argue, Steven Gilborn, Jay Hornbacher, George House, H. Robert Lanchester, William Oliver, E. Kerrigan Prescott, Sidney Roger, Edgar Schell, Bertram Schwartzchild, Jeff Weissman.

16. *The Freaking Out of Stephanie Blake* (Previews opened October 30, 1967 at the Eugene O'Neill Theatre, New York City and closed after the November 1 matinee performance).

A comedy by Richard Chandler. Director: Richard Chandler (replaced by Michael Kahn); Producers: Cheryl Crawford and Carl Schaeffer; Sets and Lighting: Ben Edwards and Jean Rosenthal; Costumes: Jeanne Button; Projection Photographs: Bruce W. Stark; Light Paintings: Jason B. Fishbein; Music and Lyrics: Jeff Barry.

Cast (in order of appearance): Jan Miner, Franklin Cover, Jean Arthur, Steve Curry, Ronald Dante, Frank Thumhart, Ronald Frangipane, John Bassette, Joy Bang, Marilyn Webb, Andrea Martin, James Fouratt, William Devane, Barton Heyman, Alberta Grant, Ellen O'Mara, Michael McClanathan, Dena Dietrich, Sidney Lanier, Joseph Hardy, Robert Hacha, David Dawson, Michael Schultz.

17. *First Monday in October* (Pre-Broadway tryout opened October 17, 1975 at the Francis E. Drury Theatre, Cleveland, Ohio. Arthur's last performance on October 29).

A comedy-drama by Jerome Lawrence and Robert E. Lee. Director: Jerome

Lawrence; Setting: Richard Gould; Costumes: Estelle Painter; Lighting: Richard Coumbs.

Cast (in order of appearance): Melvyn Douglas, Jean Arthur, George Brengel, Dennis Romer, Allen Leatherman, Ralph Neeley, Spencer McIntyre, Robert Snook, John Buck Jr., Howard Renensland Jr., Eugene Hare, Ben Letter, Earl Keyes, Andrew Lichtenberg, Frederic Sereno, David Meyer, George Simms, Dee Hoty.

TELEVISION APPEARANCES

1. *Gunsmoke* (CBS, March 6, 1965, 10 p.m.).
   Producer: Philip Leacock; Story Consultant: John Mantley; Music: Richard Shores.
   Regular Cast: James Arness, Milburn Stone, Amanda Blake, Ken Curtis.
   Guest Cast: Jean Arthur, Joe Raciti, Roy Barcroft, Hank Patterson, Suzanne Benoit, Glenn Strange, Fred Coby, Scott Marlowe.

2. *The Jean Arthur Show* (CBS, September 12 to December 5, 1966, 10-10:30 p.m. Monday nights).
   Executive Producers: Jay Richard Kennedy and Richard Quine; Producer: Si Rose; Theme Song: "Merry-Go-Round," by Johnny Keating, Richard Quine and Jay Richard Kennedy.
   Regular Cast: Jean Arthur, Ron Harper, Leonard J. Stone.
   Guest Cast: Mickey Rooney, Russ Grieve, Paul Reed, Jo de Winter, Clint Howard, Olan Soule, Richard Conte, Dick Wilson, Ernest Sarracino, Jean Huntington, Michael Constantine, Robert Hastings, Ena Hartman, Ray Bolger, Edward Faulkner, Wally Cox, Quinn K. Redeker, Roy Roberts, Raymond Burr, L.Q. Jones, Forrest Lewis, Joan Staley, Jimmy Murphy, Norbert Schiller, Lee Bergere, Frances Robinson, Jan Arvan, George Kennedy.

3. *The Merv Griffin Show* (August 1974, 90 minutes).
   Host: Merv Griffin; Musical Director: Mort Lindsay.
   Guest Star: Jean Arthur.

Index